THE SACRAMENTS OF LIFE AND WORSHIP

CONTEMPORARY COLLEGE THEOLOGY SERIES

GENERAL EDITORS: J. FRANK DEVINE, S.J.
RICHARD W. ROUSSEAU, S.J.

THE SACRAMENTS OF LIFE AND WORSHIP is one of the volumes in the Ecclesial Theology section of this series.

The Sacraments of
Life and Worship

REV. JOHN P. SCHANZ

ASSOCIATE PROFESSOR OF THEOLOGY, GANNON COLLEGE, ERIE, PENNSYLVANIA

THE BRUCE PUBLISHING COMPANY / MILWAUKEE

NIHIL OBSTAT:

John A. Schulien, S.T.D.
Censor librorum

IMPRIMATUR:

✠ William E. Cousins
Archbishop of Milwaukee
February 14, 1966

Library of Congress Catalog Card Number: 66–19748

With gratitude to my family, who first led me
to encounter Christ in his sacraments.

Editors' Introduction:
The Contemporary College Theology Series

This series begins with the presupposition that theology is necessary. It is necessary if Christian intelligence is to search for meaning in its dialogue with God, man and the world. Since Christian intelligence is not the exclusive possession of the theological specialist or the cleric, the search must be carried on in all those areas of life, secular as well as religious, including the college situation, where meaning is to be found.

This search is a peaceful one, for in some mysterious way it has already achieved its goal: the vision of faith and the fullness of love. Still it remains a relentless and universal search. Its inner certainty must radiate out not only to the edges of the mind but also into the farthest recesses of the world. We could call it "lay" theology, but this word seems too pale a description for such an exciting enterprise of the Christian life.

In view of this the editors of this series are convinced that new questions had to be asked, new structures created, and new books written. These books would be neither catechetical nor apologetic. They would be purely and simply theological. The primary audience would be believers, but all thinking men would find them useful. In scope they would be broad enough to ensure perspective. They would be scholarly enough to be intellectually relevant. They would avoid pedantry. In short, they would try to present a rich and deep understanding of Christian revelation in such a way that today's college students would be able to respond with a Christian faith and life that are both culturally mature and scientifically precise. Finally the authors of these books would be, for the most part, teachers in colleges and universities where much of the contemporary theological dialogue is now going on.

The series falls into four parts: biblical, historical, ecclesial, and ethical. The divisions were not predetermined by the editors. They follow the shape of the most vigorous theological work now being done.

The books in the biblical section are intended to go beyond the traditional treatment of Bible history and the now familiar perspectives of salvation history. They concentrate on various books of the Bible. Their method has been especially designed for college work. Tentatively it might be called "exegetical theology." Every verse is not considered after the fashion of a commentary, nor are narratives developed as a biography, nor is there any attempt to create large theological syntheses. Rather the individual books are studied in chronological sequence; key passages are treated in detail and the rest are summarized. At the same time some attention is paid to the growing theological synthesis.

Since scholastic theology is already represented by individual works and sets of textbooks, the books in our historical section study dogmatic questions from a developmental point of view. In this way the editors hope to make the college students more aware of the great wealth of theological thinking that recent historico-theological studies have uncovered. This method, which is more inductive than deductive, should happily coincide with the thought processes of the college student. The three basic poles for synthesis are: God, Christ, and Man. In each area the historical development will be studied and a significant number of basic source texts presented. The problems raised in these studies will range all the way from Augustinian pessimism to Teilhardian optimism.

The textbooks for the third part of the series will deal with issues of great contemporary importance. They will examine questions discussed by the Second Vatican Council. As the name implies, ecclesial theology must first concern itself with the Church, what the Church knows herself to be, as expressed in the insights of the new *Constitution* on *the Church* and with the more significant of the Church's allied concerns: other world religions, American Protestantism, its history, its motivating forces and spirit, and finally the new sacramental theology so enriched by the many magnificent liturgical advances. All of this growth has brought a wider and deeper appreciation of the nature of the Roman Catholic Church and her relationship, rooted in understanding and love, with the whole world.

The fourth and final section of the series is devoted explicitly to Christian moral response. The editors subscribe to the position that the proper place for the Catholic college or university to examine ethical questions is in a revelational rather than in a purely philosophical context. In addition to the "virtue" divisions of the *Summa* or the classic moral theology text, designed primarily for confessors, there is a need and a place for a "Christian ethics" that reflects the new insights which both biblical and dogmatic theology can provide. These books will strive to be openly Christian in spirit, eclectic in approach, up to date in scholarship, and will address themselves to those ethical problems which are most real to the modern American mind.

This book of Father Schanz's is made up of two distinct but obviously interrelated parts: a general study of all the sacraments, their theory and meaning, and a particular study of three of them, baptism, confirmation, and the Eucharist. In both parts are found the biblical, liturgical, historical, and ecumenical perspectives of Vatican II. He thus sets the sacraments solidly in the unrolling of God's salvation plan of history, especially as seen in the Bible. He focuses on the sacraments not so much as channels of grace as he does as signs of Christ's saving activity in the Church.

All this is seen most clearly when he turns to the three sacraments of baptism, confirmation, and the Eucharist. Here he exploits the vast riches of scriptural symbolism, liturgical development, and concrete involvement to their fullest.

In a few passages throughout the study, Father Schanz draws some explicit ecumenical conclusions. But more important perhaps even than these are the very working principles of his study. For in these days when the tension between Word and Sacrament is being fully reexplored by Catholics and Protestants alike, and when Catholics are in many ways rediscovering the riches of the Word and Protestants the riches of the liturgy, a book such as this cannot fail in advancing mutual understanding.

Finally, the editors would like to express their thanks to all those whose interest, advice, and cooperation have made this series possible. They are especially grateful to Mr. William May of The Bruce Publishing Company, who not only initiated the project and sustained it through the inevitable disappointments and complications, but contributed so much of his editorial skill to its final shape. To the individual authors who so graciously added to their heavy burden of academic responsibility by undertaking these books, we can only express the hope that their share in the shaping and influencing of the American Catholic community of today and of tomorrow will be far more meaningful to them than any meager thanks of ours.

The Editors,

REV. J. FRANK DEVINE, S.J., Boston College
REV. RICHARD W. ROUSSEAU, S.J., Fairfield University

Introduction

To live in an age of renewal and transition is an exciting, stimulating and challenging experience. While the signs of religious renewal are apparent on many fronts, yet no single factor has so largely prompted the religious awakening as the Second Vatican Council. The changes being introduced by the Council are revolutionary. New attitudes, new approaches, new insights are already at work in the Church. The Council itself, however, can do little more than chart the new paths which the Church universal is to follow. In every local community of the Church, clergy and laity must try to understand and implement the objectives which the Council has proposed.

I. AIMS OF VATICAN II

The aims of the Council are succinctly set forth in the first Conciliar document promulgated, namely, the *Constitution on the Sacred Liturgy,* December 4, 1963.[1]

> This Sacred Council has several aims in view. It desires to impart an ever-increasing vigor to the Christian life of the faithful; to adapt more suitably to the needs of our own times those institutions which are subject to change; to foster whatever can promote union among all who believe in Christ; to strengthen whatever can help to call the whole of mankind into the household of the Church. The Council, therefore, sees particularly cogent reasons for undertaking the reform and promotion of the Liturgy. [Paragraph 1, NCWC translation.][2]

The Council goals, therefore, may be summarized as: the spiritual renewal of the faithful; *aggiornamento* or updating of the Church; and the promotion of a spirit of ecumenism, both toward other Christians and toward the non-Christian world.

To help achieve this threefold goal, the Council has initiated a renewal of public worship, the center of the Church's life and the focal point of her very existence (CSL, par. 10). In an age that despises sham and hypocrisy, the Council wholeheartedly desires that Christians should find in the sacred liturgy an authentic, genuine approach to their Creator. It is in the liturgy that we meet Christ, that we hear him speak to us, that we celebrate his saving deeds for us, that we pay our respects to the Father through and with his only Son.

---

[1] Hereafter, this Constitution will be referred to as CSL.
[2] AAS, Vol. 56, No. 2, Feb. 15, 1964, p. 97.

For this worship encounter to gain in authenticity, a further dual emphasis is deemed imperative: education in the history of salvation as recorded in Scripture, and "streamlining" the Mass and the sacraments to make their structure and purpose immediately obvious to the faithful. The first emphasis results naturally from the renewal of scripture studies that has developed in the Church especially since 1943 when Pius XII issued his *Divino Afflante Spiritu,* an encyclical letter encouraging modern methods of biblical research and exegesis. To know him whom we praise is to know his saving plan for sinful man, to recall his loving deeds in past Salvation-History, and to commit ourselves here and now to Christ in the Spirit.

It is only in the broad perspective of biblical reality that God's design emerges with the clarity needed to view adequately our present family relationship with Christ. The dialogue of worship, which prolongs God's saving work in the present, cannot be a meaningful family exchange of love without attention to the inspired Word spoken in the assembly of praise. Biblical consciousness must support liturgical understanding.

Genuine liturgical encounter, moreover, cherishes an atmosphere of intelligible word and ritual. The worshipers must be able to grasp readily the chief features of their worship experience and to participate actively in this communal celebration. If the first part of the Mass, for example, is the proclamation of Christ's saving deeds for us, then his words should be announced to us from a conspicuous place traditionally used for this purpose, such as the pulpit, lectern, or the celebrant's chair (anciently, the symbol and place of teaching authority). The altar table, the place of sacrifice, should be reserved for the eucharistic offering. Furthermore, the congregation must recover its traditional role, which was gradually absorbed by the choir and the minister at the altar. Only in such a context of intelligibility can we expect to participate fully and actively in the offering of our faith and love to God.

Such adaptation to the needs of our times does not mean arbitrary change nor an antiquarianism which would blindly imitate ancient worship forms. Prudent adaptation requires first a return to the most authoritative principles or guidelines followed in the early Church in order to discover a sound norm for a creative liturgical renewal today (CSL, par. 4). Such a posture respects the Church's rightful concern for tradition, while at the same time it reflects a concern for the cultural and spiritual milieu of the present century. A certain flexibility in developing new worship forms has therefore reappeared to implement the Church's desire to be all things to all men.

The current liturgical renewal is not without its ecumenical implications. Insofar as the Church expresses her true nature most effectively in liturgical worship, the latter "shows forth the Church, to those who are outside, as a sign lifted up among the nations under which the scattered children of God may be gathered together until there is one sheepfold and one shepherd" (CSL, par. 2). Interior renewal, fostered especially by a liturgically oriented piety, will enable the Church to project to her separated brethren an image at once convincing and inviting. Moreover, even in specific elements, the reform of worship strengthens the ecumenical cause. Emphasis on the significance of God's word in worship, the use of the vernacular tongue, and the encouragement of congregational participation provides a common bond with Protestant worship, which has characteristically based its service on these features. This is not to say that Protestant forms are being imitated for their own sake; the truth lies in the Church's rediscovery of these features in her own heritage.

II. PERSPECTIVES OF OUR PRESENT STUDY

It is from such a biblical, liturgical, historical, and ecumenical perspective that this textbook takes its primary emphasis. The informed Catholic is expected to be aware of the principal intellectual trends of the time in which he lives. Underlying the liturgical renewal of Vatican II is a rich theological stratum.[3] Out of this theological awakening comes a renewed sense of sacred history, a new historical perspective in which to evaluate the experience of Christian worship. Salvation-History, or the gradual unfolding of God's plan for uniting all men with himself, provides an essential matrix for our study of worship. The saving deeds of the sacraments can be fully appreciated and understood only if they are viewed in the light of God's whole saving plan as this is revealed in Scripture. What is recorded in the Bible, the book of salvation, comes to life in the liturgy. As Pius XII put it, "Christ acts each day to save us, in the Sacraments and in His holy Sacrifice" (Mediator Dei, par. 29).

A second emphasis of the text rests on the newly evolved theology of personal encounter with Christ in his saving action in the Church, represented especially by the creative thought of the Dutch theologian, Father Edward Schillebeeckx[4] and the German Father Karl Rahner.[5] Worship is not a dead or static thing; it is not a performance or an empty drama which the congregation merely watches as an audience of spectators. It is meant to draw us into personal union with Christ. We meet Christ in the Eucharist and in the other sacraments. The theological

---

[3] Cf. Charles Davis, Liturgy and Doctrine (New York: Sheed & Ward, 1960).

[4] Christ, the Sacrament of the Encounter with God (New York: Sheed & Ward, 1963).

[5] The Church and the Sacraments (New York: Herder & Herder, 1963).

structure and meaning of this encounter will concern us as we elaborate a theology of worship.

Third, ever since June 29, 1943, when Pius XII published the memorable encyclical on the social nature of the Church, *Mystici Corporis Christi (On the Mystical Body of Christ)*, Christians have become increasingly conscious of their relationship to one another as members of God's family on earth. The sacraments of worship, then, are not mere private experiences between God and us; they are *family* celebrations which channel the worship of the community to God and, in turn, bring his saving grace to build up, to sanctify, and to solidify the Church. If the sacraments are communal celebrations, then the active sharing of the congregation makes sense, as an outward visible sign of the inward union that persists in the worshiping congregation. We are a family worshiping with the risen Christ, celebrating a meal with him, joined together in love and being drawn toward one another in the love of Christ.

Finally, as "The Mass is ended. Go in peace" implies, the Christian is sent forth from the saving event of the Eucharist to help build up the community of love among men. He must continue to live the Mass throughout his day. This calls for commitment, the Christian's response to the saving love of Christ brought to him in the sacraments. Loyalty, allegiance, dedication, surrender should follow readily from a wholehearted and meaningful worship experience. There is no dichotomy between worship and Christian living. Authenticity must be the mark not only of the Christian at worship, but also of the Christian in the community. Worship in spirit and in truth promotes the interior and social commitment so necessary in the mature Christian of the twentieth century.

The framework of Christian worship is sacramentally structured. The sacraments channel the homage of Christ and his Church to the Father; from the Father, through the Son's redemptive intercession, divine life flows sacramentally to men. After exploring the essentially sacramental design of God's saving plan and the concept of "sacraments" in the narrower sense, we shall examine the three sacraments which traditionally have served for initiation into the life and worship of the Church — namely, baptism, confirmation, and Eucharist.

Acknowledgments

The author and publisher are grateful to the following for permission to reprint copyrighted material:

A. & C. Black, Ltd. (Dacre Press), for citations from *The Shape of the Liturgy* by Gregory Dix;

Benziger Brothers, Inc., for citations from Jungman's *The Mass of the Roman Rite*;

B. Herder Book Company, for citations from *The Church Teaches* by J. Clarkson, S.J., et alii;

John Knox Press, for citations from *The Eucharistic Memorial* by Max Thurian;

The Muhlenberg Press and the Board of Publications of the Lutheran Church in America, for citations from *Luther's Works* and from *Eucharist and Sacrifice* by Gustaf Aulen;

The National Catholic Welfare Conference, for excerpts from its translation of the *Constitution on the Sacred Liturgy* and of the *Constitution on the Church*;

The Newman Press and Darton, Longman, and Todd, for citations from *Sacraments and Worship* by Paul Palmer, S.J., and from *The Mystery of Christian Worship* by Odo Casel; and The Newman Press, for citations from *The Didache*, translated by J. Kleist, S.J.;

Sheed & Ward, Inc., for citations from Charles Davis' *Liturgy and Doctrine*, Mircea Eliade's *Patterns in Comparative Religion*, Edward Schillebeeckx' *Christ, the Sacrament of the Encounter with God*, and from Max Thurian's article on transubstantiation in *Christianity Divided*;

The University of Notre Dame Press, for citations from Jean Danielou's *The Bible and the Liturgy*;

The Westminster Press and the SCM Press, for citations from J. K. S. Reid's *Calvin: Theological Treatises*.

Abbreviations

AAS — *Acta Apostolicae Sedis* (Acts of the Apostolic See).

ACW — *Ancient Christian Writers*, ed. J. Quasten and others.

ASS — *Acta Sanctae Sedis* (Acts of the Holy See).

CJC — *Codex Juris Canonici* (Code of Canon Law).

CSEL — *Corpus scriptorum ecclesiasticorum latinorum* (collected writings of Latin ecclesiastical authors, Vienna Academy, 1866 ff).

CSL — *Constitution on the Sacred Liturgy*, Second Vatican Council, December 4, 1963.

Denz — Denzinger-Schönmetzer, *Enchiridion Symbolorum*, 32nd edition, 1963 (Handbook of the Creeds).

PG — *Patrologia*, series graeca, ed. J. P. Migne (Writings of the Eastern Fathers of the Church).

PL — *Patrologia*, series latina, ed. J. P. Migne (Writings of the Latin Fathers of the West).

RJ — Rouet de Journel, S.J., *Enchiridion Patristicum* (excerpts from the writings of the Fathers)

ST — *Summa Theologiae*, St. Thomas Aquinas.

TCT — *The Church Teaches* (St. Louis: B. Herder Book Co., 1957), ed. J. F. Clarkson and others (Documents of the Church).

Contents

PART TWO: BAPTISM, CONFIRMATION, THE EUCHARIST

PART ONE

THE FRAMEWORK OF
SACRAMENTAL WORSHIP

CHAPTER I

Sacramental Plan of Saving Worship

Our life in the Church and our achievement of life's goal, union with God, can be understood only in the light of Salvation-History. The Scripture shows us how, from the beginning, God chose to enter into dialogue with man, his creature. He raised Adam to the status of a personal friend, making him divinely lovable by implanting something of godliness in him. But man willfully broke off this dialogue with God. The revolt of man in his forefather, Adam, could have made man an eternal failure; it could have separated him from his true source of life for all eternity.

Despite man's abdication from grace, God in his goodness and kindness promised to reopen the dialogue (cf. Gn 3:15). Somehow the divisive forces of evil would be conquered, the victory would be at hand for the human race. In his own good time, God chose an individual, Abraham, and promised that through his family a new beginning would be made.

Through his dealings with this race, Yahweh would educate man for the dialogue of redemption. If man by his creatureliness and his sinfulness had broken his ties of friendship and loyalty with God, and was unable to make an adequate response to the infinite Creator, then God himself, on his divine initiative, would one day send from the very stock of Abraham a spokesman truly worthy to mediate for sinful mankind: his own Son in the flesh.

The Son of God made man, Jesus the Christ, acts in a dual capacity in the dialogue between God and man. As God's Son, he is able to speak to us the word of saving love. He is able to reveal the Father's merciful desire to draw sinful man back into the family of the Father. As man, Jesus takes us up into himself, speaks and acts for us, makes his obedient "yes" to the Father's plan for drawing "second sons" into family union with the Father. He accepts his passion and death, which with his resurrection-ascension constitute his saving journey, his redemptive pilgrimage to the Father's mansions.

The saving journey of Christ's death and resurrection liberates mankind, creates a free people, a people of God, the new Israel, the Church. Through his Spirit, the risen Christ, head of the Church, is present to his Church, acting upon it to make it live with his own love. This action of the saving Christ concretizes itself especially in the sacraments, which therefore introduce us personally and communally into the long history of salvation.

From this brief survey of the leading themes in Salvation-History, it is apparent that God deals with man in the way most suited to his nature. God made us as a composite being, a union of matter and spirit, of body and soul, or as the Hebrews conceived of man, as a living body. In identifying ourselves with Jesus and returning, through and in him, to God, it is not simply a matter of "saving our soul." God wishes to draw the whole of man, indeed the whole of mankind, back to himself. So unique is the unity of man that our bodily senses are the avenue by which the exterior world impresses itself upon our psyche, and the avenue through which, in turn, we express ourselves outwardly to make contact with our fellowman.

Therefore we may see the wisdom of God in designing his master plan of salvation along sacramental lines. The external, the visible, the outward manifests and actualizes the divine, the invisible, the spiritual. The sacramental form or pattern in redemptive history may be understood better with the help of the diagram on page 5.

This diagram is an attempt to envision God's plan of reuniting men with himself, of bridging the gulf between his infinity and our finiteness, between his holiness and our sinfulness, between his pure

THE SACRAMENTAL PLAN OF SALVATION

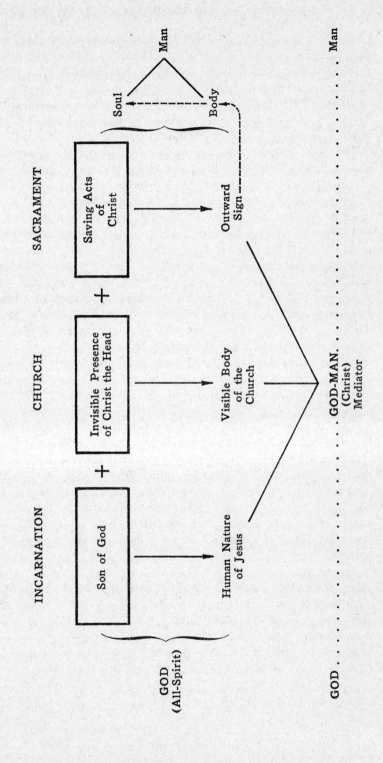

spirituality and our bodiliness. The diagram portrays three phases or dimensions of the act of salvation. The first, that of the Incarnation, makes the Son of God, who is all spirit, present and visible among men in the flesh of Jesus of Nazareth. The human nature of Jesus is the point of contact with the divinity. St. Thomas referred to Christ's sacred humanity as the instrument conjoined to his divine person.[1] When we touch Christ as man, we touch him as God.

The second step in the accomplishment of our salvation reflects the same pattern, the spiritual becoming visible and incarnate. Christ lives on in his Church. Through the Spirit, whom he and his Father send as Paraclete, Christ remains the invisible but active head of a Church which consists of visible membership, a social body of men united under authority by creed and law and worship, all of which are definite, visible realities. Thus, the Church is a mystery of the invisible becoming visible, of Christ's headship in the Church, of Christ's saving presence among men made visible in the externals of the Church's structure.

The third and final dimension portrays the activity of Christ in his Church in the form of what traditionally has been called "sacrament." The seven major signs of redemption are sacraments: the making visible under ritual and symbol of the saving actions of Christ's death and resurrection. Through the celebration of the sacraments, Christ's saving grace and love reach us. Through those same sacramental celebrations, our worship goes back to the Father with, in, and through Christ. Thus the sacraments are a mystery of saving worship in visible symbol.

The invisible world of the supernatural makes its impact upon the sanctuary of man's inner spirit, by passing through outward symbol and visible reality, through man's body to his innermost being. The whole of man is brought within the saving influence of Christ, but in a way most consonant with his nature. If the spirit expresses itself through the flesh, and the flesh is the gateway to the spirit, God will then respect the basic nature of man, by filtering the spiritual to man in a bodily way. Thus, the whole plan of salvation reflects a basically sacramental formula or pattern.

The term sacrament in its broadest sense, then, can be applied to the entire redemptive design of God. Christ is the living sacrament of God. The bodily nature of Jesus of Nazareth is the visible manifestation of the saving presence of God among men. The Church, in turn, is an extension or prolongation of Christ, the primordial sacrament. It, too, represents a mystery of spirit and flesh. The external structure of the Church — its visible authority, creed, and worship — serves to embody

---

[1] S.T., III, 64, 3.

the saving presence of Christ himself. The Church, therefore, is a kind of supersacrament of Christ living on in the world, a visible sign of his continued saving presence among us. The seven sacraments flow naturally from the Church's own sacramental nature. In addressing herself to God in worship, and in reaching out to sanctify men, it is natural for the Church to express herself sacramentally, under symbols charged with divine power. Sacramentality, indeed, lies at the heart of the divine master plan of salvation.

I. THE INCARNATION

A more detailed examination of this divine blueprint of salvation serves only to point up the wisdom and love with which it was conceived and carried out. The first step that God takes toward man, as we have seen, is to make himself visible in his own Son. Jesus of Nazareth is the invisible Son of God made visible among men in the flesh. He is the "image of the invisible God" (Col 1:15), the "interpreter of the Father" (Jn 1:18). He is "God in a human way and man in a divine way."[2] This divine Person is "personally man, and this man is personally God."[3] Christ is the personal embodiment of the Father's desire to save all men. He is God's merciful love made visible. From the moment of his incarnation, the Son of God is constituted in that mortal flesh where he makes himself subject to the conditions of sin and the sinner. He is in a state where he is subject to suffering and death. He is in that state where he is oriented toward the cross and the resurrection. Thus the incarnation is truly the beginning of salvation.[4] Since Christ is God's saving love, his saving grace made visible, we may truly call him the personal sacrament of God, the primordial sacrament of God's saving mercy.[5]

The importance of this historical encounter with the Son of God in the flesh echoes in every word of John's first epistle:

> I write of what was from the beginning, what we have heard, what we have seen with our eyes, what we have looked upon, and our hands have handled, of the Word of life. And the Life was made known and we have seen, and now testify and announce to you, the Life Eternal which was with the Father, and has appeared to us. What we have seen and have heard we announce to you, in order that you also may have fellowship with us, and that our fellowship may be with the Father and with his Son, Jesus Christ (1 Jn 1:1–3).

[2] Schillebeeckx, Christ, the Sacrament of the Encounter with God (New York: Sheed & Ward, 1963), p. 14.

[3] Ibid., pp. 13–14.

[4] Cf. Rahner, The Church and the Sacraments (New York: Herder & Herder, 1963), pp. 14–15.

[5] Ibid., pp. 14–15, 18–19.

In these words John unequivocally sets forth the value of eyewitness testimony, the ability of Christ's contemporaries to see him, to hear him, even to touch him in his risen state. The humanity of Jesus sacramentalized the Divine Word, made him visible, available to man's senses; and the personal testimony of those who knew him best has come down to us in the Scripture of the Church. Truly, God became accessible to man in the very bodiliness of Jesus of Nazareth. It is through him, in turn, that we will reach the Father. "No one comes to the Father but through me" (Jn 14:6).

II. THE PASCHAL MYSTERY

A. The Paschal Mystery, an Act of Saving Worship

The work of salvation, of reuniting mankind with the Father, is two-directional. On the one hand, its theocentric focus involves an act of total surrender to the Father on the part of the Son of God made man. "He humbled himself, becoming obedient to death, even to death on a cross" (Phil 2:8). If the first Adam had refused loyalty to God, had revolted against divine authority, had sought to elevate himself to a position of parity with God on his own terms, the second Adam, Christ, will right these wrongs in the freedom of his humanity. He will embrace his Father's will to return to him by a saving journey that will throw back the roadblocks of sin and bridge the chasm between the Father's house and his errant children. He pays the supreme homage of his very life. His life on earth and the surrender of that life on the cross are but one long act of loving worship to the Father's glory. "My food is to do the will of him who sent me, to accomplish his work" (Jn 4:34).

The other focus of the work of salvation centers upon man, to gather us together as God's children in the household of the faith. As John puts it, he was to die "not only for the nation, but that he might gather into one the children of God who were scattered abroad" (Jn 11:52). Christ's act of filial worship restores mankind to the good favor of the Father. Once again we are able to return to the Father's house, this time as members of the Church, God's family of second sons or adopted children in this world. This is the great outcome of the Paschal mystery. The saving journey to God, accomplished by Christ in his death and resurrection, liberates man in the sense that it opens to him membership in the family of the Church. This is the anthropocentric or man-directed benefit of redemption. Christ's death and resurrection, therefore, are truly a mystery of saving worship: worship to the Father, and salvation for man.

B. *The Paschal Mystery in the Light of Salvation-History*

Recent history records a succession of liberation movements, designed to recapture for oppressed and enslaved man the most precious gift of his freedom. We remember the Freedom Fighters of Hungary (1956), the struggle for freedom and independence of the emerging nations of Africa in the 1960's, freedom journeys undertaken by heroic East Germans to escape across the Berlin Wall; the sporadic efforts of heroic Cubans to overthrow the Red-tinged dictatorship of Castro, the struggle in Viet Nam to preserve freedom from Communist domination. In our own country, we think of the heroic struggle for equal rights and opportunities that oppressed minorities have had to wage in order to enjoy the great American freedoms. All of these struggles involve commitment, hardship, dedication, self-surrender, and personal sacrifice, a willingness to risk death itself for the cause of freedom.

Liberation movements of such kind find an ancient counterpart in the great freedom movement of the Israelites known as the exodus. Out of the exodus came a surcease of slavery, the birth of a new people, occupation of its own land, a sense of dignity and national identity hitherto unknown among the sons of Jacob. Left behind were the idolatries of Egypt. Israel's identity as a "kingdom of priests, a holy nation" (Ex 19:6) demanded of her a unique fidelity to its newfound God. The hand of the divine Liberator had directed a mighty saving journey that spelled death to the old ways of Egypt and the inauguration of a new life of freedom under Yahweh.

The ancient Passover from Egypt marked the beginning of a long line of divine liberations: liberation from the life in the desert to the occupation of Canaan under Joshua; liberation from invading enemies; the great liberation from the Babylonian exile in 536 B.C. All these saving acts prepared the way for the greatest liberation of all, freedom from sin and death. Until these latter were overcome, the greatest burdens of human existence remained yet to be conquered. The true Israel, Jesus, embodiment of his people, would undertake a saving journey through death to new life, a journey that would eclipse in importance all previous pilgrimages of liberation. Divine ingenuity planned this saving event to coincide with the annual festival of freedom held at Passover time. As the time approached for the Paschal *seder*, when Israel gratefully relived its ancient deliverance and prayed for the coming of the Messiah, Jesus elected to inaugurate his own passage out of this world to the Father. "Before the feast of the Passover, Jesus, knowing that the time had come for him to pass out of this world to the Father, having loved his own who were in the world, he loved them to the end" (Jn 13:1). In his mighty return to the Father through death and resurrection, Jesus would gather up all previous moments of liberation in sacred history. The moment of fulfillment, the fullness of time, had come. Man's liberation from sin and death was at hand.

To throw back the roadblocks of sin and death that barred the way to heaven for mankind, Jesus, the new Adam, would personally face up to the penalties of the sin of the first Adam and conquer them. Having freely put on the mortality of our sinful flesh, Jesus would meet death bearing with him all human sin and the sanctions it had incurred. Christ, visible sign of God's triumphant mercy and victorious grace, freely embraces the outward sign of man's sinful existence in order that henceforth that very death may be a sign and cause of man's spiritual freedom.

"Christ, our Passover, has been sacrificed" (I Cor 5:7). Jesus embraces death as the true Paschal Lamb of that year's Passover feast, but not without leaving behind the Christian memorial of his liberation. In a festive banquet, the newly delivered people, the Church, would gather like Israel of old to celebrate their birth and independence as a people of God, by reliving in the symbolic food and gestures of the eucharistic meal the victorious achievement of their founder. The Eucharist becomes the Passover meal of the Christian Church, the outward sign of the community's reunion with God in Christ, the sacrament of Christian liberation.

C. Theology of the Paschal Mystery

Christ returned to the Father through death, resurrection, and ascension. Once restored to the Father's glory, he imparted the Holy Spirit upon the Church. Each of these aspects of the Paschal mystery bears contemplation for a grasp of its theological significance.

1. The death of Christ was not a murder, the unjust killing of a victim against his will. It was a freely given sacrifice. In this, Jesus was truly the Suffering Servant of Isaiah 53:10 who "offered himself because he willed it." His words at the Last Supper indicate that he was surrendering himself to death for us. "This is my body which shall be given up for you. . . . This cup is the new covenant in my blood" (1 Cor 11:24–25). To give up one's body and to seal a covenant in one's own blood signify, in the Jewish idiom, the making of a sacrifice. The essential core of the Lord's sacrifice lies in the self-surrender of his will, "Not my will but thine be done" (Lk 22:42). The passion narrative recounts, in terms borrowed from Isaiah and the Psalms (especially Pss 21 and 68), the bloody details of the sacrifice. "He became obedient to death, even to death on a cross" (Phil 2:8).

2. The apparent defeat of Jesus' death dissolves in the joy of the resurrection. Here mankind receives a visible sign, tangible evidence that death has truly been conquered. He "burst the bonds of death and came forth as conqueror from the grave" (*Exsultet*, the Paschal Proclamation of the Easter Vigil). "By dying, he destroyed our death; by rising, he restored our life" (Preface of Easter). By conquering death, the penalty of sin, Christ shows that he has conquered sin itself. The way to heaven is open, the barrier of sin is thrown aside.

The resurrection visibily demonstrates, too, the Father's good pleasure over the return of his Son, the divine stamp of approval on Christ's work, as though the Father were to say, "Thou art my beloved Son, in thee I am well pleased" (Lk 3:22). The resurrection is the visible sign of the lordship of Christ, the moment when he is made *Kyrios* (Lord) over all creation (cf. Acts 2:36). It is the "eternally enduring act of salvation."[6] As risen Lord, Christ continues to be our Savior, through the sacraments. He lives always to make intercession for us before the Father's throne. Christ did not cast away his human nature, but rose in it and glorified it, endowed it with immortality, the highest honor to be paid to our mortal flesh. The whole man is redeemed, body and spirit.

The resurrection of Christ is the central truth of the *kerygma*, the good news proclaimed by the apostles with Pentecostal fervor.[7] And precisely because Christ has risen, we also, as St. Paul teaches, are summoned to resurrection. The resurrection of Christ our head is the surest guarantee of the resurrection of our own bodies (cf. Rom 6:3 ff.; 1 Cor 15:20 ff.; Phil 3:10). Ultimately, the risen splendor of the Head will descend upon the faithful members of his body.

3. Christ returns to the Father by resurrection-ascension. The ascension is the official installation of Christ as king over the world which he won by his blood. It is the original kingship feast, where Christ is enthroned as *kyrios*, as divine Lord, seated at the right hand of the Father in glory. In Christ the Head, we are already seated in glory with him (cf Eph 2:6). The Son of man has truly received power, victory, and dominion, as foretold in Daniel 7:13–14. If the Son has returned to the Father in glory, he can now fulfill his promise to send us the personal Pledge of his continued presence among us.

4. The Spirit of the risen Jesus, already conferred upon the Apostles on Easter Sunday evening (cf. Jn 20:22), is publicly imparted to the Christian Church on Pentecost Sunday (cf. Acts 2:1–4). The Spirit, who identified Christ's Messiahship at his baptism in the Jordan, now identifies the true messianic community by his presence in the infant Church. He

---

6 Schillebeeckx, *op. cit.*, p. 22.
7 Cf. early chapters of Acts.

is the Personal Fruit of the Paschal mystery, the Gift par excellence, the Personal Embodiment of the mutual love of Father and Son demonstrated so efficaciously in the Paschal mystery. He is that Spirit of love who has come to bind men together in love. He will make the new community of mankind, the Church. He is the soul that gives life to the Church-body of Christ on earth, a bearer of life and love to the people of the new covenant which was sealed in the Paschal sacrifice.

III. THE CHURCH, SACRAMENT OF THE RISEN CHRIST

No greater mistake could be made than to try to divorce the Paschal mystery from the Church which is its glorious outcome. Christ died that his Church might live. He traveled on the saving journey from death through resurrection-ascension in order to carry with him a new people of God along this same route into freedom. His death-resurrection is a "covenant-sacrifice," a sacrifice made to seal a covenant with the Father. It was at the Last Supper, the first Mass, that he inaugurated this covenant in his own blood (Lk 22:20). Now a covenant implies two partners to the agreement. If the Sinai covenant was sealed between Yahweh and his people Israel, then the new covenant is sealed between God and the new Israel, the Church, with his Son-made-man acting as mediator. The Church constitutes the people of the new covenant.

As a people born out of sacrifice, the Church is the posterity of the Suffering Servant of Yahweh (cf. Is 53:10–12). They are the scattered sheep gathered together into one flock by the death of Jesus (Jn 11:52). They are that kingdom of priests, cleansed for God by the blood of the Lamb (cf. Apc 5:9–10), whom Christ can claim as his own because he purified them in his own blood (cf. Ti 2:14).[8]

Unlike the founder of a nation or the leader of a movement, who after his death may live on only in spirit among his followers, Christ remains among his own because he has risen. The apostolic Church was convinced that they were bearing witness, in preaching and in the Eucharist, not to a past friend and leader now departed from among them, but to an ever present Lord and Messiah. The apostles had seen him in his risen state; as Peter boasted, they had eaten and drunk with him (cf. Acts 10:41). Most reports of the resurrection appearances of Christ make no direct mention of his vanishing from their sight; perhaps the evangelists hint that Jesus never really left them except in visible form.

Furthermore, if we grant the incarnation and even more so the resurrection, it is unthinkable that Christ and the Church should be separated. By the incarnation Christ was definitively established as the new head

---

[8] Cf. Pius XII, *On the Mystical Body of Christ*, par. 31, Paulist Press.

of mankind. Already he in a sense incorporated all mankind in himself. The resurrection established further that Christ did not cast away his humanity but glorified it, immortalized it, divinized it, and therefore has similarly glorified the people who are bound to him. In this way the Church itself remains the prolongation or extension of the glorified Christ of heaven. In this way is realized the promise of Christ, "I am with you all days, even unto the consummation of the world" (Mt 28:20). The Church is the total Christ, the Vine and the branches (cf. Jn 15), Head and members (cf. Eph 1:22–23) united together in one whole, sharing in the one same divine life, the risen life of the glorified Christ of heaven. Baptism links us directly to the risen body of Christ in all his glory; therefore, wherever the Church is, there also is Christ.

The Church then is truly the sacrament of the risen Christ.[9] It is a fellowship brought about by the common possession of the Holy Spirit in grace, in faith, and in love. The visible communion of the Church's hierarchy and faithful manifests the inward union with God in Christ. The Church thus is both sign and reality. It is the redemptive reality of grace, of Christ's triumphant mercy, present in visible form.

IV. THE SEVEN SACRAMENTS

By its very nature, the Church is Christ living on in the world, in an earthly and social body. In other words, the Church by its very nature is sacramental, the saving presence of Christ embodied in visible form. If the very nature of the Church is to be a sacrament of Christ in the world, it is then not surprising that what we traditionally call the seven sacraments should flow from the very essence or structure of the Church. It is, so to speak, natural for the Church to express itself sacramentally, that is, to accomplish its mission of sanctification and worship under outward signs. The sacraments are Christ's saving acts continued in the Church through the visible rites or functions of the Church. Sacraments are the Church acting in its official, social capacity and performing its essential functions of salvation. Without the Church, no sacramental act is possible. Therefore, whenever salvation is offered and imparted to any man, that man enters into some relationship with the Church, either explicitly or implicitly.

The Church is a sacramental organism of salvation, for in its visible form it signifies and confers grace. Christ the head of this sacramental

---

[9] In its *Constitution on the Church*, The Second Vatican Council confirms that "the Church is in Christ like a sacrament or as a sign and instrument both of a very closely knit union with God and of the unity of the whole human race." — *De Ecclesia*, par. 1, Nov. 21, 1964; AAS, Vol. 57, No. 1, Jan. 30, 1965, p. 5; NCWC translation.

organism continues to act in it, constantly infusing his Holy Spirit into the whole body and into its various members that they may fulfill the functions and services necessary for the well-being of the whole body. The sacramental acts of the Church, then, are never empty or meaningless acts. They are always full of the grace they signify because they are ultimately the personal acts of Christ himself symbolically and really made present. Thus the Church is never more itself than when it is acting sacramentally. Far from being mere occasional or incidental activities of the Church, the sacraments are its essential activity, expressing its very life, offering its praise to the Father, and receiving life from him. In short, the Church performs its essential, vital activity of saving worship in and through the sacraments.

It is important, too, to appreciate from the beginning what may be called the ecclesial dimension of the sacraments. The sacraments flow from the essential structure of the Church, and they have in view, not merely the private sanctification of the individual, but the building up of the mystical body of Christ as a whole. The Eucharist is central in the life of the Church; it is the covenant-sacrifice by which the Church is constantly vitalized. It is the meal of unity that binds all its members in charity, in the love of Christ. It is the Paschal meal ever renewed in the presence of the risen Savior. It is the covenant meal in which the new people of God renew their allegiance to their divine Covenant-Partner.

All the other sacraments and sacramentals (that is, the various blessings and blessed objects by which the Church brings all of nature under the sanctifying power of Christ) are centered around the Eucharist; they flow from it and are directed back toward it. From their relation to this eucharistic center, the ecclesial polarity of the other sacraments necessarily follows. Baptism incorporates the individual into the eucharistic community of the body of Christ. Confirmation makes him a public witness with Christ to the Father, charges him with the responsibility of helping to extend the kingdom of Christ among men. Penance and the anointing of the sick are two medicinal sacraments. Penance reconciles the sinner to full favor with the Church, so that he in turn is reconciled with God in Christ. In the sacrament of the anointing, the Church stands by the sick member in the assurance that Christ's redemption has triumphed both over sin and death. It is a sacrament that strengthens the individual's ties to mother Church in the anguished hour of suffering and may indeed restore him to his former life in the Church by curing his illness, if this is in God's providence.

Two other sacraments are functional; that is, they equip the recipient for special functions in the Church. The sacrament of Holy Orders confers the authority of building up and maintaining the existence of the

Christian community, the people of God. It confers upon the priests of the Church the power to govern, to proclaim God's word, to sanctify, especially by the celebration of the sacrament-sacrifice of the Eucharist. Matrimony expresses the sacramental nature of the Church because it creates a miniature Church in the union of husband and wife. Every couple married in Christ typifies the great union between Christ and his Church. In every Christian home the husband is the symbol of Christ, the wife a personification of mother Church. Thus the sacraments can be seen to be not mere auxiliary services or administrations of the Church, but rather the exercise of its essential powers, the expression of its essential nature, the vital acts of the body of Christ on earth.

51

CHAPTER II

Toward a Definition of Sacrament

I. GOD'S SAVING DEEDS IN
OLD TESTAMENT SALVATION-HISTORY

The history of salvation is the inspiring record of a personal God intervening by word and act in the history of man to save him from destruction and call him back into union with himself. Twelve centuries before Christ, God's mercy descended lovingly upon the Israelites, captive in Egypt, because through them the Almighty resolved to carry redemption and liberation to all men. Yahweh revealed himself to these people of his choice especially by his actions among them. He showed himself to be a saving God. By his might and power, he spared the Israelites from the death plague that afflicted the Egyptians. He led them forth across the Sea of Reeds into freedom — not mere physical or political freedom, but freedom from the idolatrous paganism of their Egyptian masters. He worked wonders for them in the desert to provide them with food and drink (manna, the water from the rock). He healed them from sickness by the brazen serpent. He bound them to himself by a covenant of love in the solemnity of Sinai. He guided them across the expanse of the desert, accompanied them across the Jordan, delivered Jericho and the Canaanite cities into their hands.

Israel was never to forget these saving acts of a loving God. Year after year in the annual celebration of the harvest festival they were to appear before the Lord with the firstfruits and to renew their covenant allegiance with God by reenacting and reliving the momentous events of the Exodus. Deuteronomy 26:5–10 recounts the words of a cultic credo or a profession of faith which was to be recited by the worshiper at the presentation of the firstfruits. It takes the form of a recital of God's great saving acts for his people Israel.

> My father was a wandering Aramean who went down to Egypt with a small household and lived there as an alien. But there he became a nation great, strong, and numerous. When the Egyptians maltreated and oppressed us, imposing hard labor upon us, we cried to the Lord the God of our Fathers and he heard our cry and saw our afflictions . . . he brought us out of Egypt with his strong hand and outstretched arm, with terrifying power, with signs and wonders; and bringing us into this country, he gave us this land flowing with milk and honey. Therefore, I have now brought you the first fruits of the products of the soil which you, O Lord, have given me.

The Deuteronomist continues in words directed to the latter-day Hebrew:

> This day the Lord your God commands you to observe these statutes and decrees. Be careful then to observe them with all your heart and with all your soul. Today you are making this agreement with the Lord. He is to be your God and you are to walk in his ways and observe his statutes, commandments, and decrees, and to hearken to his voice. And today the Lord is making this agreement with you. You are to be a people peculiarly his own as he promised you, and provided you keep all his commandments, he will then raise you high in praise in renown and glory above all other nations he has made and you will be a people sacred to the Lord your God as he promised (Dt 26:16–19; emphasis added).

These words are those of a covenant renewal. A contemporary of the Deuteronomist (eighth century B.C.?) is just as much a part of the covenant as his ancestors at Sinai. He too is personally involved in the covenant; the repetition of "today" and "you" in the above passage suggests a reenactment of the covenant. Each succeeding generation is personally involved in the covenant with God. The past, so to speak, comes to life in the annual renewal of the covenant with Yahweh. So it was to be in the future. The sacraments of the new covenant, then, were also to be a renewal of God's past saving acts for his people. They come to life, they are relived, by each succeeding generation of Christians.

Yahweh's acts of love toward his people in the first exodus hearten the faith of Israel and encourage hope for the deliverance that came much later when Israel had been captive in Babylon. The liberation of 538 B.C. marked Yahweh's continuing concern for his people and, in turn, quickened the expectation for an even greater gift of freedom in the golden Messianic Age that was to come. In this sense, Yahweh's saving deeds foreshadowed the great redeeming act of love on the part of his Son-made-man. And just as the mighty deeds of Israel's past were re-enacted and relived for succeeding generations, so also would Christ's great act of benevolence and redemptive love be reenacted and relived in the future days of the Church. This would be done especially in those ritual acts called sacraments.

II. OLD TESTAMENT RITES AND FEASTS

It was not only in the mighty deeds of the exodus that Israel met its God, but also in the ritual acts of its public worship before God from the time of Abraham on (cf. Gn 17). A male Israelite was solemnly inducted into the family of God by the ritual act of circumcision, a kind of baptism into the covenant. Sacrifice and various ceremonials of worship developed especially with the building of the ark in the time of Moses (Ex 25; Book of Leviticus), and later still reached a full flowering in the days of the temple of Solomon. Sacred meals like the annual Passover (cf. Ex 12:17 ff.), sacrificial banquets (cf. Lv 22), and the observance of holy days and special feasts during the year, served to remind the Israelites of Yahweh's presence among them and his right to their continued allegiance (for the holy days, cf. Lv 23). The ordination of Aaron and of his successors in the high priesthood sets a long-range pattern for the New Testament priesthood by which men are consecrated to the special duty of sacrificing to the Lord.

The worship of ancient Israel, then, served a twofold need: to renew God's saving deeds and covenant love for his people, and to direct Israel's homage and fidelity back to God. It is not without deep significance that the Fourth Gospel situates Christ's public life firmly within the liturgical life of Israel and makes it unfold against the rich backdrop of the Jewish feasts (cf. Chapters 2, 5, 6, 7, 10, 13). As a dutiful child of his people, Christ observed these rituals and later patterned the new worship of his Church principally on the forms of Israel's liturgy. The sacraments have deep roots in the soil of Old Testament worship.

III. GOD'S "WORD" IN SCRIPTURE AND THE SACRAMENTAL WORD

There is another aspect of Old Testament Salvation-History that will enrich our understanding of the sacraments, and that is the power and the efficacy of God's holy word.[1] To appreciate this we need to know a little of Hebrew psychology. For the Semite, man is a totality, a "one-thing." Thought also is a "one-thing," a total contact between one's whole being and outside reality. Therefore God's thought or wisdom is already an act of God's total being. God is present, therefore, and active by his word. The word of God is somehow God himself. The Hebrew vocabulary indicates that the term for "word" already implies action. The Hebrew dābār (ordinarily translated "word") meant originally "to push, to go away with, to thrust forward."[2]

God's word, therefore, precedes an event, introduces it, and brings it to fulfillment. For the prophets, God's word is invincible. God utters a word (as in the story of creation, Gn 1) and the word is already an action that is accomplished. God spoke and the heavens were made. One of the most memorable prophetic passages illustrating the efficacy of God's word is found in Isaiah 55:10 ff.:

> For just as from the heavens the rain and snow come down and do not return there till they have watered the earth, making it fertile and fruitful, giving seed to him who sows and bread to him who eats, so shall my word be that goes forth from my mouth; it shall not return to me void, but shall do my will, achieving the end for which I sent it.

Besides the word dābār in the meaning of word-action, we also find the term memrā' sometimes used as a substitute for God himself, for example, in the Targums, the Aramaic translations and paraphrases of the Hebrew Bible. In Genesis 3:8: "They heard the sound of the memrā' walking in the garden." In this latter case, the word is almost identified with God.

In the New Testament, John the apostle and evangelist calls the Son of God, the Second Person of the Blessed Trinity, the Logos or the Word of God the Father. It is this Logos that became flesh, came to live among his people, spoke to man about his Father, cured and healed often with

---

[1] Cf. Alexander Jones, God's Living Word (New York: Sheed & Ward, Inc., 1961); Carroll Stuhlmueller, "The Sacraments in Scripture," Studies in Salvation History (Englewood Cliffs, N. J.: Prentice-Hall, 1964), pp. 128–145; J. L. McKenzie, S.J., "The Word of God," Myths and Realities (Milwaukee: The Bruce Publishing Co., 1963); Louis Bouyer, The Word, Church, and Sacraments in Protestantism and Catholicism (London: Goeffrey Chapman, 1961); Gregory Baum, "Word and Sacrament in the Church," Thought, Vol. 38 (1963), pp. 190–201; Lucien Richard, "The Word and the Sacraments," Journal of Ecumenical Studies, Vol. 2, #2, Spring, 1965, pp. 234–250.

[2] Stuhlmueller, op. cit., p. 136.

a mere word of command. It is this same God-Man who suffered, died, and rose again to create the new people of God the Church, where he continues to teach us by his word and to save us by his sacraments.

If God's word worked so efficaciously in the past, as Scripture reveals, then why may it not continue to operate with power when it is spoken by the Church in her sacramental acts? The words of the sacramental rites are not merely expressions of desire or mere appeals for God's help; they contain an inward power to sanctify, to join us to Christ in the pattern of his death and resurrection. The sacraments, then, continue Old Testament Salvation-History and make us participants in God's grand design for the human race: the renewal and restoration of all things to God in Christ (cf. Eph 1:10).

With this understanding of God's saving deeds in the Old Testament and the power of his word to effect what he willed, we may now turn to the New Testament to seek more direct evidence for the sacraments of the Church.

IV. NEW TESTAMENT EVIDENCE TOWARD A DEFINITION OF SACRAMENT

Though we do not expect to find a theological treatise on the sacraments in the New Testament, we do have the right, at least in the case of baptism and the Eucharist, to try to discover the main outlines of these two fundamental sacraments of the Church's worship-life, sacraments which plunge us into the saving acts of Christ and join us to his saving worship of the Father. For it is by the sacraments that we make contact with Christ living on in the great Church-sacrament. It is through these sacred signs that we experience the same wondrous saving deeds, the same saving mercy, which the Israelites of old received from an all-loving God.

A. Baptism[3]

It is our purpose here merely to examine some of the principal New Testament allusions to baptism in order to discover the basic outlines of the sacrament, and to draw from this cursory examination some ideas for a tentative description of sacrament.

---

[3] In English there are presently available several fine works of a biblical and historical nature that study exhaustively the sacrament of baptism in Scripture as well as in the history of the Church. Among these should be mentioned: *Baptism in the Thought of St. Paul* by Rudolf Schnackenburg (New York: Herder & Herder, 1964); *Baptism and Confirmation* by Burkhard Neunheuser, O.S.B. (New York: Herder & Herder, 1964); *Baptism in the New Testament* by A. George, J. Delorme, et al. (Baltimore: Helicon, 1964).

In the Book of Acts we encounter baptism as the ordinary rite of initiation into the Christian community. Baptism appears as the response to the proclamation of the Gospel. Peter indicates what this response must be: "Repent and be baptized, every one of you in the name of Jesus Christ for the forgiveness of your sins; and you will receive the gift of the Holy Spirit" (Acts 2:38). Constantly, baptism appears as the rite of initiation into the Church (cf. Acts 8:12-13, 16; 16:31-33; 18:8). The word "baptism," from the Greek baptizein, means "to plunge" or "to immerse." Therefore, it means essentially to be plunged or immersed in water. It is of the essence of baptism that it is first of all an outward ritual; but there is associated with this outward ritual a supernatural effect: the forgiveness of sins and the reception of the Holy Spirit (cf. Acts 2:38; 10:47-48; 22:16).

For St. Paul, baptism is essentially Christ-centered. It is into Christ's body that we are baptized (cf. 1 Cor 12:13; Eph 4:4-5). We "put on Christ" (Gal 3:27) at the moment of our baptism. It is Christ's Spirit that we receive in this sacrament (cf. Rom 8:11, 15). Christ's saving mysteries, his death and resurrection, are reenacted in us by our contact with the life-giving waters of the font (cf. Rom 6:3; Col 2:12, 20; 3:3).

The synoptic evangelists stress the need of faith to accompany baptism, "He who believes and is baptized shall be saved, but he who does not believe shall be condemned" (Mk 16:16). The Matthean formula reflects the trinitarian usage of the liturgy of baptism in the Palestinian Church (cf. Mt 28:19). All three synoptics stress the difference between the baptism of John, son of Zachary, and the baptism of Jesus, who would baptize with the Holy Spirit (cf. Mk 1:8; Lk 3:16; Mt 3:11). Matthew and Luke add that Jesus would baptize "with fire" (ibid.). Just as the Spirit had appeared at the birth of the world soaring over the waters to make them fruitful (Gn 1:2), and just as he appeared at the incarnation of the Word, forming the body of Jesus in the womb of Mary (cf. Lk 1:35), so now he appears again at the birth of the Christian, with a purifying action in the soul of the newly baptized as profound as the action of fire. He takes possession of the person; and for the believer, this is like a new birth that enables him to enter, in fact, into the kingdom which John merely foretold.

The First Epistle of St. Peter, which bears many nuances of the ancient service of Christian initiation, stresses the presence of the mysteries of Christ's death and resurrection in the actual baptismal ceremony. "Baptism now saves you . . . through the resurrection of Jesus Christ" (1 Pt 3:21). Baptism makes us priests, "built into a spiritual house, a holy priesthood, to offer spiritual sacrifices acceptable to God through Jesus Christ . . . you, however, are a chosen race, a royal priesthood, a holy nation, a purchased people" (1 Pt 2:5, 9). Baptism, too, recalls the blood covenant of Sinai, since by the power of Jesus' blood, the baptized enters the new covenant and becomes a member of the new Israel (cf. 1 Pt 1:2).[4]

John's Gospel speaks of a new birth "of water and the spirit" as the necessary condition for entering into God's kingdom (cf. Jn 3:5). Several of the signs described in John may have a sacramental significance (the cure at the pool of Bethesda, Chapter 5, the healing of the man born blind, Chapter 9, the washing of the feet, Chapter 13).[5] The living waters which Christ promises (Chapter 4) in his conversation with the Samaritan woman are explained in 7:39 as referring to the Holy Spirit who is to be given at Christ's glorification. The living waters flowing from the side of the Savior are fulfilled in Chapter 19:34 in the water flowing from the pierced side of Christ on the cross (cf. also Jn 5:6–8). At this moment, the Spirit issues forth from the crucified and glorified body of Jesus. For one theologian, "at this point and only at this point does Christian baptism become possible. The death of Christ marks the institution of the sacrament."[6]

From these preliminary data, certain highlights about baptism emerge with clarity. Baptism is an outward ritual performed in water, but the baptismal event is more than merely a symbol. It causes or brings about an action of the Spirit upon the baptized. It effects the remission of his sins, it joins him to the Christian community, it makes him a believer in Christ. It conforms him to the risen Savior, whose mysteries have a transforming effect upon the inner life of the baptized. Through baptism Jesus acts by means of his Spirit to impart the fruits of salvation to the recipient. Furthermore, this sacrament of "water and the Spirit" is a ritual performed by representatives of the community of believers. It is a rite of initiation into the Christian body. From it flow all the privileges that accrue to a Christian: fellowship in the breaking of the bread (cf. Acts 2:42, 46), participation in the priestly powers of the community (cf. 1 Pt 2:5–9), union with Christ in his sufferings and his resurrection (cf. Rom 6:3 ff.; Col 2:12).

B. Eucharist

The highest privilege of the baptized is realized in the celebration of

---

[4] Cf. Carroll Stuhlmueller, C.P., "Baptism: New Life Through the Blood of Jesus" in Worship, Vol. 39, No. 4, April, 1965, pp. 207–217.

[5] Cf. Bruce Vawter, C.M., "Johannine Sacramentary," Theology Digest, VI, No. 1, Winter, 1958, 11–16, and Raymond Brown, S.S., "The Johannine Sacramentary," New Testament Essays (Milwaukee: The Bruce Publishing Co., 1965).

[6] Neville Clark, An Approach to the Theology of the Sacraments (London: SCM Press, 1958), p. 28.

the Eucharist, the "Lord's Supper" (1 Cor 11:20). At this point, we shall merely indicate the chief features of a biblical exegesis of the Eucharist, derived from the principal eucharistic texts of the New Testament (the institution accounts in Mk 14:22–25; Mt 26:26–29; 1 Cor 11:23–34; Lk 22:14–20; and the significant texts of 1 Cor 10:14–22 and Jn 6:48–59).[7]

From these accounts, the Eucharist emerges clearly as a sacred meal, the chief constituents of which are bread and wine. Behind the external sign of the meal is an event of the metahistorical order: a proclaiming of the death of the Lord (cf. 1 Cor 11:26), fellowship in the Lord's body and blood (cf. 1 Cor 10:16), the accomplishment of a new unity among the members of Christ (cf. 1 Cor 10:17), the celebration of a blood covenant in the very blood of Jesus present under the symbol of wine (all four institution accounts). It is a meal presided over in first instance by Christ himself. It is still designated as his own meal ("The Lord's Supper," 1 Cor 11:20). It is a meal distinctive of Christian worship, celebrated in the homes of Christians rather than in the temple or the synagogue (cf. Acts 2:46), and demanding faith and charity in the believer (cf. 1 Cor 11:29; Jn 6:35, 40, 66). As a meal taken in common, it serves to unite the participants with Christ and with one another or, better, with one another in Christ, all together making up one body (cf. 1 Cor 10:17).

Certain major points evolve from the above survey of the two basic sacraments reported in the New Testament. First, the sacraments are saving events or encounters with the risen Jesus that take place in faith and through some outward expression of faith. Second, they involve the presence and activity of Christ himself. Third, they are actions of the community, expressing its inner life and contributing to its upbuilding. Fourth, they unite the participant with the dead and risen Christ, they make the Christian share in the great Paschal worship of Christ's death and resurrection. Finally, they transform or transfigure the participant into the likeness of the Paschal Christ. Putting these elements from the biblical data together, we might then suggest the following as a tentative, descriptive definition of sacrament: A sacrament is (1) a symbolic saving act (2) of Christ (3) in and through the Church (4) by which we are joined to Christ's worship of the Father in his Church and (5) are formed in Christlikeness, especially in the pattern of the Paschal mystery.

---

[7] These will be dealt with in more detail below, pp. 168; 173–175.

CHAPTER III

The Sign Value of the Sacraments

Though we may not think about it very often, all our communication with one another is conditioned by the use of signs or symbols. Actions, gestures, words, and objects have come into use as a kind of sign language by which we communicate with our fellowman. The handshake, the smile on our face, the words with which we greet an old acquaintance, constitute a whole complex of signs by which we indicate our pleasure at seeing our old friend again. Whether we think of natural signs (laughing, crying), which we do instinctively, or arbitrary signs (a flag, an alphabet), which are man-made and are given a decisive meaning by the will of man, we find it necessary to make use of one or the other category of these signs in order to express our thoughts to others.

I. PRIMITIVE RELIGIOUS SIGNS

Little wonder then, that in man's earliest history he already felt the need for dealing with God through symbols. The material world around him was charged with an intrinsic sacredness. Man had a reverence for the mysteries of nature. Fire, water, air, earth exercised a certain spell over man because they spoke to him of a superior being.

To contact this superior being, man engaged in symbolic actions called rites or rituals. A living rite is not a prefabricated complex of religious ideas put together by sophisticated scholarship; rather "it is an immediate, primordial creation of religiously-minded men in which they have actively realized their effective connection with the divinity before they explain this connection to themselves. This is why at all times and in all places rites are considered to be the work of the gods . . . it is the gods who have instituted them and are the real agents of the rites, working through and beyond the action of the priests."[1]

These rites, which flow out of man's natural symbolism, are said to be of two basic types, analogous to the sacraments and sacramentals of the Church. The first type is a kind of sacred action which comes from the gods and delivers the divine life itself or blessings from the god to man. The second type includes the ordinary actions of human life, which are brought within the realm of the sacred by divine blessings. In the first type, the actions of the gods descend into the life of man by means of the ritual celebration. In the latter type, our human existence is lifted up into the sphere of the eternal.

Many of the most elementary rituals which underlie the first agrarian civilizations are associated with the theme of creation, an eternal return and a perpetual renewal of all things by returning to the beginning. Other rituals are built around the significance of water. On the one hand, the water is seen as a force of creation, a source of life. On the other hand, water can act as a force of destruction as in the waters of the Deluge, the waters that drowned the Egyptian pursuers of the Israelites, the waters of death in which all the living must finally be swallowed up and perish.[2]

Another ancient ritual is that associated with the meal, in which the taking of food unites one with the creative power or serves as pilgrim food for the return to the lost paradise. There are also the nuptial and funeral banquets. Such ritual meals underlie much of the significance attached to sacred meals in Salvation-History.

---

[1] Louis Bouyer, *Rite and Man* (Notre Dame: University of Notre Dame Press, 1963), p. 66; cf. Margaret Mead, "Ritual Expression of the Cosmic Sense," *Worship*, Vol. 40, No. 2, Feb., 1966, pp. 66–72.

[2] Cf. M. Eliade, *Patterns in Comparative Religion* (New York: Sheed & Ward, Inc., 1958), p. 188 ff.

II. MODERN PSYCHOLOGICAL NOTION OF SYMBOL

The study of primitive religious rites and symbols reveals how rich in complexity religious signs can be. Indeed, they constitute a sign language all their own. The Christian sacraments grow more intelligible to us if we learn to read them as part of man's immemorial language of religious worship. That is to say, Christ did not create entirely new religious signs for his Church. Rather, he built upon the religious sensitivity of man, developed from the dawn of creation (phase of natural religion) and brought to a certain level of religious sophistication among the Israelites (Old Testament Salvation-History). The sign language of the Christian sacraments, far from being a completely new creation, actually follows in a direct line from the ancient religious symbolism of man's worship. It was the genius of Christ to take perennially valid religious signs and invest them with a deeper significance than they had ever attained before.

Anthropology, then, can teach us much about the presacramental religious signs. But psychology also plays a part in explaining the mysteries of the religious sign or symbol. It has been suggested that we should differentiate between sign and symbol. A sign, it is contended, is a representation of a concept or judgment. It serves to present an idea to the mind. It is a one-for-one signal. It conveys a single message, it points to a single object; and once it gets this message across to my mind, it has finished its work. Red and green traffic lights, stop signs, price tags, all have such a one-for-one function.

The symbol, on the other hand, seems to be far richer than a mere sign. Whereas the sign appeals largely to the mind on a conceptual basis and conveys a mere message to my intellect, the symbol carries with it a whole background of experience, not only rational elements, but imaginative, sensitive, and emotional elements as well. All of these, on both conscious and unconscious levels, are part of the world of symbol. For example, the portrait of one we love not only shows us what that person looks like, but evokes all the happiness and affection and intimacy associated with the presence of that person. The portrait is not merely a sign, then, but a symbol that recalls and makes real all the happy experiences that we have enjoyed together — the time of our first meeting, the deepening of our acquaintance, the good times we have had together, the time when I first obtained the photograph, etc. Thus the symbol is not merely a concept-bearer, but an experience-bearer. It evokes all the rich experiences that I associate with this particular symbol. Short of the physical presence of the loved one, we have all the elements of a genuine I-thou experience.[3]

---

[3] Terrence Toland, S.J., "Christian Sacrament: Sign and Experience," *Readings in Sacramental Theology* (Englewood Cliffs, N. J.: Prentice-Hall, 1964), p. 22 f.

Such a symbol, then, has a life and growth of its own. Besides its work of referring to something else, a symbol has its own dynamic existence. Symbols are not invented, but result from a creative encounter with history. If the notion of symbol contains such a rich dimension of experience both historical and personal, it is logical to ask how such a notion may illumine our understanding of the symbol called "sacrament." Applying the above to the notion of sacrament as a symbolic act, we may better understand how the sacraments introduce us into the long line of Salvation-History.

The sacraments themselves are Sacred History prolonged and made present in our midst. Immersion in the baptismal waters, for instance, involves us in all the saving deeds that God offered through the agency of water. The Deluge at the time of Noah, the crossing of the Reed Sea at the Exodus, the waters of refreshment from the rock in the desert, the waters of life flowing from the pierced side of Christ on the cross — all these saving events clustering around the symbol of water are channeled to us at the moment of our baptism.

Or again in the symbol of the meal: the eucharistic meal evokes all the great meals of Salvation-History. The Paschal meal on the night of the exodus, the meal of wisdom (cf. Prv 9:1–5), the manna of the desert, Christ feeding the multitudes, the meals taken by Christ in the homes of sinners — all their polyvalent symbolism of nourishment, union, and forgiveness is channeled to me when I participate in the Eucharist.

On my part, of course, I must enter into the symbolic experience. I must respond to this encounter with Salvation-History, this meeting with God and his saving deeds, if it is to be a meaningful event for me, the symbol, in other words, of my faith and my loving adherence to Christ.

III. THE THREE-DIMENSIONAL SIGN FUNCTION OF THE SACRAMENTS

Since a sacrament is more than a sign, a mere one-for-one pointer or signal, it is not surprising that St. Thomas with his usual clear insight speaks of a threefold signification of sacraments. The sacraments point to the past, the present, and the future. Every sacrament is a commemorative sign, a kind of souvenir of the past, insofar as it joins us to the passion and resurrection of Christ. Every sacrament, therefore, links us with the source of Christ's saving power in his death and resurrection. In some way (to be examined later), it makes present or puts us into contact with the past historical saving acts of Christ.

In the moment of sacramental encounter, the sacrament is an effective sign which actually brings about a meeting with Christ and makes accessible to us, at the moment of sacramental reception, the saving life power and dynamic love proceeding from the passion of Christ. Grace, both sanctifying and sacramental, is available to man because of the intrinsic efficacy at the moment of sacramental celebration.

Third, as prophetic or prognostic signs, the sacraments point to the future. They are a token or pledge of the ultimate goal of sanctification, the fulfillment or perfection of God's kingdom in heaven.[4] In a prayer composed for the office of Corpus Christi, St. Thomas admirably expressed the threefold signification of the sacraments: "O sacred banquet in which Christ is received, the memory of his passion is renewed, the soul is filled with grace, and a pledge of future glory is given" (Magnificat Antiphon, Second Vespers, Feast of Corpus Christi).

IV. CONSTITUENTS OF THE SACRAMENTAL SIGN

If it is necessary to analyze briefly the components of the sacramental symbol, it can be readily seen that the sacraments are actions (usually involving the use of things) accompanied by the spoken word. In baptism, for example, the sacrament is celebrated by pouring water over the forehead or, as it was done in ancient times, by immersion into the baptismal pool. The action here is the pouring or the immersion, the thing is water.

To make the action as determinate and intelligible as possible, the spoken word is added: "I baptize you in the name of the Father, and of the Son, and of the Holy Spirit." Thus it becomes abundantly clear that the water ritual means a sacred plunging in the name of the three Persons of the holy Trinity. In the case of the Eucharist, the things employed are bread and wine, the words uttered are essentially "This is my body" over the bread, and the words "This is my blood" over the cup of wine. The words of consecration in their biblical context denote not merely the presence of Christ but also the offering of his sacrifice.

The words of the sacramental formula clearly express the Church's conviction that it is Christ in first instance who is acting in each of the sacraments (cf. Chapter IV below); it is in his name that baptism and penance are celebrated. The words of consecration in the Eucharist use the first personal pronoun "my." Christ himself is acting in the person of his priest.

Second, the sacraments are also signs that the Church is acting. The Church after all is Christ's body. Where the head is involved, so also is the body. In fact in this case Christ could not act sacramentally without the presence of a representative of his Church. The sacramental

---

[4] S.T., III, 60, 3.

economy or plan is such that Christ will act in this way only in the person of his representative, through the actions and words that constitute the sacramental experience. "I baptize," "I absolve," "I sign you with the sign of the cross and confirm you with the chrism of salvation" — formulas such as these indicate beyond doubt that the Church is at work here in this moment of sanctification in the person of her agent or minister.

V. SIGNS OF FAITH

The traditional maxim: "the sacraments are for man" does not preclude the necessity of entering into the dialectic of salvation by a personal involvement through faith and loving obedience. That we are to come to the sacraments with faith can be seen from the fact that in Scripture salvation is attributed now to baptism and now to faith, as though one or the other were all-sufficient. Actually the truth is that the one includes the other; baptism for adults presumes an act of supernatural faith on the part of the petitioner. Baptism, in other words, is itself an act of faith. In John 3:5, the new birth of water and of the Spirit is proclaimed as a prerequisite for entrance into God's kingdom. In Romans 6:3-14 and Titus 3:5 the same insistence on baptism is again apparent. In John 3:36 and Romans 10:9, faith alone is mentioned as the gateway to salvation. "He who believes in the son has everlasting life; he who is unbelieving toward the son shall not see life, but the wrath of God rests upon him" (Jn 3:36). Romans 10:9 puts it this way: "For if you confess with your mouth that Jesus is the Lord and believe in your heart that God has raised him from the dead, you shall be saved."

Again faith and salvation are found side by side if we examine the miracles of Christ, which are figures or signs of the presence of his healing and saving power among men. In many cases Christ first demanded faith in himself or at least in his power before he would work a miracle (cf. the cure of the paralytic, Mk 2:1-12; the woman with a flux of blood, Mk 5:25-34; the raising of the daughter of Jairus, Mk 5:22-43; the cure of the daughter of the Syrophoenician woman, Mk 7:24-30). Logically it would follow, then, that the sacramental wonders of Christ's healing power likewise demand faith from us if they are to reach their full effectiveness in us.

Even this response of faith to the saving hand of Christ is not wholly of our making. The initiative comes from Christ's grace, which moves us to respond freely to his offered gift. We are not justified, we are not sanctified without our cooperation. We are saved as free men, as responsible persons. God does not force his gifts upon us against our will.

The saving event which occurs in the sacraments may be said to include a descending and an ascending phase. The descending phase is the movement of God toward man; the divine saving presence of Christ through his Church in the sacramental encounter; the accessibility or availability of Christ and his grace to draw us into union with his Father by the influx of his Holy Spirit. Such a descending movement is but an extension of the movement of God toward us in the incarnation and in the Church itself. Through the incarnation the divine presence descended to earth in Jesus of Nazareth who became the living sign of God's presence among men, divinity made visible in the flesh. The Church as Christ's body and God's temple continues God's presence among men in Christ. She is "the sign set up before all nations" of the descending presence of God. The sacramental celebrations then are climactic moments when this saving presence of Christ in his Church becomes supremely actual for us, when his saving love and grace reach out to us personally and individually, directed and channeled to specific persons in the Church in terms of a personal encounter.

The ascending phase of God's saving work must likewise be traced through New Testament Salvation-History. Christ, the divine Person made man, returned to the Father as the perfect servant of the Lord in his act of final dedication and love (cf. Is 53:10; Mk 10:45). The Church, too, as Christ's body must be consciously attached to her head by loving devotion. She is his bride bound to him in love (cf. Eph 5:25 f.). Therefore, the Church, too, participates in this ascending line of loving commitment to the Savior. In every sacrament, therefore, besides God's movement toward us by his offer of saving grace (often called the opus operatum of the sacrament), there must also be the answer of man through the corporate prayer or confession of faith expressed in the liturgy of the sacraments, in other words, man's faith and loving commitment freely given in conscious and willing acceptance of God's offer of grace in the sacramental encounter (the opus operantis of the sacrament). It is in the context of this latter movement (the ascending line of the opus operantis) that the place of faith in the sacraments must be viewed.

A. Signs of the Faith of the Church

The ecclesial dimension of every sacrament is apparent from the fact that the Church determines the real meaning of the sacramental rite.[5] Any religious symbol receives its significance from the religious community in which it is employed. This also occurred in the Church under the guidance of the Holy Spirit, as the Church through the centuries

[5] S.T., III, 64, 9, ad 1.

developed a suitable matrix of rite and gesture in which to locate the central sacramental act of sanctification created by Christ. Through the things used (such as bread, wine, and oil), the gestures performed, and the words that accompanied such gestures, the Church came to express her faith in the purpose for which each sacrament was instituted by Christ. Thus a study of this outward symbol, the symbolic rite of each sacrament, will reveal to us the ultimate purpose of the sacrament according to the belief of the Church.

Especially in the sacramental words (sometimes called the "form" of the sacrament) does the Church determine more precisely the real divine meaning of the various religious symbols. Little wonder that the Fathers of the Church call the sacramental word the "word of faith." By her word of faith the Church receives the saving mercy of God descending from the Father in the Son, through the power of the Holy Spirit. Through the liturgical prayers of the sacraments, the Church expresses the supernatural meaning of the sacrament, its supernatural power and content.

Sacraments are not automation, nor are they magic by which man captures for himself something of the powers of the gods. Sacramental salvation is received from God, not created by man. Man must participate therefore in this saving event, not as a robot, not as one operating a computer or slot machine, mechanically deriving some magical saving grace by the mere performance of certain symbolic gestures. Sacraments touch the heart and core of human existence; they demand the interior as well as the outward cooperation of man.

B. Signs of Faith on the Part of the Recipient

Since the sacraments are community celebrations, they are first of all expressions of the faith of the whole Church; but, in addition to this communal expression of faith, each Christian must make a conscious adherence to Christ as an active member of the faithful of the Church. For the Christian filled with faith, this means that he looks beyond the mere externals of the sacramental signs and sees there the action of Christ. Baptism is not merely a bathing of the body; it is identification with the saving death and resurrection of Christ. The Eucharist is not merely bodily nourishment; it is primarily a meal with the risen Christ, at which his glorified flesh and blood nourish the believing worshiper.

Not only does the believing Christian approach the sacraments with the vision of faith, looking beyond the external ritual to the encounter with Christ that occurs there; but he must also come to the sacraments with the commitment of faith. Faith is more than an intellectual grasp of a supernatural reality; it is the surrender of the whole personality to Jesus the God-Man, present and active in the sacramental experience. This surrender engages one's will; it demands the gift of oneself, total service, a wholehearted dedication, the surrender of all that is deepest in one's being, a total response to the offer of God's saving grace in and through Christ.

It is this kind of faith, stimulated by single acts of God's elevating grace, that enable the adult catechumen to pledge himself unreservedly to a faithful and obedient Christian life. It is this kind of faith that enables the confirmed Christian to consecrate himself courageously and steadfastly to the mission of bearing public witness to Christ in every area of his life. It is this kind of faith that the Christian community and each individual Christian offers to God at the offertory of each Mass by means of the bread and wine. It is this kind of committed faith that the believing Christian brings to the sacred meal of the Eucharist where he receives Christ and he pledges his "Amen," as though to say "I adore, I praise, I love, I surrender myself to your service." Only if the Christian brings this kind of committed faith to his sacramental encounter with Christ will the power of the sacraments in turn influence his daily life. Only with this kind of faith will the Christian's life become gradually transformed into Christ.

Encounter in Christ with such wholehearted surrender will surely merit for the faithful member of God's people a deeper, more intimate faith in Christ and in the Father. Indeed, Vatican II assures us of the power of the sacraments to stimulate faith in the worshiper:

Sacraments strengthen faith

[The sacraments] not only presuppose faith, but by words and objects they also nourish, strengthen, and express it; that is why they are called "sacraments of faith." They have indeed the power to impart grace, but, in addition, the very act of celebrating them effectively disposes the faithful to receive this grace fruitfully, to worship God duly and to love each other mutually (CSL, par. 59).[6]

VI. THE SACRAMENTAL SIGN AND LITURGICAL RENEWAL

In the light of the foregoing it is not too difficult to see why the ritual of the sacrament should be as clear and obvious as possible to the faithful (CSL, paragraphs 59, 62). The easier it is for the Christian to understand readily the meaning of the sacramental situation, the easier it is for him to enter into the heart of the mystery with full faith. The elements of the sign, the gestures used, the actions performed, should be readily intelligible to him. Just as a smile or a handshake or a frown

---

[6] AAS, Vol. 56, No. 2, Feb. 15, 1964, p. 116.

or an exclamation of anger or command have their instant effect upon us, so should the sign of the sacrament convey its meaning to us directly and forcefully.

The sacramental rite is itself a kind of dialogue between God and man. How can I take part in such a dialogue if I don't even understand the language that is addressed to me? A sacrament is addressed not only to God but also to the participant. The early Church felt this and used the vernacular language in every instance for several centuries. It was only when the Western Mass became ossified in Latin about the ninth century that the linguistic barrier, which still prevailed into modern times, was first erected. Vatican II has restored to the faithful the privilege of the mother tongue in much of the liturgy of the Mass, the sacraments, and the sacramentals (CSL, par. 63).

In the sacramental liturgy, the actions too should reflect local cultures. Diverse cultures may express identical religious sentiments in highly different ways. It is not uncommon, for example, for Asiatic and African peoples to express intense religious emotion by means of a sacred dance (cf. 2 Sm 6, where David danced before the Ark of the Covenant as it was being escorted in triumph to Jerusalem). Western gestures like the imposition of hands, which occurs in the baptismal service as a gesture of appropriation, may have a totally different meaning in another culture. In the Orient, for a man publicly to place his hand on the head of a woman is regarded as a proposal for marriage. If the sacramental sign or ritual, then, is to be thoroughly authentic and faith-stirring, it must make sense to the assembled faithful, and must be obvious to them; it must be easy for them to understand what message the sign means to convey.

This is not to derogate from the artistry of the ceremony. The nobility of worship invites beauty of expression; but aesthetic considerations must never override the fundamental requirement of clarity. The congregation must know what it is doing if it is to do it with sincere faith. It is precisely to evoke a more lively faith and to enable the sacraments to touch our daily life that the liturgical restoration specifies clarity of sign as one of its fundamental goals.

Besides the considerations of clarity and aesthetics, there is yet another consideration involved in the liturgical sign. As the Church evolved the ritual for her sacraments, she borrowed heavily upon the treasures of Sacred Scripture. The sacraments, after all, are deeply rooted in Salvation-History; hence, the outward form of the sacraments proclaims the saving act of God in evocative biblical terms. The water of baptism, for example, is meant to recall not only the priceless value of water for the people of the near East in our Lord's time, but also its association with

Saving History (cf., above, Sections I and III). The ancient practice of baptism by immersion more vividly portrayed the Christian's association with Christ's burial and resurrection; the contemporary practice of baptism by infusion (pouring the water over the head) less vividly expresses the deepest significance of the sacrament. From this it follows that our people need an intensified biblical orientation. The better they know their Scripture, the more they will come to appreciate the message of the sacramental ceremony. Such indoctrination becomes a kind of stepping-stone to the faith; that is, to be moved by the sacraments, the faithful should have an elementary grasp of Salvation-History. With this they will come better prepared to the sacramental encounter with Christ; and they will come away from it not only united more firmly with Christ, but also better instructed in the tenets of the faith. The liturgy then becomes, as it was in the early Church, a school of learning; for it was in the liturgical assembly, the *synaxis*, the proclamation of God's word, that the catechumens received their basic orientation in the faith.

VII. FAITH AND FRUITFULNESS

As will be explained later in more detail, the intensity of faith and love that we bring to the sacraments will also affect the total efficacy of the sacraments in us. If all the requirements are met for a true sacrament (validity), then Christ actually offers us his saving grace in the sacramental encounter. The sacrament achieves a certain efficacy already from this very fact (e.g., the imparting of the sacramental seal in baptism, confirmation, and orders; the sacrifice of the body and blood of Christ in the Eucharist; the spiritual bond in marriage). The ultimate end of the sacraments, actual union with Christ through his Spirit, a sharing in his life and his love, in other words the actual production of new grace-life in us (fruitfulness of the sacrament) requires on our part a real advance toward Christ in a loving commitment of loyal faith. Once more, then, is verified the importance of the sacramental gesture in evoking our response in faith.

CHAPTER IV

The Sacraments, Acts of Christ
and of the Church

We live in an age of creeping automation. Increasingly, technology brings the wonders of science within the grasp of man by the mere press of a button or the push of a lever. Even man's food and drink become available in coin-operated machines. There is a danger that the mechanical mentality of the modern age may carry over into religion, into our relationship with Christ. We may come to think of a sacrament as some kind of magical device for acquiring the mysterious power of salvation. The sacraments may be viewed as so many compartments, each one releasing a certain type of the magic potion of salvation, so long as we contribute the coin which is necessary to initiate the transaction. It is something like driving up to the gas station to buy gas for our car or to purchase a snack at a drive-in; it is a mere *quid pro quo*, a mere payment for a service or a product.

To have such a mentality is to fail to appreciate the sacraments as the visible making present of Christ's saving love. Sacraments are the personal acts of Christ; they are a sacred experience, a person-to-person encounter with the God-Man. The profound significance of this divine reality is what we now proceed to examine.

I. THE SACRAMENTAL SITUATION

The Church's teaching on the effective value of the sacraments was considerably diluted at the time of the Reformation and afterward, when Protestant theologians came to emphasize the primacy of God's grace-giving word (preaching) and considered the sacraments as signs or seals of God's promise, employed by Christ to strengthen our faith in his word. They came to this position in part as a reaction against the liturgical status quo of the late medieval Church. Worship-forms, shrouded in mystery and encrusted with external trappings and complex rubrics, excluded the faithful from intelligent participation. A certain superstition in the "use" of the sacraments was encouraged by overemphasis on their intrinsic efficacy and deemphasis of the need for personal dispositions.

While popular preaching and piety might have taken the latter approach, the official Church teaching continued to affirm the objective reality of the sacraments as being acts of Christ among us here and now which demand our cooperation. The Church has always been conscious that she is acting in Christ's name. All we have to do is listen to the sacramental word which the Church speaks in celebrating the sacraments. In the Eucharist the Church appropriates to herself the very words of Christ at the first Mass, "This is my body. . . . This is my blood." It is not of course the flesh and blood of the ordained priest that is meant, but the flesh and blood of Christ himself. In other words, the high priest Jesus is himself consecrating and offering the eucharistic sacrifice through his priestly agent. In baptism and confirmation, the sacramental act is done in the name of all three Persons of the Blessed Trinity. In penance, the current Latin Rite formula has the confessor pray: "May the Lord Jesus Christ absolve you from your sins, and I by his authority absolve you." In the sacrament of holy orders, the bishop requests God the Father Almighty through Christ to invest his servants with the dignity of the priesthood. In matrimony the priest as official witness of the Church ratifies the contract in the name of the Blessed Trinity. Finally, in the anointing of the sick, Christ himself is appealed to for forgiveness by the holy anointing and through his most loving mercy.

That Christ is present and active in the sacraments is clearly stated in the *Constitution on the Liturgy* by Vatican II:

To accomplish so great a work [our salvation and our worship of God], Christ is always present in his Church, especially in her liturgical celebrations. He is present in the sacrifice of the Mass, not only in the person of his minister, "the same now offering, through the ministry of the priests, who formerly offered himself on the cross," but especially under the eucharistic species. By his power he is present in the sacraments, so that when a man baptizes it is really Christ himself who baptizes. . . .

Christ indeed always associates the Church with himself in this great work wherein God is perfectly glorified and men are sanctified. . . .

Rightly then the liturgy is considered as an exercise of the priestly office of Jesus Christ . . . in the liturgy the whole public worship is performed by the Mystical Body of Jesus Christ, that is, by the Head and his members.

From this it follows that every liturgical celebration, because it is an action of Christ the priest and of his body which is the Church, is a sacred action surpassing all others; no other action of the Church can equal its efficacy by the same title and to the same degree (CSL, par. 7).[1]

Herewith the Council is simply echoing what Pius XII had already said in his Encyclical on the Sacred Liturgy in 1947, "He [Christ] is present in the Sacraments, infusing into them the power which makes them ready instruments of sanctification" (par. 20); or again, "Christ acts each day to save us, in the Sacraments and in his holy sacrifice" (par. 29). We may now ask exactly how is this present activity of Christ in the sacraments to be explained.

II. INSTITUTION OF THE SACRAMENTS

It is an undisputed fact that the sacraments as such must be traced ultimately to God himself. Only God can make a visible sign a bearer of a divine reality, such as the gift of the Spirit or the forgiveness of sins, the gift of divine sonship, the gift of Christ's body and blood as food for men. Even the Pharisees in the Gospels acknowledged that only God could forgive sins (cf. Mk 2:7). Associated with baptism is the conferral of the Holy Spirit (cf. Jn 3:5; Rom 5:5; 8:9, 14 f) — a gift which can come from God alone.

All grace of the New Testament is of course the grace of Christ; that is, God's gifts are offered to us through the agency of the humanity of Christ. The sacraments, then, as bearers of Christ's grace must ultimately derive their origin from Christ himself.

There is another way of looking at the origin of the sacraments from Christ. We must remember that Christ, as the Son of God in human

---

[1] AAS, Vol. 56, No. 2, Feb. 15, 1964, pp. 100–101; NCWC translation.

flesh, is himself the great primordial sacrament of God's saving grace among men. He is God's saving mercy, God's personal love made manifest or visible among men. The presence of Jesus of Nazareth on earth is the visible sign of God's will and intention to save his people. Therefore when Christ, the great personal sacrament, founds a Church, he unites men to himself as a body to a head, creating an entity which will embody his continued presence and activity on earth. It is Christ's saving grace in a new outward sign, in the social body which is the Church. The Church herself then is the fundamental sacrament of Christ. She gives outward visibility to his continued presence on earth and to his saving action among men. Christ's will to establish certain definitive grace-giving experiences would seem to follow then from his very institution of the Church. The Church herself as primordial sacrament would necessarily express her definitive saving action in those rites called sacraments.[2]

Such an explanation obviates the difficulty of trying to discover in Scripture an explicit account of the institution of each of the seven sacraments. In fact for most of the sacraments, we do not have such an explicit affirmation of their institution by Christ. In the case of the Eucharist we have the clearest testimony of all; for the narrative of the Last Supper clearly indicates Christ's institution of a Sacrament-Sacrifice that he willed to be continually offered by his Church — "Do this in remembrance of me" (Lk 22:19; 1 Cor 11:24). For two other sacraments, namely, baptism and penance, it is also quite clear that Christ explicitly intended grace to follow as the effect of their celebration. With baptism is associated man's rebirth in God's kingdom (cf. Jn 3:3-5) and the forgiveness of his sins (cf. Acts 2:38). There is also a sacramental effect implicit in Christ's conferral of the power to bind and loose (cf. Mt 16:19) and to forgive sins (Jn 20:23) and in this way to reconcile sinners with the Church.[3] With the other sacraments, however (confirmation, matrimony, holy orders, and anointing of the sick), although there are hints at their practice in the early Church, there is no clear or explicit statement of Christ affirming his will as to their existence. Thus it must be inferred that, by his very institution of the Church, Christ already intended the Church to act decisively in these situations to extend its saving grace to man in need. In this regard Father Rahner's description of sacrament is pertinent:

A fundamental act of the Church in an individual's regard, in situations NB —) that are decisive for him, an act which truly involves the nature of the Church as the historical, eschatological presence of redemptive grace,

---

[2] Cf. Karl Rahner, *The Church and the Sacraments* (New York: Herder & Herder, 1963), pp. 61, 62.
[3] *Ibid.*, p. 42.

is *ipso facto*, a Sacrament, even if it were only later that reflection was[e] *NB*
directed to its sacramental character that follows from its connection
with the nature of the Church.[4]

Therefore it is possible to affirm the direct and immediate institution
by Christ of the seven sacraments without holding that Christ determined
everything about the sacraments in an immutable and definitive way.
That he willed each of the sacraments and their special efficacy must be
maintained. With greater or less precision he also designated the sign
for at least some of the sacraments; but the Church also seems to have
the liberty to determine other actions as well as words to express the
hidden reality contained in the sacrament which is the work of God.

III. THE SACRAMENTS AND THE PASCHAL MYSTERY

The intrinsic value of a gift is enhanced when we realize the personal
sacrifice of the donor. Christ paid the price of his death and his resurrection in order to give us the sacraments. They are, down through the
history of the Church, the lasting souvenirs of his great love for us. For
"The Paschal Mystery of the passion, death, and resurrection of Christ
[is] the font from which all Sacraments and Sacramentals draw their
power" (CSL, par. 61).

In St. John's description of the crucifixion and death of Jesus, he
draws special attention to the moment when blood and water issued from
the pierced side of Christ. "One of the soldiers opened his side with a
lance, and immediately there came out blood and water. And he who
saw it has borne witness and his witness is true; and he knows that
he tells the truth, that you also may believe" (Jn 19:34, 35). John's
careful eyewitness testimony underscores the theological import of the
spear thrust and the consequent effusion of blood and water from the
wound. For John this constitutes a sign or symbolic event charged with
saving significance. The water recalls the stream of refreshment leading
to eternal life (cf. Jn 4) and especially the Holy Spirit who was to come
at the time of the Lord's glorification (cf. Jn 7:38, 39). But a typical
interpretation by the Fathers of the Church laid stress upon the sacramental and ecclesial significance of the water and blood; water suggests
baptism and the blood typifies the Eucharist, the two fundamental
sacraments by which the Church lives.

The very fact that both an ecclesial and a sacramental significance
should be attached to the same sign (that is, that the Fathers should see
in the effusion of blood and water both the creation of the Church and
a sign of the two basic sacraments of the Church) points out how closely

[4] *Ibid.*, p. 41.

related the sacraments are to the very essence of the Church. The Church herself is derived from the passion as well as the resurrection of Christ, from the entire Paschal mystery (cf. above, p. 12 f.). Furthermore, the Church exercises her fundamental powers of sanctification and the worship of God primarily through the sacraments. Therefore, it follows that both the Church and the sacraments derive their power and efficacy from the Paschal mystery. Through the Lord's passage from death to new life, he was the efficient, meritorious, and satisfactory cause of our salvation from sin, of our own passage from sin to new risen life.[5] It is by his death that Christ merited our liberation from sin and by his resurrection that he won for us the new life of justification (cf. Rom 4:25). Therefore, the sacraments, as the great sources of the Church's vitality, must derive their life in turn from our redemption in the Paschal mystery.

In a very beautiful passage just referred to, St. Thomas expresses the theology of the sacraments as deriving from the passion of the Savior. "Sacramental grace is directed to two principal purposes; namely, to take away the failing of past sins, passing deeds for which there remains a penalty, and also for perfecting the soul and those things that pertain to the worship of God in accordance with the Christian religion. Now it is clear from what was said above that Christ freed us from our sins especially by his passion, not only as an efficient and meritorious cause but also by making satisfaction for our sins. Likewise by his passion Christ inaugurated the worship of the Christian religion 'offering himself as an oblation and a victim to God' (Eph 5:2). From this it is clear that the sacraments of the Church, in a special way, derive their power from the passion of Christ, a power which is passed on to us in some way by the reception of the sacraments. As a sign of this 'there flowed from the side of Christ hanging on the cross water and blood,' the one referring to baptism, the other to the Eucharist, which are the most powerful of the sacraments."[6]

The sacraments then have the same function as that of the passion of Christ: to direct perfect praise and worship to the Father and thus to satisfy the basic responsibility of all creatures; and, second, to make the divine life flow from God to men and thereby unite mankind with the Father by membership in the holy people of God.

Therefore, Christ did not merely "institute" the sacraments in the sense of providing for their existence in some way or other during his life on earth; but he suffered and died that divine saving grace might be available to man through the sacramental channels. He died that the

NB

---

[5] S.T., III, 62, 5.
[6] Ibid. Translation our own.

sacraments might have life to pass on to men — Paschal life that unites us with the Christ of the Paschal mystery in the likeness of his death and of his resurrection (cf. Rom 6:3 f.; 1 Cor 11:26).

IV. HOW CHRIST OPERATES IN THE SACRAMENTS

If the sacraments are personal encounters with Christ, it is highly important to realize just how this encounter is made possible. Avoiding a mechanistic interpretation of the sacraments, one recalls that the Church is the sacrament or sign in the world of the glorified, risen Christ. The Son of God, retaining his glorified and transcendent humanity, has joined to it a vast assembly of the faithful, who together with him in his risen flesh comprise one total Christ. As the risen head of this body, the Son of God still acts through his humanity and through the social body, the Church, which is joined to his risen flesh. In this way, the Church's fundamental saving acts cannot be mere human acts. As the institution of salvation among men, the definitive saving acts of that Church must also be the actions of her divine head. It is clear also that these fundamental acts of salvation cannot be mere empty signs or gestures; if they are enacted by the Church in her official capacity as body of Christ, they must be filled with the divine reality of salvation proceeding from her risen head. The Church's acts are indeed the acts of Christ.

With clear insight St. Thomas elaborates upon the way in which Christ acts in His Church through the sacraments. He points out in several articles that the Son of God acts upon men through a whole series of instruments. The Son of God, the Divine Person, is the chief agent at work in sacramental salvation. He works first through his sacred humanity which is called by St. Thomas a "conjoined instrument" (so-called because the human nature of Christ was personally united to the divinity in the Second Person of God himself). The Son of God, acting through his body joined to him, in turn works through a series of separate instruments: the priest of the Church, the objects and words of the sacramental matter and form, the senses in the body of man — a whole series of agents through which Christ's saving grace ultimately penetrates to the inmost soul of man. The sacraments then are located by Thomas in the realm of instrumental causality.[7]

V. CHRIST ACTS THROUGH THE MINISTERS OF HIS CHURCH

The Church which St. Paul had founded at Corinth was torn with

[7] S.T., III, 64, 1, 3.

many dissensions in its infancy. Certain factions or parties had arisen, each claiming loyalty to the one who had baptized them. Early in his First Letter to the Corinthian Christians, St. Paul adverts to this party strife: "Each of you says, I am of Paul, or I am of Apollos, or I am of Cephas, or I am of Christ. Has Christ been divided up? Was Paul crucified for you? Or were you baptized in the name of Paul?" (1:12, 13). In other words, Paul affirms, the baptized convert owes his primary loyalty to Christ, whose grace operated through his authorized servants. There is one ministry, one Christian priesthood, which Christ exercises through many ordained ministers. Or again, Paul is led to exclaim: "Let a man so account us as servants of Christ and stewards of the Mysteries of God" (1 Cor 4:1). As the steward or dispenser of Christ's saving grace, as the celebrant of the saving acts of Christ, Paul is conscious that he is not acting in his own name, but that he is a servant, an agent of the great High Priest working through him.

The priest then acts in a dual role. On the one hand the priest represents Christ, bringing his saving acts into contact with men. On the other hand, the priest's mediatorial role makes him a representative of the people before God (cf. Heb 5:1). Or to put it another way, we may say that the priest acts as representative of the Church in her sanctifying capacity and also as agent of the body of the faithful presenting itself before the Father in repentance, love, homage, and thanksgiving. As delegate of Christ in his Church-body, the minister of the sacrament must act, first, as a free human being (that is, knowingly and willingly) and, second, consciously aligning himself with the intention of Christ and the Church. Only in this way will the rite performed be the Church's authentic rite; only in this way will the sacrament be a true or valid sacrament. By intending to do what Christ and the Church want done when the sacrament is given, the minister of the sacrament in effect expresses the faith of the Church that this earthly symbolic act is at the same time a personal act of the risen and glorified Christ acting through his Church.

If the priest's act is all that it should be, if it is an ideal ministerial act, then he will normally add to the faith of the Church his own personal faith and apostolic love directed toward the person receiving the sacrament. In other words he must identify himself as an individual person with the sacramental saving will of the Church. This is to act in the fullest sense as delegate of Christ in his Church. Nevertheless, as a minimum requirement for the priest, he must at least manifest a willing participation in the visibility of the Church; that is to say, he must have the intention of doing what the Church does. This is the minimum necessary for a valid sacrament. "The minister must inwardly intend to perform the Church's outward rite."[8]

This means in effect that while the ordinary minister of the sacraments is the ordained priest, in cases of emergency, a layman, indeed even a non-believer, may administer baptism so long as he has the genuine intention of performing the Church's external ritual, even though he may not himself agree with the significance or meaning of that act. The intention must be that which is accepted by the faithful as an act of the Church, of which he must have at least some elementary awareness. The same is true in the case of matrimony, where the parties to the contract really administer the sacrament of union as an act of Christ in and through his Church.

It is the constant tradition of the Church, from the time of the great Fathers like St. Augustine, that despite the unworthiness of the minister, Christ's grace still flows through the sacramental act. Even heretics and schismatics (therefore, those who have broken away from the full ties of mother Church) may still be used by Christ in his sacramental ministry for the benefit of the faithful. A priest who is in the state of mortal sin, though not acting lawfully, may still render a valid absolution; for as the saying goes, the water may still flow even through a rusty pipe. The fact remains that Christ may employ even unworthy agents; his power over the agent of salvation is ordinarily accomplished by the imprint of his priesthood through the sacramental seal of baptism and confirmation (for those sacraments that may be celebrated by the laity — emergency baptism and matrimony) or the sacramental seal of orders (for the rest of the sacraments). Thus, Christ appropriates individuals to himself as special agents of salvation and sanctification for men.

VI. CHRIST'S ACT OF SALVATION IS PRESENT IN THE SACRAMENTS

Up to this point, we have seen that the sacraments draw all their efficacy from the passion and resurrection of Christ, that is from the Paschal Mystery. We have also seen the manner in which Christ continues to act in the sacraments through the instrumentality of his agents, priests and faithful, as well as through the external ritual celebrated by them. We come now, at this point, to discuss more deeply the content of the sacramental act itself. Just what is it that Christ accomplishes in us through the sacraments? It seems inadequate to maintain that the sacra-

---

[8] Denz. 854; E. Schillebeeckx, *Christ, the Sacrament of the Encounter With God* (New York: Sheed & Ward, Inc., 1963), p. 105.

ments merely bring us the grace-power issuing from the historical Calvary event. The sacraments are more than carriers of grace.

It was to deepen our understanding of what Christ achieves in the sacraments that the Benedictine monk, Dom Odo Casel, of the abbey of Maria Laach in Germany, began to explore the mystical content of the sacramental act. Dom Odo began his work by studying the pagan mystery rites of the East, which came into prominence in the early decades of Christianity. These rites, he maintained, were a kind of mystical reenactment of the life of a god by which the initiated relived the death and resurrection of the god, made contact with him, and received power from him. Dom Odo concluded that the similarity between such mystery rites and Christianity resulted from God's providence in preparing on a natural level for the gift of Christ on the supernatural level of revelation.

Now the pagan rite, which bore certain similarities to the rites of Christianity, was considered to be a "mystery" in the special sense in which Dom Odo himself defines it: "The mystery is a sacred ritual action in which a saving deed is made present through the rite; the congregation, by performing the rite, take part in the saving act, and thereby win salvation."[9]

Casel's interest in the notion of mystery naturally led him to investigate the first Christian use of this term by St. Paul. In passages like Colossians 1:20, 26, 27 and Ephesians 1:9–10; 3:9–11, St. Paul speaks of the mystery as God's plan for the redemption of all mankind — a grand design hidden from all eternity in God and revealed through Christ especially through the acts of Christ's incarnation, death, and resurrection. Dom Odo maintained that all these acts of Christ together constitute a single mystery, a single saving act identified as the Paschal mystery, the passage of the Son of God into this world and, through death and resurrection, back to the Father.

To accomplish our reunion with the Father we too must enter into the Paschal mystery of Christ's return to heavenly glory. We are able to do this, to make contact with the saving deeds of Christ in history, through a new level of the mystery, that is, through the liturgy of the Church. It is here that Casel made perhaps his most enduring contribution to current theological development. The liturgical reform has in great measure been spurred on by Casel's *mysterium* theory or the theology of mysteries. For him the whole mystery of Christ, that is, the whole saving lifework of Jesus on earth, is somehow contained in and re-presented in the sacred worship of the Church. Over and over again in his writings,

---

[9] Odo Casel, *The Mystery of Christian Worship,* translated from the German (Westminster, Md.: The Newman Press, 1962), edited by Burkhard Neunheuser, p. 54.

the monk of Maria Laach repeats his convictions on the mystery-presence. For example:

> Still in heaven with His Father, each day He [Christ] wills to sacrifice Himself with her [the Church] fighting and suffering on earth, wills to celebrate His death with her in the world by a mystical and symbolic act, and so to awaken her to a new life in and with God. Christ has given His mystery to the Church's care; she acts it out, and thereby fulfills His action, which has become hers. So Christ and the Church become one in act and passion: the mystery is made a new eternal covenant. The saving act continues and is crowned in the oneness of everlasting love, until the symbol comes to an end and only the pure reality shows itself to the seeking eye in eternity.[10]

Casel insists further on the reality of Christ's saving work being made present again in the liturgy:

> The mystery is no mere recalling of Christ and His saving deed; it is a memorial in worship. The Church does what the Lord did, and thereby makes His act present. Christ Himself is present and acts through the Church, His *ecclesia*, while she acts with Him. Both carry out the actions.[11]

Or again he maintains:

> The mystery of worship makes present among us the saving act of Christ in word and rites . . . God has made it possible for us, even in this life, to enter into the divine present and the everlasting Today; this possibility is through the sole door of the mystery of worship. . . . What is past in history, the death of Christ for example, and what is in the future of history, His parousia, are present in the mystery.[12]

Applying his *mysterium* theory to the Mass he asserts:

> It is this, the making present of the sacrificial death of Christ, which Scripture and all the ancient Fathers and liturgists hold to be the meaning of the Mass. . . . The Lord must appear in the Mass as sacrificed and not as glorified, although in heaven He is such. It is Christ's great goodness and piety toward us that, although He lives in glory in heaven, still He brings His sacrificial death before us over and over in the Mass, in a sacramental manner.[13]

Casel's statements seem to suggest therefore a quite literal and objective renewal of the past historical saving death and resurrection of Christ. He makes this point in regard to the sacraments. Quoting the ancient dictum that "The sacraments effect what they signify," he translates the verb *efficere* as "making real." "Thus what the maxim does mean is that the sacraments do not merely point to the saving action, but contain it."[14]

[10] *Ibid.*, p. 59.
[11] *Ibid.*, p. 141.
[12] *Ibid.*, p. 142.
[13] *Ibid.*, p. 152.
[14] *Ibid.*, pp. 153, 154.

If we seek an explanation as to how past history can be repeated, he points to the sacramental mode of existence in which the mysteries are renewed:

> The making present of the saving act in mystery takes place in a sacramental manner; the saving work then receives in addition to its natural mode of being, a new, sacramental mode of being. This does not imply any change in the work; this remains what it was, yet in this new manner is made present to us, so that we enter into it and can make it our own. It is therefore complete nonsense to imagine that the mystery doctrine is that at Christmas Christ comes on the altar as a tiny child. What is meant is that the whole oikonomia, the whole design of salvation from the incarnation to the parousia which has not yet appeared in point of time, does take on a sacramental presence and therefore can be the subject of our co-participation in a most vivid way.[15]

In his insistence on the objective presence of the salvation mystery in the sacraments, Casel anticipates the contemporary theology of encounter with and commitment to Christ:

> It is in the liturgy of the Church that Christ presents His saving work to us once again. The work is fulfilled in a fully objective manner, even without us. It is the very saving work which the Father accomplished, offering the Son in His great love, bringing His Son back to Him. This saving action is what is made present to us in the mystery of worship. Because it is made present we can be joined to Christ in all reality, we can do along with Him what He does. The condition is that we give ourselves to Him, that we renounce ourselves; this is the way into the action of Christ.[16]

Casel's theory, first proposed in the late 1920's, has evoked a good deal of controversy over the course of the years. The debate did not end with his death on Easter, 1948, but has continued to the present. In evaluating his theory we may first of all note its merits and then briefly summarize other scholars' chief objections to it. Pointing out the merits of the theory, we can scarcely do better than to quote the French theologian J. H. Nicolas, who wrote:

> In sacramental theology, the mysterium theory of Dom Casel has played the role of an active agent of fermentation. What is remarkable in the proliferation of studies, discussions, and critiques that it has provoked, is not so much the great diversity of solutions proposed, as rather the ever more striking agreement that is being established among theologians as to the precise manner of formulating the problem itself. That the Liturgy in general and the sacraments in particular are essentially a reactualization of the acts by which our salvation is accomplished, that the efficacy of the sacraments consists in making man have a share — spiritually and even bodily — in these mysteries which prolong them-

---

[15] Ibid., p. 154.   [16] Ibid., p. 158.

selves in him, and that in this consists salvation, no one today will any longer contest.[17]

As Nicolas suggests, no one seriously contests the concept that somehow Christ's saving work is indeed present in the liturgy; the principal concern is to explain with greater theological precision just how this can take place.

Opponents of Casel take issue with some of the fundamental ideas upon which he based his theory. They note, for example, that he accepted too uncritically the similarity between the pagan mystery rites and Christianity. In this, he may have been influenced by the very men whose theories he opposed, the Modernist writers of the nineteenth and early twentieth centuries, who read into the pagan mysteries more than was warranted and came to describe the mysteries in Christian language. This naturally made the resemblance between them and the Christian liturgy very acute.[18]

The Christian sacraments and their underlying theology of salvation rest squarely on the reality of Christ's death and resurrection. For Casel, the actual presence of this saving event in the sacramental "mysteries" may be deduced from the Pauline teaching on baptism and the Eucharist, as well as from the Eastern patristic catechesis of the fourth century. Romans 6:4 ff. speaks of a baptismal dying and rising with Christ; 1 Corinthians 11:26 affirms the eucharistic proclamation (katangéllete) of Christ's death. Scripture authorities, however, question Casel's deduction of a mystery-presence theory in Paul's teaching. Among the reasons assigned are these: (1) Paul was probably not at all influenced by Hellenistic mystery cults; his thought is better explained in terms of his Judaic background.[19] (2) Besides the image of a dying and rising with Christ, Paul employs several other analogies to develop his baptismal doctrine;[20] therefore, one is justified in looking beyond the mystery-presence concept to explain Paul's thought, perhaps, in terms of corporate personality. The sacraments unite us to Christ, who as our representative accepted the cross and the resurrection and now sacramentally allows us to share in his historical saving deed.[21] (3) Paul is not a theologian

---

[17] J. H. Nicolas, "Reactualisation des Mystères Redempteurs dans et par les Sacrements," *Revue Thomiste* (January–March, 1958), 20 (quoted in *Worship*, 34, #3, February, 1960, p. 165). For strong support of Casel's Theory by an Episcopal liturgical scholar, Theodore O. Wedel, cf. *The Liturgical Renewal of the Church* (New York: Oxford University Press, 1960), edited by Massey H. Shepherd, Jr., p. 33.

[18] L. Bouyer, *Liturgical Piety* (Notre Dame: University of Notre Dame Press, 1954), pp. 90–98.

[19] Rudolf Schnackenburg, *Baptism in the Thought of St. Paul*, tr. by G. R. Beasley-Murray (New York: Herder and Herder, 1964), pp. 139–147.

[20] *Ibid.*, p. 149.

[21] *Ibid.*, p. 148 f.

who thinks in terms of liturgy and mysteries, but rather he is primarily a preacher of the gospel belonging more to the prophetic type.[22] Even if all this be considered, the discussion is far from conclusive;[23] modifications of Casel's theory continue to enrich the theology of Christ's saving action in the sacraments.

Inspired by Casel's insights, some contemporary theologians have sought to explain how the historical deeds of Christ on earth can be present in the sacraments without being numerically repeated in space and time. For surely Christ cannot die and rise again. Charles Davis, Edward Schillebeeckx, Dom Polycarp Wegenaer, and other contemporary theologians have contributed to the development of the *mysterium* theory in the light of current liturgical considerations. What follows is an attempt to summarize this theological elaboration.

Every sacrament links us to the Paschal mystery as to its source of power and love. Thus it would be possible to maintain that God, the ultimate source of grace, establishes a causal relationship between the historical past acts of Christ and the liturgy of the sacraments today. In other words, God imparts grace to us through the sacraments precisely because of the death and resurrection of Christ. To this extent, then, we could say that the historical saving deeds of Jesus are renewed among us through the liturgy in the sense that they are "virtually" present; that is, their power, their efficacy, is present in the sacraments to effect our salvation[24] With Father Schillebeeckx, we could maintain that somehow Christ's saving acts of A.D. 30 still exist; they are "eternally actual."[25] The key is to understand the mystery of the incarnation. Jesus is God in the flesh, eternity immersed in time. The actions of Jesus the Man are the personal acts of the eternal Son of God, for all actions must be attributed to the person who acts, and Jesus of Nazareth is but one Person, and that divine. Therefore, all the acts of Jesus of Nazareth ultimately are divine acts because they are attributed to or they flow from his divine personality. Although Jesus' saving deeds on earth have an historical framework, having occurred at a given time and place, yet they also have an enduring or lasting quality; they are lasting simply because God himself is eternal, his acts constitute an eternal "now"; there is no past or future except in the limited dimensions of time.

While these historical deeds of Christ cannot be brought back as such, numerically repeated with strict literalness, not even in mystery or sacra-

---

[22] *Ibid.*, p. 187.

[23] *Ibid.*

[24] Charles Davis, *Liturgy and Doctrine* (New York: Sheed & Ward, 1960), p. 71 (cf. entire section, pp. 69–74).

[25] Schillebeeckx, *op. cit.*, p. 55 f.

ment, yet we may say that in those past deeds of Jesus' death and resurrection there is already a certain transhistorical element; there is an element, that is, that continues to exist insofar as Christ is God and insofar as his acts are divine acts. For Charles Davis, this transcendent reality is the enduring act of love in Christ — divine love expressed in the human love of the God-Man's human will.

> It was this act that lay behind all that Christ did. . . . It gave redemptive value to all the events of the *transitus* [passage to the Father through death and resurrection]. . . . The act of charity, at its deepest level, was the counterpart in the will of the vision in the intellect, and it has the same timeless and unchanging duration. This act of love still exists in the risen Christ in heaven in its unchanged reality . . . [and] can be made present in the liturgy, where it finds a sacramental or symbolic expression.[26]

Therefore, Christ's redemptive deeds have a divine and eternal quality. They still exist in the person of the risen Christ in heaven. St. Thomas speaks of the mysteries of the flesh of the risen Christ; these saving acts endure forever in the incarnate Christ of glory. The sacrifice of the cross, which reached its climax with the glorious, triumphant resurrection of Jesus, may still be said to exist in Christ in the mode of glory.[27] The Epistle to the Hebrews, Schillebeeckx notes, speaks of an eternal sacrifice at a heavenly altar.[28]

The heavenly Christ may be said to recapitulate in his glorified flesh all the mysteries of his life on earth. As the risen, triumphant Savior, he therefore persists in the final stage of his sacrifice as the triumphant Victim who has suffered and died and now enjoys the glory of the Father in risen flesh. He is what he is today in his incarnate nature because of all that happened to him while he was on earth; just as in our own case, our previous experiences have left their mark upon us and have made us what we are today. Is this not suggested by the presence in Christ's glorified flesh of his wounds, glorious badges or trophies of his victory over sin and death for our sake?

The risen Christ then is our present and personal link with his glorious, saving deeds of the past. The eternally actual mystery of worship in the risen Christ reaches us today through his glorified body prolonged in time in the Church and actuated in the sacraments. The presence of Christ in the sacraments (in the Eucharist in his very substance and in the other sacraments and the rest of the liturgy by his active power) is

---

[26] Davis, *op. cit.*, pp. 72–73.
[27] Eugene Masure, *The Sacrifice of the Mystical Body*, tr. by Anthony Thorold (London: Burns & Oates, 1954), p. 60.
[28] Schillebeeckx, *op. cit.*, p. 58. Cf. Heb 7:25, 27.

the heart of the explanation as to how we can make contact with the saving mysteries or salvation deeds of Christ when he was on earth. He is our Mediator, our link with the past; therefore, we can say that in the sacraments there is a presence of the enduring mystery of redemption. The saving deeds of Christ are recapitulated in this sense and are made over to us that we may experience them and their power of salvation. It is only when we have established this continued presence of Christ's Paschal mystery in the sacraments that we can proceed to examine the efficacy of the sacraments in conferring grace.

VII. CHRIST ACTS EFFICACIOUSLY IN THE SACRAMENTS TO CONFER SAVING GRACE

The sacraments reproduce among us in the context of the Church the Paschal mystery of Christ. This means that the sacraments, like the Paschal mystery itself, are a mystery of saving worship. They embody and make visible among us both the worship of Christ (his divine love of the Father to the point of sacrificing his very life in death and resurrection) and the saving gift of the Father's love toward redeemed mankind. The sacraments are acts of the total Christ, that is, of Christ, the head, and of his mystical body, the Church. Therefore, the Church, in her sacramental acts, associates herself with this mystery of Christ's saving worship so that the sacraments are also the Church's homage to the Father and her own bestowal of the graces of salvation. The Church is associated with Christ as the completeness or the fullness (plerōma) of Christ, a communion in grace with him. As sacrament of the risen Christ, the Church is not an empty sign; she actually does make the heavenly Christ present in the world by her saving activity. Therefore, she may be said to contain grace, which is nothing else than union with the risen Christ, his presence among his members. The Church herself is filled with Christ's holiness; and in her symbolic acts she gives expression to her union with Christ the head in faith, hope, and love. Thus the sacraments are at the same time Christ's acts of saving worship and also acts of the Church.

As the Epistle to the Hebrews intimates, the homage of Christ to the Father also includes Christ's constant intercession for us. "He lives always to make intercession for us" (Heb 7:25). A certain infallibility attaches to the prayer of Christ; there is no question of the Father's willingness to answer the plea of his Son for us. It is from this that the infallibility of the bestowal of grace is derived. The sacraments are moments in the life of the Church when in faith she joins herself to the efficacious intercession of Christ before the Father; and thus in the sacraments she enjoys the same assurance of an infallible answer of grace as does Christ her head.

The response of the Father to the suffering and death of Christ was the resurrection and ascension, the exaltation of Christ to the Father's right hand, and the consequent power of Christ to impart the Spirit upon the Church. The sacraments reproduce, in the sense explained above, the Paschal mystery of the Savior; therefore, the sacraments too bring us an infallible response from the Father through the Spirit by the presence of his saving grace. Traditionally, this power of the sacramental rite, derived from the fact that the sacraments are Christ's personal acts in ecclesial form, has been called the *ex opere operato* efficacy of the sacraments. Father Schillebeeckx thus summarizes this power of the sacraments: "When the human prayer of the glorified Son of God is sacramentally realized among us in a truly ecclesial religious act, through the sending of the Spirit by Christ, grace is really bestowed upon us in the same sacrament by the Father of Mercies."[29] *Ex opere operato* then means that "from the very rite performed" sacraments have the power to make present and visible the mystery of Christ's worship and our salvation.

Protestant Reformers opposed this concept of the sacrament largely on the basis of a misunderstanding. They feared that somehow God's freedom was limited by the sacraments, that he was bound or obliged to give grace. For them, faith alone saves. Furthermore, the Catholic doctrine seemed to border on the magic; it seemed to render salvation automatic, effective without any faith-response on the part of the recipient. By contrast, the Reformers saw the efficacy of the sacraments in God's use of these rites to reinforce his call to faith already extended through the Word of Scripture and preaching.

The Council of Trent, in turn, insisted during the Post-Reformation that the sacraments confer grace by their own power so long as the recipient is properly disposed, that is, places no obstacle in the way. The concept of *ex opere operato* may therefore be expressed negatively and positively. Negatively, the gift of grace does not depend either upon the sanctity of the minister or upon the faith of the recipient *alone*. And positively, the sacramental act is Christ's free act. The term then means ultimately that grace is made available to man through the power of Christ's saving acts made present in sacramental form.

The sacraments are seen to be signs of Christ's redemptive will, of his desire and his intention to bestow his Father's saving love upon mankind. The risen body of Christ, the established sign of salvation, actually gives what it signifies through Christ's incarnate saving activity. So also the body of Christ, the Church, actually gives the grace it signifies in its sacraments, "since this body is sacramentally identical with the heavenly

[29] *Ibid.*, p. 73.

body of Christ."[30] The redemptive act of Christ has an intrinsic efficacy about it. Since the sacraments are signs of this redemptive act, they therefore must also be causes of grace, of union with Christ in his saving act. Grace comes through the sacraments visibly, not merely in an inward way. Thus, the sacraments are effective signs or symbols that actually accomplish for man a real encounter with the risen Christ. They are Christ's loving gestures arousing a responsive love in us. If we but open ourselves to Christ, his grace reaches us and makes possible a true and personal encounter with God in Christ. Or to state it in Augustinian terms, the sacraments are Christ's words made visible; through them Christ addresses us, efficaciously summoning us to receive his gifts and to surrender ourselves in loyal commitment.[31]

Insofar as the sacraments, then, are authentically performed in the name of Christ and the Church, they are Christ's personal saving act in the Church directed to a specific person. This makes for a true or "valid" sacrament. Christ's grace is present and available to the recipient. For the sacrament to be fully complete, on the other hand, to be "fruitful," by the actual reception of grace, the recipient must reach out to Christ with faith and devotion; then the grace of Christ's presence in the sacrament, which is infallibly available and offered in a valid sacramental act, fully accomplishes its purpose in the actual sanctification of the recipient. The sacraments are truly efficacious, saving acts of Christ, visibly embodied in an action of his Church, making present both Christ's saving worship and that of his Church.

---

[30] Ibid.
[31] St. Augustine, In Joan., Hom. 80, n. 2, P.L. 35, 1840.

CHAPTER V

The Finality of the Sacraments, Communal and Personal

I. BUILDING UP THE PRIESTLY PEOPLE OF GOD

One of the chief aims of the liturgical renewal promulgated by Vatican II is a deeper understanding of the Church's worship of God. Without understanding, there can be little progress in Christian maturity. To unlock that "primary and indispensable source of the true Christian spirit" which is active participation in the sacred liturgy,[1] one must endeavor to enter into the mysteries of Christ with sincerity, understanding, faith, and devotion. Our appreciation of the sacraments will not be complete unless we grasp what Christ intends to do in his Church and in us through the sacraments. We must examine, in short, the last two parts of our definition of sacrament. The sacraments join us "to Christ's worship of the Father in his Church" and form us "in Christlikeness, especially in the pattern of the Paschal mystery."[2]

---

[1] Pope St. Pius X, *Motu Proprio*, November 22, 1903.
[2] Cf. above, p. 23.

The Church, the new Israel, is essentially, like the first Israel, a priestly people, a holy nation, a kingdom of priests (cf. Ex 19:6). This is why Peter could call the newly baptized "a chosen race, a royal priesthood, a holy nation, a purchased people" (1 Pt 2:9). Christ has founded this community of believers, this nation of worshipers, this sacred qāhal of the New Covenant to render grateful and loving praise with him to his heavenly Father, and thus to achieve union in love with the Trinity. It is precisely by sacramentally associating them with his great act of worship, the Paschal mystery, that Christ builds up the body of the faithful. The sacraments enable the great High Priest to achieve this essential work among us today, constantly re-creating or building up the community of the worshiping Church. It is only from Christ the head that "the whole body . . . derives its increase to the building up of itself in love" (Eph 4:16). Just as the father of a family cares for his children, sees that they have shelter, clothing, food, and proper training, so Christ cares for his Church and makes it grow and increase, especially through the sacraments. St. Thomas, in one of his priceless gems, says as much: "The Church of Christ is said to be built up by the sacraments which flowed from the side of Christ hanging on the cross."[3]

Theology has established that the ordinary way of salvation is by being united to Christ in his Church. Now the Church, as we have seen, is essentially sacramental in nature. It is a visible making present of Christ's will to save mankind and to join us to his worship of the Father. Through the seven major signs of Christ's saving work, the sacraments, the Church expresses her fundamentally sacramental nature; that is, she carries out her essential task of drawing men into unity with Christ and incorporating them into his body which she is, imparting to them the vitality of his divine life. Therefore, it can be seen that the sacraments have two effects: one is related directly to the Church (the ecclesial effect or the res et sacramentum); the other unites the recipient with Christ and God by communicating a share in the divine Christ-life (the grace-effect or res tantum). We shall now proceed to study each of these two effects and their function in building up the body of Christ on earth, his Church.

II. THE ECCLESIAL EFFECT OF THE SACRAMENTS (RES ET SACRAMENTUM)

A. Historical Background

The history of the first effect of the sacraments is an interesting study in theological development. As so often in the case of theological progress,

---

[3] S.T., III, 64, 2, ad 3.

the custom or practice of the Church came first; and only later did theological reflection specify and refine the theology of the practice. That is to say, the Church conducted herself habitually in a certain way, and only later did the theologians ask the question, "Why did the Church act in this way?"

The question of a first or intermediate effect of the sacraments arose in the following way. In the early centuries of the Church, the sacraments of baptism and holy orders were never repeated, once it was certain that they had been truly celebrated (validly administered). In the third century, the baptism conferred by the Novatian heretics was called in question by such men as Cyprian of Carthage (d. 258). He maintained that when such heretics applied for readmission into the true Church, they must be baptized again, for in Cyprian's mind this was the only true or valid baptism. Cyprian's view, however, was challenged by Pope St. Stephen, although the matter was not taken up in Council until the year 314 at the Council of Arles and again at the first ecumenical or general council held at Nicaea in the year 325. Pope Stephen, in answering Cyprian's charges, cites tradition in favor of the validity of such baptisms. In any case, on both sides of the controversy, there was constant agreement that there could be only one true baptism and that such a valid ceremony could not be repeated.

Somewhat later, the Donatist schism held views similar to those of Cyprian regarding the repetition of baptism and holy orders. Out of the controversy it became apparent that the orthodox Catholic position regarded baptism as somehow conferring permanent or lasting effects, since once it was given truly it could never be repeated. It remained, however, for a later mind to make the distinction between the sacrament truly or validly received and a sacrament received with complete fruitfulness of grace.

In his great treatise On Baptism against the Donatists, St. Augustine demonstrated his theological genius by establishing the possibility of a true sacrament being administered by heretics or schismatics even though it was an unlawful usurping of the Church's sacramental powers. Therefore, such a true sacrament cannot be repeated if the heretic or schismatic returns to the true Church. It must, he maintained, have a permanent effect. In the thinking of the Fathers of the Church before him, he recalls the custom of referring to baptism itself as a seal upon the member of Christ. For him, this seal remains indelible. This outward rite or seal, in turn, confers a deeper, more permanent reality. It is a mark of ownership by which an individual becomes the property of Christ. Since this lasting effect is conferred by baptism, there can be no repetition of this sacrament when the heretic or schismatic returns to Mother Church.

Furthermore, when such a reconciliation occurs, the grace-effect of the sacrament is then enjoyed. In Augustine's words, "Each of them, when he amends his ways, begins to receive profit from that which before was not profitable but was yet already within him."[4] For Augustine this effect then was distinct from sanctifying grace and independent of personal merit. This effect occurs purely through the valid administration of the sacrament.

Later in the twelfth and thirteenth centuries the Latin vocabulary of medieval theology settled on three words or phrases to designate and specify the sacrament itself and its two effects. They came to speak of the sacramentum tantum (the external rite alone), for example, the pouring of water and the recitation of the words in baptism; the res et sacramentum (this first effect of the sacrament is the spiritual res or reality effected by the external rite which in turn is a sign or sacramentum of a more profound effect, namely grace; hereafter the res et sacramentum will be called the symbolic reality); finally, the res tantum (the grace alone, that is, the ultimate reality conferred by the sacrament; hereafter called the grace-effect of the sacrament). In those sacraments which are traditionally never repeated, that is baptism, confirmation, and orders, the symbolic reality came to be called the character, variously described as a seal or a brand or a mark on the soul, which in turn was the cause of the grace that followed. The character, then, was said to dispose the recipient to receive the grace made available by the valid conferral of the sacrament and its effect. The second or ultimate effect, namely grace, would actually be received only if the party is properly disposed. The latter condition is what is known as the fruitfulness of the sacrament.

As far as the significance of the character was concerned, the Fathers of the Church considered it a sealing in the name of the Trinity or, more particularly, of Christ, since it is his imprint or image on the believer. St. Thomas, however, added an altogether new dimension to the character by considering the characters of baptism, confirmation, and orders as specifically oriented toward Christian worship. They configure or conform the Christian to Christ the priest. They delegate the Christian to share with Christ his worship of the Father.[5] Thus, for St. Thomas the character confers a certain competence or a commission within the community of the Church, a participation in varying degrees in the priestly worship of Christ toward the Father. This Thomistic view remains, however, a theological opinion, since the Church has made no dogmatic pronouncement upon the precise nature or function of the character.

---

[4] On Baptism against the Donatists, ch. 4, #5.
[5] S.T., III, 63, 3.

THE FINALITY OF THE SACRAMENTS

While the symbolic reality of baptism, confirmation, and orders came to be called the character, a symbolic reality or a certain first effect occurs also in other sacraments. In the Eucharist the symbolic reality is the body and blood of Christ present sacramentally; in matrimony it is the spiritual bond created between Christian husband and wife, a bond which lasts until the death of either party. Finally, in penance and the anointing of the sick, authors acknowledge the conferral of a certain adornment or embellishment of the soul (*ornatus animae*) which in penance is said to be the creation of an interior spirit of repentance or perhaps reconciliation with the Church, and in the anointing of the sick a spiritual anointing that remits venial sins or the scars of sin and prepares for entrance into glory.

In modern times (beginning in the last decades of the nineteenth century), theologians have come to stress the ecclesial dimension of the symbolic reality; that is, more and more they come to view this first or intermediate effect of the sacraments as creating in the recipient a special relationship to the visible Church. At the end of the past century, Matthias Scheeben maintained that the symbolic reality unites us in a special way with Christ as head of his mystical body. He likens the condition of the Christian marked by a sacramental character to the hypostatic union with Christ. Just as the humanity of Jesus of Nazareth was personally united to the Son of God and through him to the Father and the Spirit, and thereby drew down upon itself the fullness of grace, so the Christian marked with the character or symbolic reality of the sacrament is united to Christ in and through his Church, and gains access to the special sacramental graces flowing from the head to the members.[6] In support of this ecclesial dimension of the sacramental character, Father Schillebeeckx cites a constant tradition from the time of St. Augustine through the Middle Ages up to the present, a factor present despite differences in theological systems, a constant belief that "a person who bears a character or mark bears a certain relation to the visible ecclesial community."[7]

B. Scriptural Foundations for the Sacramental Character

One of the earliest names for baptism in the usage of the second- and third-century Fathers of the Church was the term "seal." It is found in the writings of the Shepherd of Hermas, Irenaeus, Tertullian, Clement, Origen, Basil, and many others. This use of the term "seal" as a synonym for baptism is probably suggested by various passages in Scripture:

[6] Paul Palmer, S.J., "The Theology of the *res et sacramentum*," in *Readings in Sacramental Theology* (Englewood Cliffs, N. J.: Prentice-Hall, 1965), pp. 111–112.
[7] Schillebeeckx, *Christ, the Sacrament of the Encounter with God* (New York: Sheed & Ward, 1963), p. 158.

Now it is God who is warrant for us and for you in Christ, who has anointed us, who has also stamped us with his seal and has given us the Spirit as a pledge in our hearts (2 Cor 1:21–22).

And in him [Christ] you . . . were sealed with the Holy Spirit of the promise who is the pledge of our inheritance, for a redemption of possession, for the praise of his glory (Eph 1:13–14).

And do not grieve the Holy Spirit of God, in whom you were sealed for the day of redemption (Eph 4:30).

In these texts, the Greek verb used is derived from the Greek noun *sphragis*, which means "a mark" or "a seal." From these texts it is clear how the Fathers of the Church came to regard baptism as a sealing of the Christian, conferring a lasting mark on his soul. While the term *sphragis* is associated in patristic writings with the imposition of the sign of the cross in the baptismal ceremony, it was an easy transition for the Fathers to apply what was said of the external *sphragis* or sign of the cross to the internal indelible seal, the sacramental character.

Another scriptural analogy that inspired rich commentary by the Fathers of the Church was a comparison already drawn by St. Paul between circumcision and baptism. "[Abraham] received the sign of circumcision as the seal of the justice of faith which he had while uncircumcised" (Rom 4:11). The seal of circumcision in the case of Abraham is now compared to baptism, which is a kind of new circumcision, a spiritual one. "In him [Christ], too, you have been circumcised with a circumcision not wrought by hand, but through putting off the body of the flesh, a circumcision which is of Christ; for you were buried together with him in baptism, and in him also rose again . . . through faith" (Col 2:11–12). Since circumcision was a visible token of entrance into the first covenant, so baptism becomes a sign of entrance into a new covenant. Just as circumcision is irrevocable, so also the seal of baptism is permanent and ineffaceable.[8]

C. The Patristic Analogies

Here we limit ourselves to some of the more common comparisons or analogies employed by the Fathers of the Church to identify the sacramental character of baptism. Just as cattle owners brand their sheep and other cattle with a distinguishing mark in order to designate their ownership of these cattle, so Christ in baptism marks off his members as being his own property or possession. John Damascene compares the Holy Spirit dwelling in us through baptism with "the royal seal with

---

[8] Cf. Jean Danielou, *The Bible and the Liturgy* (Notre Dame: University of Notre Dame Press, 1956), pp. 67–68.

which the Lord brands his own sheep."[9] Soldiers and slaves were branded or tattooed to designate the master they served and to prevent their desertion. To catechumens of his day, St. Cyril of Jerusalem proclaimed: "The Holy Spirit is on the point of setting a seal on your souls; you are coming for enlistment under the great King; make ready therefore."[10]

The baptismal imprinting upon the soul suggested to the Fathers an analogy with the impressing of a ring upon wax, a practice employed to seal authentically some public document. Again the seal is compared to a figure or image on a coin. The comparison with circumcision has already been mentioned as based on Colossians 2:11. The protective character of the seal suggested to the Fathers an analogy with the anointing of the Hebrew homes in Egypt with the blood of the Paschal lamb to ward off punishments from God. From all of these analogies it is apparent that the Fathers commonly accepted the conferral of a special baptismal seal of God upon the soul. It remains for us now to examine something of the nature and function of this seal in the light of current theology.

D. Theology of the Symbolic Reality

As already noted above, St. Thomas' significant contribution to the theology of the sacramental character was to regard it not merely as a configuration or resemblance to the Holy Trinity or to Christ, but specifically to Christ as High Priest. The sacramental characters of baptism, confirmation, and orders then "are nothing else than certain participations in the priesthood of Christ, derived from Christ himself."[11] For him the sacramental character is a power by which the faithful are delegated to receive or render to others those things pertaining to the worship of God. Since divine worship is essentially a certain profession of faith by external signs, it is fitting, he maintains, that the character reside in the cognitive power of the soul where faith also resides.[12] Thus the character is not merely a kind of moral title or legal right, but it is an ontological power of a spiritual and instrumental kind that is conferred upon the baptized, the confirmed, and the ordained.

Pius XII in his Encyclical on the Sacred Liturgy (Mediator Dei, paragraph 88) follows the Thomistic view: "By the character which is imprinted on their souls, they [the faithful] are appointed to give worship to God; thus they participate, according to their condition, in the priesthood of Christ."

From what has been said so far, the following truths emerge concerning the sacramental character: First, it is a distinguishing mark or seal that serves to create a certain structure within the Church. The baptismal

---

[9] Confess., III; P.G., 95, 285.
[10] Cat., 3:3, 4; P.G., 33, 428.

[11] S.T., III, 63, 3.
[12] S.T., III, 63, 4, ad 3.

seal distinguishes Christians from non-Christians. The confirmation character distinguishes the confirmed or adult Christian from those who are merely baptized. The character of holy orders distinguishes the ordained clergy, who alone can consecrate the sacrifice, from the laity who are able to offer the external sacrifice only through the priest. Second, it is a configurative mark that conforms the recipient to Christ in his priestly dignity, confers a resemblance to Christ the priest, and thus grants a share in his priestly powers of praising God and extending the faith. It renders the recipient of the baptismal seal capable of receiving the other sacraments of the Church. Third, sacramental character disposes the recipient for grace. It serves to consecrate the faithful for their mission of priesthood, creating the holy people referred to in the Canon of the Mass. It has been likened to the irrevocable Word of God summoning man to grace, and taking full effect in the individual who totally accepts it.[13] In other words, it is just as irrevocable as God's Word (cf. Is 55:10–11). The character is, fourth, an indelible sign or a permanent mark that makes the sacraments of baptism, confirmation, and orders unrepeatable. Last, the character is given equally to all. The intensity of grace-union with Christ that flows from the character will depend upon the fervor of the recipient.

Current theology, as we have noted, views the sacramental characters as setting up a special relation of the recipient to the visible Church, commissioning him as it were for the special task of helping to build up the Body of Christ on earth. Attempting to specify more precisely just what these tasks are to which the baptized and confirmed Christian is committed, Schillebeeckx as usual makes a fresh approach.[14]

First of all, and quite correctly, the mysteries of Christ, his incarnation, the Church, and the faithful must be linked together. The mystery of Christ is prolonged in the Church, his personal sacrament on earth, which in turn communicates the mystery of Jesus to the faithful through its great sacramental acts. For Schillebeeckx, the mystery of Jesus is a twofold earthly reflection of his eternal relationship to the Father and the Spirit in the Blessed Trinity. The mystery of Jesus' worship (or his religious sacrifice by which he returned to the Father through death and his Father's acceptance of this sacrifice through the resurrection) reflects the essential relationship between Son and Father in the Blessed Trinity —a mutual love passing from One to the Other; the love of the Father begetting the Son from all eternity, and the Son's love communicating or surrendering himself to the Father. This first earthly mystery of Jesus we

---

[13] Lucien Richard, "The Word and the Sacraments," Journal of Ecumenical Studies, Vol. 2, No. 2, Spring, 1965, p. 249.

[14] Schillebeeckx, op. cit., pp. 159–169.

shall call the mystery of his Passover. The second mystery of Jesus is the mystery of Pentecost, by which as man he was constituted in power at the right hand of the Father and became Sender of the Holy Spirit. This mystery of Pentecost, in turn, is a reflection of the Son's position in the Trinity as coprinciple of the Holy Spirit, who proceeds from both Father and Son.

Now the Church is the visibility of this twin mystery of Jesus on earth, the earthly presentation of the high priesthood of Jesus in heaven. The Church itself, therefore, is the mystery of Jesus' Paschal worship and Pentecostal conferring of the Spirit in earthly visibility. In other words, like Jesus the Church herself is a mystery of saving worship.

If, as Schillebeeckx maintains, this is the Church's essential constitution, then it is logical to maintain that the Church as sacrament or sign of the Paschal and Pentecostal mysteries of Jesus should consecrate her members by a special sacramental act to this same twofold mystery. It is into this theological line that Father Schillebeeckx inserts the sacramental character or the symbolic reality of baptism and of confirmation. For him, the baptismal character is an insertion into the mystery of Jesus' Passover, his worshipful return to the Father through death and resurrection. It is, therefore, a consecration to Jesus as Son, a consecration by which the faithful become dutiful children of the Father oriented and pledged to the Father as *filii in Filio* (adopted sons united with the true Son). Thus we return to the age-old concept that baptism makes us children of God, but with a notable enrichment of the traditional belief.

N B.

The confirmed Christian, on the other hand, through the sacramental seal or symbolic reality of this sacrament of the Spirit, is consecrated to Jesus in the Pentecostal mystery; he is likened to Christ as coprinciple of the Spirit; like Jesus he is established or confirmed in power, receiving a share in the Church's fullness and bestowal of the Spirit; he is an adult member of the Church incorporated into the fullness of its mystery as son of God in power. Thus the incorporation into the Church is accomplished by these two sacraments of Christian initiation, baptism and confirmation. Both these sacraments consecrate us, in turn, to the mystery of Jesus in and through his visible Church; and in so doing, they incorporate us into the Trinitarian relations of Jesus himself. If Jesus' work is none other than the revelation of the mystery of the Trinity understood in its fullest sense, then these two sacramental characters of baptism and confirmation seal and consecrate our entry into that very work of salvation conceived as a Trinitarian revelation.

The effects of the sacramental characters of baptism and confirmation, then, must not be regarded as merely interior, as affecting merely our spiritual life. Schillebeeckx insists that they are above all a consecration to the visibility of the Church, to its public life as saving and worshiping institution among men. Applied to baptism, this means that the person sealed with the baptismal character receives the commission and, therefore, the competence, duty, and right to participate actively in the Church's reliving of the Paschal mystery. The Church, in turn, relives this mystery primarily in its sacramental activity, particularly in the Eucharist, which fully realizes the mystery of Easter. In this way it may be seen how baptism relates the new Christian to the sacrificial worship of the Church and her organic sacramental vitality.

In the case of confirmation, the sacramental character confers the fullness of Messianic power; that is, it makes the Christian share visibly and actively in Christ's work of sending the Spirit. Just as in the early Church the Holy Spirit conferred certain kerygmatic gifts upon the faithful (cf. 1 Cor 12), so confirmation today inserts the Christian into the Church's kerygmatic activity. This is of special importance in the light of Vatican II's insistence upon the task of the layman in the Church (cf. De Ecclesia, Dogmatic Constitution on the Church, November 21, 1964, Ch. 4, par. 31, 33, 38). Specialized activity of this kind will obviously differ with the current needs of the Church. But whatever the specific ecclesial task to which the layman dedicates himself, it will consist essentially in a bearing witness to Christ who, in turn, was the visible sign of the witness borne by the Holy Spirit (cf. Jn 15:26 where Christ promises concerning the Holy Spirit that he "will bear witness concerning me" — cf. also Mt 10:18–20). In short, then, both the sacraments of baptism and confirmation through their ecclesial characters consecrate and dedicate the faithful to the ecclesial priesthood and the lay apostolate. They confer a kind of ordination upon the members of God's people, which is essentially a priestly and apostolic people.

Regarding the sacramental seal of holy orders conferred in diaconate, priesthood, and episcopacy, its specific commission and competency must be viewed in terms of the whole priestly people of God and its head, the high priest Christ. Essentially, the ordained priesthood is a priesthood of authority governing the laity. It is a pastoral and a teaching authority by which the ordained clergy act in the name of Christ as head of the priestly people of God. This priesthood is exercised in the visible Church in a visible way through the sacraments and through the preaching of God's word. The uniqueness of the sacramental seal of the priest appears in the fact that only he can consecrate the sacrifice in the name of Christ and it is he ordinarily who celebrates the other sacraments as well. Finally, it should be noted that the priest possesses his powers only as a delegate of the bishop. He is a participant in the powers of the episcopal and apostolic college. He acts as the bishop's vicar in carrying out his priestly authority.

E. The Ecclesial Effect of the Other Sacraments

So far we have considered the symbolic reality of baptism, confirmation, and holy orders. The other sacraments, too, have a first or intermediate effect concerned with the visibility of the Church. In the case of the Eucharist, the ecclesial effect is the presence of the body and blood of Christ in sacrifice as a sign of the unity of the Church in love (cf. 1 Cor 10:16–17). For matrimony, the ecclesial effect is the spiritual bond created in the soul of husband and wife, a bond which lasts until one party dies. This spiritual bond creates in the married couple a likeness to the loving union between Christ and his Church (cf. Eph 5:32). The exact nature of the symbolic reality or ecclesial effect of penance and the anointing of the sick is still controverted. In the case of penance, St. Thomas holds that interior contrition which is the ultimate disposition for the grace of forgiveness is the intermediate or first effect, the symbolic reality of that sacrament. Others, seeking a more ecclesial dimension of this first effect, consider it to be reconciliation with the Church. The formula of absolution now in use in the Western Church lends weight to this view; for the sinner must first be absolved from all bonds of excommunication and interdict before the forgiveness of sins itself is applied. In the case of the anointing of the sick, St. Albert the Great considered this sacrament to be a configuration to Christ in his resurrection, since for him the sacrament's primary purpose is anointing for glory. A leading continental theologian, Michael Schmaus, in his *Katholische Dogmatik*, considers this sacrament as basically a consecration for death. But this idea does not seem to harmonize with all the prayers of the ritual which ask instead for the recovery of health of soul, mind, and body, and restoration to the Church, if this be God's will. Besides, the sacrament of viaticum, namely, the Eucharist for the dying, would seem to be the true sacrament concerned with preparation for death. Therefore, Paul Palmer suggests that the symbolic reality of the anointing of the sick is a special bond with the Church as comforter and healer. The special configuration to Christ in this sacrament would be to the Christ of the agony where he is comforted by the visit of an angel. This would seem to be seconded by Vatican II which has accepted the name anointing of the sick rather than last anointing or extreme unction as the official name for this sacrament (CSL, paragraph 73: "Extreme Unction, which may also and more fittingly be called 'the Anointing of the Sick' is not a Sacrament reserved for those who are at the point of death; hence as soon as any one of the faithful begins to be in danger of death from sickness or old age, the most fitting time for him to receive this Sacrament has, beyond all doubt, arrived").

F. The Ecclesial Effect as Dispositive of Grace

The sacramental characters and, probably also, the symbolic reality of the other sacraments confer a certain relationship to the visible Church. Now the Church herself is sacrament or sign of the grace of salvation which it contains. It is a community of holiness, a community of grace. Therefore, such a commission to ecclesial office as that conferred at least by the characters of baptism, confirmation, and orders of its nature must include the conferral of the grace needed to carry out each specific office. This grace will be actualized in the recipient unless he positively opposes it. This is the understanding applied to the dictum of the Council of Trent, that the sacraments give grace "non ponentibus obicem," that is, to those who place no obstacle in the way.[15] The fact that sacramental characters in turn dispose the recipient for grace and make it available to the faithful, was already generally accepted in the twelfth and thirteenth centuries.[16] St. Thomas calls the sacramental character "the root of the spiritual life."[17]

Such a doctrine is simply a development of the teaching of Augustine, on the difference between a valid and a fruitful sacrament. The character or symbolic reality is given if the sacrament is a true one. But the grace available through the symbolic reality is actualized only if and when the recipient becomes properly disposed. Such "revival of grace" does not occur, however, in those sacraments which may be received with great frequency, namely, the Eucharist and penance. But in the case of the other sacraments, should one have received them validly but unworthily through the presence of mortal sin, e.g., in confirmation or matrimony, later when the recipient becomes reconciled with God through sincere contrition and confession, then the graces of the symbolic reality are actuated in him.

III. SANCTIFICATION IN THE PATTERN OF THE PASCHAL MYSTERY: THE GRACE-EFFECT OF THE SACRAMENTS (THE RES TANTUM)

Vatican II in its Constitution on the Sacred Liturgy expresses the purpose of the Sacraments as follows:

---

[15] Denzinger 849 c. 6; TCT, No. 670, p. 263.
[16] S.T., III, 63, 4, ad 1.
[17] In IV Sent., d. 22, q. 2, a. 1, ad 1.

The purpose of the sacraments is to sanctify men, to build up the body of Christ, and finally, to give worship to God. . . . They do indeed impart grace, but, in addition, the very act of celebrating them most effectively disposes the faithful to receive this grace in a fruitful manner, to worship God duly, and to practice charity.

It is therefore of the highest importance that the faithful should easily understand the sacramental signs, and should frequent with great eagerness those Sacraments which were instituted to nourish the Christian life (CSL, paragraph 59, NCWC tr.).[18]

Further on, the Council continues:

Thus, for well-disposed members of the faithful, the liturgy of the sacraments and sacramentals sanctifies almost every event in their lives; they are given access to the stream of divine grace which flows from the paschal mystery of the passion, death, and resurrection of Christ, the fount from which all sacraments and sacramentals draw their power. There is hardly any proper use of material things which cannot thus be directed toward the sanctification of men and the praise of God (CSL, paragraph 61, NCWC tr.).[19]

It is significant that the Council describes the sanctifying power of the sacraments in an ecclesial context. It does this by indicating that the purpose of the sacraments is "to sanctify men, to build up the body of Christ." By juxtaposing these two thoughts the Council reminds us that the sacraments are not mere private channels of grace from God to us as individuals, but that the sanctifying energy of Christ's Paschal mystery is imparted to us precisely in and through Christ's Church-body; and through this sanctification of men the sacraments purpose "to build up the body of Christ" or, as a commentator on the Constitution phrases it: "to build Christ into souls and to build souls into Christ."[20] In other words, it is through Christ in his body that we receive the saving power of salvation; and by receiving it, we contribute to the overall holiness of God's people and are impelled to work for the extension of Christ's kingship among men.

Such a view of the sacraments as participation in the grace-life of the Church will serve as a healthy corrective to an overindividualistic piety which has too long prevailed in recent centuries. A political "one world" must be sanctified by a supernatural "one world." Socialism, communism, schemes for the federation of western Europe, the Common Market, etc., must all eventually yield to the true unifying bond among men: the com-

---

[18] AAS, Vol. 56, No. 2, Feb. 15, 1964, p. 116.

[19] Ibid., pp. 116–117.

[20] J. D. Crichton, The Church's Worship (New York: Sheed & Ward, 1964), pp. 161–162, paraphrasing Pius XII, Mediator Dei, paragraph 20, NCWC translation.

munion or fellowship in the grace of the Holy Spirit which is the Church-body of Christ.

The Church as the great sacrament of Christ is the visibility of God's saving grace among men. Visible also then are the saving gestures, the essential actions of the Church as saving institution of grace. Through water and Word she initiates new members in baptism; through imposing hands and anointing in confirmation, she strengthens her members for witness-bearing in the Church; through the Eucharist, she gathers her children together for the meal of unity and love; through penance she imparts a healing remedy for sin by a gesture of absolution; by imposing hands in holy orders and witnessing the making of a contract of marriage in matrimony, the Church provides for her continuity through a ministry of authority and through a sanctified family life; through the anointing of the sick she prays for their bodily restoration and especially for the final spiritual healing to remove the last scars of sin. Thus the Church lives by her sacraments. She is most visible in her sacramental life.

Having seen how the sacraments confer some kind of first or ecclesial effect (symbolic reality), we now come to consider the ultimate effect, the final goal toward which the sacraments aim (grace-effect). A study of the sacramental graces will enable us to understand the ultimate effect which Christ wishes to achieve in his members.

All the sacraments confer common or sanctifying grace, either as a first gift (in baptism), or as a renewal of grace if it has been lost (in penance), or as an increase of the divine life (in the other five sacraments). But if this were the sole grace-effect of the sacraments, the reason for their diversity would not at all be apparent. Why have seven sacraments and not just one? The very fact that the Church has accepted seven distinct major signs of redemption as sacraments points to the fact that each sacrament must confer some special effect of its own. We now proceed to examine more precisely what sacramental grace involves in the case of the seven sacraments.

A. Characteristics of Sacramental Grace

Over the centuries, certain differences of emphasis can be found in the Church's attitude toward sacramental grace. The Fathers of the East laid special stress in sacramental theology on the divinizing aspect of sacramental grace. Christ is our supreme model of divine sonship; and through the sacraments, he fashions and models us as second sons, endowing us with the graces of sonship of the eternal Father in the power of the Holy Spirit. Sacramental grace, then, transforms us, makes us new creatures united with Christ in the Spirit in the homage of the Father, and accepted by the Father as his adopted children.

In the Western Church, on the other hand, the sacraments were looked upon as a restorative of man's original state of happiness. Western theology focused upon the healing power of the sacraments, the power to overcome the scars and wounds of sin. It was the genius of St. Thomas to achieve a certain balance between these two emphases; he attributed to sacramental grace the power to sanctify men by removing sin and perfecting the person for living a Christian life and thus turning man back to God in religious worship. We will come back to this point later in examining the relation between sacramental grace and the Paschal mystery.

1. **Visibility.** In contrast with the grace given outside the sacraments, what is called sacramental grace (for want of a better term) means grace that comes to us in some visible or outward form (not of course that we see the grace itself, which is a supernatural and spiritual entity, indeed a certain union with Christ who confers upon the man united to him powers that such union demands). The visibility of sacramental grace derives from the outward form in which the sacrament is celebrated. The age-old dictum, "The sacraments cause grace by signifying it," exemplifies this direct connection between outward symbol and inward grace-effect. The visible rite of the Church by which sacramental grace is made available not only assures us of the actual presence of grace in the sacramental mystery but also indicates clearly what is demanded of us in this grace-encounter with Christ. Sacramental grace, then, is first of all visible and ecclesial, that is, made present in outward form in and through the Church.

2. **Christological and redemptive.** All grace that comes through the sacraments is the grace of Christ the Redeemer. Only by his Paschal Mystery, his death and resurrection, is new life available to the people of God, the new Israel. He is the head of the new humanity; sacramental graces are nothing else than the great grace-life of the head of the Church-family enlivening his members. Just as members and organs of the body are in continuous direct contact with the head since there is one flow of life throughout the whole human organism, so also (as the mystical body doctrine makes clear) there is one life shared by the glorified Christ and his baptized and Spirit-filled members. Sacramental grace is not some kind of a liquid poured into the soul as into a vessel; rather it is an event, a situation, a personal and immediate encounter with Christ the Savior. At the moment of the sacramental encounter between Christ and a specific individual, the work of personal salvation is set in motion.[21] The objective power of Christ's redeeming love is now personalized, specifically oriented and directed to each member of the

[21] Cf. "Prayer Over the Gifts" for the Ninth Sunday After Pentecost, Roman Missal.

faithful. Here in this sacramental moment, above all, the love of Christ is drawing us into the love of the Father.

3. Trinitarian. If sacramental grace introduces us to a personal union with Christ, it necessarily follows that sacramental grace must also introduce us into the life of the Blessed Trinity. It does this, as Schillebeeckx maintains, by engaging us in the twin mysteries of Easter and Pentecost. By the mystery of Jesus' saving worship, we are taken into Trinitarian existence as other sons united to the dutiful Son of God-made-man. We become in a special way sons of the Father; and he in turn becomes, not merely Creator to us, but personal Father. From the Pentecostal mystery in which Christ became the Sender of the Holy Spirit, we have the other mystery to which we are also admitted through grace; for it is only by the power of the Spirit that we are allowed to call God Father (cf. Rom 8:15).

4. Paschal character of sacramental grace. Insofar as sacramental grace introduces us into the Paschal and Pentecostal mysteries of Christ, we may see a very significant aspect of grace. The encounter with Christ in the sacraments is not merely a kind of innocuous and pleasant visit, a mere tête-à-tête with our risen Savior. Rather the moment of sacramental grace is the moment when the risen Christ most effectively reaches us as individuals to transform us into the pattern of his Paschal mystery. Christ comes to transform us in the sacraments, to make us new men by fashioning us in the mold or model of his death and resurrection. This is why St. Paul (cf. Rom 6:3 ff.) can say that baptism immerses us into Christ's death by enabling us to die to sin; and it also joins us to Christ in his risen glorification. Rising from the baptismal font, we are to lead a risen life, a life which Paul describes as seeking "the things that are above, not the things that are on earth" and walking "in newness of life" (Col 3:2; Rom 6:4). Sacramental grace conforms us to the freedom enjoyed by the exalted Christ.

The temporal and spiritual struggles of life can now, through sacramental grace, be sanctified, merged with the death and resurrection of Christ himself. Sanctification of daily life, indeed the sanctification of the present moment, gains in depth if daily Christian existence takes its inspiration from the Paschal mystery. Each individual can best make his own application of what Paschal grace can do to his life. Christian living will take on a new dimension, Christian piety a new base. The Christian who is sacramentally oriented to the Paschal Mystery of the Savior may be less inclined toward peripheral devotions of one kind or another, and will anchor his prayer-life and his whole outlook on God and neighbor in the central redemptive act of life out of death.

5. Indwelling of God. The Christian living in faith will realize that sacramental grace, bearing us along with Christ into the heart of the Trinity, makes us present to that Holy Trinity itself. The doctrine of the divine indwelling in the souls of the just is thus seen in a new light, as the scriptural promise is fulfilled: "If anyone love me, he will keep my word, and my Father will love him, and we will come to him and make our abode with him" (Jn 14:23). Sacramental grace gives the power to live daily like another Christ, a son of God by adoption; to model one's life after the life of the natural son of God; to follow Christ's mandate "If you wish to know how to live, watch me! Come, follow me. If you would be perfect, go sell all you have, give to the poor ... and come, follow me" (Mt 19:21). The self-renunciation and self-abasement of the Paschal mystery are but the first stage of that detachment and voiding of self that seeks a new fullness in the constant presence of God who is truly Emmanuel, God with us.

6. **Sacramental life and moral life.** Frequently spiritual writers complain of an inconsistency between the sacramental experience and the daily life of the Christian. A life of faith, hope, and love centered in Christ must be the daily overflow of the sacramental encounter with the same Christ. In other words, along with the grace-contact afforded by the sacramental mystery, there is conferred an intensification of the power to know Christ, to be acquainted with him more intimately (faith), to trust in him with a childlike confidence (hope), and to love others the way God himself loves (charity). Sacramental grace, therefore, and the pledge of future graces included in the ecclesial effect of the sacraments, as well as other actual graces which are merely God's follow-up activity after the sacramental encounter, thus bridge the gap between liturgical celebration and daily living. In this life, worship is seen not as a mere routine formalism, but as a sincere turning toward Christ. And daily living on the other hand is not viewed as a secular, private, and ethically neutral existence, but rather a Christ-inspired and sacramentally energized bearing toward the world. All Christians are called to restore all things in Christ, to be the spokesmen as it were for lower nature, to fulfill the role abdicated by the first Adam, to give back to God the world of man and nature through its great High Priest and Savior Jesus Christ.

B. *The Sacramental Grace of Each Sacrament*

Commonly it is accepted that there are seven sacraments to fulfill the seven basic needs of life. The sacraments are viewed as corresponding on the supernatural level to seven principal states or experiences of man's life on the natural or human level. Birth, maturity, nourishment, remedy, authority, parenthood, suffering and death — for each of these needs, it is maintained, the merciful Christ has instituted a sacrament to sanctify and consecrate each of these moments, uplifting them, as it were, transmuting them into the sphere of the eternal. Or again, the sacraments serve to advance the Christian through the various stages of ecclesial life, especially those sacraments that confer an ecclesial commission, a certain status in the Church.

A fresh approach however to the number "seven" and therefore to the specific graces of each sacrament is provided by Schillebeeckx when he suggests that the sevenfold conferral of sacramental grace is "a manifold Messianic bestowal of grace and a commission of the ecclesial people of God as the earthly sacrament of Christ."[22] For him the number "seven" symbolizes the fullness of Christ's redemptive grace, even as we attribute seven special gifts to the outpouring of the Holy Spirit. Christ as Messiah or Savior created a following among men which is called the messianic community. This community of believers he has not left without the supporting presence of that Advocate of whom he said, "He will receive of what is mine and declare it to you" (Jn 16:14).

In this messianic community of believers, of fellowship with Christ, Christ the head configures or shapes his members progressively in his own image, in the image of himself as crucified and risen. Therefore the special grace of each sacrament will have a certain Christological focus, as well as an ecclesial one. In other words, the sacraments, insofar as they are Christ's saving acts made visible in the Church, are intended to fashion and fit us more and more perfectly into the total Christ, the Church-body united with its risen head. This dual configuration, which is really one, is the work of both the symbolic reality and the grace-effect. Current theologians, moreover, feel strongly that the sacramental grace is conferred upon the individual that he in his own personal way may carry out the goal determined by the first effect of each sacrament (the symbolic reality or the ecclesial effect, as we have called it above).[23]

Sacramental grace, then, in the Thomistic view is a certain modality or modification of sanctifying grace in general, which is given with each sacrament, in order to accomplish the specific purpose of that sacrament as indicated by the sacramental rite and by the first effect or symbolic reality of each sacrament. For some authors, sacramental grace also confers a special title or claim to future actual graces required for fidelity to the sacramental state.[24]

We may now try to specify the sacramental grace of each sacrament and to indicate its Christological and ecclesial dimension.

---

[22] Schillebeeckx, op. cit., p. 179.
[23] James Egan, O.P., "A Contemporary Approach to Sacramental Grace," *Readings in Sacramental Theology* (Englewood Cliffs, N. J.: Prentice-Hall, 1964), p. 134.
[24] *Ibid.*, p. 135.

1. The sacramental grace of baptism must be viewed in function of the symbolic reality or the character conferred as the first baptismal effect. Since the character of baptism incorporates us into the priestly people of God and imprints the image of Christ the high priest on the soul, the sacramental grace of baptism will be directed first of all to fulfilling one's status in the Church. It may be described as the grace to live as an adopted child of God, imitating in one's life the Paschal mystery of the God-Man who as true Son by nature lived once and for all a perfect filial life even unto death and resurrection. And so life as a Christian will be a life of homage or worship in union with Christ; and daily life in turn will be focused upon the climactic moments of sacramental homage and love to the Father in heaven. Since this sonship of the Father can be lived to the full only in community with God's other children, our brothers in Christ, the grace of baptism also enables us to esteem our brethren as coheirs with Christ, as fellow members of his body, as adopted brothers in Christ.

2. The confirmation character, as noted above, is a special consecration to the Pentecostal mystery. It configures us or assimilates us in a special way to Christ in his public life as a witness to his Father in the power of the Holy Spirit. Therefore the graces of confirmation coincide with this commission to be a public witness to Christ in his Church, to accept a more active part, as circumstances permit, in establishing God's kingdom among men.

3. The Eucharist is the sacrifice-meal in which the members of Christ's body on earth are gathered together in renewal of the Paschal mystery which first brought the Church into being. The special eucharistic grace therefore is the grace of the unity of the Church gathered together in the love of Christ, a grace of fraternal and Paschal charity, which the Postcommunion prayer of Easter Sunday so beautifully requests, the gift of "the Spirit of love to make us of one mind and one heart" (Roman Missal).

4. The vocational sacrament of holy orders confers a permanent likeness to Christ as priestly head of his Church-body. The fullness of the sacramental power is conferred upon the bishop; the priest is a participant or a sharer in the bishop's power and receives his delegation from the bishop. In his priestly role, the priest most directly is associated with the Paschal mystery of Christ, since he is called upon to renew it for the faithful sacramentally. His whole life then must be a special consecration to the Christ of the Paschal mystery. For this purpose, the special graces of holy orders, graces for his ministry among Christ's faithful, graces to reproduce the Paschal mystery in his own life as well as in the lives of others, are conferred upon him. They are graces im-

mediately ordered to carrying out his priestly duties of consecrating the sacrifice of the Eucharist, celebrating the other sacraments, preaching, and practicing in a superior way the spiritual and corporal works of charity.

5. The other vocational sacrament, matrimony, creates an indissoluble bond in the souls of the two to be married, a spiritual bond that remains until one of the partners dies. This bond establishes a likeness to the union between Christ and his Church. It confers the special sacramental graces needed for a lifetime of marriage, to be faithful to one another in the love of Christ, and to rear and educate children in the love of Christ.

6. Penance, the first of the two healing sacraments, may also have a certain first effect: the creation of interior repentance in the soul of the recipient or the status of reconciliation to the Church. The special sacramental grace corresponds to the first effect.

7. The anointing of the sick seems to confer a certain likeness to the suffering Christ of the Paschal mystery. It is a consecration of the faithful to Christ in his passion, conferring a special strength by merging the suffering of the member of Christ with that of the divine head. Therefore the special sacramental grace will be a grace of healing or strengthening of body (if God so intends) and of soul. Current theological emphasis, as indicated in the change of title, tends to consider this sacrament not so much as a sacrament of the dying (for viaticum — food for the journey to eternity — is that sacrament), but rather as a sacrament of comfort and strength for the Christian who is gravely ill. Therefore, as far as possible, it should not be delayed to the point where the patient is no longer able to respond to the graces conferred.

From this résumé of the sacramental graces, it is clear that every significant moment of the Christian life calls forth the saving, sanctifying gesture of a loving God. Every phase of life is sacramentalized, lifted up into the domain of the Paschal mystery; and in this way the life of each Christian becomes, like that of Christ the head, a mystery of saving worship, as all of life is sanctified for the praise and homage of the Eternal One.

PART TWO

BAPTISM, CONFIRMATION, THE EUCHARIST

Introduction: Initiation Into the Paschal Mystery

A. *Christian Initiation in the Early Church*[1]

The rites of Christian initiation, developed in the early centuries of the Church, provide a rich perspective for a deeper understanding of the sacraments of baptism, confirmation, and the Eucharist as they exist in the Church today. In the liturgy, the doctrinal convictions and belief of the Church come to life. As the ancient axiom puts it, *lex orandi, lex credendi* (the rule of prayer is the rule of faith). It will be worth our while then to examine briefly the basic outlines of the ancient service of Christian initiation in order to interpret rightly the mind of the Church, to enter into her feeling on the profound significance of the sacraments of admission into the Church. In these initiation rites, the Church betrayed a consciousness of her true self; she expressed something of her very nature, so that in studying these rites we touch the very heart and core of the Church.

---

[1] A convenient source for documentation concerning the rites of Christian initiation in the early Church is Paul F. Palmer, *Sacraments and Worship* (Westminster, Md.: The Newman Press, 1955), with special attention to the following documents: *The Apostolic Tradition of Hippolytus* (c. A.D. 215), p. 6 ff.; St. Cyril of Jerusalem, *On the Mysteries* (348/350), p. 13 ff.; St. Ambrose, *On the Mysteries* (c. 390), p. 25 ff.; and the *Gelasian Sacramentary* (c. 700), p. 37 ff.

As the Church grew larger and converts increased in numbers, particularly after the times of persecution (third century on), a lengthy period of preparation and probation called the catechumenate was organized. This was a kind of formal inquiry class in which the catechumens met from time to time for instruction, prayer, and other rites. Today a convert is usually under instruction for about two or three months before baptism; but in ancient times this preparatory period sometimes lasted as long as three years.[2] The purpose of a lengthy catechumenate was not merely to give a more intense foundation in the doctrines of the Church but also to test the sincerity of the candidate who was generally passing from sheer paganism to Christianity. Even today missionaries often postpone baptism for a long time in order to wean the native converts away from their tribal superstitions.

The final preparatory period before baptism was the season of Lent. The Liturgy of the Word or the first part of the Mass (which until recently was still called in the missals the Mass of the Catechumens) constituted the basic biblical instruction for the catechumens. Readings from the Old Testament invariably preceded the proclamation of the Gospel. In this way, the neophytes learned to view the New Testament as the fulfillment of the Old, and both testaments as revealing the Salvation-History into which they were about to enter through baptism.

Sometimes the synaxis or meeting of the catechumens also included other rites. Solemn scrutinies were held. Just as today the banns of matrimony must be announced before a forthcoming marriage to insure that the parties about to marry are free from any impediments to marriage known to the public, so also the ancient scrutiny had in part the purpose of establishing the sincerity, the good faith, and the upright conduct of the petitioner for baptism. Members of the faithful would vouch for the honesty and good character of their protégés. A scrutiny also included an exorcism, a solemn prayer beseeching God to free the catechumens from the assaults and influence of Satan and to give them strength to conquer temptation in the future. Such a scrutiny, according to the Gelasian Sacramentary, was made on the Wednesday of the third week of Lent. It included the blessing and conferral of salt as a symbol of hospitality and also of the wisdom which would come with acceptance of God's holy truth.

The Gelasian Sacramentary mentions altogether seven such days of scrutiny during Lent. The third of these, on the Wednesday of the fifth week of Lent, was called the Great Scrutiny. On this day the candidate was instructed in the Gospel, the Creed, and the Lord's Prayer. The four Gospels were solemnly introduced and the bishop in-

---

[2] Cf. Apostolic Tradition of Hippolytus, paragraph 17; Palmer, op. cit., p. 6.

structed the catechumens briefly on each of them, as well as on the articles of the Creed and the petitions of the Lord's Prayer. On Holy Saturday morning the candidates would have to know the entire Creed and recite it by heart before the bishop. The specific knowledge of the articles of the Creed and the Lord's Prayer was for a time part of the so-called "discipline of the secret"; knowledge of this kind was to be kept from pagans and was not written down, but taught orally to the catechumens.

On Holy Saturday morning, the catechumens convened in order to recite their Creed and to participate in the ceremony called "Ephpheta" or the opening of the ears, in imitation of Christ's cure of the deaf-mute in the Gospel. The nostrils and the ears were touched with spittle as a symbolic way of opening the ears to God's truth and the nostrils to the fragrance of the Gospel. This was followed by an anointing, conceived of as a strengthening for battle in the Christian militia. Next the catechumen turned to the west, symbol of darkness, and therefore of Satan's empire, and solemnly renounced all attachment to Satan and his works and temptations. Then turning to the east, symbolic of the rising sun and therefore of the risen Christ, he pledged his threefold faith in God the Father Almighty, in Christ, and in the Holy Spirit.

The final ceremonies of baptism, confirmation, and the Eucharist took place during the celebration of the great Easter Vigil beginning on Holy Saturday evening. After a lengthy service of biblical readings and meditation, the catechumens proceeded to the baptistry for their baptism. Stripping off their garments, they proceeded one by one into the baptismal pool; and after a triple immersion, accompanied by the sacramental words, they proceeded out of the pool now fully baptized members of Christ. They now received the two symbolic gifts of the white garments (symbolic of a return to the state of the first Adam) and the lighted candle (typifying a share in the light and life of Christ).

Thereupon the newly baptized proceeded to an adjoining chapel called the consignatorium where they were anointed with chrism by the bishop as a confirmation or strengthening of the new life they had just received in baptism. Through confirmation they became fully matured Christians; and now they proceeded into the church proper where they would take part for the first time in an entire Mass, the great Easter celebration of the Eucharist. There all the faithful were gathered together to welcome them into their midst with the kiss of peace. They brought their offerings at the offertory; and at the moment of their first Communion, at least in some places, they were also given some milk and honey (baby food, as it were, to remind them of their spiritual childhood, but also with an eye on the Old Testament's conception of the promised land as a land flowing with milk and honey, which was now opened to the newly baptized in the form of the Church).

In significance, the Vigil or watch service, like the sacraments themselves, was three dimensional. It looked back toward the past in commemoration of the ancient passover of the Israelites, as well as in celebration of the Paschal mystery of Christ. In the present moment, it was a celebration of the Lord's redemptive work now extended to the catechumens through the sacraments of Christian initiation and to all the faithful through the great Easter Eucharist. Finally, it was forward-looking or eschatological, insofar as it prepared for the glorious and triumphant return of Christ, of which his resurrection and ascension was a pledge and token. What better way to be found by the glorious returning Christ than as he himself commanded in the Gospel, watching and waiting in prayer?

During Easter week, a special joyful Mass was celebrated each day. The newly baptized, still wearing their white garments, occupied a place of honor in the church. The ancient Mass formularies still in our *Roman Missal* are for the most part baptismally oriented. These Masses were the occasion of a fuller explanation of the ceremonial of the sacraments of Christian initiation. Some of the great homilies of the Fathers like St. Cyril of Jerusalem and St. Ambrose, which they delivered during these Masses of Easter week, give us our best insight into the theology of Christian initiation in the fourth and fifth centuries of the Church.

B. *The Easter Vigil Today*

One of the most significant achievements of Pope Pius XII was the restoration of Holy Week and especially of the Easter Vigil in 1955. For some centuries the Vigil service had come to be celebrated in the early morning hours of Holy Saturday. Thus much of the natural symbolism of the liturgy was lost to the faithful, who came to regard the mysterious service as a series of blessings, relatively unimportant and surely poorly attended at the early hour of 5:30 or 6:00 in the morning. Some hearty spirits would manage to get to church in time for the Mass starting about 8:00. The bells were rung at the *Gloria* of the Mass, and thus Easter was already anticipated in the early hours of Saturday morning. This was in great contrast to the custom of the early Church in keeping Saturday as a day of mourning at the sepulcher of Christ. No Mass was celebrated on this day. The Vigil service commenced only in the evening and would be prolonged into the early hours of Sunday morning.

The Vigil service as it is celebrated today consists of three parts, as the adjoining schema[3] will make clear. The first part is a celebration of the mystery of light; the Paschal candle, ranging in symbolism from the column of fire in the ancient exodus to Christ the risen light of mankind, stands as a focal point in the exodus of Christians now going on. Therefore the congregation ideally is led into the darkened church by the deacon bearing the Paschal candle, a reliving of the twin exodus of the Hebrews and of Christ. The mystery of redemption, which became our mystery through the sacraments, is then solemnly proclaimed in the deacon's hymn, the ancient *Exsultet* or Paschal proclamation.

In this magnificent liturgical and poetic composition, sometimes attributed to St. Ambrose, the good news of God's saving works in the past is announced and made present once again through the sacrament of his Word. The whole theology of the Easter Vigil is contained in the Paschal proclamation. It is seen to be a celebration of the Lord's death and resurrection, or better of his passage through death to new glorious life. The proclamation reminds us of Christ's triumph over sin and death and how he has passed on that victory to us especially through the Easter Sacraments.

The central portion of the Paschal proclamation is as follows:

. . . This is that Paschal feast in which the true Lamb is slain, whose blood sanctifies the doorposts of the faithful.

This is the night in which thou of old didst lead our forefathers, the children of Israel, out of the land of Egypt dry-shod through the Red Sea.

This is the night which scattered the darkness of sin by means of the pillar of fire.

This is the very night which delivers all who believe in Christ from worldly vice and from darkness of sin, which restores them to grace and makes them co-sharers with the saints.

This is the night in which Christ burst the bonds of death and came forth as Conqueror from the grave. For unless we had been redeemed, it would avail us nothing to be born.

O wondrous condescension of thy mercy toward us!

O incomprehensible goodness of love: to redeem a slave thou didst deliver up a Son!

O truly necessary sin of Adam, which the death of Christ has blotted out!

O happy fault, that merited a Redeemer so holy and so great!

O truly blessed night, which alone merited to know the time and hour when Christ rose from the dead!

[3] Pages 80–81.

. . . The holiness of this night drives out wickedness and washes away guilt; it restores innocence to the fallen and joy to the sorrowful. It banishes enmities, establishes peace, and brings low the pride of tyrants. . . .

O truly blessed night, when Egypt was despoiled and Israel enriched!

O night, when heaven is wedded to earth, and God to man.

. . . May this candle consecrated to thine honor continue with undiminished light to dispel this night's darkness. Receive it as a fragrant and pleasing offering, and let its light mingle with the lamps of heaven.

May the Morning Star behold its flame — that Morning Star who knows no setting, who rose from the place of the dead and gently shines on man.[4]

The second part of the Vigil service is a celebration of the mystery of water. In the very night of the Lord's death and resurrection, we remember the water that poured forth with the blood from the Lord's pierced side on the cross — water and blood which Christian tradition has taken as a symbol of the sacraments of baptism and the Eucharist respectively. On this night the Church reminds us that the saving work of Christ, solemnly proclaimed in the first part of the Vigil, has been passed on to us sacramentally through our own baptism. Furthermore, what more appropriate time for the Church to initiate new members and to pass on to them for the first time the new life of the risen Christ?

THE RESTORED EASTER VIGIL
Renewal of Christian Initiation

FIRE (Light)

Part I — Light Service ... Paschal Candle: symbol of
    a) pillar of fire (God's presence) in exodus from Egypt
    b) Christ, risen light of mankind, leading a new exodus
  A. Rite:
    1. Blessing of new fire
    2. Blessing of Paschal candle (five wax nails)
    3. Solemn procession of Light (reliving all previous saving pilgrimages of Salvation-History)
    4. Paschal proclamation in praise of redemption (*Exsultet*)
  B. Significance:
    1. Offering of "evening sacrifice" of light
    2. Triumph of light over darkness (Christ over Satan)
    3. Prepares for the "illumination" or enlightenment of baptism (next part of Vigil)

---

[4] Adapted from *The Masses of Holy Week and the Easter Vigil* (Collegeville, Minn.: Liturgical Press, 1956), pp. 135–136.

WATER (Life)

Part II — Baptism . . . Font:

    a) Tomb where we bury our sins

    b) Womb from which we were born as new sons of the Church

  A. Rite:

    1. Readings from Old Testament (announce the *new creation* in baptism)

    2. Litany of Saints (Part I)

    3. Blessing of baptismal water

    4. Conferral of baptism

    5. Baptismal water carried to font

    6. Renewal of baptismal promises by faithful

    7. Blessing with new Easter water (sacramental, to renew our baptism)

    8. Litany of Saints (concluded)

  B. Significance:

    1. Historically, admission of converts into Church

    2. For us, renewal of our own baptism:

      — recall our birth into Church, family of the redeemed

      — association in Christ's death and resurrection (Paschal mystery)

      — recall our privileges as Christians and our commitment to Christ's kingdom on earth

BREAD (Life)

Part III — Eucharist . . . Altar Table

    Significance:

    1. Newly baptized partake of the family meal, sign of full acceptance into Christ's family

    2. Celebration of Paschal mystery by sharing the very flesh and blood of the glorified Christ

    3. Solemn renewal of our Covenant-union with the Father

The mystery of baptism is introduced liturgically by a Scripture service, an echo of the more ancient practice of prolonged reading of Scripture as a final instruction for the catechumens. This is a reminder that the entire baptismal and Eucharistic functions of the Easter Vigil have their historical roots in the ancient celebration of Christian initiation. The first reading is the Genesis account of creation; its function in the Vigil is to set forth the Salvation-History background of our redemption, the new creation, and of baptism the Sacrament that makes us new creatures in Christ. The second reading recalls the crossing of the Sea of Reeds on the night of the Hebrew Passover, where water is seen as a sign of punishment and destruction for the pagan pursuers, and the sign of deliverance and new life for the liberated Israelites. So also baptism marks a passage through the waters that destroys sin and casts us forth as members of God's new people. The third reading (Is 4:2–6) describes the faithful minority, the *anawim*, who will survive the exile and return to Jerusalem to establish a new Israel. Ultimately this is a figure of the Church, the messianic community, the faithful remnant of the New Covenant into which baptism admits us. The last reading (Dt 31:22–30) commemorates the central position occupied in Jewish piety by the Torah or the book of the Law. So also for the Christian, the new law of Christ, the law of the New Covenant, must claim his unflinching fidelity.

Next follows the first part of the Litany of the Saints, wherein the Christian community implores the aid of the Church triumphant on behalf of the candidates for baptism. The successful alumni of the grand fraternity of the Church on earth are petitioned to use their influence for the benefit of the new pledges being admitted.

Solemn consecration of the baptismal water now follows. After recalling the significant role that water has played in God's great salvation acts, the Church begs the Holy Spirit to impregnate water with his power so that the baptismal font may become the womb of the Church from which will spring a new creation, the children of God. Newly consecrated oils are now added to symbolize the presence of the Holy Spirit in the rite of baptism. For pastoral reasons, that is, for the instruction and edification of the faithful, all of this ritual blessing of the water is to be carried out in the sanctuary within full view of the congregation.

There follows now the actual baptism of converts. If this is done, the Church recaptures something of the community atmosphere that prevailed at the ancient ritual of Christian initiation. The congregation is present to welcome the newly baptized into their ranks. A spirit of true fraternal charity should prevail as the older "brothers" of the Christian fraternity welcome their new brothers in Christ. In former times this was visibly expressed by the exchange of the ceremonial kiss of peace. The essential rite of baptism being completed, the ceremonial gifts of the white robe and the lighted candle are next conferred. Finally the faithful renew their own baptismal allegiance to Christ, an act that invites reflection on the meaning of Christian commitment. To be a Christian in more than name only places demands of Christian action on all of the faithful, not only those involved in specialized apostolic activities. Here again liturgy and life meet; daily Christian life must be the worship of Christ overflowing in Christian service to our fellowmen. The blessing of the faithful with the new baptismal water seals the baptismal allegiance to Christ with a solemn sacramental. The Litany of the Saints is then concluded and the Eucharistic celebration is about to begin.

The climax of Christian initiation is reached with the great Paschal

Eucharist. For the ancient catechumen, this marked the first time that he was permitted to attend the entire Mass. Such a sacramental sequence shows clearly the progress of Christian initiation from baptism (admission into the Church family) to the Eucharist (admission to the family table). The Easter Eucharist furthermore is par excellence the making present of the Paschal mystery of Christ, which in turn is the font and source of all Christian life, individual and communal. It is the sacramental celebration of the New Covenant, solemnly sealed in the precious blood of Christ the true Lamb, slain for the salvation of the world. The Easter Vigil ends with a mighty Alleluia, the song of jubilation that echoes in the courts of heaven.

CHAPTER VI

Dying and Rising With Christ: Baptism

INTRODUCTION

The twentieth century, with its population explosion, technological progress, big-city growth, and mobility of people has more than ever confirmed the truth that "no man is an island." Sociologists, psychologists, and clergymen are much concerned over the increasing incidents of noninvolvement; witnesses of tragedy or crime prefer not to "get involved," even though the life of a fellow human being may be at stake. There is a tension, then, between the individual, his dignity, rights, and personal fulfillment, and the society of man in which he lives. Social, political, and technological changes have tended to create the "lost" individual, disenchanted, solitary, frustrated, anxiety-ridden, alienated, anonymous. A certain fragmentation of relationship with the primary cultural groups — the family, the church, and the local community — has thrust man back upon his own resources without the old certitudes and supports he formerly enjoyed.

The religious implications of such a loss of community are incisively drawn in the following observation:

> Man's alienation from man must lead in time to man's alienation from God. The loss of the sense of visible community in Christ will be followed by the loss of the sense of the invisible. The decline of community in the modern world has as its inevitable religious consequence the creation of masses of helpless, bewildered individuals who are unable to find solace in Christianity regarded merely as creed. The stress upon the individual, at the expense of the churchly community, has led remorselessly to the isolation of the individual, to the shattering of the man-God relationship, and to the atomization of personality.[1]

The same author goes on to say succinctly that "Belonging, not escape, is the imperative moral value."[2] The paradoxical solution of modern man's predicament would reduce itself to this, that he becomes truly himself and finds personal fulfillment precisely through meaningful associations and allegiances. Put in a theological frame of reference, this means that the individual believer realizes his fullest potential as a Christian person by a dynamic relationship to Christ's Mystical Body on earth, the Church. If the Christian community is actively informed by that charity which Christ designated as its hallmark, then each member knows and feels himself to be of worth and value before God because of the interpersonal unity that emerges in the name of Christ.

If the community must be tangible to have effect, if acceptance, identity, and status must be maintained by visible symbol and gesture, then it should be readily apparent that the Church as the visible community in Christ must necessarily grow and support itself through those visible experiences called sacraments. With basic concepts gained in previous chapters, it should be possible now to examine the three initiatory sacraments of baptism, confirmation, and Eucharist and to discover how they contribute to build up the body of believers united in Christ. It should become clear that baptism and confirmation, as first steps into the Church, endow us with a profound identity; for added to the fundamental divine image implanted in us at birth is the insuperably more wonderful "face of Christ" — that resemblance to God's very Son incarnate that makes us truly Christian, "another Christ."

Made over in the image of Christ through these sacraments, we at

---

[1] Robert A. Nisbet, The Quest for Community (New York: Oxford University Press, 1953), p. 14.
[2] Ibid., p. 26.

once take on a new social or family identity, for we share our personal likeness to Christ on a family basis. Our baptized brothers wear the same image of dignity; in common we bear the name "in Christ." In the realization that baptism and the other initiatory sacraments join us to a vast community of love, where each person really counts because of the great Body-Person to which he belongs, we have the revealed answer to the modern "quest for community."

I. PREHISTORY OF BAPTISM: BASIC HUMAN SYMBOLISM OF WATER[3]

Initiation into a visible community is unthinkable without the use of external symbols, even if they be merely words. In approaching a study of baptism, we confront a basic symbol appropriated already by primitive man to express fundamental concepts, generally of a religious nature. It is the symbol of water.

Water is but one of several primordial or archetypal images, explained by the psychologist Jung as the collective unconscious revealing itself in certain basic patterns or symbols that are the common property of mankind. These images consistently recur in one form or another in mythology, folklore, and poetry. The fact that a certain similarity appears between pagan symbolism and scriptural interpretations of images like water does not mean that one was influenced by the other or that one borrowed from the other. Speaking of the comparative meanings attached to water in various religious rituals, Professor Eliade remarks:

> All that one may call the "prehistory" of Baptism sought the same object — death and resurrection, though at different religious levels from that of Christianity. There can be no question here of "influences" or of "borrowings," for such symbols are archetypal and universal; they show man's position in the universe, while at the same time evaluating his position in regard to his god (to absolute reality), and to history. The symbolism of water is the product of an intuition of the cosmos as a unity, and of man as a specific mode of being in the cosmos.[4]

One ancient human intuition regarded water as the source of all possible existence, the principle of what is formless and potential, the basic substance from which all forms come and to which they will return. Immersion in water symbolized the dissolution of forms, a return as it were to the formlessness of preexistence; emerging from the water represented a kind of new creation, a new beginning, the assumption of a new

---

[3] This material is largely drawn from the exhaustive investigations of Professor Mircea Eliade, *Patterns in Comparative Religion* (New York: Sheed & Ward, 1958), pp. 188–215.

[4] Eliade, op. cit., p. 197.

form of life. In pagan initiation rituals, water effects a new birth. In magic rituals, it heals; and in funeral rites, it assures rebirth after death. The creation stories of most mythologies include reference to the primitive waters above and below the earth (cf. Gn 1), for example, the Babylonian *Enuma Elish* creation story. If water is the source of life, including human life, it is only one step further to consider water as a kind of universal mother. Water, it was felt, has many wonderful properties: it restores youth; it heals; it insures eternal life.

The curative and purifying function of water was attributed to the belief that in water everything is dissolved. Every form is broken up in this symbol of death. What is immersed in water dies and comes to life again in a new form. This may happen both on the cosmic level as well as on the human level. Thus the waters of the deluge or the flood wash away sin and destroy the wicked; but at the same time they regenerate a new race loyal to God (cf. the story of Noah and the Flood in Gn 6–9). The deluge is a kind of baptism; its waters are both destructive and regenerative.

Immersion in water's purifying baths is performed for the purpose of bringing back into the present the moment of creation; it is a symbolic reenactment of the birth of the world or of the new man. Thus the two basic meanings of immersion in water appear: descent into the waters is a return to formlessness and death; rising from the waters is a return to new life, a new creation. Here then on the level of universal man and common human symbolism there emerges a human basis for the theology of water that will appear in the New Testament (cf. Rom 6:3 ff.).

II. BIBLICAL SYMBOLISM OF WATER[5]

As appears from the above, a comparative study of ancient pagan religions and that of the Hebrews may be expected to yield many points of contact between the two. For primitive man as well as for the Hebrews, water was a mighty force charged with mystery. For some it represented the source of life; its cleansing power, both physical and spiritual, its sustaining and life-giving properties, its necessity for life, its importance

---

[5] Collateral readings: Oscar Cullmann, *Baptism in the New Testament* (*Studies in Biblical Theology*), No. 1 (London: SCM Press Limited, 1950), sixth reprint, January, 1961; Jean Danielou, *The Bible and the Liturgy* (Notre Dame, 1956); A. George, J. Delorme, *et al.*, *Baptism in the New Testament* (Baltimore: Helicon Press, 1964); Neunheuser, *Baptism and Confirmation* (New York: Herder & Herder, 1964); Xavier Léon-Dufour, ed., *Vocabulaire de Théologie Biblique* (Paris: Éditions du Cerf, 1962), articles on "Baptism," "Symbolism of Water," etc.; John L. McKenzie, *Dictionary of the Bible* (Milwaukee: The Bruce Publishing Co., 1965), art. "Baptism," "Water," etc.

for commerce, its benefits and its hazards are commonly acknowledged by all primitive peoples. But here we must necessarily limit our horizons to Hebrew thought as reflected in Scripture.

The ancient Hebrews, heirs of the Semitic and Babylonian tradition concerning the shape of the universe, believed that there were waters both above the firmament or sky and below the earth. But significantly these waters, like the rest of the universe, are under the control of almighty God himself. It is he who sends rain to bless the crops and nurture their growth (Gn 27:28; Lv 26:3 f., 10; Dt 28:1, 12; Pss 103, 132). If Israel is unfaithful, God shuts up the waters of the heavens in punishment (Lv 26:19, Dt 28:23) until Israel converts to God (Am 4:7). Thus water functions as a central life power for man.

Water's destructive powers are not unnoticed by the sacred authors. We remember the waters of the deluge in the time of Noah; we know how water engulfed the Egyptian armies pursuing the fleeing Hebrews. But the same water which punished the pagans allowed passage into freedom for God's people through the head waters of the Reed Sea.

In contrast to its destructive powers are its benefits for man. Water cleanses and purifies both body and soul. Among the rites of hospitality was the bathing of the feet of the guest (Gn 18:4; 19:2; Lk 7:44), a rite which Christ himself in humility and fraternal charity performed for his Apostles the night of the first Eucharist (Jn 13:2–15). Physical cleansing suggested also moral cleansing; the washing of hands was a sign of innocence; the sinner who abandoned his sins and was converted to a better life was like a man cleansed of his filth (Is 1:16). God himself is said to wash the sinner insofar as he pardons his faults (Ps 50:4). The deluge was God's purification of the earth by the extermination of the wicked (1 Pt 3:20 f.).

Jewish ritual included numerous purifications with water. The high priest had to wash himself before his investiture (Ex 29:4; 40:12) and also on the great Day of Expiation (Lv 16:4, 24). Ablutions in water were prescribed for those who would touch a corpse, for one cleansed from leprosy, or for all sexual impurity. These various bodily cleansings were a sign of interior purification of the heart necessary for one who would approach the all-holy God.

Yet these Old Testament washings were inefficacious in procuring purity of soul. In the New Testament, Christ would provide a new way of purification, namely, through baptism. Christ may be said to have announced the definitive sacrament of purification by the miracle of Cana (Jn 2:6) where he changed water destined for Jewish purifications into wine symbolizing the Holy Spirit and the purifying Word (cf. Jn 13:10; 15:3).

III. THE WATERS OF MESSIANIC TIMES

The New Testament significance of water takes on a new breadth when we appreciate its Old Testament eschatological import. Already the pre-exilic prophets employed the theme of water in sketching the future restoration of God's people. In the famous passage of Ezekiel 36:24–27, God promises an abundance of water to purify his people at the time of their deliverance from Babylon. This purification would touch the very heart of man and permit him to accomplish faithfully God's holy law.

> I will take you away from among the nations, gather you from all the foreign lands, and bring you back to your own land. I will sprinkle clean water upon you to cleanse you from all your impurities, and from all your idols I will cleanse you. I will give you a new heart and place a new spirit within you. . . . I will put my spirit within you and make you live by my statutes, careful to observe my decrees (Ez 36:24–27).[6]

The return from the Babylonian exile will be like a new exodus. Again the water miracles of the crossing of the Reed Sea, the water flowing from the rock, and all the blessings that accompanied God's people in the desert will be repeated (cf Is 35:6 f.; 41:17–20; 43:20).

For Israel's prophets, water, a scarce and therefore priceless commodity in the Near East, figured largely in their description of the "golden age" to be ushered in by the Messiah. The messianic times will be characterized by a plentiful supply of water; no more periods of aridity or famine; God will give his rain in due time (Ez 34:26), the assurance or promise of prosperity (Ez 36:29 f.). Abundant rainfall, in turn, will guarantee bread in abundance; rich pasture lands will be at the disposal of God's people (Is 30:23 f.). Fresh waters will be at hand; hunger and thirst will disappear forever (Jer 31:9; Is 49:10).

At the very center of life in messianic times will stand the new Jerusalem, the object of sacred pilgrimage. From the temple will flow living or fresh water, bringing forth a marvelous fruitfulness, indeed a veritable paradise for God's people (cf. Ez 47:1–12; Gn 2:10–14). In those waters, Israel will find purity (Za 13:1), life (Jl 4:18; Za 14:8), and holiness (Ps 45:5).

The waters of the messianic age, then, are not to be understood in a purely material sense. In its eschatological perspective, water ordinarily assumes a symbolic value. For example, Ezekiel's vision of water flowing

---

[6] In the age of the catechumenate, the Church employed passages like this for the catechesis of prospective converts. The fuller sense of the prophecy suggests baptismal themes: the ingathering of God's elect into the Church; purification; new creation; new covenant. Cf. The Roman Missal, Mass for Wednesday of fourth week of Lent.

from the temple symbolizes the vivifying power of God causing plentiful blessings for man. Water also symbolizes God's spirit which is capable of transforming the desert into a blossoming orchard and an unfaithful people into a true or faithful Israel (Is 44:3 f.). In a well-known passage (Is 55:10 f.; cf. Am 8:11 f.), God's work is compared to the rainfall that comes to make the earth fruitful. The teaching of divine wisdom likewise is a vivifying or life-giving water (Is 55:1, Sir 15:3; 24:25–31). In short, God will be the center of Israel's life showering blessing, plenitude, and abundance, of which the water is a holy symbol.

IV. WATER IN THE NEW TESTAMENT

The Old Testament theme of water is transposed into a new key in the New Testament. Here again the waters of the rock, of the temple, and of the Reed Sea reappear in their fulfillment stage in the mystery of Christ. Especially Christ's Spirit, the vivifying power of God the Creator (Jn 7:39), is symbolized by water. The paradise theme and the wisdom theme also reappear under the symbol of water (cf. Jn 4:10–14; Ap 7:17; 21:6).

The significance of the biblical symbolism of water reaches its climax in the waters of Christian baptism. Purifying water was used by John for his "baptism of repentance" (Mt 3:11 f.), indeed the very waters of the Jordan where once upon a time Naaman, the Syrian general, was cured of his leprosy (2 Kgs 5:10–14). Now Christian baptism causes the purification, not of man's body, but of his soul, of his conscience (1 Pt 3:21); it is a bath that washes us from sin (1 Cor 6:11; Eph 5:26; Heb 10:22; Acts 22:16), applying to us the redemptive power of the blood of Christ (Heb 9:13 f.; Ap 7:14; 22:14).

To the fundamental symbolism of baptismal water, Paul adds another; in the well-known passage of Romans 6:3–11, Paul interprets the baptismal immersion in water as an association with Christ in his death and resurrection. Descent into the water associates the Christian with Christ's death, which caused man's sin to be buried. By his death Christ, just as Yahweh in the past, has conquered the forces of evil so often connected with the raging waters (cf. 1 Cor 10:1 ff.; Is 51:10). Finally, in communicating to us the Spirit of God, baptism is also the principle or source of new life. Baptism is "the bath of regeneration and renewal in the Holy Spirit" (Ti 3:5; cf. Jn 3:5).

From the above résumé of the biblical theme of water, two conclusions seem warranted at this time. The first conclusion is an admonition, a caution, not to ignore the deep-lying significance of a natural resource so often taken for granted. The rich theme of water that threads its way so consistently through sacred history can only too readily be minimized in a milieu such as ours, where water is so easily obtainable from the nearest faucet. However, the critical problem of water pollution in so many lakes and streams may once again alert our people to the value and necessity of this great life resource.

The second observation underscores the importance of trying to understand and appreciate God's use of water in sacred history if we are to appreciate the great sacrament of water, baptism. For it is baptism that sums up all these previous strands of symbolism and sacred act, and inserts us as fellow beneficiaries into the long line of sacred history. We may now turn to the more direct theme of baptism itself in Old and New Testament literature.

V. BAPTISM IN SALVATION-HISTORY

God's saving work appears in Scripture as the creation of a people, a chosen race of men, who would be a kingdom of worshipers, bound to him as partner and friend, the special beneficiaries of his loving-kindness. Now the principal saving deed by which God formed this people of Israel was the exodus. The passage of the Israelites from Egypt was not looked upon as a diplomatic coup for Moses, nor as a work of Hebrew chicanery or deception, but rather as the saving act of Yahweh himself. The exodus, from which all of Israel's history flows, came to be regarded in the early Christian Church as a prelude and pattern for Christ's great work of shaping the New Testament Israel, the Church. The sacraments, which channel Christ's unifying love to us in the Church, are seen as continuing the line of Yahweh's mighty deeds for the first Israel.

Four Old Testament events are found especially linked with baptism by the Fathers of the Church. They are creation, the deluge, the exodus, and the entrance into the Promised Land. For the ancient Israelites, creation marked the first step toward the great salvation deed of the exodus-covenant. God created with a view to founding his people Israel in the Sinai covenant. Later, Israel's hopes for a golden age were expressed under the theme of a new creation yet to come (cf. Is 65:17-25).

Christ's work in the New Testament is presented as a new creation, of which the individual becomes a part through baptism. The baptized Christian is "a new creature in Christ" (2 Cor 5:17), "created in Christ Jesus" (Eph 2:10), the recipient of "a new creation" (Gal 6:15). John's report on Christ's discourse with Nicodemus (Jn 3) records the same idea under the figure of a new birth.

Two elements of the creation story suggest further parallels with baptism: water and light. Just as God gave order and direction to the primeval water chaos, so in baptism God's power orients the newborn Christian to a well-ordered life under the guidance of the Holy Spirit. It was the spirit of God who hovered over the primeval waters in the first place; now that divine influence is present again to make water powerful for new life in the Christian. Just as the separation of light from darkness is singled out as a specific act of creation (cf Gn 1:3–4), so Christ, the light of mankind (cf Jn 1:9; 8:12), communicates the light of his truth to his followers through baptism. The man born blind in John 9 receives the gift of physical sight first by the curative powers of Jesus; but such a healing takes place only on the condition that the man first wash in the pool called "Sent," which John interprets as meaning the Messiah or Jesus himself. Thus *washing* in Jesus brings *illumination*. The aftermath of the miracle finds Jesus bringing an even deeper enlightenment as he reveals his messianic identity to the man he had cured. Thus the optimum of spiritual enlightenment is reached. Not surprising, then, that the Fathers of the East should call baptism *photismós* or "enlightenment," for it is that sacrament that brings a personal acquaintance with Christ, the power to know him personally in the light of faith. The baptismal allusion suggested by the cure of the man born blind is apparent from the Church's use of this story in one of the Lenten Masses directed to the catechumens (Mass for the Wednesday after the fourth Sunday of Lent).

The writings of St. Paul confirm the New Testament view of baptism as an enlightenment. He bids the Christians of Colossae to give thanks to God "who has made us worthy to share the lot of the saints in light. He has rescued us from the power of darkness and transferred us into the kingdom of his beloved Son, in whom we have our redemption, the remission of our sins" (Col 1:12–13).

A primitive baptismal hymn seems to be quoted in Ephesians 5:14: "Awake, sleeper, and arise from among the dead, and Christ will enlighten you." Hebrews 6:4 refers to those "who were once enlightened, who have both tasted the heavenly gift and become partakers of the Holy Spirit," namely in baptism. Finally, St. Peter, addressing a group of newly baptized, perhaps during an ancient Easter Vigil, summarizes their baptismal privileges by noting that they have been called "out of darkness into his [God's] marvelous light" (1 Pt 2:9).

The second important prelude to baptism found in the Old Testament is the deluge or flood at the time of Noah. Prescinding from its historicity of detail, its Salvation-History value as a rehearsal for baptism is clearly pointed out in 1 Peter 3:20–21: "In that ark [of Noah] a few, that is, eight souls were saved through water. Its counterpart, Baptism, now saves you also . . . through the resurrection of Jesus Christ. . . ." The baptismal waters, like the waters of the deluge, destroy sin and its effects, but at the same time preserve the seed of new life. In the homilies and writings of the Fathers, Noah is compared to Christ, the ark to the Church, the dove to the Holy Spirit. The use of this reading during the former Easter Vigil testifies to the Church's fondness for this story as a type of baptism.

The third and greatest foreshadowing of baptism was the mighty exodus or deliverance of Israel from Egypt. Just as water was the medium of deliverance in the exodus, so is it in baptism. The same water that allowed the Israelites to go free flowed back over the pursuing Egyptians and drowned them (Ex 14:28–30). The Fathers of the Church were quick to see the many points of comparison between the exodus event and baptism of water. The pagan Egyptians were likened to Satan, whose power over the candidate for baptism was lost to the mightier power of the Holy Spirit. The Israelites had crossed through the waters on their way to becoming God's people through the Sinai covenant; so also the Christian by baptism crosses through the waters and enters the new covenanted people of God, the Church. The Israelites, freed from Egypt, were set on their way to the promised land; so the Christian through baptism is set on his way to heaven, the eternal land of promise. Such patristic interpretations derived their inspiration from the example of St. Paul, who, in 1 Corinthians 10:1–6, had already spelled out the parallelism between the exodus event and the Christian reality of salvation:

> For I would not have you ignorant, brethren, that our fathers were all under the cloud, and all passed through the sea, and all were baptized in Moses, in the cloud, and in the sea. And all ate the same spiritual food and all drank the same spiritual drink (for they drank from the spiritual rock which followed them, and the rock was Christ). Yet with most of them, God was not well pleased, for they were laid low in the desert. Now these things came to pass as examples to us. . . .

As the Israelites were bound to the fellowship of Moses by their exodus experience under his leadership, so Christian baptism joins us to fellowship with Christ. The cloud, symbolic of Christ's presence, is associated with the Holy Spirit in the baptismal tradition. In conferring baptism during the Easter Vigil service, commemorating the death and resurrection of Christ as well as the ancient exodus, the Church liturgically shows the same understanding of baptism as the new exodus of Christians.

One last Old Testament type or rehearsal for baptism is seen in the crossing of the Jordan by the Israelites under Joshua at the time when they came to enter the land of promise. Christ repeated this event at the moment of his baptism by entering into the waters of the Jordan in the presence of John, son of Zachary. The practice of the early Church was as far as possible to use flowing or "living" water in order better to imitate the example of Christ in his descent into the flowing Jordan waters.

The Jews who returned from the Babylonian exile developed the practice of frequent ritual washings. Although in some cases they did not entirely avoid the formalism for which the Pharisees of the Gospel are chastised (cf. Mk 7:1-5), yet, for the sincere and repentant Jew, these ablutions did help to achieve purification of heart. Toward the end of the Old Testament era and the beginning of the New, the rabbis accepted pagan converts to Judaism by a kind of baptism which, at times at least, seems to have been considered as necessary as circumcision. The Essene communities and the community of monks at Qumran frequently practiced ablutions or ritual baths to manifest a sincere desire for conversion. Archaeological discoveries at Qumran testify to the existence of baths or pools in the community buildings.

When we then come to consider the baptism of John, the son of Zachary, we see that he is the heir of a long tradition. His baptism indeed bears comparison with that of converts mentioned above; the latter introduced the convert into the people of Israel, whereas John's baptism of repentance in a sense joined the individual to the true posterity of Abraham (cf. Mt 3:9) or to the remnant of Israel, those chosen souls who would be spared from the wrath of God and were looking forward to the coming Messiah. While John's baptism was a kind of preparation for a new exodus (cf. Is 40:3 ff.), a baptism in water preparing for the appearance of the Messiah, he assured his listeners that an even greater baptism would come with fire and the Holy Spirit. It was the Messiah himself who would inaugurate the definitive sacramental baptism.

VI. THE MAKING OF CHRISTIAN BAPTISM

It is a rather naïve view of the institution of any sacrament to think that Jesus created the sacrament at one given moment, as though he were signing an edict or publishing a communiqué. Actually we can say that several actions of Christ are involved in the creation of a sacrament like baptism. There is a kind of prehistory, as we have noted in the Old Testament era. Then Christ's own baptism at the Jordan surely has great significance for the establishment of the sacrament of baptism in the Church. Furthermore, the creation of the sacraments must not be isolated from our Lord's total work of founding the Church. The Church herself is Christ's supersacrament, and the seven sacraments are but her "natural" expression and life actions. Finally the Paschal mystery of

Christ's death and resurrection is a *sine qua non* for the existence of the Church and her sacraments. Keeping this in mind, we now turn to the steps by which Christ instituted or provided for the sacrament of Christian baptism.

We begin with the study of Christ's own baptism at the Jordan. The Fathers of the Church emphasize the importance of this moment for the origins of Christian baptism. From the time when Christ descended into the waters of the Jordan, they maintained, water became amenable to God's special use of it later as an initiation rite into his Church. From this time forward, water would be a chief symbol of man's sanctification.

In submitting to the humiliating ritual of a public profession of penitence, Christ was identifying himself with the cause of sinners. He is introduced as the Lamb of God who carries away the sins of the world (Jn 1:29–36), an allusion that recalls the Servant of God, who was led like a *lamb to the slaughter* and by his death would *take away the sins* of many and win pardon for their offenses (Is 53:7, 12).

Now just as the Isaian Servant of God was also a corporate figure, standing for the whole people of Israel (Is 49:3), so Jesus comes to his baptism as the new Israel, incorporating God's people in himself. Therefore he relives or recapitulates some of the principal experiences of his people. In entering the waters of the Jordan, Jesus relives both the ancient Exodus across the Reed Sea and also the crossing of the Jordan under Joshua.

But not only did the new Israel, Jesus, re-live the exodus of the first Israel; his baptism likewise foreshadows another exodus also called a baptism, one of suffering and death (cf. Lk 12:50, Mk 10:38). Christ's descent into the Jordan, then, is both prophecy and exemplar of his descent into the waters of death, to be accomplished by the Paschal mystery of his death and resurrection.

The Paschal mystery and its association with Christ's baptism is hinted at in still another way. The theophany or appearance of God at Jesus' baptism is described in such a way as to designate Jesus as the Suffering Servant of Isaiah 53. For the voice from the cloud that overshadowed Jesus designates him as God's "beloved son" or "servant," words which were also used to identify the suffering prophet of Isaiah 42:1: "Here is my servant whom I uphold, my chosen one with whom I am pleased, upon whom I have put my spirit." Thus Jesus is marked off as God's Suffering Servant as well as his own Son. The presence of the Spirit moreover is still another facet of Christ's investiture as Messiah. For the prophets often associated the presence of Yahweh's spirit with the great prophet who was to come (cf. Is 11:2; 42:1; 61:1). Likewise this may be taken as a forerunner of Pentecost, when Jesus would pour out the plenitude of the Spirit upon his Church and make them his followers, adopted sons of his heavenly Father.

Thus we may say that Jesus' humiliation in accepting a "baptism" for sinners is crowned in the glory of the theophany. Coming forth from the waters of the Jordan in the glory of the Spirit foreshadows his glorious rising from the nether world after his passion and death. Just as the heavens opened at the Jordan and rained down God's Spirit in the form of a dove resting over the head of Jesus, so the heavens would open again to all men when Jesus ascended to sit at his Father's right hand. The baptism of Christ pledges and promises not only Christ's own death and glorification, but also that of all Christians who through baptism would enter into his life-saving Paschal mystery.

After his resurrection, Jesus, in the fullness of his power, directed his Apostles to bring his teaching to all men and to make them his followers through baptism. The words put on the lips of Christ as a farewell commission to his Apostles may well have been a liturgical formula used at baptism in the primitive Church: "All power in heaven and on earth has been given to me. Go therefore, and make disciples of all nations, baptizing them in the name of the Father and of the Son and of the Holy Spirit" (Mt 28:18–19). The Pentecostal descent of the Holy Spirit will mark the beginning of public baptism for entry into the messianic community (cf. Acts 1:5; 11:16). It is with the baptism of the Spirit that the Apostles joined new believers to the company of Christ.

The death and resurrection of Christ, the great reservoir of power from which all sacraments derive their efficacy, is itself described in the New Testament with baptismal allusions. We think of John 19:30 where it is related that Jesus, "bowing his head, gave up his spirit." This may be a hidden allusion to the handing over of Christ's holy Spirit to his followers, beginning with baptism. Or, again, the piercing of the Lord's side with the soldier's lance results in the issue of water and blood from the side of Christ, which as we have already pointed out, was a favorite patristic symbol for the sacraments of baptism and Eucharist respectively. Finally we may note how St. Paul (cf. Eph 5:25 ff.) remarks that Christ loved his Church and "delivered himself up for her, that he might sanctify her, cleansing her in the bath of water by means of the word; in order that he might present to himself the Church in all her glory . . . that she might be holy and without blemish." The bath of water accompanied by the word suggests that, by his death, Jesus baptized his Church. She is born from his pierced side. The Church begins to live with the divine life that Christ poured out for her by his own dying. This conferral of life upon the Church is a kind of baptism, flowing as it does from the supreme "mystery," the union of Christ and his Church through the Paschal mystery (cf. Eph 5:32).

Thus the making of baptism is a complex history, beginning in a sense in the days of the Old Testament and reaching fulfillment only in the Pentecostal mystery of the sending of the Spirit. To view baptism in its Salvation-History context is not a mere excursion into history or symbolism. Rather it serves a twofold advantage: (1) Such a procedure makes us realize that our own baptism grafted us into the long history of saving events that we have studied. These events of the past, forming as they do a continuous saving act of God, have all accrued to our own personal benefit through the sacrament of our initiation into the Church. (2) To study baptism in its origins is already to throw much light on the relevance and meaning of this sacrament for our own lives. For our own baptism is a kind of "rerun" of Jesus' baptism at the Jordan. At that moment we too like Jesus were designated God's sons (by adoption) and God's servants, destined to walk a sacrificial road behind him on the way to sharing his victory. Being a baptized Christian involves a front-line offensive to strengthen Christianity on earth. It means to be a member of God's militia, engaged in a death combat against would-be destroyers of man's faith. In terms of the Jordan theophany, it also means to be brought into a most intimate relationship with the three Persons of the Blessed Trinity. It means to be summoned as Jesus was from that moment forth to be a public witness to the Father in the power of the Spirit. Thus a theology of baptism in nucleus may be derived just from the study of Jesus' own baptism.

VII. THE RITES OF CHRISTIAN BAPTISM

An initiation rite is a common practice for inducting new members to organizations fraternal, social, and religious. Such a practice serves not only as a ceremonial induction into the club or organization; it also serves an informative and a social purpose. Generally, the initiation will include some historical survey of the origins of the society, followed by an explanation of its purposes and a statement of its achievements. Socially, it is the setting in which the newcomers are formally welcomed by the veteran members of the organization. They are accepted now as full-fledged members, as brothers banded together for achieving the common purposes of the organization.

The great religions of the world have followed the practice of an initiation rite. The Old Testament, as noted above, provided for the ritual of circumcision for male adherents of the Jewish faith, and a kind of baptism or ablution in water for receiving converts from paganism. Against such a background we should be surprised if Christ had not provided a similar initiation rite for his Church. This rite was to serve not merely to join an individual to a company of believers professing the doctrines of Jesus of Nazareth; but it was also to associate men in a holy fellowship whose privileged task was to celebrate their fraternal unity and the worship of God in and through Christ in the Eucharist. Baptism, it may be noted at the outset, is essentially oriented toward the Eucharist.

In the beginning, this ritual of admission into the fellowship of Christ was naturally very simple. The matrix or nucleus was provided by Christ; but to his Church he gave the liberty of working out a suitable ritual to frame the essential ablution at the heart of baptism. The added ritual would serve both to solemnize this important occasion in the life of the Church and of the individual joining it, and also to teach the catechumen the significance of the great step that he was taking by requesting admission into Christ's Church.

Centuries of development have gone into the ritual of baptism just as in the case of the other sacraments. The Church, receiving from Christ the right to organize these rituals in the first place, may change them from time to time to suit various historical and cultural conditions. The history of the baptismal liturgy is an example of such liturgical adaptation. The first recorded baptism into the infant Church was apparently a mass baptism of some three thousand persons on Pentecost (cf. Acts 2:37–41). The members of the Christian community gathered around the Apostles, some one hundred and twenty souls, had apparently not been baptized except with the baptism of John. Christ himself had constituted the apostolic college as the beginning of the Church of the New Testament. They and other disciples had personally known Christ; and the events by which they were bound to the company of believers were climaxed with the "baptism" of the Holy Spirit on Pentecost. From Pentecost on, the original community was conscious of its right to admit other members to its company by baptism and the imposition of hands or confirmation. The conferral of baptism is mentioned over and over again in the Acts of the Apostles and in the Epistles of St. Paul.[7]

As far as the form that baptism took, immersion into the water (the word "baptize" means "to dip" or "immerse") was presumably the normal practice (cf. Acts 8:38–39, the baptism of the Ethiopian by the deacon Philip; and also Pauline allusions to baptism as a bath of water

---

[7] Cf. A. George, S.M., "The Literary Catalogue of New Testament Passages on Baptism" in Baptism in the New Testament (Baltimore: Helicon Press, 1964), pp. 13–22.

in Eph 5:26; Ti 3:5, and as a burial with Christ in Rom 6:3 ff.). The early second-century Syrian work called the *Didache* specifically mentions baptism by pouring the water where immersion is impossible. When the custom of reserving a special indoor place for baptisms came into vogue, these baptistries (from the first part of the fourth century on) contained pools sunk below the level of the floor. The shallowness of the pools, however, and supporting evidence in the catacombs suggest that it was a common practice to pour the water over the head while the catechumen stood in the pool of water.

By the beginning of the third century, the custom of blessing the water set aside for baptismal use seems to have been well established.[8] Today the baptismal water is solemnly blessed during the Paschal or Easter Vigil. The prayers serve as a fruitful reminder of the significance of baptism itself.

Along with the ablution with water, baptism included the candidate's profession of faith in answer to the priest's interrogation. At some early date in the first century, the catechumen made an explicit profession of faith in the Blessed Trinity. The triple profession of faith was accompanied by a triple immersion. This threefold questioning of the candidate's belief in the three Persons of the Blessed Trinity and the works attributed respectively to them eventually became the basis for the formulas of belief called "creeds" (e.g., Apostles' Creed, Nicene Creed, etc.). When infant baptism became the rule, the current trinitarian formula, "I baptize you in the name of the Father and of the Son and of the Holy Spirit," came into use by the minister of baptism as the so-called "form" of the sacrament.

By the beginning of the third century, the Church also began to organize a more formal preparation for this sacrament. A catechumenate or preparatory period of instruction and probation was developed, sometimes lasting as long as three years.[9] Like the "pledge" period of college fraternities, which indoctrinates the "pledge" in fraternity traditions and fosters loyalty to the brotherhood, so the catechumenate functioned to catechize and to form applicants in the spirit of Christian love. The testing period came to an end with the great baptismal experience of Easter night.

Over the span of centuries, the catechumenate underwent several changes too complex and varied to be gone into here. Eventually (by the eleventh and twelfth centuries) the custom of baptizing infants im-

[8] Charles Davis, *Sacraments of Initiation* (New York: Sheed and Ward, 1964), p. 44. For a detailed discussion of the history of the rites of baptism, the second chapter of this book, pp. 39–70, may be consulted.

[9] Cf. above, p. 76 f.

mediately after their birth led to a simplification of the baptismal ritual in which the prolonged and spaced-out ceremonies of the catechumenate were shortened and compressed into one ceremony. Two versions of baptism, one for adults and one for infants, came to be included in the Roman Ritual of 1614. Both texts borrowed more ancient prayers taken from adult baptismal rituals, and only slight modifications were made in the ritual for baptizing infants. Because the form for adult baptism is so lengthy, the Church granted permission for the use of the shorter form, that which is specified in the ritual for infants.

On April 15, 1962, a decree was issued allowing once more the spacing out of the different stages of adult baptism, so that there would be six ceremonies before the actual baptism (the seventh and last stage). These prebaptismal rituals are to accompany the gradual instruction of the convert. Some modifications were made in these ceremonies pending a more complete revision of the baptismal rite. Since the rite for adult baptism as it now stands is unduly long and repetitive, we shall take for our commentary the Rite for the Baptism of Infants, which is also commonly used for baptizing adult converts. This rite preserves the essential features of the more ancient catechumenate. In describing the current rite, we shall make some historical observations to clarify the origin of the various ceremonies.

We may distinguish three principal stages in the present rite for infant baptism: the ceremonies of acceptance into the Church; the combat with evil and apprenticeship to Christian life; the celebration of the actual baptism.

A. The ritual begins at the entrance to the church; as the ceremony unfolds there is a gradual approach to the font — a pattern no doubt suggesting that the Church on earth is "on the move," on pilgrimage toward heaven. After an initial greeting of peace, the name of the candidate is requested. This custom originated with the ancient practice of inscribing the names of the catechumens in the baptismal register or "book of life," a sign of official acceptance as a member of the catechumenate. The original dialogue between priest and catechumen recalls the preliminary inquiry and first instruction in the faith.

The Priest: What do you ask of the Church of God?
Catechumen: Faith.
Priest: What does faith offer you?
Catechumen: Eternal life.
Priest: If, then, you wish to enter into life, keep the commandments. You shall love the Lord your God with your whole heart, and with your whole soul, and with your whole mind, and your neighbor as yourself.

Next comes a first exorcism, accompanied by a gentle blowing on the face of the candidate three times, and then the words "Depart from him, unclean spirit, and give place to the Holy Spirit, the Consoler." This ceremony, called an "exsufflation" or a blowing off, reflects the primitive manner in which the Church expressed her intention of driving off the influence or power of Satan and drawing the catechumen into the protective influence of Christ's Spirit.

Next the priest makes the sign of the cross with his thumb on the forehead and breast of the catechumen, saying:

Receive the mark of the cross on your forehead and within your heart. Embrace the faith with its divine teachings. So live that you will indeed be a temple of God.

With this ceremony, the candidate is enrolled under the sign of Christ's cross. It is under this banner that he shall henceforward march in the army of the Church militant. The cross is the great emblem of the faith, as well as the emblem of redemption. Signed and sealed with the cross, the catechumen has received his "badge of membership" by which he is consecrated to the Paschal mystery of the Lord's suffering and death. The prayer that follows asks protection upon his chosen one through the never failing power of Christ's cross.

Next the priest imposes hands on the catechumen and prays for God's favorable assistance upon the neophyte who is taking his first steps in the faith. There follows the blessing and giving of the salt, which in the course of its liturgical usage has received several different meanings. In the Orient, giving salt to a guest was a gesture of hospitality. Here it is called the first food to help the recipient on the way to the heavenly Bread of the Eucharist. The salt also is called the "symbol of wisdom," which gives us some insight into the mind and works of God and preserves us from being spoiled by a corrupt world.

The first part concludes with a prayer to God the Father, asking him to lead the catechumen to the waters of new birth (baptism) and the Bread of heaven (the Eucharist).

B. The second part of the baptismal rite reflects the Christian's combat with evil and offers him an apprenticeship for life. In highly condensed form, it summarizes the sixth-century Lenten scrutinies held for the catechumens in preparation for their Easter baptism. A chief feature of the scrutinies or probationary meetings was the exorcism of the devil. The second part of the baptismal service today begins with such an exorcism, in which the unbaptized person, considered to be at this point still part of unredeemed humanity, must be taken out of Satan's dominion and handed over to God, transferred from the status of a person without grace to that of a grace-filled member of the family of Christ. Once again, after an initial prayer of exorcism, the sign of the cross is imposed upon the forehead; this is followed by the imposing of hands and a prayer for the protection of the candidate.

There follows now a short procession into the church up to the entrance to the baptistry. For this ceremony, the priest places the end of his stole on the shoulder of the candidate and admits him into God's temple "so that you may have part with Christ in everlasting life." Now follow ceremonies that originally were held on Holy Saturday morning. The candidate or his sponsors recite with the priest the Apostles' Creed and the Lord's Prayer. In ancient times during the Lenten catechesis, the catechumens learned these two prayers; and then on Holy Saturday morning they had to recite them or give them back to the bishop or priest.

The Creed historically is based upon the triple questioning of faith that formed part of the actual baptism. It is fitting as a baptismal prayer since it summarizes the chief articles of faith, every one of which is also an act of God's generosity toward us. The Lord's Prayer, taught us by Christ himself, is likewise an eminently suitable baptismal prayer, since baptism makes us for the first time God's children in the rightful and strict sense of the term. We ought to remember the baptismal significance of the profession of faith (the Creed) and the Lord's Prayer when we recite them at Mass. The Creed at our Sunday Mass is the solemn public renewal of our baptismal faith. The common recitation of the Lord's Prayer at the beginning of the Communion part of the Mass reminds us that our right to share in the family meal of the Eucharist derives only from our baptism. Our entrance into God's family through baptism gives us the right to approach the family table of the Eucharist.

A final exorcism asks that the baptismal candidate may become a "temple of the living God" and that "the Holy Spirit may dwell in him."

Next the priest touches the ears and nose of the candidate, with or without saliva at the discretion of the celebrant, in imitation of Christ's cure of the deaf-mute (Mk 7:31–37). The same word that Christ used, "Ephpheta," which means "Be opened," accompanies the gesture and explains its meaning. The symbolism given to it is indicated in the words, "So that you may perceive the fragrance of God's sweetness."

The renunciation of Satan now follows. This ceremony was dramatically performed on Holy Saturday morning when the candidate turned his back to the West (the place where darkness sets in, therefore a symbol of the empire of Satan) and solemnly abjured all attachment to Satan. The devil's "pomps" or allurements originally referred to the processions and games which were part of pagan worship and were therefore "out of bounds" for a baptized Christian.

After the renunciation of Satan, there follows an anointing on the breast and between the shoulders with the oil of catechumens. The Fathers of the Church interpreted this as an anointing for the struggle with Satan, after the analogy of an athlete's rubdown before the contest. The catechumen is reminded that he is entering the Church militant, the fighting Church, and that his principal struggle will be against the forces of evil. For this, baptism will confer a special strengthening, symbolized by this anointing.

C. The third and last part of the ritual now takes place. It is the actual celebration of baptism, preceded by a profession of faith (which used to be a part of the baptismal rite itself) and followed by the anointing with chrism and the conferral of the two ceremonial gifts, the white robe and the lighted candle. The triple profession of faith formerly accompanied the triple immersion in the waters of baptism. It is now, in the present ceremony, a final declaration of allegiance or loyalty to the Holy Trinity, Father, Son, and Holy Spirit. During the Easter Vigil as it is celebrated today, and on other occasions too, such as first Communion and confirmation, the renunciation of Satan and the triple assertion of faith are repeated under the name of the baptismal vows. This is a way of renewing a lifelong commitment that we ourselves made or our sponsors made for us at the time of our baptism. Baptism is a personal attachment to Christ, a surrender, a dedication, a giving of one's self into the hands of Christ. Hence the seriousness that should accompany this solemn reaffirmation of baptism.

The heart of the baptismal rite is reached with the pouring of the baptismal water three times on the head of the candidate in the form of a cross. At the same time the priest pronounces the words: "I baptize you in the name of the Father, and of the Son, and of the Holy Spirit." At the beginning of the formula, he mentions the new Christian name to be given to the recipient of baptism, usually the name of a saint who will act as a model or patron, a model for our imitation and a patron or intercessor for our assistance. The giving of the baptismal name should perhaps be emphasized more than it is. It suggests that we become a new person in Christ, we take on a new relationship and become members of Christ's family. We are John or Mary in Christ; and the name that we bear reminds us of the sacred lineage that is now ours.

The celebrant now anoints the newly baptized person with the most precious of the three oils, the oil of chrism (the name is related to "Christ" or Christos, "the Anointed one"). Tradition has viewed this cruciform anointing on the crown of the head as an outward sign of the conferral of a priestly power, the power to join Christ in the priestly worship of the Church. It is a kind of external reminder of the inward character or seal of baptism, the spiritual power that makes one a member of the priestly kingdom, the royal priesthood, designated and delegated to gather up the world about him and restore it to the Father through Christ.

Following the anointing, there is the conferral of the two ceremonial gifts. Investiture with the white garment recalls the ancient practice of clothing the newly baptized with a white tunic after the ascent from the font. Stripping off the old garment before entering the baptismal pool and putting on a new garment afterward were given a multiple symbolism in the homilies of the Fathers.[10] St. Ambrose (*De Mysteriis*, 34) suggests a fundamental significance when he says, "after baptism, you have received white garments that they may be the sign that you have taken off the clothing of sin and that you have been clad in the pure garments of innocence." We recall St. Paul's words: "You have been baptized in Christ, you have *put on Christ*" (Gal 3:27).

Besides purity of soul, the white garments also suggest incorruptibility of the body. They liken the newly baptized to the transfigured Christ, indeed to the glorious risen Christ, and thus illustrate the role of baptism in putting us on the road to immortality. Baptism makes us share Christ's resurrection. Another line of thought finds the white baptismal robe typifying the restoration of the original integrity and holiness in which the first Adam was created. Baptism returns us to Paradise (cf. the custom of decorating the baptistry walls with a paradisal motif — the sheep [the newly baptized] surrounding Christ the young shepherd boy, in a setting like the Garden of Paradise [the Church]).

Finally, as the prayer in the present baptismal rite suggests, the white garments have an eschatological significance, pointing to our future union with God in heaven. "Receive this white garment. Never let it become stained, so that when you stand before the judgment seat of our Lord Jesus Christ, you may have life everlasting." In the Book of the Apocalypse, the martyrs, having triumphed over death, are clothed in white robes of glory (cf. Ap 3:5, 18). In the same vein, the third-century writer Tertullian, describing the baptismal robes as the "symbol of the hope of the flesh," considered them to be symbols of the resurrection of the body.

In fine, a threefold typology becomes evident, centering around Adam, Christ, and future glory. Referring to Adam, the white garments suggest a return to primitive innocence; referring to Christ, they remind us that he, the second Adam, restored grace lost by the first Adam; third, they prefigure and anticipate our future glory in heaven.

---

[10] Danielou, *The Bible and the Liturgy*, pp. 49–53.

The lighted candle is handed to the newly baptized or to the sponsor in the case of infant baptism, with the words "Receive this burning light, and keep the grace of your baptism throughout a blameless life. Observe the commandments of God. Then, when the Lord comes to the heavenly wedding feast, you will be able to meet him and all the saints in the halls of heaven, and live forever and ever." In the Gospels, Christ himself is called the "light of the world" (Jn 8:12). The Greek fathers called baptism "the enlightenment" (photismós). Baptism is a coming to share in the light of Christ which is his very life. Life in Christ means to know him by faith, to be united to him through grace-life, and in turn to be a light to one's fellowman. Like John the Baptist, we must radiate our baptismal light as a witness to the true Light (cf. Jn 1:8; Mt 5:14).

The baptismal ritual closes abruptly with the Christian greeting of peace: "Go in peace, and the Lord be with you."

VIII. THEOLOGICAL SYNTHESIS

The effects of baptism upon the Christian may be stated in different ways. One way is to follow the thought patterns of the theologians in the schools of the twelfth and thirteenth centuries (Scholastic theology). In the terminology of the Scholastics, baptism confers as its first effect the sacramental seal or character which incorporates one into the Church and makes him a member of the priestly people of God, configuring him to Christ, the priest, delegating and qualifying him to join in Christian worship through Christ to the Father.

This priestly character, in turn is a pledge of grace — grace that is actualized in the infant or in the contrite adult not only as common or sanctifying grace (a share in the life of the Blessed Trinity) but also as a special sacramental grace, the power to live as an adopted child of God in imitation of Christ, Son of God by nature. From these radical powers would flow in turn all the privileges that belong to an adopted son: intimacy with Christ; the powers of Christian living known as the virtues, especially faith, hope, and charity; the gifts of the Holy Spirit; and the assurance of helping or actual graces when they are needed. Finally the inheritance of heaven itself is held out to the child of God who perseveres until the end in loyal brotherhood of Christ and filial, reverent sonship of the eternal Father.

But the effects of baptism may perhaps more felicitously be described in biblical terms. Baptism grants incorporation into the Church; it unites us with Christ in the pattern of the Paschal mystery; it confers the Holy Spirit and the remission of sins; it gives the adopted sonship of God. All these effects have been touched upon in one way or another, either in the discussion of general sacramental principles (Chapters 4 and 5) or in our brief discussion of the liturgy of baptism earlier in this chapter. For the sake of synthesis, however, we may briefly review each of these effects in a scriptural context.

A. Incorporation Into the Church

Baptism clearly appears in the Acts of the Apostles as the rite of initiation into the community of believers in Christ. Beginning with Pentecost, the Apostles preached the necessity of repentance for sin, a true metanoia or conversion of heart, and an adherence to Christ in faith. These dispositions or attitudes, coupled with the external rite of baptism, effected membership in the body of Christ. In Acts 2:38, 41, entrance into the community of believers at Jerusalem follows this pattern: repentance and faith, baptism, forgiveness of sins, gift of the Holy Spirit, and acceptance into the company of Christ.

By baptism we become the true children of Abraham. St. Paul was convinced that "the men of faith are the real sons of Abraham" (Gal 3:7) and a little further on he says:

For you are all the children of God through faith in Christ Jesus. For all you who have been baptized into Christ have put on Christ. There is neither Jew nor Greek; there is neither slave nor free man; there is neither male nor female. For you are all one in Christ Jesus. And if you are Christ's, then you are the offspring of Abraham, heirs according to promise (Gal. 3:26–29).

Not only are we offspring of Abraham helping to make up one mighty family of believers, but we are also members of the New Covenant, the new people of God. Just as circumcision was the visible sign of membership in the covenant of Abraham, so now baptism is the visible sign of our entrance as sons into the new covenant, the covenant of Christ:

In him [Christ] too you have been circumcised with a circumcision not wrought by hand, but through putting off the body of the flesh, the circumcision which is of Christ. For you were buried together with him in Baptism and in him also rose again . . . (Col. 2:11, 12).

This incorporation is an insertion into Christ's very body, "For in one Spirit we were all baptized in the one body, whether Jews or Gentiles, whether slaves or free; and we were all given to drink of one Spirit. . . . Now you are the body of Christ member for member" (1 Cor 12:13, 27). The baptismal insertion into Christ's body is not a mere impersonal happening; rather it is a personal union with Christ, the Head of this Church-body. It is a union with the risen Christ, an attachment to his very risen body. "All you who have been baptized into Christ, have put on Christ" (Gal 3:27). This may well suggest putting on a new body rather than merely new garments.[11] Furthermore the phrase to be "in Christ," which occurs so frequently in St. Paul, is generally recognized as an ecclesiological formula, that is, it signifies "to belong to the Church."[12]

B. Dying and Rising With Christ

In defining just how this union with Christ in the Church comes about and what its nature is, St. Paul carries us further along christological and redemptive lines. Baptism achieves for us our first initiation into the Paschal mystery of Christ. What Jesus accomplished for us is not merely an historical death and resurrection, whose benefits are passed on to us through time. We do not merely reap the graces of Jesus' saving work. In his Passover, Jesus opened a new way to his Father's house, a way that for him involved suffering, detachment, self-surrender, total self-giving to the point of death; and only in this way did he achieve the state of risen happiness with the Father. We too, then, as Christians, followers of Christ, must experience this same mystery, this same event. We must live out sacramentally in the baptismal experience and in our daily life the very death and resurrection of Christ. Of ourselves we are powerless to achieve such a death to sin and a rising to new life; but through the power of the baptismal waters, activated by Christ's own Spirit, we are truly able to enter into the Lord's death, to die personally to sin in the sense of sharing Christ's conquest of it, and to rise with Jesus in the new triumphant life of the order of the resurrection.

This is the meaning of three cardinal texts in St. Paul's writings which formulate our baptismal identification with Jesus by sharing the Paschal mystery. The first classic passage is in Romans 6:3–11:

> Do you not know that all we who have been baptized into Christ Jesus have been baptized into his death? For we were buried with him by means of baptism into death, in order that, just as Christ has arisen from the dead through the glory of the Father, so we also may walk in newness of life. For if we have been united with him in the likeness of his death, we shall be so in the likeness of his resurrection also. For we know that our old self has been crucified with him, in order that the body of sin may be destroyed, that we may no longer be slaves to sin; for he who is dead is acquitted of sin. But if we have died with Christ, we believe that we shall also live together with Christ; for we

---

[11] Cf. Col 3:9–15; Neville Clark, An Approach to the Theology of the Sacraments (London: SCM Press, 1958), p. 24. But for the "garment" interpretation, cf. Schnackenburg, Baptism in the Thought of St. Paul (New York: Herder & Herder, 1964), pp. 23–25.

[12] Cf. Clark, loc. cit. Cf. also George Montague, S.M., The Living Thought of St. Paul (Milwaukee: The Bruce Publishing Co., 1966).

know that Christ, having risen from the dead, dies now no more, death shall no longer have dominion over him. For the death that he died, he died to sin once for all, but the life that he lives, he lives unto God. Thus do you consider yourselves also as dead to sin, but alive to God in Christ Jesus.[13]

St. Paul seems to be thinking here of baptism by immersion, as practiced for adult converts in the primitive Christian community. Submersion under water is a symbol of our being buried with Christ. But this symbolic union with Christ's death under the figure of a burial in water is not a mere symbol; we are really acquitted of sin and made to live with the risen Christ. Thus the Paschal mystery is personally transmitted to each of us through the sacramental experience of baptism.

The second classical passage is found in Colossians 2:12. In this later Epistle, we see a development in St. Paul's thought, at least to the extent of a more explicit affirmation of baptism as a union with Christ in his resurrection as well as in his death, and an emphasis on the role of faith in the celebration of the sacrament:

For you were buried together with him [Christ] in baptism, and in him also rose again through faith in the working of God who raised him from the dead (Col. 2:12).[14]

Finally in the Epistle to the Ephesians (2:4–6), Paul explicitly expands the stages of the Paschal mystery into which baptism elevates us. Along with the death and resurrection of Christ, his ascension and enthronement in heaven are also communicated to us in the sacramental experience of baptism:

God, who is rich in mercy, by reason of his very great love wherewith he has loved us even when we were dead by reason of our sins, brought us to life together with Christ . . . and raised us up together, and seated us together in heaven in Christ Jesus. . . .

We already then have a foothold in heaven by our union with the triumphant, royal Christ of heaven. The baptismal reproduction of the Paschal mystery in us is central in St. Paul's teaching on baptism.

C. Baptism and the Holy Spirit

Jesus' baptism was distinguished from that of John the Baptist by the promise that Jesus would baptize with fire and the Holy Spirit. Just as the Spirit appeared at the messianic baptism of Jesus at the Jordan, so

---

[13] For a detailed exposition of this classical text, cf. Schnackenburg, *Baptism in the Thought of St. Paul*, Chap. 3, pp. 30–61.

[14] For a detailed commentary, cf. Schnackenburg, *op. cit.*, pp. 67–73; Y. B. Tremel, "The Incorporation of the Christian into Christ," in *Baptism in the New Testament* (Baltimore: Helicon, 1964), pp. 194–198.

also the Spirit appeared on Pentecost in the form of tongues of fire to "baptize" the apostolic community. Under the impulse of the Spirit, then, the Apostles proclaimed the Paschal mystery and began to confer baptism "in water and the Holy Spirit" (Jn 3:5). This Holy Spirit brings the remission of sins (Acts 2:38) to those who are truly repentant. He makes the Christian a child of God, an adopted son made in the image of the true Son and constituted a fellow inheritor of heaven (cf. Rom 8:14–17). It is the Holy Spirit who joins the baptized faithful to the glorified Church-body of Christ (cf. 1 Cor 12:13), a body which the Spirit continues to animate or vivify on earth as a kind of soul, uniting and vivifying all the body members.

The Paschal mystery has merged into the Pentecostal mystery, as the glorified Christ confers his Spirit upon his followers. This Spirit is the seal of the mutual love of Father and Son for each other; he is the Gift par excellence. And so he is infused into us through baptism to make us adopted sons in the true Son (filii in Filio), to carry us into the inner life of the Blessed Trinity. We are led by the Spirit in Christ to the father. Grace-life, baptismal life, Paschal life, Trinitarian life — all are apt designations of the new life infused into God's creature through baptism.

The Spirit is given us as the fruit of God's love (cf. Rom 5:5 ff.); his coming, then, is intended not only to render each of us a loving and lovable individual but also to join us into Christ's community of love on earth. Just as the Paschal mystery itself was essentially motivated by divine love (cf. Jn 3:16; 13:1), so also our insertion into this mystery by baptism impels us to a life of concern and charity for our fellowmen. Baptism into Christ's mystical body is the most compelling motive for the practice of fraternal charity.

If God is love (cf. 1 Jn 4:8), then our baptismal insertion into God's love must necessarily bring us to the very heart of God's inner life. Baptism truly consecrates us to the Trinity. We become sons of the Father, brothers of Christ, temples of the Holy Spirit. Thus our baptismal life in Christ is not static but dynamic, propelling us forward with a mighty thrust toward our common Father. Characteristically the ancient liturgy of the Church led the faithful in prayer to the Father through or with the Son in the Holy Spirit (cf. the Orations or Collect prayers of the Roman Missal). To be authentic, prayer-life must overflow from the God-life within us.

D. *The Kingdom of Priests*

As already discussed above where we treated the baptismal character, the Holy Spirit is said to seal us for the worship of God. By baptism we become "a chosen race, a royal priesthood, a holy nation, a purchased people" that we may "proclaim the perfections of him who has called [us] out of darkness into his marvelous light" (1 Pt 2:9). This priestly power to join Christ in his laudatory love for the Father is attributed in a special way to the anointing or sealing of the Spirit:

> In him [Christ] you too, when you had heard the word of truth, the good news of your salvation, and believed in it, were sealed with the Holy Spirit . . . (Eph 1:13).

Or again in the same Epistle:

> Do not grieve the Holy Spirit of God, in whom you were sealed for the day of redemption (Eph 4:30).

> . . . now it is God who is warrant for us and for you in Christ, who has anointed us, who has also stamped us with his seal and has given us the Spirit as a pledge in our hearts (2 Cor 1:21–22).

As noted above, texts like these have supported the theological development of the *character*, that power conferred on the faithful to make them co-worshipers with Christ. Here a key principle of the liturgy comes to the fore; baptism through its sacramental seal makes us a worshiping people, delegates and empowers us to exercise our highest duty and privilege of rendering homage to God. To celebrate the Eucharist and to receive the other sacraments, then, it is necessary first to receive baptism. The latter is the gateway to all the other sacraments, the door to the Church, the beginning of salvation. Thus a nonbaptized person attending Mass may well receive actual graces from God through his pious act; but he cannot participate in the same way as a baptized Christian in the offering of the family gift of praise and love to God.

IX. BAPTISM AND OUR SEPARATED BRETHREN

Ecumenism or the movement toward religious unity has forced a theological reappraisal of the question of membership in the Church. Following the lead of Vatican II in its *Decree on Ecumenism* and its *Constitution on the Church*, it is incumbent upon us to recognize the very deep spiritual bond that unites all baptized Christians: Catholics, Orthodox, and baptized Protestants. A valid baptism exists outside the limits of the Catholic Church if it is given with the requisite intention of doing what the Church does in baptism, if genuine water is used, accompanied by the Trinitarian formula.[15]

---

[15] C.J.C., c. 732; cf. Anthony B. Boylan, "The Conditional Baptism of Converts," *The Clergy Review*, Vol. 49, No. 12, Dec., 1964, pp. 733–737, for pertinent citations in ecclesiastical documents.

The bonds of such a valid baptism in some way unite all who believe in Christ. Vatican II deals with this problem in its *Constitution on the Church*, November 21, 1964, paragraph 14, After reaffirming the necessity of faith and baptism for salvation (cf. Mk 16:16; Jn 3:5) and thereby also the necessity of the Church to which baptism admits us, the Council Fathers continue:

> They are fully incorporated in the society of the Church who, possessing the Spirit of Christ, accept her entire system and all the means of salvation given to her, and are united to her as part of her visible bodily structure and through her with Christ, who rules her through the Supreme Pontiff and the Bishops. The bonds which bind men to the Church in a visible way are profession of faith, the Sacraments, and ecclesiastical government and communion (*Constitution on the Church*, NCWC tr., par. 14).[16]

Here the Council Fathers were speaking of *institutional* union with the Church of Christ, verified in the Catholic Church. Such full membership however is not an automatic guarantee of salvation. The Council continues:

> He is not saved, however, who, though part of the body of the Church, does not persevere in charity. He remains indeed in the bosom of the Church, but as it were, only in a "bodily" manner and not "in his heart." Catechumens likewise who explicitly intend to be baptized are by their intention already joined with the Church (*Constitution on the Church*, NCWC tr., par. 14).[17]

But besides such institutional union with Christ in the visible Church, the Council Fathers also recognize the spiritual bond among all who are baptized in Christ:

> The Church recognizes that in many ways she is linked with those who, being baptized, are honored with the name of Christian, though they do not profess the faith in its entirety or do not preserve unity of communion with the successor of Peter. For there are many who honor Sacred Scripture, taking it as a norm of belief and a pattern of life, and who show a sincere zeal. They lovingly believe in God the Father Almighty and in Christ the Son of God and Savior. They are consecrated by Baptism, in which they are united with Christ. They also recognize and accept other Sacraments within their own Churches or ecclesiastical communities. Many of them rejoice in the episcopate, celebrate the Holy Eucharist and cultivate devotion toward the Virgin Mother of God.[18] They also share with us in prayer and other spiritual benefits. Likewise we can say that in some real way they are joined with us in the Holy Spirit, for to them too He gives his gifts and graces whereby He is operative among them with His sanctifying power. Some

[16] AAS, Vol. 57, No. 1, pp. 18, 19.

[17] *Ibid.*, p. 19.

[18] This refers in a special way to the Eastern Orthodox communions who retain a valid priesthood and valid sacraments.

indeed He has strengthened to the extent of the shedding of their blood. In all of Christ's disciples the Spirit arouses the desire to be peacefully united, in the manner determined by Christ, as one flock under one shepherd, and He prompts them to pursue this end. Mother Church never ceases to pray, hope, and work that this may come about. She exhorts her children to purification and renewal so that the sign of Christ may shine more brightly over the face of the earth (*Constitution on the Church*, NCWC tr., par. 15).[19]

Vatican II's *Decree on Ecumenism*, published at the same time as the *Constitution of the Church*, also takes note of these invisible and visible bonds that link baptized non-Catholics with the Church. It notes that outside the visible boundaries of the Catholic Church there can exist "some, even very many of the most significant elements and endowments which together go to build up and give life to the Church itself" (*Decree on Ecumenism*, Vatican Polyglot Press tr., par. 3).[20] These elements are noted as "the written word of God; the life of grace; faith, hope, and charity, with the other interior gifts of the Holy Spirit, as well as visible elements. All of these, which come from Christ and lead back to Him, belong by right to the one Church of Christ" (*ibid.*).[21] The Council Fathers also point out that the separated brethren "also carry out many liturgical actions of the Christian religion. In ways that vary according to the condition of each Church or Community, these most certainly can truly engender a life of grace, and, one must say, can aptly give access to the communion of salvation" (*ibid.*).[22]

The Council, then, does not hesitate to speak of "separated Churches and Communities" which the Holy Spirit uses "as means of salvation which derive their efficacy from the very fullness of grace and truth entrusted to the Catholic Church" (*ibid.*).[23] Regarding those who are members of these separated Communities, the Council Fathers assert:

> However, one cannot charge with the sin of the separation those who at present are born into these Communities and in them are brought up in the faith of Christ, and the Catholic Church accepts them with respect and affection as brothers. For men who believe in Christ and have been properly baptized are brought into a certain, though imperfect, communion with the Catholic Church. . . . All who have been justified by faith in baptism are incorporated into Christ [here the Council refers to the *Council of Florence*, Session 8, 1439]; they therefore have a right to be called Christians, and with good reason are accepted as brothers by the children of the Catholic Church (*Decree on Ecumenism*, Vatican tr., par. 3).[24]

This brotherhood of all baptized Christians constitutes the theological basis of ecumenism; and in setting forth its ecclesiological teaching in

---

[19] *Ibid.*, pp. 19, 20.   [21] *Ibid.*   [23] *Ibid.*
[20] *Ibid.*, p. 93.   [22] *Ibid.*   [24] *Ibid.*

these two documents on the Church and on Ecumenism, the Council has advanced considerably beyond the teaching of Pius XII in *Mystici Corporis* (1943). There, membership in the Church was conceived primarily in a canonical or juridical way, in terms of the institutional structure (profession of the Catholic faith, baptism, and communion with the Apostolic See). In effect, the Body of Christ was made co-terminous with the Catholic Church. Vatican II takes a more Pauline approach. Emphasis is placed on the Church as "the community of faith, hope, and charity" (*Constitution on the Church*, NCWC tr., par. 8), a communion of life with Jesus in the Spirit (*ibid.*, paragraphs 4 and 7). Christ's Church is "an entity with visible delineation through which He [Christ] communicated truth and grace to all" (*ibid.*, par. 8). Now the Catholic Church and the Mystical Body "are not to be considered as two realities, nor are the visible assembly and the spiritual community . . . rather they form one complex reality which coalesces from a divine and a human element" (*ibid.*). The Church of Christ "constituted and organized in the world as a society, *subsists* in the Catholic Church . . . although many elements of sanctification and of truth are found outside of its visible structure. These elements, as gifts belonging to the Church of Christ, are forces impelling toward catholic unity" (*ibid.*).[25]

A leading ecumenical theologian offers the interpretation, based on the *Constitution on the Church*, that "the body of Christ is present in the Catholic Church, but at the same time, without losing its historical and incarnate character, transcends it. . . . The transcendence of Christ's mystical body beyond the historical limits of the Catholic Church permits Chapter II [of the Constitution] to say that other Christians are incorporated in the Church of Christ and offers theological justification for regarding other Christian Churches as realization, albeit institutionally defective, of the Church of Christ. According to Catholic faith, only the Catholic Church perfectly embodies the Church of Christ on earth, but, because of the transcendence of Christ's Church, this does not preclude the possibility that there may be partial realizations of this Church among men."[26]

If this be an accurate appraisal of Conciliar teaching, it is clear that we are on the threshold of an exciting ecumenical era. We must, then, recognize the influence of the Holy Spirit among our separated brethren.

[25] All the references in this paragraph are found in AAS, Vol. 57, No. 1, pp. 11, 12 (for *Const.*, par. 8); pp. 6, 7 (for *Const.*, par. 4); pp. 9, 10 (for *Const.*, par. 7).

[26] Gregory Baum, "The Constitution on the Church," *Journal of Ecumenical Studies* (Duquesne University Press), Vol. 2, No. 1, Winter, 1965, pp. 6, 7. Cf. also, by the same author, "Who Belongs to the Church?" *The Ecumenist*, Vol. 1, No. 4, April–May, 1963, 49–51; "What are Other Churches?" *ibid.*, Vol. 2, No. 1, Nov.–Dec., 1963, pp. 1–4; "A Note on Ecumenism at Vatican II," *ibid.*, Vol. 3, No. 1, November–December, 1964, pp. 1–3.

The bonds of baptism, charity, and the Spirit must draw together all Christians in the ecumenical movement. This movement of prayer and study is not reserved merely to the experts, the theologians, and the Scripture scholars. It must be realized on the grass-roots level by works of cooperation with our separated brethren, such as in civil rights, housing, better government, and whatever promotes the common welfare. As common prayer services, study sessions, retreats, and the like increase, more and more the laity will have access to the workings of ecumenism. The common dignity of our baptism and the presence of the Holy Spirit in us should be a powerful motive impelling every educated Christian to take an enlightened and leading role in the effort toward Christian understanding, to heal the split in Christendom, and to pave the way for that divinely willed unity that Christ prayed for at the Last Supper: "that all may be one, even as thou Father in me and I in thee; that they may be one in us, that the world may believe that thou hast sent me" (Jn 17:21).[27]

X. CONCLUSION

We must never forget that we owe our radical dignity as Christians to the sacrament of baptism. Our baptism itself is a sign of God's providence in our regard, for out of countless souls he has chosen us, even as he chose the great figures of Salvation-History, Abraham, Moses, and the others. This mystery of divine election or choice rests upon each of us who are recipients of the grace of faith and the gift of holy baptism. If circumcision of old introduced the Hebrew child into all the blessings of the covenant with Abraham and Moses, today Christian baptism initiates us into the people of the New Covenant, the recipients of God's mercy in Christ.

As American citizens, we enjoy the blessings of many freedoms; if we stop to think of it, it is these very freedoms that make us proud of our American heritage. Someone has noted that in every succeeding generation we must fight to preserve these freedoms, we must fight as though to win them all over again. Now what is true of our privileges as

---

[27] For other literature on ecumenism, cf. Paul Broadhurst, "A Short Bibliography of Ecumenical Literature" in *Ecumenical Theology Today* (Paulist Press, 1964), pp. 245–256; Henry St. John, O.P., *Essays in Christian Unity* (Westminster, Md.: Newman Press, 1955); Willebrands, *Problems Before Unity* (Baltimore: Helicon Press, 1962); John A. O'Brien, *Steps to Christian Unity* (New York: Doubleday, 1964); *Liturgy and Unity in Christ*, proceedings of the twenty-first annual North American Liturgical Week (Washington: Liturgical Conference, 1961); Bernard Leeming, *The Churches and the Church* (Westminster: Newman Press, 1963); Gregory Baum, *Progress and Perspectives: The Catholic Quest for Christian Unity* (New York: Sheed and Ward, 1962).

American citizens can be predicated also of our status as Christians. Our *esprit de corps* as Christians rests squarely upon our baptismal dignity. The privileges of knowing God intimately, of receiving his holy truth, sacramental union with Christ and with all our fellow members united in the charity of Christ's Spirit — all of these privileges constitute the positive benefits of being a Catholic and are therefore the cause of a legitimate and justifiable pride of heritage. They are more than worth the daily struggle to maintain them in the face of an increasingly pagan and sensuous world.

But this corporate enthusiasm over our Christian privileges should be tempered by humility, gratitude, and zeal. Humility bids us never forget the divine initiative in our regard. Gratitude bids us have that attitude of which St. Paul speaks, the attitude of giving thanks, which reaches its summit in the celebration of the Eucharist, the great act of thanksgiving. Zeal impels us to live our Christian faith enthusiastically before men, not with ostentation but as witnesses to Christ's love, since we are part of that Church which is "the sign raised up for the nations" (Is 11:10).

The baptismal commitment is a lifelong mission — a free dedication to a way of life, to a set of principles, to an attitude of mind emanating from God Himself. Therefore we need to use every opportunity to remind ourselves of our baptismal status. Along with the celebration of birthday anniversaries, parents might well encourage celebration of the anniversary of baptism. If this is not done individually, at least the whole Church has a common celebration for our baptismal anniversary in the Easter Vigil. It is there that we renew our solemn commitment to Christ undertaken at the moment of our baptism. All of Lent should lead up to this solemn renewal of baptismal commitment, and all of Eastertide should be a time of joyful and prayerful reflection on the noble life to which Christ called us in baptism. Use of holy water, both on entering the church and in our homes, is another baptismal reminder. At Mass the public recitation of the Creed and the Lord's Prayer, traditional baptismal prayers, should reinforce our baptismal consciousness; for here in the eucharistic celebration we experience the summit of our activity as members of the faithful, the celebration of sacrifice and personal union with the risen Christ. Fittingly then we ought to keep in mind the admonition of St. Paul in Ephesians (4:1-6):

I . . . exhort you to walk in a manner worthy of the calling with which you were called, with all humility and meekness, with patience, bearing with one another in love, careful to preserve the unity of the Spirit in the bond of peace; one body and one Spirit, even as you were called in one hope of your calling; one Lord, one faith, one baptism; one God and Father of all, who is above all and throughout all and in us all.

CHAPTER VII

Witnessing With Christ in the Spirit: Confirmation

INTRODUCTION

The loneliness of modern man cries out for community. Not that the individual wants to be lost in the crowd; but rather he desires social acceptance, he wants to belong, he seeks rightful status among his fellowmen. Within the larger society of man, one generally craves the special love, loyalty, and acceptance of one or a few persons to whom he is willing to open himself in return. Friendship, as distinct from mere acquaintance, is more than gestures or gifts of esteem; it is a real giving of oneself to the other to form a new unity of persons, a new bond of oneness. Such human self-giving and interpersonal communion reaches its climax in marriage; yet all genuine friendship reflects this openness, loyalty, commitment, and reliance upon one another.

Baptism has committed us to the friendship of Christ. There we were brought face to face with him, as he offered to us his unutterable depths of friendship and love. But since Christ is divine, he must first make us sinful finite beings worthy to be loved divinely; this he did in the baptismal encounter by putting something of his own life, perfection, and lovableness into us. Baptismal character and grace ennobled us to the extent that now at least some reciprocity, some mutuality of friendship is possible between God and his creatures.

The free response of the baptized infant to the proffered friendship of Christ is delayed until he attains the age of reason. Confirmation, as it is usually given, affords the opportunity for a solemn, adult adherence to Christ and his love. It is the sacrament that matures and ripens the seeds of divine friendship planted in baptism. The call to service and friendship with Christ is accepted anew with greater intensity, resoluteness, and dedication.

A vocation to love Christ cannot be divorced from a summons to love him in all his creatures, especially fellow members of his own body. Confirmation as the sacrament of Christian maturity therefore urges us to a self-sacrificing service of Christ in community, a genuinely deep concern for the redemption of all men. Such generous supernatural involvement in the lives of others presumes sacramental strength, as well as adult prudence, decisiveness, and courage. It is confirmation as finisher of baptism that moves us to join Christ in his witness to the Father's saving love for men.

Discovering the mind of the Church on the meaning of confirmation reveals a consistent understanding of this sacrament as a *conferral of the Holy Spirit*. Although baptism is also a sacrament of "water and the Spirit" (Jn 3:5), yet confirmation appears as an outpouring of the Spirit with a special fullness and for a specific function in the Church. To determine this more accurately, it will help us to examine first the place of God's "Spirit" in Saving History, then to study the ritual of confirmation as it developed in the Church, and finally to synthesize basic theological conclusions as to the significance of this sacrament in our Christian lives.

I. THE HOLY SPIRIT IN SALVATION-HISTORY

Our excursion into Saving History will lead us to consider the work of the Holy Spirit in the following four stages: first, the Holy Spirit foreshadowed in the Old Testament; second, the Holy Spirit communicated to Christ; third, the descent of the Holy Spirit upon the Apostles and the infant Church; and, fourth, the communication of the Spirit to each of us in our own confirmation.

A. "Spirit" in the Old Testament

The term frequently used in the Old Testament to describe the action of God in the Saving History of Israel is the phrase ru'ah Yahweh. The term ru'ah originally meant "breath" or "air." It is identified as the source of life in man and indeed in all creation. It came to connote God's inner actions and influence within men.[1]

It is in the Hebrew story of creation that God's breath is first active as a bearer or bringer of life. In Genesis 1:2, God's breath or spirit stirred above the primeval waters; in the Yahwist account of man's creation, it is this same spirit that breathed life into Adam (cf. Gn 2:7; Jb 27:3). Much later, in the vision of the prophet Ezekiel, God's spirit raised up the whole dead army of Israel (cf. 37:1–14). Thus God's breath gives life to the whole people of God, a foreshadowing of the work of the Spirit in vivifying the Church.

Not only does the "spirit" vivify the whole people of God, but also it rests upon certain individuals designated by God to be his spokesmen to the people, namely the prophets. Thus the spirit of God rests on Moses (cf. Nm 11:17, 25); it is imparted to Joshua (cf. Nm 27:18; Dt 34:9); David receives the Spirit (cf. 1 Sm 16:13), which speaks through him (cf. 2 Sm 23:2). God's spirit speaks through the prophets to deliver his commands to the people (cf. Za 7:12; Neh 9:30) and is given for the same purpose to the wise men (cf. Jb 32:8, 18; Sir 39:6; Wis 7:7; 8:17).

In a special way, Yahweh's spirit or ru'ah will rest upon the messianic king and his assistants (cf. Is 11:2; 28:6), on the prophetic servant of God (cf. Is 42:1), as well as on the prophet who brings the good news of liberation to the people (cf. Is 61:1).

In a famous passage, the prophet Joel (fourth century B.C.?) foretold that, in the messianic age, Yahweh's spirit or power would be manifested in a special way, not only for Israel or its prophets, but for all mankind:

> Then afterward I will pour out my spirit upon all mankind. Your sons and daughters shall prophesy, your old men shall dream dreams, your young men shall see visions; even upon the servants and the handmaids, in those days, I will pour out my spirit (3:1, 2).

In his Pentecostal sermon, Peter directly quoted this passage to explain the mysterious happenings of that day (cf. Acts 2:17–18).

The one possessed of God's spirit was said to have been "anointed" — that is, set aside, consecrated, dedicated to the service of God in some special office or mission. Thus the postexilic prophet, in words later to be appropriated by Christ himself, proclaims:

---

[1] Cf. John L. McKenzie, Dictionary of the Bible (Milwaukee: The Bruce Publishing Co., 1965), art. "Spirit."

The spirit of the Lord is upon me, because the Lord has anointed me; he has sent me to bring glad tidings to the lowly, to heal the broken-hearted, to proclaim liberty to the captives and release to the prisoners . . . (Is 61:1).

It was this passage, quoted before the synagogue at Nazareth, that Jesus applied to himself and his mission (Lk 4:18, 19).

B. *The Holy Spirit in Christ*[2]

It is especially in St. Luke's writings that Jesus and the messianic community he founded appear in a prophetic role under the aegis of the Holy Spirit. Fulfilling the prophetic role of the new Moses foretold in Deuteronomy 18:15, Jesus appears as the great Prophet-Messiah endowed with the power and wisdom of the Holy Spirit.

Already at his annunciation and birth, all the personages and circumstances attending these events are affected by the Holy Spirit. Zachary, Elizabeth, Mary, and Simeon are enlightened by this Spirit concerning the momentous design of God that has come to pass. The Incarnation of the Son of God is effected by the third Person of the Godhead, as the angel proclaimed to Mary: "The Holy Spirit shall come upon you and the power of the Most High shall overshadow you" (Lk 1:35) — words redolent of the cloud of glory with which Yahweh "overshadowed" the ark of the covenant. Thus Mary is the new Ark of the Covenant, enshrining the New Covenant personified, Jesus the Christ. The Incarnation is Christ's first "anointing"; as man, that is, he is singled out by God's Spirit and consecrated *christós* (the Anointed One) for man's salvation.

Christ's "anointing" with the Spirit at the moment of the Incarnation is not revealed publicly until his baptism at the Jordan, when Jesus is about to commence his public ministry. Here the dove as a sign of the Spirit is seen to abide over and rest upon the head of Jesus (cf. Jn 1:33); that is to say, the Holy Spirit will remain with the Messiah. The dove, traditional symbol of peace, presages the reconciliation which Christ will effect between God and man; the Spirit is the seal of redemption to be accomplished through Christ. Jesus will "baptize with the Holy Spirit and with fire" (Mt 3:11) because ". . . God anointed Jesus of Nazareth with the Holy Spirit and with power" (Acts 10:38 ff.). From the moment

---

[2] For a fuller treatment of this subject, cf. Adrian Hastings, *Prophet and Witness at Jerusalem* (Baltimore: Helicon Press, 1958), pp. 76–97; Marian Bohen, O.S.U., *The Mystery of Confirmation*, (New York: Herder & Herder, 1963), pp. 76–100; Leonard Bushinski–P. van Imschoot, "Spirit of God," in *Encyclopedic Dictionary of the Bible* (New York: McGraw-Hill, 1963), translated and adapted from A. van den Born, *Bijbels Woordenboek*, col. 2299–2309.

of his messianic inauguration at the Jordan, Jesus will bear public witness to his Father in the power of the Spirit.

Following the baptism, Jesus, "full of the Holy Spirit, returned from the Jordan and was led about the desert by the Spirit for forty days, being tempted all the while by the devil" (Lk 4:1–2). After thus reliving the desert temptations of ancient Israel and conquering them, he returns once more "in the power of the Spirit into Galilee" (Lk 4:14). Coming to his home town of Nazareth, he participates in the Sabbath service, reads from the scroll of Isaiah, "the Spirit of the Lord is upon me" (Is 61:1 ff.) and applies it explicitly to himself (Lk 4:21).

In function of the presence of the Spirit in him, Christ appears as witness to and revealer of his Father. "He bears witness to that which he has seen and heard and his witness no one receives. He who receives his witness has set his seal on this, that God is true" (Jn 3:32, 33; cf. Jn 14–17).

As he approaches the crisis in his life when he will face the supreme test of his loyalty to the Father, Christ steadfastly proclaims:

> I have not spoken on my own authority, but he who sent me, the Father, has given me commandment what I should say . . . and I know that the commandment is everlasting life. The things, therefore, that I speak, I speak as the Father has bidden me (Jn 12:49, 50).[3]

Christ did not flinch from making the supreme witness of his earthly career — his death and resurrection. In fact, this great passage through death to new life (his "glorification," according to John) is the necessary condition preceding the gift of the Spirit to his followers.

> If any man thirst, let him come to me and drink. He who believes in me, as the Scripture says, "From within him there shall flow rivers of living water." He said this, however, of the Spirit whom they who believed in him were to receive; for the Spirit had not yet been given, since Jesus had not yet been glorified (Jn 7:37–39).

It was at the Last Supper, on the eve of his glorification, that Jesus promised to send his Spirit upon the Apostles and his Church as another Paraclete or Protector and Guardian of truth, to insure accurate, courageous witness:

> But when the Advocate has come, whom I will send you from the Father, the Spirit of truth who proceeds from the Father, he will bear witness concerning me. And you also bear witness, because from the beginning you are with me (Jn 15:26 f.).

---

[3] For the role of Christ as witness to the Father, cf. Jn 5:16–47; 6:27, 39, 40; 8:18–19, 28–29, 38, 54–58; 12:44–50; 14:31; 17 (entire chapter — prayer of Christ to the Father at the Last Supper).

It is expedient for you that I depart. For if I do not go, the Advocate will not come to you; but if I go, I will send him to you (Jn 16:7).

When he, the Spirit of truth, has come, he will teach you all the truth (Jn 16:13).

You shall receive power when the Holy Spirit comes upon you, and you shall be witnesses for me in Jerusalem, and in all Judea and Samaria, and even to the very ends of the earth (Acts 1:8).

C. The Holy Spirit and the Apostolic Community

It was on the day of his triumphant resurrection that Jesus first imparted his Spirit to the Apostles, with special emphasis upon their role of forgiving sins (Jn 20:22, 23). Now that he had completed his saving worship of the Father and had reconciled sinful man to the Father's love, he authorized the leaders of God's people to carry that redemptive, saving love to all who contritely aspire to salvation. His Spirit would personify the Father's willingness to receive back the errant, wayward, and straying son.

But the Easter gift of the Spirit was to be followed by a more public investiture, a conferral of the unifying Spirit in power, to implement the ingathering of God's people into the Church. Therefore, before Jesus took final leave of the Apostles, he directed them to remain in Jerusalem until they received new power from on high. After nine days of prayer (the first Pentecostal novena) in the upper room, the Apostles, together with Mary and the company of the brethren (about 120 altogether — Acts 1:15), received the fullness of the Spirit amid the visible symbols of a violent wind and parted tongues (a charism or special divine gift), not only an external sign of the inner gift of the Spirit, but also a mark of the universality of the good news of redemption which they were about to preach.

Divine Providence conferred the fullness of the Spirit on the day of Pentecost, when pious Jews thronged the Holy City to give thanks for the spring harvest and to commemorate the covenant of Sinai. The New Covenant, a covenant "in spirit and in truth" (Jn 4:23), was publicly proclaimed to the world on this day by the forceful and inspired sermons of Peter and the others, as they gave witness to the resurrection of the Messiah and converted some three thousand souls (Acts 2:41). Clearly the company of Christ appeared before the world as that community of believers where the Holy Spirit permanently dwelled (the messianic community).

Let us summarize what we find here: (1) The Holy Spirit fired the Apostles with zeal and courage to be public witnesses to Christ, especially witnesses to his resurrection (the Paschal message of the Lord's death and glorification, i.e., his entire redemptive work). (2) The Spirit indicated his powerful presence in the fledgling community of Christ by certain signs (wind and fire) and by the charismatic gifts (which continued to be bestowed upon confirmed Christians for a time, as an aid in conversion and for the expansion of the Church; cf.: Peter and John confirm at Samaria, Acts 8:5-6, 14-17; Paul confirms or imposes hands at Ephesus, Acts 19:5, 6). (3) Therefore confirmation is above all an ecclesial sacrament, a sacrament that builds up the Church by giving her strong, articulate leaders and loyal spokesmen.

D. *The Holy Spirit in Us*

Our own Pentecost was the day of our confirmation. It was at that time that, like the Apostles, we received a commission to become public witnesses to Christ and his redemptive work; it was at that time that the Holy Spirit came to deepen our friendship, our commitment to Christ. He who showed his power by outward signs in the apostolic age has conferred divine power upon us, that we may take our Christian commitment seriously, live our faith manfully, and help Christ build up his benevolent reign over men.

II. THE LITURGY OF CONFIRMATION

A. *Historical Development*

The baptism celebrated on Pentecost (Acts 2:37-41) accomplished forgiveness of sins and the initial gift of the Spirit as well as admission to the company of believers. Now the Book of Acts supplies us with at least two clear instances where baptism was followed by another sacramental rite:[4]

> Now when the Apostles in Jerusalem heard that Samaria had received the word of God [through the preaching of the deacon Philip], they sent to them Peter and John. On their arrival they prayed for them, that they might receive the Holy Spirit; for as yet he had not come upon any of them, but they had only been baptized in the name of the Lord Jesus. Then they laid their hands on them and they received the Holy Spirit (Acts 8:14-17).

In this text it is clear that the deacon Philip had done the original preaching and baptizing. It was reserved for the Apostles Peter and John to pray, to impose hands solemnly, and to confer the spirit. Thus there is the external rite or gesture of the "laying on of hands," symbolic of conferring spiritual power. The imposition of hands, accompanied by prayer, causes the Spirit to be given amid certain external manifestations just as

---

[4] Cf. also Heb 6:1-6.

in the case of the first Pentecost, and also in the case of Cornelius (Acts 10:44–46). For at the Samaritan "Pentecost," Simon the magician "saw that the Holy Spirit was in him through the laying on of the Apostles' hands" (Acts 8:18) and offered to them money to obtain a similar "magical" power. This event is understood by the Church as the conferral of the Holy Spirit with special power in that rite which we call confirmation.

The second text of Acts which suggests a confirmation rite is found in Acts 19, where Paul's work at Ephesus is described. When Paul arrived at the city, he found certain disciples who had been baptized only with John's "baptism of repentance." On hearing that they were not baptized with Christ's baptism, Paul baptized them "in the name of the Lord Jesus; and when Paul laid his hands on them, the Spirit came upon them, and they began to speak in tongues and to prophesy" (Acts 19:5–6). In this summary passage a clear distinction appears between the baptism of John, the son of Zachary, baptism into Christianity celebrated by Paul, and the imposition of hands to confer the Holy Spirit in confirmation.

From the above New Testament allusions to confirmation, it seems clear that this sacrament of the Holy Spirit was celebrated with prayer and the outward gesture of imposing hands. As the rite of confirmation developed, however, an anointing and signing with the cross were added; and in the East the latter came to displace the imposition of hands altogether.

Certain practices of the early Church make it difficult to trace the historical development of the ritual of confirmation. The first is the fact that in primitive Christianity, baptism and confirmation were administered together as part of Christian initiation, which was regarded as one continuous event, that of entering the Church by reliving Christ's death and resurrection. After baptism, the Christian was anointed, the bishop imposed hands upon him, and he received the sign of the cross on his forehead. Only then was he permitted to join with the faithful in the Eucharistic sacrifice. The whole ceremony preceding the Eucharist was often called "baptism" or "the seal" (sphrágis). Therefore, while the Church certainly regarded the imposition of hands and the anointing as signs of the gift of the Spirit, it did not coin a distinct name for the sacrament of the Spirit until the fifth century, when the term "confirmation" appears in documents of the Councils of Riez (439) and Orange (441).

Nevertheless, the two sacraments do appear as fairly distinct in the *Apostolic Tradition* of St. Hippolytus (c. A.D. 215), dealing with the practices of the Church at Rome. After describing the actual baptismal immersion, the author continues:

And afterward when he [the newly baptized] comes up [from the baptismal pool] he shall be anointed by the presbyters with the oil of thanksgiving saying: I anoint thee with holy oil in the name of Jesus Christ. And each one drying himself, they shall now put on their clothes and after this let them be together in the assembly [church].

(This anointing still belongs to the baptismal ceremony).

The confirmation ceremony proper is then described as follows:

1. And the bishop shall lay his hand upon them invoking and saying: O Lord God, who didst count these worthy of deserving the forgiveness of sins by the laver of regeneration, make them worthy to be filled with thy Holy Spirit and send upon them thy grace, that they may serve thee according to thy will; to thee the glory, to the Father and to the Son with the Holy Ghost in the Holy Church, both now and ever, world without end. Amen.

(Confirmation:)

Imposition of hands

Prayer

2. After this, pouring the consecrated oil and laying his hand on his head, he shall say: I anoint thee with holy oil in God the Father Almighty and Christ Jesus and the Holy Ghost.

Anointing

3. And sealing him on the forehead, he shall give him the kiss and say: The Lord be with you. And he that has been sealed shall say: And with thy spirit. And so he shall do to each one severally (Apostolic Tradition, Sec. 21, par. 19; Sec. 22, par. 1–3).[5]

Kiss of peace

The kiss mentioned in paragraph 3 is the kiss of peace, the ancient Christian greeting with which the bishop officially welcomed the confirmed as a full and perfect Christian. When infants were confirmed, as they still are in the East, the bishop merely administered a fatherly tap on the cheek. A medieval development (beginning with the Pontifical of Durandus at the end of the thirteenth century), no longer cognizant of its origin, misinterpreted this gesture and called it a blow on the cheek, reminding us as soldiers of Christ to be ready to defend the faith. Hence there still persists the anomaly of a blow on the cheek accompanied by the greeting: "Peace be to you"!

In summary, then, the outward sign or ritual of confirmation has undergone a complex development. Three distinct ceremonies appear in the Roman rite of confirmation: a collective imposition of hands accompanied by a solemn invocation of the Holy Spirit, an anointing, and

---

[5] Translation: Paul Palmer, Sacraments and Worship (Westminster, Md.: The Newman Press, 1954), p. 11.

a signing with the sign of the cross. In the fifth century or before, the anointing and the signing came to be combined. Since the eighteenth century, an individual imposition of hands has been added to the signing so that the bishop first holds his hand on the head of the candidate to be confirmed and then signs him with the chrism on the forehead.

Thus it seems that the original ceremony of the imposition of hands described in the Book of Acts has now become, even in the Western Church, an accessory rite to that of the anointing, and generally speaking in the Eastern Church has disappeared altogether. Such an occurrence challenges theologians to explain the Church's power to change the outward rites of a sacrament and yet leave intact the substance of the sacrament as coming from Christ.[6]

B. *The Present Rite of Confirmation*

Regarding the ritual of confirmation, the *Constitution on the Sacred Liturgy* (1963) has decreed:

> The rite of Confirmation is to be revised; the intimate connection which this Sacrament has with the whole process of Christian initiation is to be more clearly set forth; for this reason it is fitting for candidates to renew their baptismal promises just before they are confirmed.

> Confirmation may be given within the Mass when convenient; when it is given outside the Mass, the rite that is used should be introduced by a formula to be drawn up for this purpose (*CSL* par. 71).

Pending a more complete alteration of the rite of confirmation by the Post-Conciliar Commission on Liturgy, the following provisions have been made in the United States.[7] With a view to enriching the present provisional rite of confirmation, there are two possibilities for celebrating this sacrament. It is highly desirable that the sacrament be administered during Mass and if possible that the bishop himself should celebrate this Mass and preach the homily. If this is done (according to the *Instruction*, Chapter III, Section III, Nos. 64–67) the Mass may be the second class *Votive Mass of the Holy Spirit*. After the Gospel of the Mass and the homily, there follow the renewal of baptismal promises by the candidates for confirmation (the same formula in use during the Easter Vigil ceremony) and the actual celebration of confirmation.

If the sacrament is celebrated outside of Mass, the following ceremony is suggested:

---

[6] Cf. Karl Rahner, *The Church and the Sacraments* (New York: Herder & Herder, 1963), pp. 51–58.

[7] This schema for the rite of confirmation was proposed to the conference of the bishops of the United States meeting in Rome on October 26, 1964, in accord with the "Instruction for the proper implementation of the *Constitution on the Sacred Liturgy*" approved by Paul VI, September 22, 1964.

1. The Liturgy of the Word, consisting of the reading of the Epistle and Gospel of the votive Mass of the Holy Spirit (Acts 8:14–17 and Jn 14:23–31). This is to be followed by the homily.

2. The renewal of the baptismal promises.

3. The conferral of the sacrament of confirmation.

C. The Actual Text of the Complete Rite

THE RITE OF CONFIRMATION

1. **Liturgy of the Word.** If Mass is not celebrated, the Epistle and Gospel of the votive Mass of the Holy Spirit may be read.

After the entrance hymn or chant, a lector reads the following: a reading from the Acts of the Apostles 8:14–17:

> In those days, when the apostles in Jerusalem heard that Samaria had accepted God's message, they sent Peter and John who went down to the Samaritans and prayed that they might receive the Holy Spirit. For it had not yet fallen on any of them; they had only been baptized in the name of the Lord Jesus. Then the two laid hands on them and they received the Holy Spirit.

Between the readings from Scripture, psalm verses or other chants may be sung. Then a deacon or priest reads the following:

The Lord be with you.
All: And with your spirit.
A Reading from the Holy Gospel according to John.
All: Glory to you, O Lord.

JOHN 14:23–31

> At that time Jesus said to his disciples. "If anyone loves me, he will keep my word. Then my Father will love him, and we shall come to him and make our dwelling-place with him. Whoever does not love me does not keep my word; yet the word that you hear is not my own but comes from the Father who sent me. All this have I spoken to you during my stay with you. But the Paraclete, the Holy Spirit, whom the Father will send in my name, will teach you everything and remind you of all that I told you myself.

> " 'Peace' is my farewell to you. My 'peace' is my gift to you, and I do not give to you as the world gives it. Do not let your hearts be troubled or fearful. You have heard me say to you, 'I am going away,' and 'I am coming back to you.' If you loved me, you would rejoice to have me go to the Father, for the Father is greater than I. But I have told you this now even before it happens so that, when it does happen, you may believe. I shall no longer speak at length with you, for the Prince of the world is coming. Actually,

he has no hold on me; but the world must recognize that I love the Father and that I do exactly as the Father has commanded me."

After the Gospel the Bishop preaches a homily.

2. **Renewal of Baptismal Promises.** After the Gospel and homily of Mass, or after the Gospel and homily of the rite outside Mass as given above, the baptismal promises may be renewed.

Bishop: Let us renew the promises of holy baptism, by which we once renounced Satan and his works, as well as that world which is the enemy of God, and promised to serve God faithfully in the holy Catholic Church.

Bishop: Do you renounce Satan?
All: We do renounce him.
Bishop: And all his works?
All: We do renounce them.
Bishop: And all his allurements?
All: We do renounce them.
Bishop: Do you believe in God, the Father almighty, creator of heaven and earth?
All: We do believe.
Bishop: Do you believe in Jesus Christ, his only Son, our Lord, who was born into this world and who suffered?
All: We do believe.
Bishop: Do you believe also in the Holy Spirit, the holy Catholic Church, the communion of saints, the forgiveness of sins, the resurrection of the body and life everlasting?
All: We do believe.
Bishop: Now let us pray to God together, as our Lord Jesus Christ has taught us to pray:
All: Our Father, who art in heaven, hallowed be thy name; thy kingdom come; thy will be done on earth as it is in heaven. Give us this day our daily bread; and forgive us our trespasses as we forgive those who trespass against us; and lead us not into temptation, but deliver us from evil. Amen.
Bishop: And may almighty God, the Father of our Lord Jesus Christ, who has given us a new birth by means of water and the Holy Spirit and forgiven all our sins, keep us by his grace in the same Christ Jesus our Lord, so that we may have life everlasting.
All: Amen.

3. **The Sacrament of Confirmation.** After the renewal of baptismal promises, the Bishop, without the miter, faces those to be confirmed. They kneel before him, and he says, with his hands joined:

V.: May the Holy Spirit descend upon you and the power of the Most High preserve you from sin.
All: Amen.

Then with his right hand he signs himself with the sign of the cross, saying:

V.:   Our help is in the name of the Lord.
All: Who made heaven and earth.
V.:   O Lord, hear my prayer.
All: And let my cry come to you.
V.:   The Lord be with you.
All: And with your spirit.

Next, with his hands extended toward those to be confirmed, he says:

V.:   Let us pray.
      Almighty and eternal God, who in your kindness gave to these
      your servants a new birth through water and the Holy Spirit, and
      granted to them remission of all their sins, send forth from
      heaven upon them your sevenfold Spirit, the Holy Consoler.
All: Amen.
V.:   The Spirit of wisdom and understanding.
All: Amen.
V.:   The Spirit of counsel and fortitude.
All: Amen.
V.:   The Spirit of knowledge and piety.
All: Amen.
      Mercifully fill them with the Spirit of your fear, and seal them
      with the sign of the cross of Christ, that they may obtain ever-
      lasting life. Through the same Jesus Christ, your son, our Lord,
      who lives and reigns with you in the unity of the Holy Spirit,
      God, forever and ever.
All: Amen.

The Bishop, after sitting on the faldstool, receives the miter and inquires the names of those to be confirmed. Each one is presented to him by a sponsor and kneels to be confirmed. The Bishop dips the tip of the thumb of his right hand into the chrism and says:

"N., I sign you with the sign of the cross."

While saying this, he makes the sign of the cross on the candidate's forehead. He then continues:

"And I confirm you with the Chrism of salvation. In the name of the Father, and of the Son, and of the Holy Spirit."

The newly confirmed: "Amen."

Striking him gently on the cheek, he says: "Peace be with you."

After the anointing the Bishop wipes his thumb with a bit of bread and washes his thumb and hands over a basin. The water from this washing, together with the bread, is thrown into the sacrarium.

While he washes his hands, the following antiphon is recited by the ministers or sung.

Ant.: Strengthen, O God, what you have wrought in us, from your holy temple, which is in Jerusalem.

V.: Glory be to the Father and to the Son and to the Holy Spirit.

All: As it was in the beginning, is now, and ever shall be, world without end. Amen.

The antiphon "Strengthen, O God," is repeated.

The Bishop then removes his miter and stands facing the altar, with his hands joined before his breast, and says:

V.: Show us, O Lord, your mercy.

All: And grant us your salvation.

V.: O Lord, hear my prayer.

All: And let my cry come to you.

V.: The Lord be with you.

All: And with your spirit.

V.: Let us pray.

O God, you gave the Holy Spirit to your apostles, and willed that through them and their successors he be given to the rest of the faithful. Look with favor upon our humble service, and grant that the Holy Spirit, descending into the hearts of those whose foreheads we have anointed with holy Chrism and signed with the sign of the holy cross, may, by dwelling there, make them a temple of his glory. You who with the Father and the same Holy Spirit live and reign, God, forever and ever.

All: Amen.

Then he says: "Behold, so will the man be blessed who fears the Lord."

Turning toward the newly confirmed, he makes the sign of the cross over them, saying:

May the Lord bless you from Sion, so that you may see the prosperity of Jerusalem all the days of your life and may have life everlasting.

All: Amen.

III. THE THEOLOGY OF CONFIRMATION

A. Completion of Baptism

Vatican II's *Constitution on the Church* (November 21, 1964, par. 11) interprets confirmation as follows:

They [the faithful] are more perfectly bound to the Church by the Sacrament of Confirmation, and the Holy Spirit endows them with special strength so that they are more strictly obliged to spread and defend the faith, both by word and by deed, as true witnesses of Christ.[8]

[8] AAS, Vol. 57, No. 1, p. 15; NCWC tr.; cf. St. Cyril of Jerusalem: Catechesis 17,

When it asserts that confirmation binds the Christian more perfectly to the Church, that it adds another perfection to baptism, the Council merely echoes a long-standing tradition. For the earliest Christian writers, commenting on the role of confirmation in Christian initiation, where it follows immediately after baptism, insist that this second sacrament perfects, seals, and confirms God's work begun in us through baptism. Baptism is our birth into God's people; confirmation empowers us to take a more adult role in the Church and in society. Baptism is the sacrament of new life; confirmation, the sacrament of Christian maturity. Confirmation makes us perfect Christians, that is, Christians in the fullest sense, by a more complete sharing in the mission of Christ conferred by the sending of the Spirit.

According to some contemporary theologians, the complementary nature of these two sacraments consists in this, that baptism makes us adopted sons of God and Christ's brothers, whereas confirmation constitutes us adopted sons in power; that is, the latter unites us more fully to the active messianic mission of Christ in the world. This deepening of our vocation to union with Christ makes his work our own; like him, we are summoned to be prophets and witnesses in promoting God's kingship over men.

Besides perfecting or finishing the work of baptism, confirmation historically and ritually was oriented toward the climax of Christian initiation: the celebration of the Eucharist. There is a school of thought, championed especially by French and other continental scholars (e.g., Fr. Bonifaas Luykx), which regards confirmation as primarily a priestly consecration deepening the baptismal deputation to worship and leading the Christian to a fuller and more active role in Christian worship. It is this school that is particularly interested in restoring as far as possible the ancient sequence of these three sacraments — baptism, confirmation, and then first Holy Communion.

The fact that confirmation was originally one of the Paschal sacraments celebrated during Christian initiation suggests still another line of investigation. For if baptism is a dying and a rising with Christ to a new life, confirmation is the sacrament "of the fire and unction of the Spirit of love, Who seals and completes this dying and rising";[9] the Eucharist is the sacrament of perfect union with Christ, the sacrament of that fellowship which is begun on earth and perfected in eternity.

On the Holy Spirit, II, 35–37: P.G., 33, 1009–1012; St. Thomas Aquinas, S.T., III, 65, 3; 72, 1 and 5.

[9] Bohen, op. cit., p. 188.

B. Seal of the Spirit

From the above description, a general theological sketch of confirmation begins to emerge. It remains only to flesh in the details.

One of the earliest patristic names for the ceremony of initiation, including both baptism and confirmation, was the Greek word *sphragis* which means "seal" or "stamp" or "signature." Just as the Spirit resting upon Christ at the moment of his baptism was God's seal or signature upon the whole messianic work of Christ (cf. Jn 6:27), so his presence in the confirmed Christian was regarded as a seal or signature upon the initial saving event of baptism.

St. Paul had already referred to a sealing by the Holy Spirit in the soul of the Christian:

> And in him you too, when you had heard the word of truth, the good news of your salvation, and believed in it, were sealed with the Holy Spirit of the promise, who is the pledge of our inheritance, for a redemption of possession, for the praise of his glory (Eph 1:13, 14).

If this seal of the Spirit be connected with confirmation, then in the view of a leading Protestant theologian it may be compared to a covenant act:

> One might say that baptism of water is a treaty which establishes an alliance, and that baptism of the Holy Spirit [what we call Confirmation] is the signature and seal which guarantee God's commitment and protect the treaty against any violation.[10]

The Pauline concept of a sealing with the Spirit enjoyed a rich development in the writings of the Fathers of the Church.[11] For example, Cyril of Jerusalem in his *Catechesis on the Resurrection of the Body* describes confirmation as "the seal of the communion of the Spirit."[12] St. Ambrose, like Cyril, notes that "Baptism is followed by the spiritual seal [*signaculum*] because after the beginning, perfection is still to be achieved. This takes place when, after the invocation of the priest, the Holy Spirit is poured out" (here follows the mention of the seven gifts of the Spirit). Then he continues: "These are the seven virtues that you receive when you are marked with the seal."[13]

Another development takes its inspiration from statements like Ephesians 4:30, where St. Paul speaks of the Christian being sealed in the Holy Spirit of God "for the day of redemption." If this be associated with confirmation, the gift of the Holy Spirit after baptism is regarded as a seal that stamps the believer for the day of redemption. "This seal

---

[10] Max Thurian, *Consecration of the Layman*, tr. W. J. Kerrigan (Baltimore: Helicon Press, 1963), p. 29.

[11] Cf. Danielou, *The Bible and the Liturgy* (Notre Dame, 1956), p. 117 ff.

[12] Danielou, *op. cit.*, p. 118.

[13] *De Sacramentis*, III, 8, cited in Danielou, *op. cit.*, p. 119.

of the Holy Spirit insures the keeping of the alliance of Baptism and confers perseverance unto the end: then on the last day it will be a proof, a sign of this perpetual alliance."[14] Or again:

> The seal of the Spirit is a sign which, by the tokens or fruits of the Spirit, testifies here and now that God's faithful belong to him, and which will be testimony in their favor on the Day of Redemption; as a seal insures the integrity of an official act, the seal of the Spirit insures the integrity of the baptismal alliance, guarantees its perpetual validity, and holds both parties to fidelity: fidelity on the part of God to his promise, and fidelity on the part of the believer by perseverance until the end.[15]

Thus the seal is a guarantee of immortality; it pledges eternal life and glory.

In summary, according to this ancient analogy of the confirmation "seal," the Holy Spirit's work in us involves:

1. An official completion or perfection of baptism;
2. A deepening of our friendship with God (we belong to him more fully);
3. A personal union with the Holy Spirit of Christ;
4. A pledge of God's commitment toward us;
5. The strength to persevere as a good son of God's family;
6. The promise of eternal happiness with God.

C. Anointing by the Spirit

It is St. Paul who brings together the notions of sealing and anointing by the Holy Spirit:

> Now it is God who is warrant for us and for you in Christ, who has anointed us, who has also stamped us with his seal and has given us the Spirit as a pledge in our hearts (2 Cor 1:21, 22).

Undoubtedly, Paul had in mind the Old Testament practice of anointing kings and priests and sometimes prophets also, as a way of consecrating them for a sacred office assumed in the name of Yahweh himself. Now all three offices were to be united in the person of the great "Anointed One" (Messiah), the royal priest-prophet par excellence.[16] And in this threefold office, every baptized and confirmed Christian has a share. As a "Christian" ("anointed," i.e., set apart, consecrated), he is con-

---

[14] Thurian, op. cit., p. 30.

[15] Ibid., pp. 31, 32.

[16] Recalled by the Church when she consecrates the chrism on Holy Thursday (cf. Roman Pontifical). The sweet-smelling chrism, made from olive oil and fragrant balsam, symbolizes our spiritual "fragrance" before God and our fellowmen. The presence of his Spirit, effected by the anointing with chrism, makes us pleasing to God and docile to his inspirations (cf. gifts of Holy Spirit).

secrated to a priestly and prophetic mission. It seems that confirmation in a special way is directed to accomplish this twofold "consecration."

1. A Priestly Anointing. The anointing with chrism in confirmation acts as a consecration to a new stage of the royal priesthood of the faithful. It corresponds to an amplification and intensification of the sacramental character of baptism, which is also a priestly character. The interior "seal" or character of confirmation, seen in this light, draws the Christian more deeply into the mystery of eucharistic worship, and makes him enter more intensely into Christ's Paschal mystery reenacted there.

Proponents of this thesis may point to the liturgical tradition and practice of the early Church, as well as to patristic testimony. In the ancient liturgical tradition of Christian initiation, as we have already seen, baptism and confirmation may be viewed as twin sacramental rites, a kind of twofold baptism — in water and in the spirit,[17] leading up to and structured toward the celebration of the Eucharist. Since the Eucharist is the highest worship of God's people, and the rendering of such worship to God is the primary function of the Church as worshiping community, both baptism and confirmation then would seem to confer some kind of permanent consecration and orientation toward worship.

Ancient liturgical prayer further corroborates this view. The beautiful Preface for the consecration of the chrism on Holy Thursday, taken from the Gelasian Sacramentary (seventh or early eighth century), petitions God the Father to consecrate the oil and

> to commingle therewith the efficacy of the Holy Spirit through the power of your Christ, from whose holy name chrism has taken its name, with which you have anointed priests, kings, prophets, and martyrs . . . that it may be the chrism of salvation to those who shall be born of water in the Holy Spirit, and that you may make them partakers of eternal life and sharers in the glory of heaven.[18]

Therefore either in baptism or confirmation or in both, a chrismal anointing makes Christians share in one way or another the priesthood, kingship, prophetic office, and martyrdom of Christ.

Patristic testimony may also be marshaled in favor of such a view, particularly in the commentaries and homilies on the significance of the sacred chrism. However, a certain obscurity sometimes persists, since there were two anointings with chrism, as noted earlier. Cyril of Jerusalem[19]

---

[17] Cf. Luykx, "Confirmation in Relation to the Eucharist," in Readings in Sacramental Theology (Englewood Cliffs, N. J.: Prentice-Hall, 1964), p. 194.

[18] Roman Pontifical, Consecration of the Chrism.

[19] In his Third Catechetical Instruction on the Mysteries, par. 6: cited in Palmer, Sacraments and Worship, pp. 22–23.

sees the Old Testament anointing of Aaron as high priest and Solomon as king reflected in the anointing with the chrism in confirmation. Therefore this anointing has a priestly and a royal character. In a similar vein, St. Ambrose notes: "We are all anointed with spiritual grace to make up the kingdom of God and an assembly of priests."[20] St. Augustine wrote: "As we call all of them Christs by reason of their mystical chrism, we call them all priests inasmuch as they are members of the one Priest."[21]

Current investigation in part tends to highlight this priestly significance of confirmation. The distinguished liturgical scholar, Father Bonifaas Luykx, who has made a thorough study of the subject,[22] insists that "Confirmation is the proper Sacrament of the priesthood of the faithful."[23] If baptism brings a person into the people of God and gains admittance into God's house, confirmation gives him a function in that house. "He becomes an adult with his own responsibility in the bosom of the people of God . . . which enables him to exercise validly the acts that belong to that function."[24] Now since the people of God is destined first of all to be a worshipping community, then the new member of the people of God must be empowered to carry out this primary function of worship. It is confirmation, says Fr. Luykx, that confers this special orientation toward the celebration of the Eucharist.

The same author develops his thesis further with another approach. Confirmation brings us the fullness of the Holy Spirit. Now in Christ's case, the fullness of the Holy Spirit was his priesthood. If confirmation makes us share the gift of the Holy Spirit bestowed upon Christ, then it must confer upon us also a certain share in his priesthood, directing us in a very active way toward the celebration of the mystery of Christian worship.

Agreeing in part with Luykx but viewing the confirmation anointing in a broader light, Max Thurian, the monk of the Reformed community at Taizé (France), contends that confirmation makes the Christian "prophet, priest, and king with Christ."[25] He sees confirmation as conferring a threefold mission upon the Christian, a mission which is catechetical, liturgical, and fraternal. The catechetical mission flows out from his consecration as a prophet or witness to God's truth. His liturgical mission flows from the special priestly consecration of confirmation. His

---

[20] De Mysteriis, VI, 30; cited in Thurian, op. cit., p. 37.

[21] City of God, XX, c. 10; tr. Walsh-Honan, The Fathers of the Church, Vol. 24, 1954, p. 281.

[22] La Confirmation, Doctrine et Pastorale (Bruges, 1958).

[23] Luykx, art. cit., p. 204.

[24] Ibid., p. 205.

[25] Thurian, op. cit., p. 37.

fraternal mission as witness to the love of Christ for his fellowmen flows from his royal character as a member of Christ the King.

2. **Anointing for Witness.** In his fine text *Sacraments of Initiation* (Sheed & Ward, 1964), the British theologian Father Charles Davis parts ways with the above theory, at least in emphasis. He suggests that it is baptism which anoints the faithful as priests and kings in Christ; confirmation makes the Christian a prophet and a martyr, in other words, a witness of Christ.[26] This concept, that confirmation establishes the Christian in his status as witness to Christ before the world, may still be reconciled with the notion of a priestly anointing in confirmation. For the priest is not only the offerer of sacrificial worship but also the guardian of the word or a prophet, who proclaims the good news of Christ's death and resurrection in order to gather together the worshiping community of the redeemed. Thus confirmational witness is both a priestly and a prophetic function.

Certainly the scriptural evidence accumulated above[27] would seem to give substantial support to the "witness" character of confirmation. It would seem logical to expect the Holy Spirit to continue in this sacrament the operation especially attributed to him in earlier Salvation-History. Now the presence of God's "Spirit" accounts for the witness function of the Old Testament prophets, of Christ, and of the Apostles in the early Christian community. Since we are a social body immersed in the larger "body of mankind," the witness of our Christian commitment would seem to be an essential function of a Christian before the world. Would it not, therefore, be in line with Christ's sacramental plan to have provided a distinct sacramental consecration for this mission? Confirmation as *the* sacrament of the Holy Spirit would seem to have this primary orientation toward Christian witness — a witnessing *with Christ in the Spirit!*[28]

Along these lines, Mother Marian Bohen, O.S.U., in her extensive study on the *Mystery of Confirmation*, comes to a similar conclusion: that confirmation is in a special way the sacramental sign of charity and as such may be called the sacrament of witness. The Holy Spirit, she contends, is the love of God poured forth into our hearts (cf Rom 5:5). Therefore the purpose of confirmation is to make baptized Christians into confirmed witnesses to God's love manifested in Christ:

By sealing and completing the Christian in his status as child of God,

[26] Davis, *Sacraments of Initiation*, pp. 151, 152.
[27] Cf. above, pp. 118–122.
[28] For a similar conclusion, cf. Pierre Camelot, "Towards a Theology of Confirmation," *Theology Digest* (VII, 2), Spring, 1959, p. 70.

the second sacrament of initiation constitutes him — now by a double title — as witness to God's love for man. The confirmed Christian, led by the Spirit of God, is to manifest to his fellowmen something of the Father's love for them; led by the same Spirit, he is to "manifest" to the Father something of the filial love of the Son.[29]

The confirmed Christian's intimate association in the life of the Blessed Trinity and the bearing of the three Divine Persons toward man is brilliantly explicated in an original study by a leading Belgian catechetical scholar, Fr. Georges Delcuve.[30] Taking the same point of departure as Mother Bohen, he begins his study by reviewing the activity of the Holy Spirit within the Trinity, then proceeds to analyze the action of the Spirit in Christ, and finally applies the Trinitarian concept to Christian life.

In regard to the first point (that is, the place of the Spirit within the Blessed Trinity), it is asserted that since the Holy Spirit proceeds from all eternity from both Father and Son, and is as it were the personification of the mutual love of Father and Son, we may go on to distinguish the way in which he proceeds from the Father toward the Son and the way in which he proceeds from the Son toward the Father. The Father breathed out the Spirit in the paternal love he bears the Son and in this sense the Holy Spirit may be called the love of the Father for the Son or the *Spirit of the Father.* The Son on the other hand breathes out the same Holy Spirit in the love of Sonship that the second Person bears toward the Father; and in this sense the Holy Spirit would be the love of the Son for the Father or the *Spirit of the Son.*[31]

If we analyze more carefully the presence of the Spirit in Christ the God-Man, especially at the great moments of Christ's public career (Father Delcuve suggests three moments or three stages in the drama of salvation accomplished by Christ: his baptism at the Jordan, his transfiguration, and the Paschal event of his death, resurrection, and ascension), we may by careful distinction of the Trinitarian relations assert that, at Christ's baptism, the formal and visible aspect of the gift of the Holy Spirit is that of the Spirit of *Sonship,* for the biblical accounts of the Jordan event heavily emphasize the divine Sonship of Jesus. The Spirit that rests above Christ at his baptism in the form of a dove, therefore, is especially the Spirit as the love of the Son for the Father, that Spirit

---

[29] Bohen, *The Mystery of Confirmation* (New York: Herder & Herder, 1963), p. 185.

[30] Georges Delcuve, "Is Confirmation the Sacrament of the Apostolate? The Theological and Pastoral Meaning of Confirmation," *Lumen Vitae,* Vol. 17, No. 3, September, 1962 (Brussels, Belgium), pp. 467–506; cf. *Theology Digest,* XIII, 3 (Autumn, 1965), pp. 198–205.

[31] *Lumen Vitae, loc. cit.,* pp. 474, 475.

in whose power Christ will bear witness to the Father's love for mankind, shown forth in the whole wondrous plan of redemption. With his baptism at the Jordan, Christ commences his public life of total devotion to his Father. Sent by the Spirit, the God-Man must proclaim the good news of salvation.

On the other hand at the transfiguration (a kind of second baptism or baptism with fire), Christ is anointed with the Spirit and with power (cf. Acts 10:38). Here on the mountain, Christ is especially the recipient of the Spirit as breathed forth by the Father toward him, in other words, the recipient of the Father's love for him. And thus he receives the Father's glory, not the glory of an immediate resurrection, but the glory of becoming High Priest (cf. Heb 5:5) to offer sacrifice in the Holy Spirit (cf. Heb 9:14), the sacrifice that will include both the offering of his life and the crowning glory of the resurrection. Once that moment of triumph is achieved, Christ will diffuse the Holy Spirit as Spirit of the Father. Thus both "baptisms" prepare Christ for a definitive "baptism of fire" in his passion, death, and resurrection.

If Christ experienced a twofold "baptism" on the way to the Paschal mystery, the apostolic Church also may be said to have relived these mysteries of Christ's life. Like Christ at the Jordan, the Apostles are obedient sons, holding fast to the teachings of Jesus, which he had proclaimed from the time of his baptism by John onward. Then on Pentecost they received the Spirit of the Father, that is, a share in the love of the Father toward his Son, with which they are loved in him as second or adopted sons, united with the true Son. After citing texts like 1 John 5:5–12 (which speaks of the Father testifying to his son) and John 15:26 ("When the Advocate has come whom I will send you from the Father, the Spirit of truth who proceeds from the Father, he will bear witness concerning me"), the author suggests that the different Trinitarian relations involving the Spirit may now be applied to our own baptism and confirmation.

Baptism is the sacred moment when, like Christ at his baptism, we receive the Spirit and love of the Son toward the Father. It is at this baptismal moment that we become children of God and heirs of heaven, and we receive the grace to imitate Christ's own love for the Father. Confirmation, on the other hand, is the moment when we receive the Spirit as Spirit from the Father, and become sharers in the Father's love toward his own Son.

Or again, confirmation is a reflection or an echo of the transfiguration mystery of Christ. Just as Christ received the Spirit of the Father as a kind of anointing for his priestly sacrifice through suffering to glory, so also our own confirmation has priestly overtones insofar as it prepares us to be both priests and victims in a sacrificial life modeled after and united to the priestly life of Christ who "through the Holy Spirit offered himself unblemished unto God" (Heb 9:14). In this view baptism becomes the "seal of the Spirit of the Son" while confirmation is the "seal of the Spirit of the Father."[32]

In sum, through baptism, the Spirit "first assimilates us to the Son-Servant of God, and unites us to him in his *élan* toward the Father." Standing before the Father, united to Christ, in the sacrament of confirmation, we receive in him the "gift of the Most High God," the Kiss of Peace par *excellence*, the Love of the Father, who bears witness to his Son in our innermost being, and gives us the strength to offer ourselves up in and with Christ.

Both these sacraments unite us to Christ in his passion-resurrection-ascension; baptism more under the aspect of Son-Servant, Victim obedient until death, to whom a glorious posterity is promised; confirmation more under the aspect of the Father's favors, one of the effects of which is precisely to give us in the strength of love, power to share actively in the very offering of the High Priest and thus to attain glory. Baptized and confirmed, we share the "royal priesthood," we are members of a "priestly people" with a double title of "victims and priests."[33]

D. Anointing for Illumination

The Greek Fathers often called baptism the sacrament of enlightenment because it introduced the newborn Christian to Christ, the light of mankind, who in turn confers the new vision of faith. But something of the idea of enlightenment also came to be associated with confirmation. In 1 John 2:20, 27, the evangelist seems to connect the two ideas of a confirmation anointing and the idea of knowledge or illumination:

> But you have an anointing from the Holy One and you know all things.
> . . . Let the anointing which you have received from him dwell in you,
> and you have no need that anyone teach you. But as his anointing
> teaches you concerning all things, and is true and is no lie, even as
> it has taught you, abide in him.

May we not recall the farewell supper discourse in the Gospel of St. John, where Jesus promised the Spirit as the Teacher of truth, the Enlightener, who would further indoctrinate the Apostles with all truth and call to their minds what he himself had already taught them?

As Preceptor of truth, the Holy Spirit causes in the confirmed Christian a deepening or intensification of those gifts of wisdom, understanding, and knowledge, which make our mind docile and amenable to what

---

[32] *Ibid.*, p. 499.
[33] *Ibid.*, p. 503.

God asks of us. Wisdom increases in the confirmand a relish for things divine and an insight into them springing from love. Counsel enables the Christian to judge soundly and prudently in matters of Christian practice. Understanding means a basic grasp of the doctrines of the faith. Knowledge inspires in the recipient a proper appreciation of material goods and of all created things.[34] This is why St. Ambrose in his De Sacramentis and De Mysteriis explains that the chrism is received upon the head, symbol of the faculty of wisdom.[35]

In this way, confirmation prepares the Christian for that life of wisdom he is expected to lead in helping to build up Christ's community on earth. Knowing and appreciating his own faith more intensely, he is stirred with zeal to communicate this same urgency of belief and commitment to others.

E. Sacrament of the Christian Militia?

It may be observed that the catechism emphasis on confirmation as a sacrament that makes us soldiers of Christ has been played down in the above discussion. The reason for this emerges from a brief résumé of the origin of this notion. In a Pentecost sermon, Faustus of Riga (d. 590), a bishop in the southern part of Gaul, used this explanation of confirmation to distinguish it from baptism. After noting that confirmation provides an increase of grace above that of baptism, he went on to say that "in baptism we are born again to life; after baptism we are confirmed for combat."[36] In the ninth century this answer on the significance of confirmation was included in a fictitious letter attributed to a nonexistent Pope Melchiades (Miltiades). The letter was included in a group of forged documents which have come to be known as the False Decretals, documents compiled with the object of enhancing the authority of the bishops.[37] Theologians have known for some time of the later origin of this supposed sixth-century text; but when widespread attention was given to the discovery of this hoax in which a minor sixth-century bishop's sermon was magnified into supposed papal teaching, then a new search into the authentic meaning of confirmation was set off. Though a long-standing tradition had developed from this, yet such an interpretation of confirmation as an arming for spiritual combat

[34] Charles Davis, Sacraments of Initiation (New York: Sheed & Ward, 1964), p. 153.

[35] De Sacramentis, Book 3: I, 1; De Mysteriis, VI, 30; cf. J. Quasten, Florileguim Patristicum (Bonn: Hanstein, 1936), Fascicle 7, Part III, pp. 151 and 127 respectively.

[36] Quoted in B. Leeming, Principles of Sacramental Theology (Westminster, Md.: The Newman Press, 1956), p. 625; cf. pp. 620–634.

[37] Cf. Colman O'Neill, Meeting Christ in the Sacraments (New York: Alba House, 1964), pp. 165–167; cf. also Henry Bettenson, Documents of the Christian Church (New York: Oxford University Press, 1947), p. 133.

must surely be understood as accessory or subordinate to the principal meaning of the sacrament.[38]

F. Confirmation in the Light of Ecumenism.

What did the reformers of the sixteenth century think about confirmation?[39] Luther, after much hesitation, considered it a ceremony instituted by the Church, a kind of sacramental blessing, but not a sacrament in the strict sense. Melanchthon, Luther's "lieutenant," believed that in the primitive Church confirmation had been essentially a catechetical questioning of the candidates in view of a public renewal of faith accompanied by a blessing.[40] Calvin, leader of the Reformed tradition, took the same view as Melanchthon. He refused to acknowledge confirmation as a sacrament, but merely as a form of instruction so that children or adolescents may be able to defend the faith that is in them in the presence of the Church.[41] The later Swiss Confession of Faith persists in denying sacramental status to confirmation, extreme unction, penance, orders, and matrimony, but does regard the last three as of divine institution.

The reformers' position may be interpreted as a reaction against the typical medieval notions of confirmation which lacked theological depth and tended to overshadow the importance of baptism. In the Western Church, by the year 1200, confirmation had become a rite more or less independent of baptism. Ignorant of the early history of the sacraments of initiation and their close association with one another, the reformers were led to disparage the whole idea of confirmation as a sacrament.

In analyzing the Protestant rejection of the sacramental nature of confirmation, one might ask: How did the reformers interpret the texts of Acts 8:17 and 19:6, which relate the Apostles' imposition of hands and transmission of the Holy Spirit? Calvin's answer was that this pertained to the once-and-for-all unique nature of the apostolic Church. "In the time of the apostles one might work miracles, effect cures, confer the Holy Spirit by the imposition of hands but now all that is finished . . . there now exist, as means of grace, solely the Word, and the two sacraments of baptism and the Supper."[42]

In our time, however, beginning with the Anglican theologians, there has been a renewed interest in the subject of confirmation. As the

---

[38] Thurian, Consecration of the Layman, pp. 59, 60; Colman O'Neill, ibid.

[39] Cf. Thurian, op. cit., pp. 1–9, 65–68.

[40] Gregory Dix, Theology of Confirmation in Relation to Baptism (Westminster: Dacre Press, 1946), p. 28.

[41] John Calvin, Institutes of the Christian Religion, tr. Henry Beveridge (London: J. Clarke & Co., 1957), Vol. 2, Bk. IV, Chap. 19, pp. 625–632.

[42] Thurian, op. cit., p. 7.

scholarly works of Dom Gregory Dix (Anglican) and Brother Max Thurian (Reformed) suggest, there seems to be a new willingness to re-examine not only the scriptural data but also tradition, which research in the past decades has once more opened up to us. The ceremony of confirmation retained in many Protestant denominations has for the most part the character of a renewed public profession of faith at the time of adolescence. The retention of at least this much of the ancient rite affords a bridge of understanding that might in time lead to a renewed acceptance of the sacramental status of confirmation in the Churches of our separated brethren.

IV. SUMMARY AND CONCLUSIONS

From our study of confirmation in the light of Scripture, history, liturgy, and doctrine, there emerge certain major ideas of its nature, purpose, and its value for our life.

1. Confirmation has the general purpose of deepening our Christian life. It is a maturing encounter with Christ, in which the Spirit of Father and Son is given us to bind us more intensely to them in their mutual love. In short, it is a more intense orientation toward the life, happiness, and friendship of the Blessed Trinity.

2. Through its sacramental character or seal, confirmation imprints more deeply into us the image of Christ — Christ as filled with the plenitude of the Spirit for his messianic career; Christ as High Priest of the Paschal mystery; Christ as public Witness to the Father.

3. It is especially the sacrament of social maturity, charging us with the power and commission to follow Christ in his openness toward the world he is sent to redeem. Our deeper involvement in worship becomes both sign and cause of our deeper involvement in witness.

In the fullness of the Spirit, Christ witnessed to the Father's saving love for men in word and deed. As the Father's very Word, he uttered that love in every discourse and in every deed of mercy, even to the point of death and resurrection.

The Apostles, imbued with the same Spirit of witness, proclaimed to the world the saving deed of Christ and extended his reign among men. Like their risen Head, whom they knew to be among them, they also testified in blood to their loyalty to the cause of spreading the kingdom.

The confirmed Christian continues the line of Christlike and apostolic witness. The kind of witness he bears will always be conditioned to his specific situation; but the general features of his redeeming encounter with the world are not hard to delineate.[43]

His basic witness is that of faith and love. His faith witness springs first of all from sincere conviction, grounded upon a firm intellectual grasp of doctrine, fortified by prayer. A man of principle, he will try to set the example of a Christian life lived in depth; with humble gratitude for his own vocation to the faith, he will be eager and enthusiastic to carry the faith to others.

As a Christian parent, he will take seriously his responsibility of handing on the faith to his children. Outside the home, in his neighborhood, in business and professional relationships, he will acquit himself sincerely of his Christian and ecumenical duty to project the most favorable image of Christ's Church. Politics, law, medicine, science, teaching, public service, business, or whatever other career he chooses must claim from him not only a commitment of excellence, but also the witness of a redeeming love. He will seize every opportunity to bring his Christian ideals to bear upon his sphere of influence, to restore "all things in Christ."

If he is called to a more direct form of the apostolate, he will pursue it single-mindedly as his share of the witness of Christian love. If he is loved by the Father and convinced that he bears within himself, in the Person of the Holy Spirit, the very Love of the Father toward the Son, then his mandate of fraternal charity to others is clear.

All social responsibility, all organized charity, all Catholic Action must be motivated by and spring from the presence of the Spirit of love in us. All Christian life is a work of witness to the love of God for us in Christ. The corporal and spiritual works of mercy or charity which the Gospel presents as the very basis of judgment are not antiquated or obsolete in our fast-moving twentieth century. Indeed to many the supernatural and the disinterested love of true Christian charity is the last sign that there is a God. The selfless love of devoted service to our fellowmen is the most accurate test of the depth of our Christian conviction. It is the mystical body doctrine come to life! Christ himself made it the hallmark of fellowship with him: "By this will all men know that you are my disciples, if you have love for one another" (Jn 13:35). The challenge of world peace, freedom in the Church, civil rights, antipoverty, national defense, integrity of home life — the multiple challenge faced by the Christian today requires the active pursuit of Christian charity and justice in the power of the Holy Spirit of confirmation.

---

[43] Among a growing host of books on the apostolate, one might very profitably read Dennis Geaney's You Shall Be Witnesses (Fides, 1963); Philip Berrigan, No More Strangers (New York: Macmillan, 1965).

CHAPTER VIII

Fellowship in the Body of Christ:
The Sacrifice-Meal of the Eucharist

I. THE EUCHARIST, CLIMAX OF CHRISTIAN INITIATION

Vatican II, in its *Constitution on the Sacred Liturgy*, after describing the creation of the Church out of the Paschal and Pentecostal mysteries of Christ, goes on to say:

> From that time onwards the Church has never failed to come together to celebrate the Paschal mystery; reading those things "which were in all the scriptures concerning him" (Lk 24:27), celebrating the Eucharist in which "the victory and triumph of his death are again made present" and at the same time giving "thanks to God for his unspeakable gift" (2 Cor 9:15) in Christ Jesus, "in praise of his glory" (Eph 1:12), through the power of the Holy Spirit (CSL, par. 6).

The Eucharist is the sacramental renewal of the whole Paschal mystery of Christ, the celebration of his death and resurrection, in which the people of God are most efficaciously gathered together into that fellowship and unity of which St. Paul speaks (1 Cor 10:16–17):

> The cup of blessing that we bless, is it not the sharing [fellowship] of the blood of Christ? And the bread that we break, is it not the partaking [fellowship] of the body of the Lord? Because the bread is one, we, though many, are one body, all of us who partake of the one bread.

St. Paul insists here that it is the Eucharist which makes Christians one body by uniting them with the flesh of the risen Christ. The Eucharist is above all the meal of fellowship, the heart of the Church's family life, the source of unity with Christ in his Paschal mystery.[1]

Nowhere does the celebration of the Eucharist appear more clearly as the summit of the Church's life, the supreme cause and visible expression of that *koinonia* or fellowship of which St. Paul speaks, than when it is viewed in its ancient Paschal setting as the climax of Christian initiation. In this context, the Eucharist appears as the chief function of the Church, that supreme "action" toward which Christian initiation leads: namely the great act of *saving worship* that gathers God's people together in Christ.

Furthermore, toward this Eucharistic act converge the four major perspectives of this study: Scripture, ecclesiology, encounter, and commitment. The Paschal Eucharist gathers up all the decisive *biblical* moments of Salvation-History to make them present to the newly baptized. Yahweh's exodus-deliverance of Israel and Christ's death-resurrection exodus are brought into sacramental focus, are actualized in the Eucharistic mystery. Christ himself personally presides over this victory celebration, sharing his triumph over sin and death with the newborn sons of the Church.

Clearly, the Paschal Eucharist is a major *ecclesial* event, one that touches the heart of the Church's existence. Here the Church is most visible, most in evidence. Just as a family enjoys one of its most cohesive moments at the evening meal or the Sunday dinner, or just as a large relationship meets annually at a family reunion, so the Church-family is most conscious of her ties with Christ when she gathers around him in the Easter Mass.

At the Easter Vigil, the Church recognizes her own beginnings in the mystery being celebrated. Easter is like Founder's Day or Independence Day, for the Church-body of the redeemed emerged historically from

---

[1] M. E. Boismard, O.P., "The Eucharist according to St. Paul," in *The Eucharist in the New Testament* (Baltimore: Helicon Press, 1964), pp. 130–131.

the death struggle of Christ and from his victory over death in the resurrection. At every Easter, the Church renews herself by the sacramental reliving of that great freedom victory, in the central constitutive sacraments of baptism and the Eucharist. The sacraments make the Church! The Church lives by its sacraments!

It is in the Easter Eucharist that we are able to meet the risen Christ most directly. Not merely is his power present, as in baptism or the other sacraments; the Eucharist makes him present in very substance. We encounter him in his risen flesh and blood on the very night of his own supreme self-commitment unto death and resurrection. We meet him in those redemptive sacraments which grew out of this very self-giving.

II. PATRISTIC TESTIMONY TO THE PASCHAL EUCHARIST

Some of the earliest Christian writings we possess testify to the climactic position of the Eucharist in the celebration of the ancient Paschal Vigil and its concomitant service of initiation. A document of mid-second century called *The First Apology* of St. Justin the Martyr (a pagan philosopher and convert to Christianity who explains the Christian faith and practice to the Roman emperor) describes the service of Christian initiation beginning with paragraph 61. In paragraph 65, Justin comes to describe the Paschal Eucharist of the Christian initiation as follows:

After thus baptizing the one who has believed and given his assent, we escort him to the place where are assembled those whom we call the brethren, to offer up sincere prayers in common for ourselves, for the baptized person, and for all other persons wherever they may be, . . . At the conclusion of the prayers we greet one another with a kiss. Then, bread and a chalice containing wine mixed with water are presented to the one presiding over the brethren. He takes them and offers praise and glory to the Father of all . . . and he recites lengthy prayers of thanksgiving to God. . . . At the end of these prayers and thanksgiving, all present express their approval by saying "Amen." . . . And when he who presides has celebrated the Eucharist, they whom we call deacons permit each one present to partake of the Eucharistic bread, and wine and water.[2]	Baptism

Prayers of the Faithful

Kiss of peace

Offertory

Consecration

The great "Amen"

Communion under both kinds |

[2] Justin the Martyr, *The First Apology*, par. 65, as cited in Paul Palmer, *Sacraments and Worship* (Westminster, Md.: The Newman Press, 1955), pp. 4–5. For the critical text cf. J. Quasten, *Florilegium Patristicum* (Bonn: Hanstein, 1935), Fascicle 7. Part I, pp. 16–17.

An early third-century witness to the Paschal Vigil of initiation is *The Apostolic Tradition* of St. Hippolytus (c. A.D. 215), which reflects the liturgy of Rome at this early date. Having described the celebration of baptism and confirmation, the document presents the ritual schema for the Paschal Mass:

And then let the oblation at once be brought by the deacons to the bishop, and he shall eucharistize first the bread into the representation of the flesh of Christ; and the cup mixed with wine for the antitype of the blood which was shed for all who believed in Him . . . and when he [the bishop] breaks the Bread in distributing to each a fragment he shall say: The Bread of Heaven in Christ Jesus. And he who receives shall answer Amen.[3]	Offertory Consecration Breaking of the Bread Communion

For the newly baptized, there follows the reception of water; then milk mingled with honey is given them, and, finally, the precious Blood. The milk and honey are reminders that the new Christians have now entered that land of promise described in the Old Testament as a place "flowing with milk and honey" (all prosperity and good things), which in the New Testament is fulfilled in the Church.

A final witness from the early Church of the West is St. Ambrose of Milan, *On the Mysteries* (c. A.D. 390). Again, Christian initiation is brought to a close with the celebration of the Eucharist:

Rich with these adornments[4] the cleansed people hastens to the altar of Christ, saying: "And I will go in to the altar of God; to God who giveth joy to my youth" (Ps 42:4). Having shed the scales of ingrained error [the old paganism], renewed with the youth of the eagle, she hastens to approach that heavenly banquet. She comes, and on seeing the sacred altar arranged, exclaims: "Thou hast prepared a table before me" (Ps 22:5).[5]

It is not unlikely that these psalms quoted by St. Ambrose were chanted by the newly baptized Christians as they proceeded solemnly from the baptistry into the church, where they were to celebrate the entire Eucharist for the first time and make their first Holy Communion.

In the church proper, they would be invited to sit at God's table as his personal guests, to exchange gifts with him, to join the family and Christ in offering the eucharistic sacrifice to the Holy Trinity in

---

[3] *The Apostolic Tradition of Hippolytus,* par. 23, as cited in Palmer, *op. cit.,* pp. 12–13; cf. Quasten, *op. cit.,* pp. 32–33.

[4] "Adornments" probably refer first to the outward symbols of baptism which are the white garments and then to the interior reality conferred by the sacraments.

[5] For the Latin text, cf. Johannes Quasten, *Florilegium Patristicum,* Fascicle No. 7, Part III (Bonn: Peter Hanstein, 1936), p. 19 (131); translation from Palmer, *op. cit.,* p. 32.

celebration of the New Covenant to which they now belonged, and to eat the covenant-meal of the eucharistic Communion. The Eucharist was and still is the sign of *full incorporation into the Church* and into Christ's Passover.

Already plunged into his death and risen with him in baptism, the Christian, in newfound solidarity with his brothers, met the risen Christ, the triumphant Conqueror of sin and death, in the sacramental sacrifice of the Eucharist. With the Christ of the Easter Eucharist, he began — and he would continue to do so in every Mass thereafter — to pass over little by little from this world to the world of Christ:

> Brethren, if you have risen with Christ, seek the things that are above where Christ is seated at the right hand of God. Mind the things that are above, not the things that are on earth, for you have died and your life is hidden with Christ in God. When Christ, your life, shall appear, then you too will appear with him in glory (Col 3:1–4).

III. THE PRIMACY OF THE EUCHARIST AMONG THE SACRAMENTS

The Eucharist is the chief high-priestly work of Christ continued in his Church. As mediator between the Father and us, Christ continues his saving work, constantly aggregating to himself a holy people, the family of his Father, a redeemed race. This "downward" or man-centered movement is enshrined or capsuled in the central sacrament of our salvation, the Eucharist.

But besides this "downward" or man-directed movement from God toward us, Christ's work also rises "upward" in a movement of supreme homage rendered to the Father from the sons of the family. As God-Man, High Priest of his Church, Christ gathers his members into his own manly praise of the Father, climaxed in his death and resurrection and renewed for us again in the eucharistic sacrifice. The Eucharist becomes the great sacrament of our worship of the Father. The Eucharist is the principal mystery of *saving worship* in the ecclesial community of Christ on earth.

Insofar as the other sacraments are likewise "mysteries of saving worship," though to a lesser degree than the Eucharist, they may be said to flow from the Eucharist, from which they derive all their efficacy; and in turn they are directed back to the Eucharist as the summit of the Church's worship.

The centrality of the Eucharist in the sacramental system is often brought out by using the image of the solar system. Just as the sun stands in the center of the solar system and the other planets revolve around it, so also the Eucharist holds the central place in the liturgy of the Church. All other sacraments and sacramentals revolve about the Eucharist as a kind of magnetic center.

St. Thomas maintains that the Eucharist is the most powerful of all the sacraments for three reasons.[6] *First,* in the sacrament of the Eucharist Christ himself is contained in very substance; in the other sacraments there is contained a certain instrumental power derived from Christ. *Second,* all the other sacraments are ordered toward the Eucharist as toward a certain goal or end. *Third,* the other sacraments generally reach their ritual "consummation" in the Eucharist — i.e., their celebration normally leads to the Mass.

We will set forth an explanation of the Eucharistic Presence in a later chapter; here we pass to the second and third points. How are the other sacraments oriented or directed doctrinally toward the Eucharist? The sacrament of orders clearly is directed to the consecration of the Eucharist. The sacrament of baptism is directed toward the reception of the Eucharist. Confirmation strengthens one so that he does not have to fear to withdraw from such a great sacrament. Here we would perhaps enlarge upon St. Thomas and show how baptism and confirmation, together with the Eucharist, really constitute the Church. They gather together that eucharistic community, that people of God whose highest privilege and essential character is to join Christ in his most priestly work of acknowledging the Father's excellence and love. While baptism confers the first right to share in offering the Eucharist and to receive Christ in Holy Communion, confirmation seals us by its sacramental character for the worship of God as active and public witnesses to Christ. The Mass itself is an act of supreme witness to our faith in Christ before our fellowmen. Penance may be called the gateway to the Eucharist because it removes the barrier of sin, which prevents us from full eucharistic union with Christ. The anointing of the sick likewise prepares for the reception of Communion and strengthens the Christian to persevere as a faithful member of Christ during the ordeal of suffering. Matrimony likewise is related to the Eucharist, for both are symbols in "miniature" of the union of Christ and his Church. Thus the Eucharist, which makes present the redeeming sacrifice of the Lord, pours out its abundant fruits to man through all the other sacraments.

As to their liturgical orientation, the other sacraments are generally completed or consummated by the celebration of the Eucharist. This was clearly brought out in the ancient practice of Christian initiation, where baptism and confirmation were followed by the Paschal Eucharist and the first Communion of the new converts. Even today baptism should

---

[6] See S.T., III, 63, 6; 65, 3.

be followed as soon as possible by Mass and Communion on the part of an adult convert. Likewise the *Constitution on the Liturgy* encourages celebration of confirmation during Mass if at all possible. Furthermore, the consecration of the oils (which are used in four sacraments — baptism, confirmation, holy orders, and the anointing of the sick) at the Chrism Mass of Holy Thursday in the cathedral is another way of illustrating how the graces of the other sacraments flow from the Eucharist. The Eucharist is the normal setting for the conferral of holy orders and the celebration of matrimony. It is during the Liturgy of God's Word that the bishop celebrates the ceremony of ordination, after which the new priests concelebrate with the bishop, offering together with him their first Mass.

Matrimony most appropriately is solemnized within the context of the Eucharist to bring out the covenant aspect of both sacraments. The Eucharist celebrates anew the great covenant between Christ and his Church, sealed in his own sacrificial blood sacramentally offered in the Eucharist. It is in this holy setting that the spouses pledge their covenant to each other in Christ and merge their own adventurous commitment to each other for the rest of their lives with the great loving surrender of Christ to his Church, a surrender perpetually enshrined in the celebration of this sacrament.

Thus all the other sacraments focus upon the Eucharist, particularly under its aspect of sacrifice. The sacrifice of the Eucharist is the central realization in our midst of the supreme worship of Christ by his death and resurrection. All the other sacraments point to this redemptive center, this focus of salvation. From the Mass they draw their life, their power, their energy; and in turn they lead us back to the center of our own life in Christ, the table of sacrifice, the altar of the Eucharist.

IV. THE EUCHARIST IN SALVATION-HISTORY

A. *Covenant-Sacrifice and Covenant-Meals in the Old Testament*

The Eucharist is an especially rich and profound sacrament. Unlike the other sacraments, which contain a single supernatural reality, the Eucharist may be said to contain three mighty, integrated realities, namely Christ's sacrifice, Christ's meal, and Christ's real presence. It is not surprising that a sacrament of such plenitude, enshrining God's gift of the New Covenant, should be prepared for, rehearsed, and hinted at by a number of Old Testament realities. At this point we select for discussion the biblical concept of covenant-sacrifice and covenant-meal, ideas which are essential for an understanding of the New Testament Eucharist.

The notion of "covenant" itself is fundamental. Among the Israelites, covenant or *beriṯ* signified a "communal relation between two parties, along with all the rights and duties which follow."[7] A covenant, like a treaty or contract, had the effect of producing peace and guaranteeing the personal welfare of the contracting parties. Major covenants, like those between tribal chieftains, would often be formalized by a special ritual called "cutting the covenant." An example of such a covenant-ceremony appears in the patriarchal story of Abraham (cf. Gn 15).

God had chosen Abraham to head a new people, the beginning of God's great plan for reuniting all men to himself. In return for Abraham's loyalty to his newfound God, Yahweh made impressive promises: (1) that he would have a great progeny as numerous as the sands of the seashore and the stars of the heavens; (2) that he and his descendants would have their own land; and (3) that somehow all nations of the earth would be blessed in him (Gn 12:1–3). To ratify this promise, as Genesis 15 describes it, God ordered Abraham to slay certain animals and to lay the halved beasts on the ground opposite each other. Then as it grew dark "a smoking oven and a fiery torch passed between the pieces. On that day the Lord made a covenant with Abraham saying 'to your posterity I will give this land' . . ." (Gn 15:17–18).

What occurred in this strange covenant-rite was typical of desert procedure. After splitting the animals, the two parties to the agreement would walk up and down between the halved carcasses, and in the meantime would take an oath, saying in effect: "May the same thing happen to me that has happened to these animals, may my blood be spilled like theirs, *if I fail to keep my word.*" Like a desert chieftain, then, Yahweh binds himself to keep his word to Abraham and seals the promise in the blood of the slain animals.

When Jacob, grandson of Abraham, reached a peaceful agreement with his father-in-law Laban, they also formalized a covenant by offering sacrifice in the highlands, and concluded this treaty of understanding with a covenant meal (Gn 31:44–54). The common meal following the exchange of oaths and the sacrifice is a sign of the friendship and peaceful relations established between the partners to the covenant. Sharing the same food is the sign of sharing a common life.

By far the most evocative example of a Hebrew blood-covenant is that which was solemnized on Sinai between Yahweh and the Israelite refugees from Egypt. Like the covenant with Abraham, the Sinai pact was initiated at God's own benevolent choice. It was he who named Israel as his own possession, his priestly people, dearer to him than all

---

[7] P. van Imschoot and Bruce Vawter, "Covenant" in *Encyclopedic Dictionary of the Bible* (New York: McGraw-Hill, 1963), c. 432.

other nations on the face of the earth (cf. Ex 19:5, 6).

In Exodus 24:3–11, the sacred author describes the ceremony of the ratification of the covenant. An altar is erected and sanctified to Yahweh; blood from the bulls slain by young men of the tribe is placed in bowls. After he has proclaimed Yahweh's covenant-love and code of obedience and received the people's assent, Moses, the highest human dignitary present, seals the solemn agreement by the sprinkling of blood, half on the altar and half on the people, and proclaims: "This is the *blood* of the *covenant* which Yahweh has made with you in accordance with all these words of his" (Ex 24:8).

Since blood is the carrier of life (Lv 17:11), the mutual sprinkling of the blood signifies that God is sharing his very life with these people, that from this moment on, the Israelites become his blood relatives. The sprinkling of the blood on the altar, symbol of God himself, also suggests the recognition that all life originates with him and therefore "returns" to him under the sign of the blood. In such a return, it gains new vigor; life is revitalized at its origins. The creature returns to God in order to be re-created. At Sinai, the whole people of Israel enters into union with God, "turns" toward him through the blood of sacrifice, and thereby acquires a new status as God's own people. This is the deep meaning of covenant-sacrifice. It signifies and causes, seals, ratifies, and proclaims man's entry into God's own life as a "holy nation," a redeemed race, a free and responsible people — the people of God.

Finally, the covenant-sacrifice is concluded with a sacred banquet (cf Ex 24:11) between God and the elders of Israel. "After gazing on God, they could still eat and drink." Set in such a framework, the meal testifies to the new life in common that Yahweh begins to share with his chosen people. It presages a continuation of God's covenant blessings, his enduring friendship, protection, and constant care for Israel.

The covenant of Sinai indeed made a people out of the Israelite tribesmen, who up to that time had been a nomadic clan, settled in Egypt as foreigners and finally reduced to the status of slaves. With the Sinai covenant, the Israelite exiles won a new freedom, gaining national religious identity as Yahweh's people in addition to political independence.

Freedom brings responsibility; and so succeeding generations of Israelites were challenged by judge, prophet, and king to remain faithful to the ideals of this holy partnership with God. Annually, Israel was to renew its gratitude for divine deliverance from Egypt and to pledge its continued fidelity to the covenant by the celebration of the sacrifice-meal of the Passover.

But despite God's continued forgiveness of Israel's shortcomings, the people time and again broke the covenant and fell into idolatry and immorality. Against a backdrop of increasing abuses of covenant-freedom and privilege, the prophets threateningly announced a day of destruction. The Old Covenant would perish, yet God would not abandon his people altogether; out of the ruins of the Old Covenant he would establish a new and more wonderful partnership with his people. Especially in the prophecies of Jeremiah, Ezekiel, and in Second and Third Isaiah, the promise of a New Covenant appears with increasing clarity. The classic announcement of the New Covenant is found in Jeremiah 31:31–34:

> The days are coming, says the Lord, when I will make a new covenant with the house of Israel and the house of Judah. It will not be like the covenant I made with their fathers the day I took them by the hand to lead them forth from the land of Egypt; for they broke my covenant, and I had to show myself their master, says the Lord. But this is the covenant which I will make with the house of Israel after those days, says the Lord. I will place my law within them, and write it upon their hearts; and I will be their God, and they shall be my people. No longer will they have need to teach their friends and kinsmen how to know the Lord. All, from least to greatest, shall know me, says the Lord, for I will forgive their evildoing and remember their sin no more.

From such a passage it appears not only that God will someday introduce a new order for his followers but also that this new age will involve a much more profound intimacy between him and his covenanted people. If the first covenant was inscribed on tablets of stone, the New Covenant will be interiorized, spiritualized, "written in men's hearts." God's people will be intimately associated with him: they will know him, they will be united to him as intimate friends; and this very friendship, shown forth in the lives of the people, will serve to instruct others in the knowledge of God. Finally, the New Covenant will result in a purification of God's people by the remission of their sins. The stage is now set for us to understand the drama of the New Covenant publicly proclaimed by Christ, sacramentally inaugurated at the Last Supper, and definitively established by his bloody death on the cross and his resurrection.

B. The Institution of the Eucharistic Covenant

Investigation into the essential nature of an event or an institution always leads us back to its origins. If we can discover the circumstances and setting of the original event, if we can trace back the origins of a thing as it proceeded from the mind of its creator, then we are in a better position to analyze and understand the essential nature of that event. To understand the Eucharist, then, let us turn to the New Testament accounts of its institution by Christ.

There are four chief sources recounting the institution of the Eucharist in the New Testament: Matthew 26:17–30; Mark 14:12–26; Luke 22:7–38; and 1 Corinthians 11:23–25. John's Gospel deals with the Last Supper in Chapters 13 to 17, but does not explicitly mention the institution of the Eucharist; therefore we shall postpone consideration of John's teaching until later.[8]

We shall first analyze the texts from a literary and historical point of view, following the opinion of current biblicists; then we shall try to reconstruct the context or setting in which the words of the first Eucharist were uttered; this in turn will prepare us for interpreting the texts from a theological point of view.

If we compare the four New Testament accounts that directly describe the first Eucharist, we observe both striking similarities and some noteworthy differences. The fact that these narratives all agree on essential points suggests an original common source. The differences, so the scholars tell us, can be explained on the basis of later influences, especially of a liturgical nature. Although there is not unanimity of opinion, yet a majority of exegetes seem to favor the following explanation.

The four accounts are reducible to two chief formulations of what the Lord Jesus said and did on the night of the Last Supper. There are two basic traditions: one a primitive Palestinian tradition associated with Peter and reflected in the Gospels according to Mark and Matthew; the other account, going back to Luke and Paul, is based on a traditional narrative handed down in the Greek Church at Antioch.

Paul-Luke Tradition
(Palestinian-Antioch Origin)

1 Cor 11:23–26

For I myself have received from the Lord (what I also delivered to you), that the Lord Jesus, on the night in which he was betrayed, took bread, and giving thanks broke, and said, "This is my body which shall be given up for you; do this in remembrance of me." In like manner also the cup, after he had supped, saying, "This cup is the new covenant in my blood; do this as often as you drink it, in remembrance of me. For as often as you shall eat this bread and drink the cup, you proclaim the death of the Lord, until he comes."

Mark-Matthew Tradition
(Palestinian Origin)

Mk 14:22–25

And while they were eating, Jesus took bread, and blessing it, he broke and gave it to them, and said, "Take; this is my body," and taking a cup and giving thanks, he gave it to them, and they all drank of it; and he said to them, "This is my blood of the new covenant, which is being shed for many. Amen I say to you, that I will drink no more of the fruit of the vine, until that day when I shall drink it new in the kingdom of God."

[8] Cf. pp. 167–168, below.

Lk 22:19–20

And having taken bread, he gave thanks and broke, and gave it to them, saying, "This is my body, which is being given for you; do this in remembrance of me." In like manner he took also the cup after the supper, saying, "This cup is the new covenant in my blood, which shall be shed for you."

Mt 26:26–29

And while they were at supper, Jesus took bread, and blessed and broke, and gave it to his disciples, and said, "Take and eat; this is my body." And taking a cup, he gave thanks and gave it to them, saying, "All of you drink of this; for this is my blood of the new covenant, which is being shed for many unto the forgiveness of sins. But I say to you, I will not drink henceforth of this fruit of the vine, until that day when I shall drink it new with you in the kingdom of my Father."

The basic agreement among these four accounts testifies to a single ultimate source. That this ultimate source is actually the Last Supper itself is indicated by the general Semitic background for all the elements of the words of institution. Linguistic scholars have established the general Semitic tone of the language used; and though the texts of the Gospels come down to us in the Greek tongue, nevertheless there is evidence in these passages of an original Palestinian tradition.

But there are incidental differences, as even a casual comparison will show. A literary and historical study would try to establish the inter-relationship of these accounts; and although there is not universal agreement among scholars on this point, there seems to be a general acceptance of the fact that these two passages reflect independent traditional accounts of the Last Supper. That is, there is no immediate literary dependence of one tradition on the other. The earlier tradition (although this also is disputed) seems to be that of Paul and Luke, both of whom may have borrowed from an ancient nonliturgical source no longer extant. In any case their accounts seem to reflect the primitive celebration of the Eucharist as it took place in the Church at Antioch and Corinth.

On the other hand the Mark-Matthew tradition betrays a Palestinian origin directly; and since Mark's Gospel is generally accepted as the earliest of the three synoptic accounts, Matthew would simply be an expansion of Mark.

It is generally believed that these accounts are not verbatim reports of the Last Supper; rather they are liturgical formulas for the celebration of the Eucharist actually in use in Jerusalem, in Corinth, and in Antioch, which were taken into the sacred text to preserve for successive generations of Christians the remembrance of what the Lord Jesus said and did at the first Eucharist. "The *Sitz im Leben* [the actual historical occasion, circumstances, or setting] of the accounts of institution is the primitive liturgy."[9] A résumé of some of the scholarly arguments for maintaining the liturgical character of these passages provides an interesting insight into the literary and historical method of analyzing Scripture.

1. The Marcan account of the first Eucharist gives some indication of having existed as an independent pericope before it was incorporated in St. Mark's passion narrative. Mark 14:18 introduces the supper scene with the words "And while they were at the table eating, Jesus said . . ." A little later, verse 22 needlessly repeats a reference to the context, "And while they were eating, Jesus took bread, etc." Such unnecessary repetition of detail is not customary in Mark's relatively smooth style and suggests that verses 22 and following were not originally part of Mark but rather represented an account ready at hand which he simply incorporated into the text without smoothing over the insertion.

2. All of the accounts as we find them are reduced to the bare essentials which would interest a Christian audience. They lack the detail which would be expected of a more historical and graphic portrayal of the occasion. For example, there is no mention of the Paschal lamb nor of the very complex procedure followed at a Paschal meal, although there are hints here and there. Such conciseness of expression is fitting for a liturgical formula, which would have eliminated all details of purely Jewish interest and have retained only those elements that pertained immediately to Christian worship.

3. Another characteristic of the accounts is their use of parallelism, a literary device frequently found in liturgical formulas. This parallelism is most obvious between the words spoken over the bread on the one hand and those spoken over the wine on the other. To maintain that these are liturgical formulas in no way questions their historical value; it simply suggests that when the sacred authors or editors came to this part of the passion narrative, they incorporated into it the succinct account familiar to them from the liturgy of the local church, which in turn represented a tradition traceable to the actual historical event of the Last Supper itself. A condensed version retained only those words and gestures of Christ which the Church considered necessary for the representation of the first Eucharist. Furthermore, St. Paul's introduction to the eucharistic institution might also be understood as a reflection of a fixed and traditional text (cf. 1 Cor 11:23; 15:3). Conclusively, then,

[9] Edward J. Kilmartin, S.J., *The Eucharist in the Primitive Church* (Englewood Cliffs, N. J.: Prentice-Hall, 1965), p. 29.

both of these traditional texts are authentic and precious, probably the very words used at Mass in the primitive Church.

C. *The Context of the First Eucharist*

In order to place the Eucharist in proper perspective, the next task of the scholar is to reconstruct the original setting (*Sitz im Leben*) of the Last Supper as best as possible.[10] A reconstruction of this kind will help us greatly to enter the mind of our Lord and to learn his intention and purpose in giving us the Eucharist.

The Synoptic Evangelists seem to affirm explicitly that the Last Supper was a Paschal meal (cf. Mt 26:17; Mk 14:12; Lk 22:8). One of the major difficulties, however, is that John apparently contradicts the Synoptics, since in his passion narrative the official Pasch begins only on Friday evening after our Lord's death and burial (cf. Jn 18:28; 19:31, 42). Different solutions have been proposed by scholars in the effort to solve the apparent contradiction. One conjecture is that the Synoptic chronology is correct, but that John for theological reasons deliberately changes the chronology (since he is concerned with Salvation-History and is not writing strict factual history in every detail). According to this view, John's account puts Christ on the cross precisely at the time when the rabbis are slaying the Paschal lambs in the temple in preparation for the feast which is to begin Friday evening at sundown. Thus in John's Gospel Christ appears as the true Paschal lamb of that feast, by whose blood the whole world is redeemed (cf. Jn 19:14, 34–36). Another explanation suggests that Jesus anticipated the Passover meal because his death would prevent his eating it at the appointed time. Such a proposed anticipation would gain some corroboration if, as supposed, Christ used a priestly calendar different from the official calendar of the Sanhedrin. There is no ready answer to this problem, but most scholars would agree that the Last Supper was at least a religious and fraternal festive meal taken in the atmosphere of the Paschal feast.[11] Furthermore, Jesus seems to intend a Paschal symbolism in the meal when he commands his disciples to repeat it in remembrance of him, even as Yahweh in the Old Testament had commanded an annual celebration of the original Passover event as a memorial of his great saving work (cf. Ex 12:14–17; Nm 9:2, 12, 13).

If, therefore, Jesus consecrated the first Eucharist within a Paschal setting, can we reconstruct in any detail the ritual of that meal? Despite

---

[10] Cf. Kilmartin, *op. cit.*, pp. 37–53.

[11] Cf. Kilmartin, *op. cit.*, pp. 43, 44; Dix, *The Shape of the Liturgy* (London: Dacre Press, 1945), p. 50 ff.; J. Delorme, "The Last Supper and the Pasch in the New Testament," in *The Eucharist in the New Testament* (Baltimore: Helicon Press, 1964), pp. 57–67.

an inevitable evolution in the ritual of the Passover, it seems possible to say that the Last Supper took place somewhat as follows:[12]

1. Double blessing over the first cup of wine by the father of the family or leader of the group (a blessing for the feast and a blessing for the wine).

2. The washing of the right hand. (Was this the moment when Jesus washed the feet of his disciples? Cf. Jn 13:5 ff.).

3. The eating of the first course (a kind of *hors d'oeuvres*), consisting of bitter herbs dipped in vinegar sauce to remind the Israelites of the bitter years of their ancestral captivity in Egypt. (This might have been the moment of Judas' betrayal of Jesus; cf. Jn 13:21–30.)

4. The explanation of the meaning of the feast and the symbolism of the foods. The father or the host recalled the historical background of the bread, the lamb, and the wine in the light of the ancient Exodus event. The unleavened bread recalled the bread hastily made without yeast on the night of Israel's departure from Egypt; the lamb recalled the blood smeared on the doorposts to ward off the death plague; the wine testified to the joy and thanksgiving of Israel at her deliverance.

5. The singing of the first part of the *Hallel* (Pss 113 or 113–114).

6. The drinking of the second cup of wine and the washing of both hands.

7. The blessing and distribution of the matzoth or unleavened bread. This ceremony, which usually occurred at the very beginning of a meal, occurred at this point in the Paschal meal, just before the main course. The father or leader recited a prayer of thanks over the bread, broke it, and handed a piece to each participant. In this way all those at table came to share in the blessings which God had already bestowed upon Israel, as well as in those promised for the messianic future. It was probably at this moment, as the Gospel account suggests, that Christ departed from the prescribed ritual prayer and performed instead the first consecration of the Eucharist, proclaiming that this was "his body" and that they, the Apostles, should now eat of it.

8. The main course, consisting of the lamb.

9. The blessing and distribution of the third cup of wine (the great "cup of blessing"). It was probably at this moment of the most solemn wine-blessing that Christ performed the second consecration of the first Eucharist — offering his blood as covenant-blood to the Father and sharing it then with his Apostles, to signify their own participation in his approaching covenant-sacrifice on the cross.

10. The close of the meal with the singing of the rest of the *Hallel* (Pss 114 or 115–118). The reference in Mk 14:26 to the singing of the hymn probably corresponds to this final chant of the Paschal meal.

---

[12] Kilmartin, *op. cit.*, pp. 40, 41; P. Benoit, O.P., "The Accounts of the Institution and What They Imply," in *The Eucharist in the New Testament*, pp. 74–76.

D. *Deductions From the Paschal Context of the First Eucharist*

1. The Eucharist is the fulfillment of the Old Testament Passover.

The Paschal atmosphere of the first Eucharist would indicate that Christ intended the latter to have a meaning for the Church similar to that which the ancient Passover feast had for the Israelites. The first Passover was to be commemorated annually by a sacred meal, a meal involving worship and thanksgiving to Yahweh for his saving work. Hence Christ must have intended that the Eucharist which he instituted at the Last Supper be the new Passover of the Church. The Hebrew Passover was an annual commemoration in symbolic reenactment of God's great act of deliverance at the time of the exodus; and the effect of the annual celebration was to confer upon succeeding generations of Israelites the continued benefits of the original act of salvation. By celebrating the memorial meal each year, latter-day Jews would experience the abiding benefits of the original act of deliverance.

In a similar way, the new Passover of the Eucharist is also a memorial feast in the Jewish sense, as Jesus himself indicated when he said "Do this in remembrance of me." Like the ancient Pasch, annually making present the benefits of Yahweh's saving deeds for Israel, the Eucharist too as a memorial celebration must include the re-presenting or making present again the saving work of Jesus, so that his followers might also share in its benefits.[13]

The Paschal celebration of the Old Testament was bound up with the covenant of Sinai; similarly the Eucharist of the New Testament must be a covenant celebration that renews the profound relationship between God and the people of the Church.

2. The Eucharist is the meal of the messianic Servant of God.

Among the great expectations of the Israelites was the festive banquet that would announce the messianic age to come. Just as the sacred meals of the Old Testament were understood as symbols of the unity between Israel and Yahweh its God, so the meal of the Messiah would symbolize the gathering of Israel and indeed all peoples in the presence of Yahweh and his Messiah. This banquet would inaugurate the new age of promise fulfilled, an era of divine favor and mercy, far transcending anything that Israel had previously experienced.

At the Last Supper Jesus intimates that in his role of Messiah he is about to usher in the true messianic age. He casts himself in the role of *Servant-Savior* (cf. Is 53), a role whose meaning was not well known or popular among his contemporaries; like a slave, he stoops to wash the

---

[13] Cf. below, p. 165 f.

feet of his disciples. Thus the meal at which he presides is none other than the messianic meal, when Jesus gathers the first leaders of the new Israel, the Church. Here he already begins to fulfill the role he had predicted for himself: "The Son of man has come not to be served but to serve and to give his life as a ransom for many" (Mk 10:45). "Which is greater, he who reclines at table or he who serves? Is it not he who reclines? But I am in your midst as he who serves" (Lk 22:27). The ultimate service which Jesus renders as God's Servant at the Last Supper is precisely the giving of himself as sacrifice and food, in order to involve the participants of this eucharistic meal in his own redemptive work.

In giving his Apostles and his Church the eucharistic banquet of the new age, Jesus inaugurates the new kingdom of the Church. This seems to be implied in his words: "I appoint to you a kingdom, even as my Father has appointed to me, that you may eat and drink at my table in my kingdom" (Lk 22:29–30). Thus the Eucharist is the eschatological meal that inaugurates sacramentally the new Church-Kingdom, about to be completed in Christ's death, resurrection, and conferral of the Spirit.

E. *The Meaning of the First Eucharist as Deduced From the Actual Texts of Institution*

1. **Preliminary observations on the words used.**

Referring to the distinction between the two traditional accounts (the more primitive Antioch-Palestinian account, represented by Paul and Luke, and the second or later account of Mark and Matthew), we may note a certain difference in theological outlook. The Pauline-Lucan account presents Jesus as the Suffering Servant of Yahweh (cf. Is 42–53) offering himself in sacrifice for sinners, while the Mark-Matthew account presents Jesus as the new Moses presiding over a ritual sacrifice like that of the Sinai covenant (cf. Ex 24:8).

A second point to be noted in the analysis of the words of institution centers around the sayings of Jesus: "This is my body" and "This is my blood." Scholars versed in biblical languages assure us that in each of these phrases, whether Jesus is speaking of his body (flesh) or later after the meal of his blood, what Jesus means to say is that he is giving his whole person for the redemption of mankind. To state it succinctly, body (flesh) equals the whole person; blood equals the whole person.[14]

2. **At the Last Supper, Jesus as messianic Servant of God surrenders himself to the Father as Redeemer of sinful man.**

The whole atmosphere of the Last Supper makes it clear that Jesus

---

[14] Kilmartin, op. cit., pp. 57–59.

is about to die. The whole movement of events suggests it. He speaks
of the supper as his last meal; "I will drink no more of the fruit of the
vine, etc." (Mk 14:25); "I have ardently desired to eat this Pasch with
you before I suffer" (Lk 22:15). At the bread ceremony which immediately precedes the main course, he relates the bread to his body, that is,
to his whole person; then he goes on to say that this body is to be given
for others, an allusion to his role as Suffering Servant, the innocent
sufferer dying freely for the guilty (cf. Is 53:10, 12 passim). At the
benediction over the last cup of wine, he proclaims that it is his blood
being poured out for many (Mk 14:24; Mt 26:28). To speak of one's
flesh or body being given up and one's blood being shed are surely figures
suggestive of death. As Suffering Servant, then, Jesus gives himself with
complete freedom to his Father; as his prayer in Gethsemani later brings
out, his will is perfectly aligned with that of his heavenly Father: "Not
my will but yours be done." The most important element of the Lord's
sacrifice is found here in the giving of his will.

Something else of importance may be pointed out in connection with
the Lord's words and gestures at the first Eucharist. The study of the
Old Testament has revealed the existence of what is called a prophecy-
in-action or acted prophecy. Two of the best examples are found in the
Book of Jeremiah. In Chapter 19, God commands the prophet to break
an earthen flask in the sight of the people, as a warning that sinful Judah
itself would be broken up in a similar way by the enemy. Or again in
Chapters 27 and 28, Jeremiah carries a yoke on his shoulders as an exhortation to the people and the king to be willing to serve the Babylonian
king Nebuchadnezzar, who had already gained control of Jerusalem and
made its king his vassal. Jeremiah's warning attempted to forestall an
even greater punishment, a threat which actually materialized when the
people of Judah foolishly revolted and caused Nebuchadnezzar to return,
totally destroying Jerusalem, and deporting its leaders into exile. Other
examples of acted prophecy may be found in Ezekiel 4:1–3 and 5:1–5.

Such a prophecy-in-action meant that the prophet acted out in symbol
and gesture and in a sense already initiated the future event which he was
predicting.[15] If we now turn to the Gospel accounts of the words of
institution, we note that Mark-Matthew insert the Last Supper account
in the middle of seven prophecies spoken by Jesus. This prophetic context highlights Christ's prophecy-in-action over the bread and wine. Here
Jesus is acting out an event which will come to pass in the physical order
by his death; on the level of effective symbol or gesture, Jesus is already
pledging himself to die like the Suffering Servant of Isaiah 53, who gave
his life freely for his guilty brethren. Announcing that his body (his

---

[15] Cf. below, p. 164 f.

flesh) is to be "given up" for man, his blood to be poured out, Jesus now acts out his approaching death in that kind of ritual gesture which we have come to call "sacrament." At this moment of the Last Supper Eucharist, Jesus already gives himself to his Father in a sacrifice acted out in prophetic gesture and word, in the symbolic form called sacrament. The first Eucharist, then, is a *sacrament-sacrifice*.

The sacramental symbols of this prophecy-in-action are the words over bread and wine. Can we see a deeper meaning in the twofold consecration of these elements? Although at the first Eucharist, the two consecrations were probably separated by the main course of the Paschal meal, the Gospel accounts, having eliminated purely Jewish details no longer of concern to the Christian Church, place the two consecrations in direct sequence. This juxtaposition of bread (flesh) and wine (blood) would evoke the nuances of Jewish sacrifice, where flesh appears beside blood but separate from it. In the sacrificial ritual of Israel, the flesh and blood of the victim were separated from one another to provide the material of sacrifice (Lv 17:5–6; Dt 12:27).

Further sacrificial resonances emerge from the death symbolism that may be associated with the bread and wine, as Father Benoit points out.[16] The bread must be *broken* for distribution; the wine is called "the blood of the grape" (Gn 49:11). Furthermore the grapes must be crushed (cf. Is 63:1–6, the treading of the winepress). The red color is suggestive of blood. The word "cup" often denotes tragedy (cf. Mk 10:38; 14:36, and parallels; cf. also Ap 14:10; 16:19). Therefore the separate consecrations of the bread and wine may express on the level of symbolism or sacrament the separation of the body and blood of Christ as a figure of his death.

3. Jesus seals the New Covenant in his own sacrificial blood.

There is further evidence that Jesus offered a sacrifice at the Last Supper. All four accounts in the New Testament contain the phrase "blood of the covenant." These are most meaningful words if we appreciate their Old Testament context. The Apostles, well versed in the sacred writings of the Old Testament, were familiar with the concept of a blood-covenant. They would have remembered the covenants of the patriarchs, and especially that of Sinai. Further, they would have recalled the more recent promise of the sixth-century prophet Jeremiah, who gave solemn assurance that:

The days are coming, says the Lord, when I will make a *new covenant* with the house of Israel and the house of Judah. . . . This is the cove-

---

[16] Pierre Benoit, "The Accounts of the Institution and What They Imply," in *The Eucharist in the New Testament*, p. 77.

nant which I will make with the house of Israel after those days, says the Lord. I will place my law within them, and write it upon their hearts; I will be their God, and they shall be my people. . . . All from least to greatest shall know me says the Lord, for I will forgive their evildoing and remember their sin no more (Jer 31:31-34, *passim*).

Now according to the Semitic mind, to seal a covenant with blood means to perform a sacrifice.[17] Therefore, Christ's words over the cup mean that his own blood, soon to be poured out physically, is already present sacramentally under the sign of wine as the solemn seal of the New Covenant or new partnership between God and mankind realized in the form of the Church. Christ is inaugurating the New Covenant, not in the blood of animals, but in his own sacrificial blood. The Eucharist must be a sacramental covenant-sacrifice.

Furthermore, Christ's words over the bread also have a certain covenant significance. If under the form of bread he gives his flesh to his followers as covenant-food, Jesus thereby expresses a desire to draw his followers into an "I-thou" relationship with himself on the supernatural level; on the very level of being, they are to become one with him — as the author of Genesis put it, "two in one flesh." By eating the flesh of Christ, we become one with him and one with each other in the New Covenant of the Church. Thus it can be said that at the Last Supper or the first Eucharist, Christ was inaugurating the Church of the New Covenant, a task he would perfect by his death, resurrection, and conferral of the Holy Spirit. Like a second Moses, he was mediating a new partnership between God his Father and his Church in the person of his Apostles.

In the light of this first Eucharist, our Sunday parish Mass or college community Mass takes on new meaning. The Mass is that occasion when we solemnly renew our pact with God in the blood of Christ. In the fullness of our freedom, we consent humbly and gratefully to be that people of God sacramentally inaugurated at the first Eucharist and continually renewed at every celebration of the same Eucharist. In short, the Eucharist is the dynamic moment when the Church is not only most visible, most communitarian, most actively the people of God, but also the moment when the Church receives a new divine life-impulse necessary for her continuance in being. The Church is never more "Church" than when she gathers to celebrate the Eucharist.

4. Jesus gives his life as covenant-food.

In ancient times, especially among the Hebrews, a sacrifice was often concluded with a meal in which the participants ate some of the sacri-

---

[17] Cf. above, pp. 149–152.

ficial food.[18] This was a way of dramatizing the worshipers' newly found favor with the divinity, for to eat holy food was a way of being associated with the divinity itself. The worshiper felt himself a table guest of God; and since he was sharing food with God, he was also sharing something of God's own life.

Therefore at the Last Supper, when Jesus instructs his Apostles to eat the bread which has been made his body and to drink the wine which has been made his blood, he is in effect inviting his followers to eat a covenant-meal with him. Here the ancient Jewish significance of table fellowship, established by the breaking and sharing of the one bread and the drinking of the same cup of wine, comes to full flower; for the participants of this meal are assimilating into their own bodies not mere ordinary food, but food that has been consecrated into the Lord's own flesh and blood. Thus in assimilating his flesh and blood, they are drawn into personal union not only with Jesus but also with one another. Hence the Eucharist is the great meal of the Church's unity; it is the sign and cause of that union of love or fraternal charity of which Christ himself spoke at the Last Supper: "A new commandment I give you, that you love one another as I have loved you" (Jn 13:34; cf. the whole "sermon" — Chapters 14–17).

Furthermore the eating of blessed food at the Passover meal especially signified that all at table were sharing the blessings of their ancestors in the exodus. God's act of deliverance, wrought on their behalf, was now made present again and renewed, reactualized for the benefit of the latter-day generation of Jews. In like manner, we can begin to see how the meal and sacrifice of the Eucharist is meant to reactualize the saving act of the Lord's death, even as he himself had commanded it to be renewed: "Do this in remembrance of me" (Lk 22:19; 1 Cor 11:24, 25). The eating of the food by the Apostles implies a share in Christ's redemptive activity. The surrender of Christ's own mind and will to the Father by way of sacrifice summons forth from the Apostles a similar commitment, a sharing in his own passion and death. All this is implied by their eating the sacred food commemorating the Lord's sacrifice.

5. The Eucharist contains the redemptive act of Christ in sacramental form.

We have noted so far that Jesus effectively offered himself to his heavenly Father as the Suffering Servant, the innocent sufferer for the guilty, prophesied some eight centuries before. Again, Jesus concluded at the Last Supper a covenant-sacrifice, in which his death was visibly symbolized by his words and gestures. When he invites his Apostles to eat

---

[18] Cf. above, pp. 149–152.

this sacrificial food, the implication is that in the meantime the offering must have been accepted by the Father; it must have been successful in obtaining from the Father the blessings which Jesus now bestowed upon his followers in the form of bread and wine. Thus Jesus enacts in the presence of his disciples the complete drama of redemption (offering; acceptance by the Father; blessings upon man).

St. Paul asserts that every time the Christian community consecrates the bread and wine of the Eucharist, they "show forth the death of the Lord until he comes" (1 Cor 11:26). To do this implies that this sacred banquet is both a memorial and a re-presentation, not only of the Lord's death but also of his risen presence. The phrase "until he comes" implies that he must still be alive in order to come; in other words, at the meal of the Eucharist, he presides as the risen and glorious Christ, who often appeared to his disciples after the resurrection especially when they were at meals. Thus the Eucharist is the continuation of those precious post-resurrection meals recorded in the Gospels (cf. Lk 24:30, 35, 41–43; Jn 21:9 f.; Acts 10:41; note, too, that the "breaking of the bread" or the Eucharist took place on the Lord's day, the first day of the week, the weekly anniversary of the resurrection — Acts 20:7–11; Ap 1:10). Therefore the Eucharist is not merely a memorial of the Lord's death connected with the Last Supper, but it is also a meal shared with the present and living Christ of glory, a resurrection-meal recapitulating and reliving those precious moments when the Apostles enjoyed the sight of the risen Christ while they were at table. The essentially joyful and festive character of the Eucharistic celebration is crystal-clear.

That there is a sacramental real presence of the sacrifice of Christ every time the Eucharist is renewed is, according to scripture scholars, also apparent from the notion of prophecy-in-action discussed above. Such acted prophecy, it is pointed out, is actually a part of the event it prognosticates. It is the overture to the event, and is therefore in part a cause of that event. So Jesus' action at the Last Supper as acted prophecy effects what it signifies: his self-surrender to the Father and the latter's acceptance of this gift of his life. His action effectively anticipates in the form of bread and wine, in the form of a ritual sacrifice (sacrament-sacrifice), a saving event to be physically and historically fulfilled in his death and resurrection.

The annual celebration of the ancient Passover was not merely a dramatic memorial of the historical exodus under Moses, but rather an actual making-present of that saving deed, so that all future generations of Israel actually entered into the exodus of their forefathers through the annual celebration of the Paschal festivity. For the Jews the notion of memorial therefore is a very rich and dynamic concept. It means not only remembering or recalling (in the accepted sense), but a real making-present, a reliving of the historical deed. In their ritual services, the Jews traditionally recalled the saving deeds that God had accomplished for their people; and according to the Hebrew mind these past acts of salvation were never really past. Only that which no longer had any effect was considered to be over and done with. In the Semitic understanding of time, there was a continuity between God's past acts on behalf of his people and the present moment — a continuity which permitted the latter-day Israelite to experience in his own lifetime God's saving interventions of the past. This was especially true in the annual celebration of the greatest of all Old Testament saving acts, the Passover. Yahweh himself had promised: "In every place where I cause my name to be remembered, I will come to you and bless you" (Ex 20:24).

By his words "Do this in remembrance of me," Jesus assigns the Eucharist to the same category of memorial celebrations. It is his intention that this memorial supper will re-present his entire saving work; that it will continue to re-present the new covenant-act of the Last Supper-Cross sacrifice. As the new Passover, it will renew and re-present the saving death and resurrection of Jesus, even as the ancient Passover relived God's redeeming work of the first exodus. Hence Jesus makes a memorial gift of himself both to the Father and to the Church. As a gift to his Father, the Eucharist will make present again the same self-surrender of Jesus, his Father's Servant, as was given in the once-for-all sacrifice sacramentally rendered at the Last Supper and physically offered on the cross. As a memorial gift to his Church, the eucharistic supper enables the company of Jesus to unite actively with his sacrifice and to obtain its benefits every time the sacrifice is renewed by form of the sacrament.[19]

6. Jesus himself is really present in the eucharistic food of the Last Supper.

It should be apparent that the New Testament institution accounts present the Eucharist of the Last Supper as a meal within which Jesus offers himself as a sacrifice to the Father to seal the New Covenant he is inaugurating with his Church (personified at the Last Supper by the Apostles) and also that he is giving himself to the Apostles and to the Church as food to keep them united not only with him but with one another (cf. 1 Cor 10:16, 17; Jn 14–17). Now we come briefly to discuss the further implication that follows as a necessary corollary or consequence

[19] For a detailed treatment of the subject of the Eucharist as a memorial, consult Max Thurian, *The Eucharistic Memorial* (Richmond: John Knox Press, 1961), Part II, translated by J. G. Davies, pp. 34–107; also Edward J. Kilmartin, S.J., op. cit., pp. 67–73.

of the above two truths of the Eucharist; namely, that under the form of the eucharistic food and drink Jesus remains really present with his Church. Although this point will be dealt with in more detail later, it is appropriate at least to sketch the basic outlines of the New Testament evidence at this point.

When Jesus gives the consecrated bread and wine to the Apostles and commands them to "take and eat of this" and "take and drink of this," it is quite obvious that he is giving the Apostles a sacred food and drink by which they will be associated with his sacrifice which he has just offered to the Father. But we want to see now that Christ also intended that there be a physical presence of himself under the forms of the bread and wine. He chose the elements of bread and wine precisely to indicate his gift of food; his presence in the form of food needs further analysis.

To argue from the words "This is my body" and "This is my blood," we must realize that the verb "is" was probably not used by Christ at all; as far as we know, he spoke Aramaic in which this verb is not expressed. A noted scholar suggests that the original words might have been simply *den bisri* (This my flesh) and *den idhmi* (This my blood).[20] And even with the verb "is" being understood, in itself it would not express real identity. The verb often appears when our Lord is teaching in parables. For example, in the parable of "The Sower," Christ interprets the parable as follows: "The seed *is* the word of God. And those by the wayside *are* they who have heard," etc. (Luke 8:11–12). Here the word "is" obviously means "symbolizes." But at the Last Supper, Jesus speaks of his body which he is about to give up for his followers and of his blood which he is about to pour out for the salvation of man. The bread and wine are not readily seen as symbols of body and blood without some further explanation. Their first appeal through man's senses is as food and drink; their essential purpose is to nourish us. How do we know, then, that we are to take Christ's words realistically?

For this it is necessary to go beyond the mere words of institution and analyze the extended commentary of Paul (1 Cor 11:23 ff.), as well as the great "Bread of Life" sermon in John (Chapter 6). After describing the institution of the first Eucharist, Paul draws a practical conclusion concerning the reception of the Eucharist:

> Whoever eats this bread or drinks the cup of the Lord unworthily, will be guilty of the body and the blood of the Lord. But let a man prove himself, and so let him eat of that bread and drink of the cup; for he who eats and drinks unworthily, without distinguishing the body, eats and drinks judgment to himself (1 Cor 11:27–29).

[20] Joachim Jeremias, *The Eucharistic Words of Jesus* (Oxford: Blackwell, 1955), p. 142 ff.

There is no reason for doubting Paul's realistic understanding of the terms "the body and the blood of the Lord." For him, to receive the eucharistic food unworthily constitutes a sacrilege which is subject to punishment from God. What constitutes the unworthy eating of the Eucharist, according to Paul, is a failure to "distinguish the body" — a phrase which is subject to various interpretations. Generally it would seem that Paul means to proscribe or condemn one's failure to distinguish the eucharistic food from mere ordinary food. Another interpretation, recalling the context in which Paul is writing (mainly to correct certain abuses of fraternal charity at the eucharistic supper), understands Paul to mean here a failure to distinguish the Mystical Body of Christ, the Church, by a proper observance of brotherly love. Such abuses of fraternal charity would constitute a failure to "distinguish the body," to see Christ in one's colleagues. Finally another opinion holds that the phrase "without distinguishing the body" means "without recognizing the Eucharistic body in its specific claim to fraternal charity."[21] On the contrary, the worthy reception involves a "proving" of oneself in order to bring one's interior dispositions into line with the social nature of the Eucharist. Sinning against one's neighbor, as was being done at Corinth, was therefore a failure to recognize that Christ is being received in the Eucharist not merely as a private gift for the individual, but as the Christ who is communicating himself to "the many." It is a failure to recognize the unifying purpose of the Eucharist: to draw together the one people of Christ by the eating of the one bread (cf. 1 Cor 10:17).

John is even more forceful than Paul. In the latter part of the "Bread of Life" discourse, which is generally accepted as referring to the Eucharist, Jesus asserts:

Unless you eat the flesh of the Son of Man, and drink his blood, you shall not have life in you. . . . For my flesh is food indeed, and my blood is drink indeed. He who eats my flesh, and drinks my blood, abides in me and I in him. As the living Father has sent me, and as I live because of the Father, so he who eats me, he also shall live because of me (Jn 6:54–58).

What John is asserting then is plainly this: to be united with Jesus in the most intimate way demands an eating of his flesh and a drinking of his blood as they are found in the Eucharist. But now, since his resurrection, Jesus exists in a spiritualized and glorified state; that is, he retains his human nature which has now taken on spiritual properties, though it still remains a truly human nature. His body still bears the wound marks (cf. Jn 20:27); he orders his body to be touched by the dismayed disciples (cf. Lk 24:39–40; Jn 20:27); he can still eat with his

[21] Kilmartin, op. cit., p. 88.

bodily powers, even though he no longer needs to eat (cf. Lk 24:42–43; Jn 21:13–15). Now in his risen and glorified state, Jesus can no longer be broken up into parts. Wherever there is actually present his body or his blood, there the whole Christ must be really present by what the Scholastics call the principle of "concomitance." The *total* Christ exists under each species, that of bread and that of wine. If we communicate under only one species, we are not receiving any less of Christ, because he is totally present under even the tiniest recognizable portion of the species of either bread or wine.

To speak of the real presence of the whole Christ in the Eucharist better accords with the divine plan of salvation. Since it is the whole human person, not just his "soul," that is to be saved, it is fitting that Christ should bestow his sanctifying energies upon us precisely by our bodily contact with his own risen flesh. Body sanctifies body; the risen figure of Christ radiates to our own person his glorious risen life. The incarnational or sacramental plan of salvation (noted in Chapter I) comes to full term with the due value that God has placed upon our human nature. He dignifies us by allowing us to assimilate the very flesh and blood of his own Son eucharistically present; and by reason of our eating this most sacred and nourishing food, we have the divine assurance that our body as well as our soul is summoned to the final resurrection. "He who eats my flesh and drinks my blood has life everlasting, and I will raise him up on the last day" (Jn 6:55).

In summary, the Eucharist as it appears in the New Testament contains not just one mystery but three realities closely intertwined with each other. These three "mysteries" or divine realities are the eucharistic meal, the sacrifice, and the real presence of Christ. All three of these mysteries are enclosed within one and the same sacramental sign: the words of consecration spoken over the bread and wine. As the accompanying diagram makes clear, the outward ritual of the Eucharist, its outward sign, expresses all three of these realities. Christ could have arranged distinct sacraments to fulfill these three purposes; but in his wisdom he has combined all three in one and the same wondrous sacrament. Covenant-sacrifice, covenant-meal, and covenant-presence — these three realities constitute the incomparably rich content of this, the most excellent of all sacraments. Christ offered in sacrifice, Christ received as food, Christ really among us — no wonder the Eucharist is the center of the Church's life and liturgical worship.

The Eucharist is the sun around which revolve all the other sacraments and sacramentals; it is the sun that gives light and warmth to the people of God. It is the focal point of the Church's unity, drawing all men

THE EUCHARISTIC MYSTERY

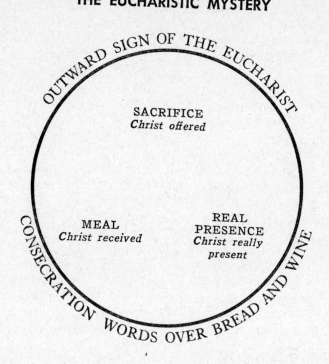

OUTWARD SIGN OF THE EUCHARIST

SACRIFICE
Christ offered

MEAL
Christ received

REAL PRESENCE
Christ really present

CONSECRATION WORDS OVER BREAD AND WINE

together in the sacrificial meal of Christ. It is the central sacrament of our salvation because it renews so effectively under the sacramental signs the death and resurrection of Christ, the entire Paschal mystery. After this analysis of the basic outlines of the Eucharist as it appears in the New Testament, it will now profit us to examine with more detail the theological development of the Eucharist in the history of the Church. This we proceed to do in the following chapters.

CHAPTER IX

Theology of the Eucharist
as Sacrifice

I. BASIC NOTIONS OF SACRIFICE

Basic to all religions from time immemorial has been the effort on the part of man to make contact with the divinity here and now. Man does not wait until the afterlife to meet his God, but feels impelled by his inner consciousness of God to strive for the divine presence in the temporal and spatial limitations of the here and now. Undoubtedly one of the most fascinating aspects of man's efforts to meet God is the phenomenon called *sacrifice*. While on the one hand sacrifice constitutes the very summit of religious experience, on the other hand the exact and original meaning of sacrifice has proved very elusive. Twentieth-century developments in anthropology have given further impetus to this study, so that we seem to be approaching a certain synthesis in our understanding of the original significance of sacrifice and the curious secondary meanings that have come to be attached to it in the long history of religion. Obviously a clearer understanding of this fundamental religious phenomenon, practiced by men of all times, should throw considerable light on our appreciation of the Eucharistic sacrifice, the central and climactic worship of the Christian community.

The word sacrifice has a clear enough meaning in our ordinary usage. The history of our country and our contemporary national experience make clear enough the claim upon certain individuals to surrender themselves for the common good in an act aptly called sacrifice. Not only have our statesmen and our fighting men down through history given of their very lives to insure our independence and our freedoms as a people; but today, and in every successive generation, the same freedoms, privileges, and rights must be won anew. The contemporary struggle for civil rights, perhaps the most challenging domestic phenomenon of the mid-twentieth century, has already claimed its martyrs. The dedicated involvement of people like Mrs. Viola Liuzzo, the Rev. Mr. Reeves, and Jonathan Daniels provides convincing examples of a selfless commitment for justice even to the risk of death. The cold war between East and West, erupting time and again into hot wars on many a front, has accustomed our civilization to the challenge of personal sacrifice for the defense of our whole Western culture and its emphasis on the personal dignity of man. The lesser daily sacrifices demanded of all of us by our state in life — the challenge of work, of human suffering, of community living — these too have made their mark upon our social consciousness. Clear enough then from all these examples is the notion of sacrifice as a kind of self-surrender, a giving of oneself for others.

But when we come to the religious practice of sacrifice and especially the ritual developments surrounding it, it is easy to lose our way in the labyrinth of ceremonial and interpretation.

Because blood came to have a very prominent role in sacrifice, especially in the Old Testament, the notion of sacrifice has in some circles come to be coterminous with the slaying of a victim. But cultural anthropologists and historians of comparative religion suggest a somewhat different approach to a precise understanding of sacrifice.[1]

To begin with, three projected notions of sacrifice must be reexamined. Etymologically, the phrase sacrum facere, from which the word "sacrifice" is taken, has perhaps a less definite connotation than "to make sacred" by transferring an object from the profane world to the divine. Originally

---

[1] An authoritative work in this area is R. K. Yerkes, Sacrifice in Greek and Roman Religions and Early Judaism (New York, 1952), on which Father Louis Bouyer, Rite and Man (Notre Dame, Ind.: Notre Dame University Press, 1963), leans very heavily. Cf. Bouyer's excellent chapter, "Sacrificial Rites and Their Ambivalence," pp. 78–94.

man thought of the whole world around him as being sacred. There was no such thing as the profane.[2] The division between sacred and profane came in a later stage of man's development when he began to become more civilized, to learn to control nature; he lost his sense of the sacredness of that which he could easily dominate by his own natural powers. The word "sacrifice," etymologically derived, is perhaps more accurately interpreted as simply "to do a sacred act"; and this obviously tells us very little about its nature.

Correlative with this idea, sacrifice cannot be made to consist solely in an offering to God of something which previously did not belong to him, for the simple reason that primitive man considered God to own all things. This appears frequently in the Old Testament (cf Gn 1; Ex 19:5–6; Ps 49:10–11). Men have not been satisfied, either, with the explanation that sacrifice essentially consists in the slaying of a victim, an immolation. On the one hand, the gory, bloody spectacle of ancient sacrifices repels modern man and furthermore does not answer the problem as to how the Eucharist can be a sacrifice, since there is no slaying of a victim in the Mass.

Against all such theories of sacrifice, it has recently been asserted that, in its primitive character, sacrifice is a *meal*, conceived as a *meal of the gods*.[3] Every meal is already sacred, since food comes from God. But a sacrifice-meal has a special sacred character, since man wishes thereby to enter into union with the deity. He associates himself with such a meal, either by providing the food at his own expense, securing it and preparing it, or actually taking part in it in some way or other. Even when the food is totally consumed, as in a libation or holocaust, or when man himself consumes all the food, the basic connotation of the sacred act is reducible to that of a meal with God. Sacrifice means essentially the attempt to draw into union with God, to enter into his presence, to become one with him. If this is the true notion of sacrifice, then its paramount place in all religions is obvious because it touches upon the fundamental religious experience, that of being united with God.

The sharing of the meal with God and one's fellowmen becomes an experience of both giving and receiving. In nourishing himself, he realizes his union with the cosmos which provides him with sustenance for life; he feels a bond of union with God himself who provides this food.

---

[2] Perhaps some allowance in this theory should be made for the notion of "zones of special sacredness" to which gifts could be brought and transferred to the divine power through their special ministers. This could be linked with the preparations for a sacred meal, according to the theory proposed below. Cf. A. H. Armstrong, "Rites and Man," *The Downside Review*, Vol. 81, No. 263, April, 1963, p. 102 — a critique of Bouyer's *Rite and Man*.

[3] Cf. Bouyer, *op. cit.*, pp. 82–85.

From this awareness of his dependence on God for life, man is prompted to give himself back to the One who possesses the fullness of life. When such a meal is taken in common with one's fellowmen, the common bond of life is recognized among them, for eating the same food is a sign of sharing life. Man is bound up with the life of his fellowmen, as well as with the life of God. According to this view, sacrifice is the meeting par excellence between God and man. All other variations of sacrifice both in form and in meaning are thought to be a later development (e.g., the holocaust, the sin offering, the scapegoat, etc.).

Now it becomes clear why blood should figure so prominently in the sacrifices of the Old Testament. To the Semite, pouring out blood, the seat of life, means simply a return of the worshiper to God through the blood, a reunion with God's own life. The use of blood in formalizing a covenant connotes the same idea of sharing divine life with the people. With this in mind, we are in a better position to examine the Eucharist as the Christian sacrifice. Our concern will be essentially with the theological development of this idea in the growing consciousness of the Church.

II. NEW TESTAMENT ALLUSIONS

Besides the institution texts considered in the previous chapter, there are other New Testament allusions, more or less explicit, to the Eucharist as sacrifice. In keeping with the phenomenological analysis of ancient sacrifices given above, it will be seen how the idea of sacrifice and meal come close together in the Christian Eucharist. The first text to be considered is from that very early letter of Paul to the Corinthians (cf. 1 Cor 10:14-22). A case of conscience had arisen in Corinth over the eating of meat that had been consecrated or sacrificed to idols. Could a Christian participate in a meal of this kind? The conclusion Paul draws is that, by eating such meat, one was in effect participating or sharing in the worship of devils. "You cannot drink the cup of the Lord and the cup of devils; you cannot be partakers of the table of the Lord and of the table of devils" (1 Cor 10:21). Just previous to this, Paul had stated concisely: "The cup of blessing that we bless, is it not the sharing of the blood of Christ? And the bread that we break, is it not the partaking of the body of the Lord? Because the bread is one, we though many, are one body, all of us who partake of the one bread" (1 Cor 10:16-17). Paul's argument then runs as follows: to eat meat that has been sacrificed to idols associates the participant in idolatrous and sinful worship; in effect he is guilty of sacrificing to the idols, or, since this is false worship, to the devil himself. When the Christian shares in the breaking of the bread and the drinking of the cup of the Lord, he is thereby associating with Christ's very body and blood. Therefore, in setting the "cup of the Lord" and the "cup of devils" in contrast, Paul implies that the former must also be, like the latter, a sacrifice. The Eucharist is that sacrifice that unites Christians with the Lord. Here again sacrifice and meal are one in their objective to draw man into union with God.

The sacrificial concept of the Eucharist may at least be hinted at in another New Testament pericope — the "bread of life" discourse in John 6. In the latter part of this discourse, John includes much material borrowed from the Last Supper narrative. In verse 52, he records the words of Jesus: "If anyone eat of this bread he shall live forever; and the bread that I will give is my flesh for the life of the world." To give (didomi) his flesh means to bestow himself upon men; but implicitly Jesus refers to the saving or redemptive value of his flesh, for it is only by his death and resurrection that his flesh can redeem mankind.

Even clearer in its allusion to sacrifice, however, is the later mention of blood, verses 54–57. When Christ commands the drinking of his blood as a necessity for attaining eternal life, he implies that it is his sacrificed body that must be eaten, that body which will have poured out its lifeblood. The emphasis, then, on drinking the blood of Christ as well as eating his flesh certainly connotes sacrifice.

Finally, in two of the Epistles there are at least hints at the eucharistic sacrifice of the primitive Church. The Epistle to the Hebrews, probably written by a disciple of Paul, compares the sacrifice of the Old Law, especially the ceremonial of Yom Kippur or Day of Atonement, with the sacrificial event of Jesus' death and resurrection. Just as the high priest entered into the holy of holies once a year and sprinkled sacrificial blood upon the propitiatory, so Christ entered once and for all into the heavenly "holy of holies" by the shedding of his own blood. Here is a real "passing over," a crossing from this world to the world of the Father by means of his death and resurrection.

Although the Epistle emphasizes Jesus' once-and-for-all sacrifice on Calvary, where he definitively established the New Covenant by the physical shedding of his own blood, it also seems to make a passing allusion to Christ's continuing eucharistic sacrifice in the Church. After making a plea for not succumbing to "various and strange doctrines," the author of Hebrews points to the true source of grace in Christian worship. "We have an altar from which they have no right to eat who serve the tabernacle. . . . Through him [Christ], therefore, let us offer up a sacrifice of praise always to God . . ." (Heb 13:10, 15). The sacrifice of praise which the Christian priestly people offer at the altar of the Lord might well be the Christian Eucharist itself, especially in its original meaning of thanksgiving for God's great saving acts, poured forth in faith and surrender to God's saving plan by a life of charity to one another.[4]

Finally, a consideration may be given to the First Epistle of St. Peter, which seems to be based upon a Paschal homily delivered to newly baptized Christians during an ancient service of Christian initiation. The newly baptized, like "newborn children" (1 Pt 2:2), are exhorted to desire "pure spiritual milk" and to taste and see "that the Lord is sweet" (2:3). The latter, a reference to Psalm 33, which was often sung as a communion song, already establishes a certain relationship to the Eucharist. This is the "pure spiritual milk" which the baptized are now to experience as they draw near to the altar for the celebration of the Easter Mass.

The privileges of their baptism are now recalled for them; they have been built "into a spiritual house, a holy priesthood, to offer spiritual sacrifices acceptable to God through Jesus Christ" (1 Pt 2:5). And again: "You are a chosen race, a royal priesthood, a holy nation, a purchased people; that you may proclaim the perfections of him who has called you out of darkness into his marvelous light" (1 Pt 2:9). Baptism establishes a catechumen as a member of a priestly people, whose chief privilege is to offer sacrifice. This could be none other than the sacrifice of the Eucharist.

III. TOWARD A DOGMATIC SYNTHESIS ON THE EUCHARIST AS SACRIFICE

In the previous chapter, where we studied the first celebration of the Eucharist at the Last Supper, it was emphasized that the Lord first offered himself to his Father in a sacramental sacrifice and then gave himself to his Apostles in the sacrificial meal of the New Covenant. That Christ willed this celebration of his sacrifice to be continued in his Church is clear from the rubrical command: "Do this in remembrance of me" (Lk 22:19b; 1 Cor 11:24b, 25b). It is now our purpose to show that, from the beginning, the Church was conscious of this command from Christ to go on celebrating this sacrifice-meal, and that she always considered the Eucharist not merely as a meal but also as a sacrifice.

A. The First Three Centuries

The early Church was very conscious of its Old Testament heritage. Some of the earliest eucharistic testimony we possess points to the

---

[4] Bouyer, The Spirituality of the New Testament and the Fathers, translated by Mary P. Ryan (New York: Desclée, 1963), pp. 149–150.

Eucharist as that universal sacrifice foretold by the late Old Testament prophet Malachi. Unhappy with the blemished sacrifices of the post-exilic priests, the prophet foresees a day when all nations will offer a worthy sacrifice to the Lord God:

> I have no pleasure in you, says the Lord of hosts; neither will I accept any sacrifice from your hands, for from the rising of the sun, even to its setting, my name is great among the nations; and everywhere they bring sacrifice to my name, and a pure offering; for great is my name among the nations, says the Lord of hosts (Mal 1:10–11).

The early Syrian document called the *Didache* (the *Teaching of the Twelve Apostles*), dating from around A.D. 90 or 100, contains the following directions for the typical Sunday Eucharist of the first century:

> On the Lord's own day, assemble in common to break bread and offer thanks, but first confess your sins so that your sacrifice may be pure. However, no one quarreling with his brother may join your meeting until they are reconciled; your sacrifice must not be defiled. For here we have the saying of the Lord, "In every place and time offer me a pure sacrifice, for I am a mighty King, says the Lord, and my name spreads terror among the nations" (*Didache*, par. 14).[5]

Here the eucharistic "breaking of the bread" (1 Cor 10:16) is explicitly linked to the universal sacrifice foreseen by the prophet.

Similarly in A.D. 150 in his *Dialogue with Trypho* (par. 117), Justin the Martyr, after quoting the prophet Malachi, continues: "But of the sacrifices offered to him in every place by us the Gentiles, the sacrifices, that is to say, of the bread of the Eucharist and likewise of the cup of the Eucharist . . . of these he prophesied when he said that we glorify his name, but you profane it."[6]

Justin was prompted to make these remarks about the Eucharist to counteract the crass material sacrifices practiced by the Jews and pagans. He wished to show that God was no longer satisfied with bloody animal sacrifices; but now he desired the spiritual sacrifice of the Eucharist to be offered, the sacrifice of Christ's own body and blood under the outward forms of bread and wine.

A little later, Irenaeus, Bishop of Lyons, France (c. A.D. 177) continued the fight for sincere interior sacrifice on the part of the worshipers joining in the Eucharist. Like Justin, he also appealed to the teaching of Malachi to substantiate his plea for a genuine interior offering. Tracing the origins of the Eucharist to the Last Supper, Irenaeus narrates:

---

[5] Cf. J. Quasten, *Florilegium Patristicum* (Bonn. Hanstein, 1935), Fascicle 7, Part I, pp. 12–13; tr. J. Kleist, *Ancient Christian Writers*, Vol. 6 (Westminister, Md.: Newman Press, 1948), pp. 23–24.

[6] S. *Justin the Martyr: Dialogue with Trypho*, *The Fathers of the Church*, Vol. 6, tr. Thos. B. Falls (New York: Christian Heritage, 1949), p. 327 f.

He [Christ] took that which is from creation, bread, and gave thanks, saying: "This is My body." And likewise the cup, which is of the same creation as ourselves, He confessed to be His blood, and taught a new oblation of the New Testament. This the Church receives from the Apostles and offers to God throughout the world, to Him who gives us nourishment, as the first fruits of His own gifts in the New Testament. In reference to this oblation, Malachi, in the twelve Prophets, attached the following meaning in advance: "I have no pleasure in you, says the Lord Almighty, and I will not receive a sacrifice from your hands. For, from the rising of the sun even to the going down my name is glorified among the Gentiles, and in every place incense is offered to My name, and a pure sacrifice; since great is My name among the Gentiles, says the Lord Almighty." By these words he clearly means that the older people will cease to make an offering to God, but that in every place a sacrifice would be offered to Him, and this a pure one; for His name is glorified among the Gentiles" (*Against the Heresies*, IV, 17, 5).[7]

No less clearly than the above witnesses, a spokesman of the third century, St. Cyprian of Carthage, assures us that the Church continues to offer a true sacrifice:

If our Lord and God, Christ Jesus, is Himself the high priest of God the Father, and offered Himself as a sacrifice to the Father, and commanded this to be done for a memorial of Himself, certainly that priest truly performs his office in the place of Christ who imitates that which Christ did, and then offers in the Church to God the Father a real and complete sacrifice, when he begins to offer as he sees Christ Himself offered (*Epistle 63*, par. 14).[8]

B. *The Fourth to the Thirteenth Centuries*

As the Church reflected on the meaning of her central act of worship, she faced especially two problems. First, exactly how is the Eucharist a sacrifice? Second, if Christ offered the perfect sacrifice once and for all (Heb 9:26–28), how then can the Church continue to offer sacrifice? Regarding the first question, Cyril of Jerusalem in the fourth century reflects a well-established tradition that the Eucharist is a sacrifice of propitiation, as witnessed by the Church's early custom of offering Masses for the dead, and including prayers for the living and the dead at each Eucharist. St. Cyril explains the connection between these petitions and the propitiatory nature of the Eucharist:

After the spiritual sacrifice or bloodless worship has been completed, we entreat God over the *victim of propitiation* for the common peace of the Church . . . in a word, we all pray and offer *this victim* for all who stand in need of help. Then we commemorate as well those who have

---

[7] Quoted in Palmer, *Sacraments and Worship*, pp. 273, 274; *P.G.* 7, 1023.

[8] CSEL (Vienna, 1866 ff.) 3, 2, 713; translation from Palmer, *op. cit.*, p. 276.

fallen asleep before us. . . . We offer up Christ sacrificed for our sins, and make God, in His loving kindness toward men, propitious toward them as well as toward ourselves.[9]

The propitiatory character of the Eucharist, insisted upon by Cyril, reinforces the Church's understanding of the Eucharist as a sacrifice. The next Father of the Church to be cited attacked the above-mentioned problems on the Eucharist more directly. In the year 402, St. John Chrysostom commented on the Epistle to the Hebrews with a special reference to Hebrews 10:12–14, which speaks of the eternal efficacy of the one single sacrifice of Christ. In justification of the Church's practice of continually celebrating the sacrifice of the Eucharist, Chrysostom proceeded as follows:

> . . . What then? Do we not offer every day? Certainly we offer, making a memorial of His death. And His death is one and not many. . . . For we ever offer the same person. . . . Therefore, the sacrifice is one. From this line of reasoning, does it follow that, since the offering is made in many places, there are many Christs? By no means! For Christ is everywhere one, complete here and complete there, one body. . . . there is but one sacrifice. Our high priest it is who offered the sacrifice which cleanses us. So we offer now that which was then offered, and which cannot be exhausted. This we do as a remembrance of that which was then done. For "do this" He said, "in remembrance of Me." We do not offer another sacrifice, as the high priest of old, but we ever offer the same; or rather we make a remembrance of His sacrifice.[10]

For John Chrysostom, then, the Mass is a sacrifice because it is the offering of the body of Christ; the Church is able to make this continuous offering by way of a memorial or remembrance. Here is a typical patristic solution as to how the Mass renews Calvary and the Last Supper, without being a basically new or different sacrifice or repeating the historical death of the cross.

If Chrysostom sees the unity of the cross- and the Church-sacrifice in the Eucharist as memorial of the Calvary-sacrifice, another Eastern writer views the Mass as the heavenly sacrifice of Christ made visible on earth in the sacrament. If Christ is still offering himself in heaven, still accepting the death he has undergone and the risen state he now enjoys, then the Eucharist serves to make present on earth these same sacrificial sentiments of Christ.

---

[9] St. Cyril of Jerusalem, On the Mysteries, Lecture 5, par. 8 and 10; tr. Palmer, op. cit., pp. 277–278 (emphasis mine); for complete text, cf. A Select Library of Nicene and Post-Nicene Fathers, Second Series (New York: The Christian Literature Co., 1894), ed. Schaff-Wace, Vol. 7, pp. 154–155.

[10] John Chrysostom, Homilies on Hebrews, 17:3; P.G., 63, 131; quoted in Palmer, op. cit., pp. 279–280.

Although in the food and the drink we make commemoration of the death of Our Lord, it is clear that in the liturgy it is as if we accomplished a sacrifice, without its being anything new, nor its being his own sacrifice that the Pontiff carries out, but it is a kind of image of the liturgy taking place in heaven. . . . Each time, then, that the liturgy of this dread sacrifice is carried out — which is obviously the likeness of earthly realities — we must consider that we are like one who is in heaven; by faith it is the vision of heavenly realities of which we see the outlines in our understanding, considering that Christ, Who is in heaven, Who for us died, rose again, ascended into heaven, it is He Himself Who even now is immolated by means of these figures.[11]

Perhaps here we have an acceptable interpretation far better than many later theological hypotheses.[12]

St. Augustine's contribution to the developing theology of the Eucharist as sacrifice centers also around the notion of the Mass as a sign or symbol of an invisible sacrifice. Speaking of sacrifice in general he explains: "A visible sacrifice, therefore, is a sacrament or a sacred sign, of an invisible sacrifice."[13] The Eucharist as celebrated by the Church is none other than the sacrament or sign of Christ's own self-offering.

. . . He [Jesus] was made the mediator between God and man by assuming the form of a servant, the Man Christ Jesus — although in the form of God He receives sacrifice along with the Father, with whom He too is God — yet, in the form of a servant He preferred to be rather than to receive a sacrifice, lest anyone should take occasion from this to believe that sacrifice is to be offered to any creature whatever. For this reason He is also priest, the very one who offers, and the very offering. And He willed that the sacrifice of the Church should be the daily sacrament (sign) of this. Since she is the body of this head, through Him she is taught to offer herself. . . .[14]

Clearly Augustine describes the continuing priesthood of Christ in his Church. Just as on Calvary Jesus was both priest and victim, so also in the sacrifice of the Church, Jesus is both principal priest and offering. The Church's part in this sacrifice is delineated in another passage from the same work:

---

[11] Theodore of Mopsuestia, *Catechetical Sermons*, XV, 14, 20; quoted in Danielou, *The Bible and the Liturgy* (Notre Dame, Ind.: University of Notre Dame Press, 1956), p. 137.

[12] For a recent hypothesis comparable to that outlined here, cf. Bernard Cooke, S.J., *Christian Sacraments and Christian Personality* (New York: Holt, Rinehart and Winston, 1965), p. 132 f. Also Jungmann, *The Mass of the Roman Rite*, Vol. II, p. 135.

[13] *City of God*, 10, 5; trans. Walsh-Monahan (New York: Fathers of the Church, Inc., 1952), Vol. 14, p. 123.

[14] *The City of God*, 10, 20; cited in Palmer, *op. cit.*, p. 283; cf. complete text in Walsh-Monahan translation, p. 153.

It follows that the whole redeemed city, that is to say, the congregation and community of the saints, is offered as a corporate sacrifice through the great Priest, who also offered Himself in His passion for us, in the form of a servant, that we might be the body of so glorious a head. As a servant He offered Himself; in this form was He offered, because in this form is He mediator, in this form priest. . . . This is the sacrifice of Christians: "we, the many, are one body in Christ" (cf. Rom 12:5). And this also is the sacrifice which the Church continually celebrates in the sacrament of the altar — which is known to the faithful. In it the Church learns that in the offering which she makes she herself is offered.[15]

In these inspiring words, Augustine lays the principle for understanding how the Mass is the work of the whole Church. The Eucharist is that "corporate sacrifice" by which the whole Church offers itself through "the great Priest," Christ himself our mediator. At Mass, the Church-body offers itself to the Father in union with its head. In celebrating the Eucharist, the Church offers itself along with Christ the Priest; but the gift that is offered is not only Christ, but the Church also, as covictim along with its head. Thus Augustine stresses the spiritual participation of the members of the Church in the offering of the Eucharist. The external ritual must always signify the authentic participation of the whole Church along with its head. This notion of the Church's sacrifice as sign or symbol of the interior spiritual sacrifice of Christ and his Church provides a basic understanding of the Mass for all future theological inquiry.

Augustine's emphasis on Christ's mediatorship in the Mass evokes another important liturgical principle that needs to be restored in Catholic thinking on the Mass today. The eucharistic offering is directed not merely to Christ as God, but also through Christ as priestly mediator to the Father. This emphasis places new value on the humanity of Christ; in his risen glorified body, Christ is still high Priest of his Church-body on earth.

Augustine's teaching on the Eucharist paved the way for the more systematic theology of St. Thomas Aquinas (1224–1274). Among other points, Aquinas takes up the question as to just how the Eucharist is an immolation of Christ. If Christ was immolated or sacrificed on the cross, how can he be immolated again in the sacrament? The answer Thomas gives is twofold. First, the Mass is immolation of Christ because it is "a kind of representative image of Christ's passion, which is his true immolation." Second, because the effects of Christ's passion are truly extended to Christians in the celebration of the Eucharist. Here Thomas quotes the prayer over the gifts from the Mass for the ninth Sunday after Pentecost:

---

[15] *City of God*, 10, 6; cited in Palmer, *op. cit.*, pp. 282–283; cf. Walsh-Monahan translation, p. 127.

"As often as the commemoration of this sacrifice is celebrated, the work of our redemption is set in motion" (*Summa Theologiae*, III, 83, 1). Thus Thomas also comes to the point of viewing the Eucharist as a memorial of the sacrifice of Christ on the cross.

C. Reformation Theology

The next major development in the theology of the eucharistic sacrifice was to come as a result of the Reformation. It cannot be denied that by the time of the Reformation there were certain abuses in the Church associated with the celebration of Mass. Problems like those of the multiplication of Masses, traffic in stipends, overemphasis on Masses for the dead, the notion that the Mass is simply a good work, infrequent Communion by the faithful — all of these shortcomings helped to set the stage for the Reformers' dissatisfaction with contemporary eucharistic practices.

However, it was not merely failures of this kind that ultimately caused the Reformers' rejection of the sacrifice of the Eucharist. While personal factors were not entirely absent (as in the case of Luther who as a young priest was seemingly afflicted with a scrupulous sense of personal unworthiness to celebrate Mass),[16] the ultimate and basic reason for the Reformers' rejection of the Eucharist as sacrifice is to be found in their theological system.[17]

The most fundamental challenge of the Reformers was against the incarnational principle of Catholicism, against the notion of *mediation*. As described above in Chapter I, Catholic belief centers on the visible and the human as a medium for reaching God and his saving grace. Christ himself is the Son of God become visible; his Church is the visible sign of Christ's continued presence among men; and the sacraments are Christ's activities embodied in visible rites. Thus Christ, his Church, and the sacraments are viewed as an integral pattern of mediation between the Father and mankind — a pattern which best suits our matter-spirit constitution.

The Reformers, on the other hand, maintained that religion is a personal encounter of the individual with God's mercy and grace; no mediator is necessary, for the individual has direct access to God in Christ. Such a doctrine is implicit also in the great Lutheran concept of justification by faith alone. It is not the "work" of the Church or of the sacraments or of the Mass that infuses divine grace in man and therefore effects his salvation, but rather God's favor freely given to the

---

[16] Francis Clark, S.J., *Eucharistic Sacrifice and the Reformation* (Westminster, Md.: The Newman Press, 1960), pp. 113–115.

[17] *Ibid.*, p. 103 ff.

elect whose sins are pardoned because of the merits of Christ and who attain this pardon by saving faith. The Lord's Supper, in this view, is a promise and pledge of that pardon to the individual worshiper; it is essentially a gift of God to men, not a gift of man to God. And with the stress on the necessity of faith to obtain pardon and mercy from God, the Lord's Supper can help only the individual; it cannot be offered for others, either living or dead.

Luther, however, as will be shown subsequently, did retain a notion of the real presence of Christ in the Eucharist. But the Swiss Reformers, who shared Luther's objections to the Mass as a "work," went further than he by reducing the sacraments to mere signs or figures and rejected any real presence of Christ in the sacrament. Under this view, it was logical to reject the notion of the Lord's Supper as an offering of Christ's body and blood to God, since Christ was not present in the bread and wine in the first place.

A common doctrine of the Reformers which also contributed to their rejection of the Mass was their notion of redemption. Christ, acting in place of sinful mankind, having once appeased the wrath of his Father and averted his anger from man, had essentially completed his work. Emphasis was put upon the once-for-all efficacy of the cross-sacrifice (e.g., Hebrews 10:12, 14). Redemption as atoning sacrifice is a thing of the past; any attempt to continue offering sacrifice in the Mass must be rejected as blasphemous, since this would imply the insufficiency of Calvary. Christ has left himself to his Church (either really or figuratively) not to be offered, but to be received as food in a memorial supper of thanksgiving and as a token of forgiveness through his past act of redeeming us.

In the light of these theological premises, it becomes clear why the Reformers attempted to remove from the service of the Mass every vestige of sacrifice. In the earliest of his eucharistic writings, titled *The Blessed Sacrament of the Holy and True Body of Christ, and the Brotherhoods* (Dec., 1519), Luther views the Mass principally as the sacrament of Christian unity, a fellowship meal uniting Christians with one another and with Christ.[18] In this early work nothing is said about the Mass as sacrifice, and only a passing reference is made to the real presence of Christ. Beginning with the next work *A Treatise on the New Testament, that is, the Holy Mass* (1520),[19] Luther came to speak of the Mass as a testament conceived not so much in the biblical sense as in a legal sense. A testament or a will is essentially something bequeathed by the

---

[18] M. Luther, *The Blessed Sacrament of the Holy and True Body of Christ, and the Brotherhoods*, tr. by Jeremiah J. Schindel, *Luther's Works*, Vol. 35 (Philadelphia: Muhlenberg Press, 1960), pp. 49–67.

[19] *Ibid.*, pp. 75–111.

testator or will-maker to his heirs; therefore it is essentially a gift. Christ is the testator, we are the heirs who receive the testament, the words "This is my body" and "This is my blood . . . a new eternal testament" are the testament itself; the seal or token is the sacrament, that is, the bread and wine under which are Christ's true body and blood. The blessing bestowed upon us, signified by the words, is the remission of sins and eternal life. As Christ's heirs, we have the duty to remember with gratitude his generosity to us; and therefore we should preach his love and grace and by meditating upon his word be moved and preserved to love and hope in him.[20]

If this orientation was paramount in Luther's mind, we can understand his reluctance to accept the Mass as a good work, a meritorious achievement of man, an act of atonement, an offering made to God to compensate for man's sins. After all, we are powerless of our own accord to do anything meritorious before God. The Mass therefore is God's gift to us, not our gift to God. Christ made the unique atoning sacrifice once and for all on Calvary; it would be blasphemy to attempt to complement or to add anything to this sacrifice by trying to repeat or renew it. It is with this document then that Luther began an explicit attack upon the Mass as a sacrifice of atonement. For him the body and blood of Christ really present in the sacrament are a pledge or token that God forgives our sins if we receive this gift in faith.

Yet surprisingly Luther is not unwilling to use the word "sacrifice" in some connection with the Mass. Making a clear distinction between the sacrament itself, the sign of bread and wine, and Christ's presence therein, he concedes that the congregation may offer a sacrifice of prayer, praise, and thanksgiving and of themselves as well. He explains this as follows:

To be sure this sacrifice . . . we are not to present before God in our own person. But we are to lay it upon Christ and let Him present it for us. . . .

. . . We do not offer Christ as a sacrifice, but Christ offers us. And in this way it is permissible, yes, profitable, to call the Mass a sacrifice; not on its own account, but because we offer ourselves as a sacrifice along with Christ. That is, we lay ourselves on Christ by a firm faith in His testament and do not otherwise appear before God with our prayer, praise, and sacrifice except through Christ and His mediation. . . . Christ takes up our cause, presents us and our prayer and praise, and also offers Himself for us in Heaven. If the Mass were so understood and for this reason called a sacrifice, it would be well. Not that we offer the sacrament, but that by our praise, prayer, and sacrifice we move Him and give Him occasion to offer Himself for us in heaven and ourselves with Him.[21]

---

[20] *Ibid.*, pp. 86–87.   [21] *Ibid.*, p. 99.

While these words sound very orthodox to Catholic ears, Luther a little later in the same document explicitly affirms "You will never make out of a sacrament or testament of God a sacrifice or work of satisfaction; indeed satisfaction itself is more of a human than a divine law."[22]

What is to be said of Luther's use of the word "sacrifice" in relation to the Mass? A distinguished Lutheran theologian commenting on this subject has remarked that Luther uses the word "sacrifice" in different senses:

> If we are to try to obtain a general view of what Luther has said about the Eucharistic sacrifice, we must differentiate between two kinds of sacrifices. On the one hand, we are dealing with the "offering" which we, or the Church, bring, and on the other hand, with Christ's offering of himself. In regard to the former we find that Luther uses this expression in various connections. He speaks often of how we bring our need, our sin, and our suffering as a "sacrifice." Such points of view are congenial to his thinking. Nothing could be more foreign to him than that the "offering" which we bring to God should possess any kind of "merit." At this point Luther directed his most violent and unrelenting attack against the conceptions he found connected with the sacrifice of the mass.

> The ideas of sacrifice which Luther otherwise connects with the eucharist are, as we have seen, praise, prayer, and willing service. . . . As Christ carries our burden so we are to bear one another's burden. . . .

> Prayer and intercession is for Luther something essential in worship life. Prayer is an approach to Christ, for in him man meets God. Christ is the altar, says Luther, on which the one who prays is offered, and through which our prayers appear before God. It is natural, therefore, that "the offering of prayer" should belong to the celebration of the eucharist. . . . [This prayer is for Luther not so much a prayer of petition for selfish reasons but rather a prayer of praise and thanksgiving.] When the thankfulness for God's gift had found its due place in the offering of praise, then only could the offering of prayer be rightly used.

> . . . To celebrate the eucharist is to bring thanksgiving and praise to Christ and to give to Him the honor which belongs to Him. The subject of praise is especially the death of Christ. . . . A strong emphasis on Holy Communion as a commemoration of the death of Christ has often tended to eliminate the eucharistic element and has given a somber character to the celebration. This happened frequently in later Lutheran history. But Luther himself looked at this differently. The death on the cross signified that the act of sacrifice was finished; it included the victory and the completion of the work of redemption. The Lord's Supper becomes then a celebration of the finished work of redemption and of the unfathomable mercy of God in Christ.[23]

---

[22] *Ibid.*, p. 103.

[23] Gustaf Aulen, *Eucharist and Sacrifice*, tr. by Eric H. Wahlstrom (Philadelphia: Muhlenberg Press, 1958), pp. 87–89.

In short Luther favors a "sacrifice" of intercession and praise rather than of atonement or propitiation.

In the light of current reforms in the Catholic Mass, it is interesting to note the complaints against the medieval Mass that Luther then brings forward in his *Treatise on the New Testament*. Since the Mass is not a good work or service but the reception of a gift from God in faith, one cannot observe or hear Mass for another but only for himself.[24] The Mass therefore cannot be a sacrifice for the faithful departed; for it is essentially as sacrament a word and pledge of the forgiveness of our sins which must be received in faith. It is only the one sacrifice of Christ's death that is profitable to the souls of the departed. To pray for the faithful departed at Mass is encouraged; but this is not the same as offering the "sacrament" for them as a sufficient work to release them for heaven.[25]

Again, since the Mass is essentially a word of faith directed to us, it is inconceivable that the Mass should be celebrated in a language foreign to the congregation. The Mass should be in the vernacular so that the congregation can make an active response of faith. Masses where there is no sermon, where the Canon or consecration prayers are said in silence, where there are few or no Communions on the part of the faithful, perhaps no congregation present at all, Communion under only one kind — these are abominations and abuses of the worst kind in Luther's estimation.[26]

Luther's next works on the Eucharist add little to what he had already said in rejection of the Mass as sacrifice. These works: *Prelude on the Babylonian Captivity of the Church* (Sept., 1520), *the Misuse of the Mass* (late 1521), and the *Abomination of the Secret Mass* (1525) are of a more polemic tone and become part of a broader attack against the whole Roman system of sacraments and authority. More explicitly and clearly than before, Luther explains the Catholic view of the Mass-sacrifice as something we do that automatically (*ex opere operato*) exerts an influence on God. The teaching on the Mass therefore must be integrated within Luther's broader teaching on works; the Catholic view according to him turns the Christian into one who earns his own salvation from God, whereas Luther stoutly maintains that salvation from beginning to end is "a reception in faith of the forgiveness of a gracious God."[27] In summary, Luther maintained "The whole power of the mass consists in

[24] *Luther's Works*, Vol. 35, p. 94.
[25] *Ibid.*, p. 103.
[26] *Ibid.*, p. 90, 91, 102, 106–108.
[27] James F. McCue, "Luther and Roman Catholicism on the Mass as Sacrifice," *Journal of Ecumenical Studies* (Pittsburgh: Duquesne University Press, 1965), Vol. 2, No. 2, Spring, 1965, p. 222.

the words of Christ, in which he testifies that forgiveness of sins is bestowed on all those who believe that his body is given and his blood poured out for them."[28]

Luther's later writings on the Eucharist add nothing from the viewpoint of sacrifice; they do show however a development in his concept of how Christ is present in the Eucharist. This will be the subject of a later chapter.

Luther's opposition to the sacrificial character of the Eucharist was echoed by the other Reformers. Ulrich Zwingli, a Swiss Reformer from Zwingli the Mass cannot possibly be a sacrifice. Even though the

> Christ is offered when He is slain and His blood is shed; and conversely when He is slain, then is He offered. But Christ was slain only once, and His Blood was shed only once. Therefore He was offered only once.[29]

Since there is no actual slaying of Christ in the Mass, therefore for Zwingli the Mass cannot possibly be a sacrifice. Even though the Catholic defenders took Zwingli to task for restricting sacrifice to a destruction of life and insisted that the Mass-sacrifice is commemorative, mystical, and sacramental, yet the Swiss Reformer refused to change his mind.

Like the above Reformers, John Calvin, a Frenchman who settled at Geneva, Switzerland, was adamant in his rejection of the Mass-sacrifice. Complaining of the horrible "abomination" which Satan spread far and wide, Calvin condemns as a "most pestilential error" the belief "that the Mass was a sacrifice and oblation for obtaining the remission of sins . . . a work by which the priest who offers Christ and the others who in the oblation receive him, gain merit with God."[30] According to a sympathetic interpreter of Calvin's eucharistic doctrine, it is asserted that:

> In his *Short Treatise on the Lord's Supper*, Calvin expressed himself more categorically against the idea of sacrifice; but he was criticizing the Mass as "a sacrifice for acquiring the remission of sins," in the sense of a repetition of the Cross. He accepted the idea of a representation of the sacrifice, as found in the Fathers, but rejected, as Judaic, a form of celebration which recalled only the Old Covenant. We do not offer or sacrifice, but "we take and eat that which has been offered and sacrificed." He even rejected the idea of the "application of the unique sacrifice" which he was prepared to admit in his Commentary on 1 Cor 11:24. But the center of his attack was the Mass without communion, which was in danger of appearing to be a repetition of the unique

---

[28] *Luther's Works*, Vol. 36, p. 43.

[29] *De Canone missae*, quoted in Francis Clark, S.J., *Eucharistic Sacrifice and the Reformation* (Westminster, Md.: The Newman Press, 1960), p. 395.

[30] John Calvin, *Institutes of the Christian Religion*, tr. Henry Beveridge (London: Clarke & Co. Ltd., 1957 reprint), IV, 18, p. 607.

sacrifice of the Cross and not a participation in the unique sacrifice and an application of the sacrifice of redemption.[31]

In keeping with his eucharistic views, Calvin's liturgy or Sunday service added to the first part of the Mass a long series of petitionary prayers not unlike the ancient prayers of the faithful, concluding with a lengthy prayer of some sixty lines. But the Offertory and the Canon were entirely omitted. Communion was distributed, followed by a thanksgiving prayer for the communion received.[32]

The influence of the continental Reformation was felt in England, particularly after the death of Henry VIII (1547), which gave a free hand to Thomas Cranmer, archbishop of Canterbury. One of Cranmer's early statements on the nature of Christ's sacrifice in the Mass reads as follows:

> The oblation and sacrifice of Christ in the Mass is so-called not because Christ indeed is there offered in sacrifice by the priest and the people (for that was done but once by Himself upon the Cross) but it is so-called, because it is a memory and representation of that very true sacrifice and immolation which before was made upon the Cross.[33]

Cranmer's mind on the Eucharist is further clarified in his *Defense of the True and Catholic Doctrine of the Sacrament* (1550):

> Popish Masses are to be clearly taken away out of Christian churches, and the true use of the Lord's Supper is to be restored again, wherein godly people assembled together may receive the Sacrament every man for himself, to declare that he remembereth what benefit he hath received by the death of Christ, and to testify that he is a member of Christ's Body, fed with His flesh and drinking His Blood spiritually.[34]

From this statement, it is clear that the Mass for Cranmer is an occasion for remembering what the death of Christ has accomplished for us, for testifying that we are members of Christ's body, and partaking of Communion. What Cranmer means by the latter, he explains a little further on in the same document:

> His holy Supper was ordained for this purpose, that every man eating and drinking thereof should remember that Christ died for him, and so should exercise his faith, and comfort himself by the remembrance of Christ's benefits; and so give unto Christ most hearty thanks and give himself also clearly unto Him.[35]

In other words for him "to eat the Body and drink the Blood of Christ"

---

[31] Max Thurian, *The Eucharistic Memorial*, Part II, p. 81, footnote 3.
[32] Cf. Palmer, *Sacraments and Worship*, p. 300.
[33] Gregory Dix, *The Shape of the Liturgy* (London: Dacre Press), p. 641.
[34] *Defense*, V, 9; quoted in Dix, op. cit., p. 649.
[35] *Defense*, V, 13; quoted in Dix, op. cit., p. 650.

means "to remember the Passion with confidence in the merits of Christ."[36] The only sacrifice that occurs in the celebration of the Eucharist is a purely subjective one on the part of the congregation, as the following passage indicates:

> In this eating, drinking, and using of the Lord's Supper, we make not of Christ a new sacrifice propitiatory for remission of sin. But the humble confession of all penitent hearts, their knowledging of Christ's benefits, their thanksgiving for the same, their faith and consolation in Christ, their humble submission and obedience to God's will and commandments, is a sacrifice of laud and praise, accepted and allowed of God no less than the sacrifice of the priest.[37]

Gregory Dix, himself an Anglican, concludes on the basis of this statement:

> It would appear, therefore, that the sacrifice and oblation in the Eucharist consists for Cranmer in the emotions and ideas of those present at the Eucharist, and not in anything appertaining to the rite itself.[38]

Cranmer was responsible for the original liturgical changes made in England after the Reformation had taken hold. His two prayer books (1549 and 1552) constitute the basis of the Anglican liturgy even today. In this rite, there is no Offertory of bread and wine at all; this was deliberately set aside. Any idea of "consecrating" bread and wine in the sense of sacrificing or changing them into Christ's body and blood has been watered down to that of "setting apart to a holy use," even though the words of institution are still repeated. There remains however the communion service, which Cranmer insisted was only a token act, taken in memory of Christ's death.[39] As Dix remarks, "The real Eucharistic action for Cranmer . . . is something purely mental and psychological — 'This is the eating of Christ's Flesh and drinking of His Blood, the feeling whereof is to every man the feeling how he eateth and drinketh Christ' which he insists means 'believing that Christ died for me.' "[40]

The purpose of Reformation testimony on the eucharistic sacrifice has been to show the general rejection on the part of the Reformers of any true notion of sacrifice in the Mass and their reasons for this attitude. Any ecumenical understanding today will have to begin with such clearly drawn positions as those undertaken at the time of the Reformation itself. The seemingly harsh language and belligerent accusations that appear in so many of the Reformation writings regrettably testify to the intense

---

[36] Dix, op. cit., p. 656.
[37] Cranmer, Defense, V, 13; quoted in Dix, op. cit., pp. 654–655.
[38] Dix, op. cit., p. 655.
[39] Dix, op. cit., p. 671.
[40] Ibid.

passions that were aroused on both sides of the theological controversy and to the acrid spirit of polemics into which the Reformation degenerated. As Gregory Dix laconically remarks "That was in the manner of the times."[41]

D. *The Council of Trent, the Post-Reformation Council (1545–1563)*

Twenty-eight years after Luther initiated the reform movement, the Church marshaled her own forces of reform and renewal by summoning the Council of Trent. Unhappily by the time the council convened in 1545, the theological battlelines were deeply entrenched; and in an atmosphere of charge and countercharge, it is not surprising that the council adopted an essentially defensive posture, aimed at restating and justifying the traditional doctrines of the Church that had come under fire by the Reformers. In its decree on the holy sacrifice of the Eucharist (1562), the very first chapter seeks to justify the Mass alongside the uniqueness and permanent efficacy of the cross-sacrifice:

> Therefore, our Lord and God, although He was about to offer Himself but once by way of death to the Father on the altar of the Cross, there to accomplish an eternal redemption, yet — since His priesthood was not to be brought to an end with His death — at the Last Supper, on the night He was betrayed, declaring that He had been ordained a priest according to the order of Melchizedek, offered to God the Father, under the appearances of bread and wine, His own body and blood, and under these same symbols He gave them to be consumed by His Apostles, whom He then ordained as priests of the New Covenant. Furthermore, by the words: "Do this in commemoration of Me, etc.," as the Catholic Church has always understood and taught, He commanded them and their successors in the priesthood to offer. This He did, that He might leave to His beloved spouse, the Church, a visible sacrifice, such as the nature of man demands, that by it the sacrifice in blood to be accomplished but once on the altar of the Cross might be represented, that the memory thereof might remain to the end of the world, and its salutary effects might be applied to the remission of such sins as we daily commit.
>
> For, after He had celebrated the ancient Passover, which the children of Israel were accustomed to immolate in memory of their passage out of Egypt, He instituted a new Passover, His very self, to be immolated under visible signs by the Church through the ministry of priests, in memory of His passage from this world to the Father, when, through the shedding of His blood, He redeemed us, and rescued us from the power of darkness and transferred us into His Kingdom (Col. 1:13).[42]

Herein the council emphasized on the one hand the continuing priest-

---

[41] *Ibid.*, p. 647.

[42] Council of Trent, *Decree on the Holy Sacrifice of the Mass*, Chap. 1; quoted in Palmer, *Sacraments and Worship*, p. 305.

hood of Christ and on the other the way in which this priesthood is enacted in the Mass. The Eucharist is seen as the representation, the memorial, and the application of the benefits of the cross-sacrifice to the remission of sin. Finally the council likens the Mass to the Passover meal which included the sacrificial lamb.

Chapter 2 of the conciliar decree proceeds from the unity of the Mass with the cross-sacrifice to deduce the propitiatory value of the eucharistic sacrifice. In so doing, the council explicitly affirms the unity of the cross and the Mass-sacrifice in terms of identity of priest and victim, the form of the sacrifice alone being distinct:

> Moreover, in this divine sacrifice which is enacted in the Mass, one and the same Christ is contained and immolated in a bloodless manner who but once offered Himself in blood on the altar of the Cross (Heb. 9:27). For this reason, this Holy Synod teaches that this sacrifice is truly propitiatory, and that through it, if we come to God with a true heart and right faith, with fear and reverence, in contrition and penitence, we obtain mercy and find grace to help us in time of need (Heb. 4:16). For appeased, surely, by the offering of this sacrifice, the Lord grants grace and the gift of repentance, and forgives sin, yes, even the greatest of crimes. For the victim is one and the same; and He who now offers through the ministry of priests is the same as He who once offered Himself on the Cross, the manner of offering alone being different. In fact, the fruits of that oblation — the one in blood, we mean — are received most abundantly through this which is bloodless, with the result that this latter is far from detracting in any way from the former. Therefore, in conformity with Apostolic tradition, this sacrifice is properly offered not only for the sins, penalties, satisfactions, and other needs of the faithful who are living but also for the departed in Christ who are not yet fully cleansed.[43]

Therefore, since the Mass is not a new sacrifice but rather the same sacrifice as that of Calvary offered in a new form, then like Calvary, it also is efficacious for the remission of sin, by applying the fruits of the cross-sacrifice due to the eucharistic intercession of Christ and the Church (propitiation). If this is true, then this sacrifice may be offered not only for the individual who requests it, but for others both living and dead, a fact which the Reformers strenuously denied.

In this same twenty-second session (cf. *Denzinger*, 948–951), the council summarized this teaching in the form of canons or dogmatic syntheses of conciliar teaching. The negative phrasing of these statutes and the flinging of anathemas at the dissidents reflect the doctrinal tensions of the times. The principal canons that concern us are as follows:

---

[43] Trent, *Decree on the Mass*, Chap. 2; quoted in Palmer, *op. cit.*, pp. 306–307.

1. If anyone says that in the Mass a true and proper sacrifice is not offered to God or that the sacrificial offering consists merely in the fact that Christ is given to us to eat: let him be anathema.
2. If anyone says that by the words "Do this in remembrance of Me" (Lk 22:19; 1 Cor 11:24) Christ did not make the Apostles priests, or that He did not decree that they and other priests should offer His body and His blood: let him be anathema.
3. If anyone says that the sacrifice of the Mass is merely an offering of praise and thanksgiving or that it is a simple memorial of the sacrifice offered on the cross, and not propitiatory, or that it benefits only those who communicate; and that it should not be offered for the living and the dead, for sins, punishments, satisfaction, and other necessities: let him be anathema.
4. If anyone says that the sacrifice of the Mass constitutes a blasphemy to the sacred sacrifice that Christ offered on the cross, or that the Mass detracts from that sacrifice: let him be anathema.[44]

E. The Unity of Sacrifice

On the basis of Trent's formulation of eucharistic doctrine, it may be possible to show the interrelationship of what might be called three moments of sacrifice: the sacrifice of the Last Supper, that of the cross, and that of the Mass today. The sacrifice of the cross may be called an absolute or natural sacrifice since it is neither the commemoration of a past sacrifice nor the prefigurement of a future sacrifice. It is complete in itself, the freely willed death of Christ. It is Christ who truly offers his life for the redemption of man; his death is not a murder, nor is his life taken from him against his will. "I lay down my life that I may take it up again. No one takes it from me, but I lay it down of myself. I have the power to lay it down, and I have the power to take it up again" (Jn 10:17–18). Christ is the priest or offerer of the gift of the cross, yet he is also that gift itself. It is he who is offered in the supreme sacrifice of his human death. Thus Christ is both priest and victim, offerer and gift of the cross-sacrifice. The form of the gift is a most bloody death, the heroic surrender to the last drop of his lifeblood.

Christ's sacrifice, however, was not concluded with his death. What Jesus accepted was the whole process of passing through death to a risen life of new freedom. He wills not only to "lay down" his life, but also "to take it up again" in resurrection. His humanity must enter into a new order of existence with the Father, a life of freedom from suffering and death, as well as freedom from the constraints of time and space. In this risen state, Christ's sacrifice may be said to endure, insofar as he still acts freely in acceptance of his past death and his present risen state.

In contrast to the natural or absolute sacrifice of Christ, his historical

---

[44] The Church Teaches (St. Louis: B. Herder, 1956), 756–759, p. 295.

death and resurrection-ascension, we may speak of the Last Supper, the first eucharistic sacrifice, as a *relative* sacrifice, a kind of preview of the cross-and-resurrection. The Last Supper is related to Calvary insofar as the former sacrifice borrows its inner content, its inner reality, from the sacrifice of Good Friday-Easter. Already at the Last Supper, Christ pledges himself as the victim of that sacrifice — pledges his humanity to immolation and resurrection. His interior will-act is already sacrificial. He expresses his sacrificial intent outwardly, by word and gesture, over bread and wine. In short, he offers himself as Victim under sacramental forms — he offers a *sacrament-sacrifice*. In this state in which he is at that first Mass of the Last Supper, Christ is able to put himself under the sacramental forms so that his Church will always have the rich content of this gift whenever it renews the sacramental forms in the proper context (by a duly authorized priest with the intention of doing what Christ did at the Last Supper). Christ, who wished his Church always to have a worshipful gift of homage and praise to render to the Father along with him, left to his Church the gift of his sacrifice. The content of this gift is his very own self as offered for the redemption of man; the "wrappings" of the gift are the forms of bread and wine. Whenever the Apostles or their successors in the Church reproduce the gestures, the words, and the signs of Christ at the Last Supper, they reproduce or make present the same interior sacrificial will of Christ, as well as his immolated and risen flesh. This we call sacrament-sacrifice.

The "third" moment of sacrifice is the Eucharist or the Mass today. It is essentially identical both with the sacrifice of the Last Supper and that of the cross-resurrection. The same Priest celebrates, only now Christ offers through an agent, a sacramentally ordained priest at the altar (here the sacramental nature of the Mass-sacrifice is further extended). The priest lends his lips to Christ as he pronounces the sacred words of the offering: "This is my body; this is my covenant-blood." The gift again is Christ, risen from death. The same sacrificial will of Christ prevails today in the Eucharist as at the Last Supper and in his death-resurrection. Christ the head is still offering himself, still accepting the death he died on earth and his present state of risen freedom — all part of his sacrifice; but now he offers, not in earthly, bloody form, nor by a new resurrection, but in the sacramental forms used at the Last Supper — bread and wine.[45]

There is however a further difference between the sacrifice of the Supper and of the cross on the one hand, and that of the Mass today. In the former cases Christ was offering directly in his own Person; today

---

[45] Cf. pp. 49–50 above, for discussion of "sacramental world"; also, A. Vonier, *A Key to the Doctrine of the Eucharist* (Westminster: Newman, 1946), pp. 35–44.

he offers through the person of his priest and also in union with his followers, his Church. For the eucharistic sacrifice is truly the celebration of the whole Church, of Christ the risen head, of the priest in holy orders, and of the priestly people of God, the faithful, qualified by baptismal seal to share in the privilege of offering the family gift and eating the family meal.

F. Eucharistic Sacrifice in Theological Speculation

The study of the scriptural data in the preceding chapter focused on the central actions of Christ at the first Eucharist; that is, the offering of himself under the double species of bread and wine and sharing his body and blood with the Apostles in the festive, sacrificial meal. Over the centuries, the reflection of the Church has established the double Consecration in the Mass as the precise moment when the sacrificial action of the offering occurs. In the centuries since the Council of Trent, one of the primary questions that theologians have tried to answer is: How *exactly* does the double consecration, that over the bread and over the wine, signify and embody the sacrifice of Christ? In other words, what makes the Consecration a sacrificial action?

First, it should be noted that the Church has not settled this problem; it remains open to theological study. While the Church insists that the Eucharist is indeed the sacrifice of Christ made present again under sacramental signs, just *how* the sacrifice is *symbolized* there is still open to debate.

Generally speaking, theological theories about the sacrifice symbolized in the double consecration take the form of either of two patterns, depending upon the notion one has of the essential meaning of sacrifice itself. For those who feel that sacrifice consists essentially in some kind of destruction or change in the gift, their explanation of the sacrificial character of the twofold Consecration demands some kind of real destruction or change in the sacrificial gift. The earliest theorists of this school reacted to the Reformation denial of true sacrifice in the Mass. While Suarez asserted that the sacrifice consists in the destruction of the substances of the bread and wine through transubstantiation and the consequent production of the body and blood of Christ, other theologians, De Lugo and Franzelin among them, too realistically regarded the body and blood of Christ as present in a kind of deathlike condition under the appearances of food and drink. Others, e.g., Bellarmine and Soto, regarded the communion as signifying destruction and therefore sacrifice. Scheeben saw the necessary sacrificial change in the conversion of the substances of bread and wine into Christ's body and blood. But the common difficulty of most of these theories of destruction or change is that there can be no real change in the body and blood of Christ as such; his risen glorified body is no longer subject to suffering and death or to any change at all. If there is a change brought about by the Eucharist, it must occur only in the bread and wine or their species.

A variation of the destruction theory capitalizes on the idea that the words of the first Consecration (that over the bread) refer only to the body of Christ, while the second consecration refers only to the blood. Therefore on the level of sacramental signification, there is a representation here of a real change in Christ which was previously effected (opinion of Vasquez). Or again, the theologian Lessius maintains that the consecration words in themselves intend a real separation of Christ's body and blood; but accidentally, because Christ's glorified body can no longer suffer, this separation is no longer effected in the order of reality. Finally, according to Billot, the sacramental separation of body and blood is enough to signify Christ's inward act of offering (theory of sacramental immolation). A difficulty, especially with the first two opinions, however, might be that since a sacrament ought to signify what it causes here and now, the above theories seem to have the sacraments signify something that is no longer actually brought about here and now.

A second line of thought proceeds from the premise that sacrifice does not consist essentially in destruction but rather in offering. For these theologians, Christ personally (either actually or virtually) offers himself in the Mass. Thalhofer, asserting that Christ continues to offer himself to the Father in heaven as a true sacrifice, believes this sacrifice is made present in the Mass. The heavenly sacrifice enters time and space.

The French theologian De la Taille holds for both oblation (offering) and immolation (sacrificial slaying). According to his view the offering takes place at the Last Supper and in the Mass today, but the immolation takes place only at the cross. This would seem to make the Last Supper and the cross-sacrifice fuse together into one sacrifice only, thus reducing the completeness of the Calvary-sacrifice. The Mass today then would be not the renewal of the cross-sacrifice but only that of the Last Supper.

Dom Odo Casel and the school of Maria Laach, while perhaps holding for a too literal, objective re-presenting of Christ's historical death and resurrection in the Eucharist (mystery-presence theory), nevertheless have served to stimulate eucharistic theology and liturgical study with a fresh new vigor. The Eucharist seems to be not a mere lifeless figure or representation of Christ's historical deeds of salvation, but rather an actual making-present of Christ, who in some way at least by his inner act of oblation brings his sacrifice along with him.

Canon Masure, a contemporary French theologian, would seem to combine Casel's theory with something of the earlier theories like that of Suarez. He sees an immolation in the conversion of the substances of bread and wine into Christ's body and blood. The loss of their true substantiality constitutes a kind of immolation for the bread and wine, since only their species or outer forms remain. Furthermore, the glorified Christ, he maintains, brings with him in the Eucharist all the previous states of his life on earth, including the passion-death phase as well as the present glorious phase of his sacrifice.

Whatever may be said for all these varied theories, perhaps the simplest and freshest approach is to return to the Gospels as interpreted in the light of their Old Testament context. This would see the presence of sacrifice as a kind of prophecy-in-action as explained in Chapter VIII.[46] It would also certainly include the presence of the sacrificial will of Christ, who at the Last Supper pledged himself as Suffering Servant to lay down his life as a ransom for many. Under the figure of the Old Testament victim, whose sacrificial state was sometimes expressed in terms of its flesh and its blood (cf. Gn 9:4; Lv 17:11, 14), Christ enshrines and makes present already at the first Eucharist, the sacrament-sacrifice that he will continue to offer in union with his Church-body until the end of time. The Eucharist, too, is the *covenant*-sacrifice of the new people of God inaugurated, not in animal blood as that of Sinai (cf. Ex 24:5, 8), but in the sacrificial blood of the Suffering Servant himself.

The Eucharist is able to renew this covenant-sacrifice of Christ in the Church because Christ has risen and remains as head of his Church in his glorified state. In fact, the Church-body of Christ, according to interpreters of Pauline theology, is united to the risen body of the Savior. Thus the Eucharist is not merely the action of Christ, but rather the action of the whole Christ, the head and his members acting together. We offer in and through and with him. If our offering is to be sincere, it must be made in the spirit of that same genuine commitment or openness to the Father that Christ demonstrated at the Last Supper and on the cross. For we cannot conceive of his inner attitude being anything other than a complete and total acceptance, indeed a positive eagerness to fulfill his Father's will. Christ does this freely, acting with a fully human capacity of surrender.

But even in Christ this act of selfless giving was possible only because of the grace that descended upon his human nature through its union with divinity. So in our case our decisiveness in commitment to Christ, or willingness to do utterly in life whatever he asks — this can be done on our part only with the graces that flow to us as members of the body

---

[46] Cf. above, p. 164 f.

of a glorious risen head. Our sharing in the eucharistic sacrifice then will be more than singing and praying together as a show of unity. Such external acts will have to be interiorized.

Underlying the external expressions of community will have to be a truly Christian sense of common love in Christ, that spirit of Christ's willingness to lay down his life for his brethren. Our common meal of thanksgiving will make us realize how our individual lives are tied in with the lives of those around us; what we do even in our inmost self must redound to the benefit of our fellowmen. Therefore the restraint of sinful impulse, of selfish reflection, of prideful assertion, will lead us more deeply into the sacrificial intent of Christ, dynamically present in the Eucharist.

G. *Ecumenical Observations*

The Reformers' reluctance to accept the Eucharist as sacrifice in the Catholic sense is being tempered somewhat by their latter-day followers. European Lutheranism has displayed a much greater liturgical momentum than its American counterpart. Although the Augsburg Confession, a primary source of Lutheran faith, stated: "We readily accept that the Mass be understood as a permanent sacrifice," the sacrificial nature of the Eucharist nevertheless remains a delicate point for Lutheran theology. On the other hand the Lutheran insistence on the real presence of Christ in an objective sense puts them closer to the Catholic position on this point than to most of their Protestant colleagues.

In Calvinism, interest in sacrifice is reviving. One text goes so far as to note: "His [Christ's] sacrifice is now a living sacrifice; it is himself as alive from the dead that he offers to the Father on our behalf; and in the sacrament he unites us with himself in the action of his self-presentation."[47] Another representative of the Calvinist tradition, frequently quoted in previous chapters, has devoted an entire study to the eucharistic sacrifice: Max Thurian's *The Eucharistic Memorial*. For example he maintains:

> Of itself the Church can neither offer nor present anything to God except its misery, but in Christ it can offer a true sacrifice of thanksgiving and intercession, because it can present to the Father the sacrifice of the Cross by being united to the heavenly intercession of the Son; it presents the Body of Christ and presents itself as the Body of Christ.[48]

Perhaps under the influence of Odo Casel, he sees a presence of Christ's historical act of redemption in the Mass:

---

[47] Wotherspoon-Kirkpatrick, *A Manual of Church Doctrine According to the Church of Scotland*, quoted in Tavard, "The Eucharist in Protestantism," *Worship*, XXXV:3, February, 1961, p. 187.

[48] Max Thurian, *The Eucharistic Memorial*, Part 2, p. 107.

A balanced Christian theology supports the view that in Christ the historical act of redemption is made present in faith and in the sacrament. When the Church is united through the Eucharist to the heavenly intercession of Christ, it is united to Him as crucified, and thus makes present the historical act of redemption to apply it to man now, that it may be received in faith and by faith.[49]

Thurian will not accept the expiatory nature of the Mass in the sense of a sacrifice that here and now offers compensation for sins already atoned for on the cross. In this, he is at one with the teaching of Trent (Denz. 950). But he is willing to accept the word "propitiatory" if it means a presentation or intercession. Clearly he asserts: "The Eucharist then, which is a sacramental presence of the sacrifice of the Cross and a liturgical presentation of that sacrifice to the Father, is not an expiatory sacrifice. . . ."[50] The Mass is rather the application of the fruits of the one expiatory sacrifice of the cross.

Anglican scholarship, at least in some quarters, seeks to resolve the problem of the Eucharist as sacrifice in terms of the mystical body doctrine. If the Evangelicals assert that we are offered and Catholics insist that Christ is offered, this need not involve any contradiction since the doctrine of the Church as the total Christ includes both Christ and Christians in the offering. Perhaps along these lines modern Anglicanism may feel able to accept a more Catholic doctrine on sacrificial worship.

Finally, the Faith and Order Conference of the World Council of Churches, meeting in Montreal in July, 1963, devoted some study in its Committee on Worship to the problem of sacrificial worship. Catholic observers at the conference came away heartened at the apparent willingness of many eminent Protestant theologians to accept the need for sacrifice (however this is understood) in the worship of the Church. While the committee Report on Worship necessarily remains vague on some points and does not descend to particular theological explication, yet its general tenor is hearteningly ecumenical:

The holy Supper which God has bestowed upon His Church is a Sacrament of the presence of the crucified and glorified Christ. This presence will endure until His second coming. The sacred meal, furthermore, is a means for making operative in the Church the Cross-sacrifice which we proclaim. In the holy Supper, the members of Christ's body are strengthened in unity with their Head and Savior who offered Himself on the cross. Through Him, with Him, and in Him, our high priest and mediator, we offer to the Father in the power of the Holy Spirit our praise and our contrite hearts as a living and holy sacrifice. This sacrifice must express itself in our daily life. United in this way with our Lord

---

[49] Ibid., p. 102.   [50] Ibid., p. 79; emphasis added.

and with the Church triumphant and in concert with the universal Church over the whole earth, we will continue to participate over and over in the Covenant which is sealed by the blood of Christ.[51]

---

[51] *Report on Worship*, Fourth World Conference on Faith and Order, Montreal, July 12–26, 1963, *passim*, esp. pp. 16–22; cited in Augustine Cardinal Bea, "Eucharistie und die Einheit der Christen," *Stimmen der Zeit*, Vol. 176, 12, September, 1965, p. 404 f. For interesting observations on ecumenical understanding in the realm of worship, cf. Cyril C. Richardson, "Word and Sacrament in Protestant Worship," *Ecumenical Dialogue at Harvard* (Cambridge, Mass.: Belknap Press of Harvard, 1964), pp. 168–171.

CHAPTER X

The Eucharistic Meal

I. MEALS IN SALVATION-HISTORY

Hospitality and friendliness are much appreciated virtues in a rather impersonalist and fast-moving age. Because businessmen, factory workers, clerks, and students so often have to take a quick lunch during the noon hour, the social and human values associated with a meal in common are likely to be neglected. On the other hand, perhaps this is the very reason why a leisurely meal enjoyed with one's family on a Sunday or in the evening with special friends takes on an added note of relaxation, joy, and conviviality. When a friend comes to your house, you offer him a drink or a snack, or perhaps you invite him to join in the family meal. Dining together has always been understood as a way of cementing a human relationship.

Moreover it seems very natural to conclude all the most significant celebrations of human life with a banquet or a repast of some kind. Whether it is the simple birthday anniversary, or the more elaborate wedding banquet and reception, or the occasional social and seasonal

events of the year, or the testimonial dinner to mark a significant milestone of achievement in one's life, all of these have a common meaning
of deep value for interpersonal relations; taking food and drink together
is a sign of sharing life together. Because we partake of the same nourishment that sustains our life, we are drawn together by that which we
become for in a true sense we are what we eat.

If taking a meal together has always been a sign of friendship and
hospitality, it is not surprising that, in his primitive religious consciousness, man should seize upon the experience of a meal to express his
desire for union with the deity. As amply explained above (pp. 172–173),
primitive man acknowledged at every meal his dependence upon the
Superior Being who provided the sustenance of his life from the resources
of the material world around him. Thus the meal manifests man's kinship
with nature as well as with the Creator. In this view, every meal is
sacred, for man is in effect sharing in a life-source provided him by God.

As expected, the ancient Israelites retained this primitive devotion
to the meal as a religious symbol. In the cycle of patriarchal stories, we
read that Abraham entertained the three mysterious strangers (cf. Gn
18:1–8), sometimes taken to symbolize the Blessed Trinity.[1] The meal
story highlights Abraham's intimacy with God as well as his prized virtue
of hospitality. It is by a meal that a covenant or alliance is sealed, as
between Isaac and Abimelech (cf Gn 26:26–31), between Jacob and
his father-in-law Laban (cf. Gn 31:53 f.), between God and his anointed
King Saul (cf 1 Sm 9:22), between God and his priests (cf. Lv 24:6–9),
and between God and the whole people of Israel (cf. Ex 24:11; Dt
27:7). In this connection the yearly Passover feast would recall Yahweh's
wondrous deeds in the exodus (cf. Ex 12:13); and eating the firstfruits
was considered a reminder of the continual providence of God who
watched over his own (cf. Dt 26).

The Book of Deuteronomy emphasizes the communal or social aspect
of the meal with God as a joyous festival in his presence (cf. Dt
12:4–7, 11 f., 18; 14:22 f.; 15:20; 16:10–17). The only sacred meal is
that which reunites all the people in the place chosen by God for his
presence; the meal becomes the occasion for thanking God for all his gifts.

In the New Testament, the meal acquires its full significance when
Christ is present there. Christ frequently appears at meals; he is invited
to the house of Lazarus (cf. Lk 10:38–42) and to the wedding feast of
Cana (cf. Jn 2:1–11). Frequently his attendance at a meal symbolizes
the entire redemptive work he has come to accomplish. The meal is a
time of forgiveness, of reconciliation (cf. the repentant woman at Simon's

---

[1] Cf. In Russian iconography, Andrei Rublev (early fifteenth century); also the
sixth-century mosaic in San Vitale at Ravenna.

house [Lk 7:36–50]; the meals taken with the despised tax collectors Levi [Mt 9:10] and Zachaeus [Lk 19:2–10]). The meals Christ attends often echo the characteristics of the messianic age: joy (cf. Mt 9:15), pardon (cf. Lk 7:47), salvation (cf. Lk 19:9), the superabundance of Jesus' own meal when he multiplied the loaves in the desert (cf. Mt 14:15–21). The meals and works of Christ not only recapture the joy of Paradise and renew the miracles of the exodus (cf. Jn 6:31 f.; Ex 16:18) but also serve to announce another banquet, the Eucharist, and beyond it the eschatological feast itself.

Pending his return, Jesus inaugurates the meal of the New Covenant sealed in his own blood. In place of the manna he gives his flesh as nourishment, the true living bread that offers life to the world. The Eucharist would continue those meals which Jesus habitually took in the company of his disciples. On the day of his resurrection, it is in the course of a meal that the risen Savior allows himself to be recognized by his followers (cf. Lk 24:30, Jn 21:13). The Jerusalem community relived and renewed those precious meals with the risen Christ at the breaking of the bread, an occasion of joy and brotherhood (cf. Acts 1:4; 2:42, 46).

Paul proclaims the primary prerequisite for sharing in the Eucharist — charity toward the brethren (cf. 1 Cor 11:17–33). It is the meal that unites one with Christ and with his fellow Christians (1 Cor 10:17). Finally, it is the meal that announces the Lord's death "until he comes"; that is, it proclaims that the Savior is to come again for the heavenly feast, the eschatological banquet.

This banquet of the future, associated with the coming of the Messiah, was expressed under various images. It was to be the joyful banquet provided by Wisdom (cf. Prv 9:1 f.); it is the banquet to be provided by Yahweh at the end of time for all peoples (cf. Is 25:6; 65:13), in which all who are hungry will participate. It is the meal which Jesus promises to the poor in spirit (anawim) and to those who hunger and thirst for justice (cf. Mt 5:3, 6). It will be realized or will take place only at the Parousia, the final coming of Christ. All those who have responded in faith to the invitation of the king shall take their place at the feast with Abraham, Isaac, and Jacob in the kingdom of God (cf. Mt 8:11), provided they wear the nuptial garment (cf. Mt 22:11–14). It is the meal which the Master himself serves his faithful, vigilant servants (cf. Lk 12:37). It is finally the assembly of all the redeemed; yet each guest enjoys the personal attention of the Host: "Behold I stand at the door and knock. If any man listens to my voice and opens the door to me, I will come in to him and will sup with him, and he with me" (Ap 3:20).

II. THE FATHERS INTERPRET THE
EUCHARISTIC MEAL

If there is any doubt that the Fathers read and interpreted the ceremony of the Eucharist in the light of Salvation-History, one may reassure himself by reading the great fourth- and fifth-century instructions on the Eucharist which the Fathers delivered during Easter week to the newly baptized Christians. To interpret the sign of the Eucharist, the Fathers constantly had recourse to God's own system of pointers, by which all through the history of salvation God prepared the way for the great meal of his Church, which in turn would foreshadow, anticipate, and promise the eternal meal of heaven.

Even before the days of the great sacramental catecheses, the Church was well aware of how eucharistic-centered her life really was. In the *Didache* or *Teaching of the Twelve Apostles*, a second-century Syrian compilation of material originally dating from the end of the first century, the Eucharistic Prayer over the bread clearly interprets the Eucharist as a symbol of the unity of the Church. The prayer is as follows: "As this piece of bread was scattered over the hills and when gathered together has become one, so may your Church be gathered from the ends of the earth into your kingdom."[2]

At about the same time, St. Ignatius of Antioch (died about A.D. 107) writes to the Christians of Philadelphia in Asia Minor: "Be resolved to celebrate one Eucharist only; for there is only one flesh of our Lord Jesus Christ and only one chalice for unification with his blood, only one altar, as there is only one bishop with the presbyters and the deacons" (Philad. 4). Again as in the *Didache*, the Eucharist is the symbol of unity, unity with Christ and visible unity with the Church under the local bishop. In another epistle, the same martyr-bishop reiterates his teaching on the Eucharist as focal point of ecclesial unity:

> Let that be considered a valid Eucharist which is celebrated by the bishop or by him to whom he has given authority. Where the bishop appears, there let the gathering (of the faithful) be, just as where Christ Jesus is there is the Catholic Church.[3]

The early third-century writer Tertullian notes that the reception of the body of the Lord in the Eucharist is both "participation in his sacrifice and the execution of one's duty."[4]

. Another writer of the same period, Irenaeus of Lyons (c. 140–c. 202),

---

[2] *Didache*, Chap. 9, verse 4; in *Florilegium Patristicum*, fascicle 7, edited by J. Quasten (Bonn: Peter Hanstein, 1935), pp. 10–11.

[3] Ep. to Smyrnians, 8; R.J., 65.

[4] On Prayer, Ch. 19; R.J., 301.

emphasizes the ultimate effect of the Eucharist on our bodies by implanting in us the seed of resurrection:

> Therefore when the chalice has been mixed and the bread has been made, receive the word of God and become the Eucharist of the blood and the body of Christ, from which the substance of our flesh is increased and supported. How do they [the heretics] deny that the flesh is capable of the gift of God which is life eternal, which is nourished by the blood and the body of Christ and is his very member? . . . So also our bodies nourished by them [the body and blood of Christ] and placed in the earth . . . shall rise in their own time when the Word of God grants them resurrection unto the glory of God the Father.[5]

A similar evaluation of the Eucharist as communicating eternal life appears in the catecheses of the Fathers, especially when the Eucharist is compared with the manna, the food of the Israelites during the Exodus. We may cite St. Ambrose as typical of this train of thought:

> The manna was a great marvel, the manna that God rained down on the Fathers. . . . But this nourishment that you receive, the Bread descended from heaven, communicates to you the substance of eternal life. It is the Body of Christ. As the light is greater than the shadow, the truth than the figure, so the Body of the Creator is greater than the manna from heaven (On the Mysteries, 46).[6]

In another of his works St. Ambrose likened the Eucharist to the feast of Wisdom in the Old Testament (cf Prv 9), which was a foreshadowing of the universal meal in which the Messiah would gather all the redeemed:

> You wish to eat, you wish to drink. Come to the feast of Wisdom which invites all men by a great proclamation, saying: "Come, eat my bread and drink my wine that I have mingled." Do not fear that in the Feast of the Church you will lack either pleasant perfumes, or agreeable food, or varied drink. . . . There you will eat the bread that strengthens the heart of man, you will drink the wine so that you may grow to the full stature of Christ (Of Cain and Abel, I, 5).[7]

Holy Communion, then, is both a communal and a personal event; it generates a mighty strengthening and transforming power to make us more Christlike.

Another line of thought developed by the Fathers is to link the Eucharist with the Jewish Passover meal. This enables them to conclude by implication that the Eucharist, as the new Passover, is both a Covenant-meal and also the sacrament of the Passover Lamb that puts

---

[5] Against the Heretics, 5:2, 3; R.J., 249.
[6] Cited in Danielou, The Bible and the Liturgy (Notre Dame, Ind.: The University of Notre Dame Press, 1956), pp. 148–149.
[7] Ibid., p. 158.

us in contact with the passion of Christ. St. Cyril of Alexandria, who developed the eucharistic symbolism of the Paschal meal most fully, teaches:

> The communion in the holy body and the drinking of the saving blood contains the confession of the Passion and the death received for us by Christ, as He said Himself in instituting for His own the laws of the sacrament: "Whenever you eat this bread and drink of this chalice, you announce the death of the Lord" (*Glaphyres*, LXIX, 428C).[8]

From the same symbolism of the lamb, St. Cyril also teaches how the Eucharist should help us to grow in the dispositions, the spirit, and the ways of Christ.

> . . . He who has taken part in Christ by the communion of His holy Body and Blood, should also have His spirit and live to enter into His interior dispositions in having the understanding of what is in him . . . (*On Adoration*, LXVIII, 1072A).[9]

Many more examples could be cited, especially from the catecheses of Easter week, but these passages give us a general idea of patristic teaching on the eucharistic meal.[10] They show us the fulfillment aspects of the Eucharist as the new Manna, the new Passover, and the banquet of the new Wisdom, Christ himself. They show the Eucharist, furthermore, as our sharing in the Paschal mystery of Christ — a participation in the sacrifice of his passion and death and the implanting of the seed of resurrection pledged by the risen Christ.

III. RITUAL TRADITIONS OF THE EUCHARISTIC MEAL

The reform of liturgical worship inaugurated by Vatican II has been concerned to reemphasize the meal aspect of the Eucharist. This concern is reflected in the fact that the council has encouraged the restoration of Mass facing the people, and also the wider practice of Communion under both species in the Western Church, as has been traditional in the East.

A. *The Altar Table*

It is obvious from the institution accounts in the New Testament

---

[8] *Ibid.*, pp. 169–170.

[9] *Ibid.*, p. 170.

[10] The student might well read the inspiring works of St. Ambrose, *On the Mysteries* and *On the Sacraments*, available in English translation by T. Thompson, with introduction and notes by J. H. Srawley (London: The Society for Promoting Christian Knowledge, 1950); also Roy J. Deferrari, *The Fathers of the Church*, Vol. 44 (Washington, D. C.: The Catholic University of America Press, 1963).

that Christ celebrated the first Eucharist within an actual meal, in fact, a religious meal taken at least in the atmosphere of the Paschal solemnity. The Gospel accounts note that Jesus and his disciples reclined at table, the customary posture for the Passover celebration at the time of our Lord. For some decades, under the auspices of the Apostles or the presbyters, the early Christians imitated the meal framework of the first Eucharist. The Jewish Christians, of course, would scarcely have repeated every Sunday the whole Paschal ritual which Christ probably followed at the Last Supper; they would rather have used an adaptation either of the Sabbath meal or of the *Chaburah* (brotherhood) meal celebrated by various Jewish confraternities; both of these meals had religious connotations and included the blessing and sharing of bread and wine.

In Greek communities, the meal preceding the Eucharist attempted to express the atmosphere of charity and friendship which the Eucharist itself was meant to cement and solidify. This was done by having a kind of tureen dinner, to which the wealthy brought additional food for the poor. But this expression of charity came to be abused, as Paul indicates in a letter to the Corinthian Church:

> So then when you meet together, it is no longer possible to eat the Lord's Supper. For at the meal, each one takes first his own supper, and one is hungry, and another drinks overmuch. Have you not houses for your eating and drinking? Or do you despise the church [i.e., the assembly] of God and put to shame the needy? (1 Cor 11:20–22.)

Such a passage testifies to the meal practice still in vogue in the Church at Corinth around A.D. 55 or 57. Because of such abuses it is likely that this banquet of charity or *Agape* was soon separated from the Eucharist. Some scholars derive such a conclusion from a study of the *Didache* and also from a letter sent by the Roman governor Pliny to the Emperor Trajan (c. A.D. 111), which seems to describe two distinct services of Christian worship, one on Sunday morning and the other in the evening.[11]

Another factor which would have contributed to the separation of the Eucharist from an actual meal is the growth of congregations. As the number of converts to Christianity increased, it became more and more difficult to celebrate a "domestic" Eucharist (in private homes) with everyone seated at a table. Therefore, the tables disappeared from the

---

[11] Cf. Joseph Jungmann, *The Mass of the Roman Rite* (New York: Benziger Bros., 1950), Vol. 1, p. 18. The *Didache* speaks twice of a "breaking of bread" and "giving thanks." Some authors held that the first reference (opening section of Ch. 9) is to the Agape, while Ch. 14 is properly Eucharistic. Cf. Jungmann, *The Early Liturgy* (Notre Dame, Ind.: University of Notre Dame Press, 1959), p. 35 ff.; Gregory Dix, *The Shape of the Liturgy* (London: Dacre Press, 1960), pp. 90–93. For original text cf. Quasten, *op. cit.*, Part I, pp. 10–14.

room except for the one at which the president of the assembly pronounced the thanksgiving prayer over the bread and wine (the celebrant still faced the faithful gathered around him). With such a simple table arrangement, it was still possible to retain rather clearly the meal-character of the Eucharist.[12]

With the edict of Constantine (A.D. 313), which freed the Church by granting it legal recognition, the Church began to take over special buildings for divine worship and to erect new buildings for this purpose. The emperor himself set the example by constructing the magnificent basilicas over the burial place of Peter on Vatican Hill, at the site of Paul's martyrdom outside the walls of ancient Rome, as well as the church in honor of Mary (St. Mary Major) and the Pope's cathedral church at St. John Lateran. In these basilica-type churches, which were cruciform in shape, the altar stood in the center of the intersecting arms of the cross and the celebrant would face the congregation during the liturgy. For the liturgy of God's word (the first part of the Mass, including the Epistle, Gospel, and homily), the celebrant was seated on a chair or a throne behind and above the level of the altar so that he might easily be seen and heard by the congregation. He advanced to the altar table only for the offertory of the Mass. Thus the altar table was highlighted as the place of sacrifice and of the meal with the risen Christ.

In the period of Gothic architecture developing in the later Middle Ages, the altar was moved back to the wall of the apse. The celebrant no longer faced the congregation but turned his back to it. The wall space immediately behind the altar lent itself to artistic embellishment and encouraged the construction of highly ornamental altar screens in the Renaissance and Baroque periods. The end result of this architectural development tended to obscure the table concept of the altar and therefore the meal-character of the Eucharist itself. The altar table was totally dwarfed by the mighty sculptural and artistic structures behind the altar. No longer was it clearly the place for a meal with Christ. Furthermore, the size of the great Gothic cathedrals, with seating for numerous clergy and choir between the sanctuary and the congregation, tended to remove the congregation farther and farther from their meal table. The liturgy became more and more a spectacle, a pageant to be watched and admired rather than a family meal to be shared by all present.

In the light of such developments, we can appreciate why the Fathers of Vatican II encouraged the restoration of a simpler altar table standing

---

[12] For an interesting discussion of these early developments of the Eucharist cf. Jungmann, The Early Liturgy, pp. 10–49; Gregory Dix, op. cit., pp. 48–102; E. J. Kilmartin, The Eucharist in the Primitive Church (Englewood Cliffs, N. J.: Prentice-Hall, 1965), pp. 141–159.

free in the center of the sanctuary, permitting the priest celebrant once again to face his people.

B. *The Rite of Communion*

Beginning in the fourth century and continuing in some places until the twelfth century, there grew up the custom of an Offertory procession in which the faithful and clergy brought gifts to the altar. Besides gifts used for the support of the clergy and for the poor, it became a well-established custom to bring bread and wine to be used in the sacrifice. For some eight or nine centuries, even in the Western Church, this took the form of leavened bread, probably in the shape of small loaves or rolls. Enough bread and wine to satisfy the needs of the faithful at a given Mass was set aside at the altar for consecration. Later at Communion time the faithful would again proceed to the altar to receive the sacrament.

In preparation for the Communion of the faithful, it would be necessary to break up the leavened bread into smaller particles. This ceremony, called the *fractio panis* (breaking of the bread), was performed by the assisting clergy at a Pope's or bishop's Mass. At Communion time for several centuries it was customary for the faithful to approach the altar and to receive the sacrament standing.[13] The communicant received the consecrated bread into his open hand, answering "Amen" to the celebrant's words: "The body of Christ."[14] Reverentially the communicant gave himself the consecrated bread and later returned to participate in the chalice.[15]

An interesting description of the celebration of Communion in the fourth century appears in one of Cyril of Jerusalem's catechetical instructions:

> When you approach, do not go stretching out your open hands or having your fingers spread out, but make the left hand into a throne for the right which shall receive the King, and then cup your open hand and take the body of Christ, reciting the *Amen.* Then sanctify with all care your eyes by touching the Sacred Body, and receive It. But be careful that no particles fall, for what you lose would be to you as if you had lost some of your members. Tell me, if anybody had given you gold dust, would you not hold fast to it with all care, and watch lest some of it fall and be lost to you? Must you not then be even

---

[13] Jungmann, *The Mass of the Roman Rite,* Vol. 2, pp. 375–378; Dix, *op. cit.,* pp. 13, 137. At the time of the Council of Nicaea (325), the faithful stood for the whole Mass. For a long time, the Eucharist was celebrated only on Sundays and feast days and preserved an Easter character. Thus standing seems to be associated with the resurrection (cf. Jungmann, *op. cit.,* Vol. I, p. 368).

[14] Jungmann, *ibid.,* p. 379, footnote 33 for additional evidence.

[15] *Ibid.*

more careful with that which is more precious than gold and diamonds, so that no particles are lost? Then, after you have partaken of the Body of Christ, approach the chalice with the Blood without stretching out your hands, but bowed, in a position of worship and reverence, and repeat the Amen and sanctify yourself by receiving the Blood of Christ. Should your lips still be moist, then touch them with your hands and sanctify your eyes and your forehead and the other senses. Then tarry in prayer and thank God who has made you worthy of such mysteries.[16]

In addition to the liberty of communicating with the sacred Particles, the faithful also for a time were permitted to take consecrated Particles home with them to receive daily during the week. Such an arrangement, of course, presented certain dangers of irreverence and abuse; so the custom was gradually abandoned. Danger of abuse was also involved in receiving the Eucharist into the hands. A person who would receive the Eucharist and not eat It would be considered guilty of sacrilege.[17]

Growing reverence for the sacrament, then, eventually led to a change in the method of celebrating Communion. A related factor that occurs about the ninth century is the change in the Western Church from leavened to unleavened bread. The introduction of small waferlike hosts invites the form of celebration that still prevails today: the placing of the Host in the mouth of the communicant by the priest. This method of communicating reduced the worry over losing small Particles of the consecrated Bread and eased the problem of purifying the fingers, as had now become customary for the priest. Concern of the former kind led to the adoption of a Communion cloth, and since 1929 the Communion paten or plate.

While these changes were taking place in Communion under the form of bread, reception of the chalice continued for a much longer time. This was done in various ways at different times and in different localities. In one case all drank from the same chalice, generally a special ministerial chalice for the use of the faithful. There could be several of these for a large congregation of communicants. A second possibility for communicating in the cup was to pour but a small portion of the consecrated Wine into several chalices of unconsecrated wine. This custom dates at least from the seventh century, as the Roman ceremonial books testify. The unconsecrated wine was considered to be sanctified by its commingling with the blood of Christ.[18] Sometimes the wine was sanctified by touching a Particle of the consecrated Host to it, especially in the case of Communion for the sick.

---

[16] Cyril of Jerusalem, *Mystagogic Catechesis*, V, 21 f.; quoted in Jungmann, *Mass of the Roman Rite*, Vol. 2, p. 378.

[17] Cf. Jungmann, *ibid.*, p. 381.

[18] Cf. Jungmann, *op. cit.*, Vol. 2, p. 383.

Besides drinking from the cup, another possibility was the use of a tube, either of silver or of gold. Communion by intincture was also used in the Western Church, as it is still commonly practiced in the Byzantine rite of the East. In this method, a consecrated particle is dipped in the precious blood and then placed upon the tongue of the communicant.

Since the twelfth century, Communion under the species of wine was discontinued more and more in the Western Church. Concurrently with this change was the theological development of the notion that the whole Christ is already contained under the species of bread (concomitance); therefore the communicant is not receiving any less of Christ if he communicates under one species alone. Besides there was also an historical tradition of Communion under one species dating back to the earliest times — namely, in the case of Communion to infants and young children, and Communion to the sick and imprisoned.

Since, however, Communion under both species more fully represents the total sign-value of the Eucharist as life-giving food and drink for man, the Second Vatican Council has permitted the restoration of Communion under both species, at the discretion of the bishops, on certain occasions, e.g., for the newly ordained in their Mass of ordination, for the newly professed in their Mass of religious profession, for the newly baptized adults in the Mass that follows their baptism, and for weddings and wedding anniversaries. Since the council has restored this privilege in principle, we may well look for its gradual extension on more numerous occasions. This restoration also has ecumenical implications of some importance, since other Christian bodies for the most part have maintained the Lord's Supper or Communion under both kinds.[19]

In its recommendations on Communion of the faithful, the Vatican Council encourages the reception of Particles consecrated at the same Mass. "That more perfect form of participation in the Mass whereby the faithful, after the priest's Communion, receive the Lord's Body from the same sacrifice, is strongly commended."[20] This in no way prohibits the use of Particles consecrated at a previous Mass; but rather it sets forth an ideal which demonstrates the unity of action in the Mass. The particles to be consecrated at a given Mass symbolize the gift of the faithful, ultimately the gift of themselves (whether there be an Offertory procession or not); the offerings of the faithful then are transformed by the Consecration into a sacrificial Gift worthy of God's majesty. This Gift is returned to the faithful at Communion. Thus the cycle of offering and receiving is more clearly signified by the use of the same Particles for a given Mass.

---

[19] CSL, in AAS, 56, 2, February 15, 1964, par. 55, p. 115.
[20] Ibid., N.C.W.C. tr.

C. Frequency of Communion[21]

In the primitive Church, Communion was regarded as an integral part of the Eucharist. Christ himself had set the pattern when, after offering himself sacrificially to the Father, he directed the Apostles to "Take and eat" and "Take and drink." The earliest eucharistic documents, e.g., that of Justin Martyr (about A.D. 150), take for granted that all in attendance at the Eucharist participate by receiving Communion. This custom was to prevail until about the fourth century.

For some time it was customary to celebrate the Eucharist only on Sunday. During this period the faithful were permitted to take the consecrated Bread home with them and give themselves Communion every day.[22] In this case, however, Communion was usually taken before any food. At times also one might be allowed to take the Eucharist along on a journey.

In the meantime, with the attainment of freedom under Constantine (A.D. 313) and the consequent building of churches, the Church in the West increased its liturgical services, including the celebration of Holy Mass. Since more frequent reception was now possible in church, prohibitions were instituted by the fifth century against taking the Eucharist out of church. But now suddenly we find frequent Communion disappearing, at least in some countries. Typical of complaints voiced already by some of the Fathers are those of Chrysostom in the East and Ambrose in the West, who is disturbed at those who receive only once a year. Regional councils of the Church had to insist on Communion at least three times a year up to the height of the Middle Ages. In the Carolingian period (early ninth century) a certain reform tried to reintroduce weekly or Sunday Communion, but it was only temporarily successful.

From the eighth century on, Communion once a year had become more and more the customary practice. Even among lay Brothers and in convents, infrequent Communion had often become the rule. It was several centuries of the practice of infrequent Communion, then, that led to the decree of the Fourth Lateran Council in A.D. 1215 which established as a minimum the reception of Communion during the Easter time.

What caused such a change in the pattern of frequent Communion? Partial blame may be assigned to the many superficial conversions in the Roman Empire after the time of Constantine, and among the German tribes following the great missionary effort there. But a far more serious

---

[21] Cf. Joseph Jungmann, S.J., *The Mass of the Roman Rite*, Vol. 2, pp. 359-367, 396; M. J. Nicolas, O.P., *What is the Eucharist?* (New York: Hawthorn, 1960), translated from the French by R. S. Trevett, pp. 111-116.

[22] Cf. Jungmann, *op. cit.*, Vol. 2, p. 360, footnotes 1 and 5.

cause of infrequent Communion was the heresy of Arianism. Arius, who
gave his name to the movement, had denied the divinity of Christ. This
led the Church to counter by a reemphasis on his divinity, sometimes
at the expense of his mediatorship. The humanity of Christ gradually
receded from the focus of eucharistic piety; in the East and in Gaul, the
Church came to regard the Eucharist as a fearful and awesome mystery.
Theologically, eucharistic reception was discouraged by an oversensitive
fear and reverence for Christ's presence there. It was in Rome, where
the structure of liturgical prayer remained unchanged the longest, that
frequent Communion still endured through the seventh and eighth centuries. Here the tradition of prayer through Christ as High Priest and
Mediator, an emphasis flowing from his humanity, had persisted despite
the anti-Arian reaction.

Another factor contributing to decrease in frequent Communion was
the change in penitential discipline, that is in the practices associated with
reparation for sin. From the tenth century on, more and more demands
were made for confession before each Communion. With limited opportunities for confession on the parish level due to defects in organization of
parishes and lack of personnel, it became increasingly difficult for one
to communicate even if he wished to do so. A growing pattern of rigidity
in eucharistic discipline tended to restrict more and more the reception
of the sacrament. After the manner of Jewish purification laws, certain
restrictions were placed upon married people and women barring them
from the Eucharist. Preparatory requirements were extended in some
places to include abstinence from meat for almost a week or a fast of half
a week (Synod of Coventry, 1237).

At the end of the twelfth century, a new wave of eucharistic devotion
swept over Europe; its emphasis was not on Communion, however, but
rather on adoration of the eucharistic presence. The idea took hold that
looking at the Blessed Sacrament was hardly less efficacious than sacramental Communion.[23] Worshipers turned to the practice of "spiritual
communion," a devotion that included Christ-centered acts of faith and
love, meditation on the sacred passion, devout assistance at Mass, and a
prayerful looking up at the Host. In the later Middle Ages, the spiritual
communion turned into a kind of communion of desire; at a time when
restrictions barred more and more people from sacramental Communion,
the spiritual desire to receive Christ sacramentally must have become a
sincere and serious expression of eucharistic piety.

The Middle Ages attempted to justify the practice of infrequent
Communion in the thought that the celebrant, who necessarily communicates as part of the Mass-liturgy, receives not only for himself but

---

[23] Jungmann, op. cit., Vol. 2, p. 364.

also for the congregation. Time and again, the documents of preaching and lay spirituality emphasized this representative role of the priest. From this it was but a further step to have the faithful begin to receive for others, e.g., for the sick and the faithful departed. Thus arose the notion of offering one's Communion for another, a trend which prevailed up to recent times in the formulation of so-called spiritual bouquets. While of course one may utilize the moments after Communion to petition Christ for one's personal intentions, one cannot transfer the sacramental grace of this eucharistic encounter to another person.

In the light of Protestant objection to Mass without Communion for the faithful, the Council of Trent was moved to encourage once again the practice of more frequent Communion. It was left, however, for our present century to witness the efforts of Pope St. Pius X (1903–1914), who lowered the age for first Holy Communion to the age of reason and at the same time encouraged eucharistic reception as a normal function of every Mass. The great liturgical movement of this century reached its culmination in Vatican II's *Constitution on the Sacred Liturgy*, where the Fathers insist with reference to the Eucharist that the faithful "should be instructed by God's Word and be nourished at the table of the Lord's Body."[24]

In order to encourage frequent Communion, recent popes have mitigated the eucharistic fast. Obviously this is an area subject to Church regulation, since the Church has the general duty of overseeing the worthy celebration of the Sacraments. In the early decades, as pointed out previously, there was no fasting legislation, since the Eucharist was part of an actual meal as it was at the Last Supper. But quite early after the separation of *Agape* and Eucharist, the practice of taking the Eucharist before any other nourishment came into vogue. Some authors conclude that fasting was already considered obligatory at the time of Tertullian (end of second century, beginning of third century). By the end of the fourth century, allowing for exceptions like Holy Thursday, when the setting of the Last Supper was re-created, fasting before Communion was more or less explicitly imposed as the general norm for the Western Church. During the Middle Ages, fasting was maintained not only before Communion, but was prescribed or at least counseled even for attendance at Mass.

With the advent of World War II, modifications in the eucharistic fast were granted for those in military service as well as for nighttime factory workers. Postwar industrial developments led many bishops to ask for further concessions. On January 6, 1953, Pius XII reduced the

---

[24] *CSL*, in *AAS*, loc. cit., par. 48, p. 113.

fast to three hours from solid foods and one hour from liquids except water, which no longer was considered to break the fast. More recently still, Paul VI has reduced the fast to one hour for both solids and liquids, a condition which greatly facilitates reception of Communion, especially since Mass itself may be celebrated around the clock — morning, noon, or night.[25]

As all food nourishes and strengthens life, the eucharistic food is designed to strengthen our life in Christ. Besides approaching this sacrament in the state of grace, we should also approach the Eucharist with sincere faith and a genuine desire to let Christ's transforming action take effect in our life. To approach Communion with a right and pure intention means to have an openness toward Christ as friend to Friend, a willingness to let Christ take over in our life. If friendships grow by a cultivation of mutual likes and interests, then it goes without saying that we must steadily put on the mind of Christ, make his interests ours, his zeal for the salvation of mankind our own overriding purpose in life.

Since the task of putting on the mind of Christ is of lifelong duration, granted the weakness of our human nature, then frequency of communicating in Christ's flesh and blood is clearly indicated. Christ's power to transform us is omnipotent; but our weak will tends to hold us back from authentic surrender to the Christ of the eucharistic encounter. Our self-giving is always deficient; too often we hold something back, a small attachment here, a petty selfishness there. In some way or other our faults tend to curb our freedom, the freedom of our growth in Christ's love.

Frequent Communion, therefore, is a logical necessity to have us grow in the mind of Christ. We need frequent Communion, not as a reward for our goodness, but as a remedy for our weakness. The details of this spiritual growth and the specific benefits that accrue from frequent reception of the Eucharist may be gleaned from the following dogmatic synthesis.

IV. DOGMATIC SYNTHESIS

A. Communion as the Consummation and Fruit of Sacrifice

For a sound eucharistic piety, it is essential to preserve a proper balance among the three sacramental realities of sacrifice, meal, and real presence of Christ. While, for purposes of analysis, we treat each of these concepts separately, yet we must never fail to integrate them in practice.

---

[25] Announced November 21, 1964, at general session of the Vatican Council; published in AAS, Vol. 57, #2, February 27, 1965, p. 186.

Wonderful as Holy Communion is, it would be an imbalance to suggest that the Mass exists purely for the sake of Communion. Surely it is a distortion of proper spiritual values to receive Communion before Mass without necessity (as has been done even in some religious houses) and to think of the Mass that follows as a thanksgiving for the Communion. Even when Holy Communion is given apart from Mass, as for example to the sick, the eucharistic food must never be separated in our mind from its true source, which is the sacrifice celebrated at the heart of the Mass. To place Holy Communion in proper perspective, it is imperative to view it in the context of sacrifice. Communion is the consummation, the end-result, the overflow, the humanly oriented benefit of the eucharistic sacrifice of Christ in his Church.

There is more than one way of viewing this perspective. It may be seen in the ancient connection of sacrifice and meal established by the studies of primitive man. It may be seen in the biblical context of covenant-sacrifice and covenant-meal, where the latter serves to dramatize the bond created by the former. The covenant-meal is the final outward expression of the return to God by the worshiping community.

In terms of the eucharistic Covenant in the Upper Room, Christ first pledges himself to death and resurrection; he hands Himself over to his Father as the Suffering Servant, already committed to die and rise again for sinful man. He himself is the sacrificial gift visibly embodied in the form of food. Turning from his Father to the Apostles, Christ offers them a share in his oncoming Paschal mystery by allowing them to eat his consecrated Person in the eucharistic forms. Consuming sacrificial food and drink, the Apostles already enter into the Lord's Paschal sacrifice. For them this implies a readiness to enter into Christ's own dispositions, to put on his way of thinking, in short to be covictims with their Leader. But if in the eating they are pledging themselves to their own part in the Master's passion and death, they are also receiving the assurance, the pledge, the token of a share in the messianic resurrection.

Precious food is given to man, then, in the eucharistic bread and wine, food that is bought at a great price. It cost Christ nothing less than the gift of his very humanity, marked out for sacrifice to his Father, to bestow himself upon us as the strengthening food for our own sacrificial pilgrimage to the Father.

Thus Christ paid the price of his own life in order to give himself to us in the Eucharist ("This is my body which is given up for you. . . . This is my blood which is shed for you . . . unto the remission of sins"). And in his presentation of the Eucharist, Paul reminds us that it is the sacrificial *victim* that we receive in communion. "As often as you shall eat this bread and drink the cup, you proclaim the death of the Lord" (1 Cor 11:26).

Communion-encounter with such a self-sacrificing Friend must impel us to a parallel generosity. Already at the offering of the gifts, the Church urges us to a spirit of surrender, a willingness to die to self — to keep his word and to help channel his saving grace to our fellowmen. Only if we have first given with the whole of our being in the ascending line of Offertory and Consecration-surrender do we deserve the divine invitation at Communion: "Come to me all you who labor and are burdened and I will refresh you."

Communion is no time for parasites. To participate worthily, intelligently, and fullheartedly in Christ's and the Church's offering demands that we adopt as far as possible the very mind of Christ himself as he embraced his death-resurrection Passover to the Father. If the Eucharist serves to enshrine for all time the sublime commitment of a Divine Being embracing humiliation and death in our name, then we his adopted brothers through baptism cannot stand idly by as detached observers. Like the Apostles, we accept the challenge of joining Christ in his Passover when we eat his flesh and drink his eucharistic blood.

Communion requires commitment. The simple dialogue restored at the moment of Communion must be the articulation of a genuine willingness to accept our share of the Paschal mystery whatever the cost. The "Amen" with which we answer the priest's declaration "The Body of Christ" is a hearty affirmation of our faith and faithfulness toward Christ encountered at that significant moment. Like Peter we might be led to exclaim, "Lord to whom shall we go? You have the words of eternal life"; or again, "Depart from me for I am a sinful man, O Lord." Our "Amen," our "Yes," involves us in a mission of charity, of witness, of zeal, of generous obedience, and of filial piety. Viewed in this light, Communion is seen as a challenge to grow more and more like Christ, to let ourselves be changed by him, to live a more selfless life dedicated as he was to the good of others. Desire, love, loyalty, sincere friendship, genuine openness, aversion from deep-seated, friendship-rupturing sin — all these constitute the mind that we are to bring to Christ in the Communion-encounter of the Eucharist. What the handshake is between trustworthy business partners finds its far nobler parallel in our Communion pledge to the risen Christ. It is here that the fidelity of Christ to us in covenant-love meets our own covenant-loyalty most articulately. Our sacramental union with Christ becomes not a matter of passing moment nor a mere routine, but a real pledge to live a better life, a readiness to let Christ's justice and charity radiate to our fellowmen through us. Only in this way does our Communion commitment revitalize our daily life. Communion is inseparable from Christian conduct; it renews, extends, and prolongs the commitment of our baptism and confirmation; it is the final seal on our eucharistic experience of the Paschal mystery.

B. *The Meal of Freedom*

The Paschal context of the Last Supper Eucharist invites reflection on sacramental Communion as the meal of true Christian freedom. The annual Jewish Passover memorialized Israel's deliverance from Egypt and its debut as a free people among the nations of the world. Gathering for the Paschal banquet, successive generations of Israelites actually entered into the freedom of their fathers through the liturgical meal-celebration. By the time of Jesus, the ancient custom of taking this meal in a standing position (cf. Ex 12:11) had been modified to imitate the reclining posture of the free citizens of Rome.

Within such an atmosphere of freedom, Jesus inaugurated His great work of liberating mankind from the tyranny of sin and death. The creation of a free people, the new Israel of the Church, is marked by the sacramental covenant of the eucharistic sacrifice-meal. At that very meal, Jesus not only pledges himself to accept his passage through death into risen freedom, but he also establishes the new memorial sacrifice-meal that will serve to draw all his followers into the same dimension of liberty in which his resurrection places him. The Church meets Jesus in his risen humanity in the eucharistic celebration.

That the Apostles understood the Eucharist or the "breaking of the bread" as a meal with the risen Savior is clear from their choice of the first day of the week, resurrection day, as the time for their weekly gathering as a community of faith and worship (cf. Acts 2:42, 46; 20:7). The Lord's Supper or the Eucharist was thought to recapitulate those precious postresurrection reunion meals. Traces of this may be seen in the eucharistic overtones evident in the New Testament accounts of Christ's resurrection-appearances; most of these visits took place when the Apostles were gathered for a meal (cf. Mk 16:14; Lk 24:30, 41 ff.; Acts 1:4; 10:41). The scene at Emmaus is described with the phrase that came to be an accepted name for the Eucharist, "breaking of the bread" (Lk 24:30, 35). For Peter, one of the chief characteristics of the official witnesses of the risen Jesus was that they had eaten and drunk with him (cf. Acts 10:41). Thus it may be safely assumed that the breaking of bread, the primitive Christian Mass, prolonged for the Apostles the meals they had enjoyed with their risen Leader.

Now the risen Jesus has entered into a new dimension of freedom, an existence that knows no time-space barriers or limitations of suffering or death. The risen Jesus, conqueror of death, presides over every Eucharist where he gathers up his followers into his own freedom, the freedom of the "sons of God" (Rom 8:21; Gal 4:31; 5:13). When we assemble to celebrate the Eucharist, we are called to enter with Jesus into his own Passover, to continue the Paschal journey begun in baptism by entering more deeply into the Lord's death-resurrection and in this way to come to share in his own wondrous gift of freedom. The power to overcome sinful attachment, egotism, pride, sensuality, injustice, and all the other roots of sin that we find in our life is the mighty gift of the risen Jesus to his eucharistic table companions.

At this banquet table, there are no barriers — racial, national, or social. We are all one body in Christ; no more slavery, no more caste system here. The freedom of equality before God in Christ takes visible form in the company of believers who are one in faith and charity. The Church, the free people of the new Covenant, opens out the redeeming power of Christ to all peoples; free from the restrictions of the synagogue, it opens its ranks to all sincere believers in Christ.

As the meal of free men, the Eucharist is also the pledge of freedom from eternal death. Here the risen Christ becomes the personal guarantee of immortality. "He who eats my flesh and drinks my blood has life everlasting and I will raise him up on the last day" (Jn 6:55). The eucharistic meal makes it possible for us already in this world to begin living in that dimension of freedom that Christ enjoys with the Father and the Spirit. "As the living Father has sent me, and as I live because of the Father, so he who eats me he also shall live because of me" (Jn 6:58). The Eucharist is an abiding and intimate union with the immortalized flesh and blood of the glorified Christ. "He who eats my flesh and drinks my blood abides in me and I in him" (Jn 6:57).

Thus the life-giving bread of Jesus has a transforming power, leading us into that life of interior wholeness that alone guarantees true happiness. The risen Christ stands before us in the Eucharist as that truly Whole Man who, as victor over the disintegrating effects of Adam's sin, invites us to know once more the integrity of the risen man. Though in this world we still remain finite, and suffering and death still have a claim upon us, yet the seed of a true integrity germinates within us in our present union with the risen Christ. When this God-life comes to full radiance in the splendor of God's unveiled presence, then eucharistic integrity will give way to eternal transfiguration.

Can such a feast with the risen Jesus be anything else than a meal of joy, a celebration of friendship? Will not deep interior satisfaction always pervade the family feast of freedom? All the great festivals of the year — Thanksgiving, Christmas, Easter, and the great milestones of life — seek joyous expression in the heart of the family at a happy reunion meal. Here is true freedom in the relaxed atmosphere of one's own home. It is here that we are truly open to one another. All of this and more must be said of that celebration of freedom in the heart of the Church-family, the festival of eucharistic liberty.

C. Communion and Community

In our reflections on Communion, we need to realize that Christ does not merely visit us as Friend to friend. Indeed we need to realize that Communion, while it certainly puts us in personal touch with Christ, does not end there; its full extension and meaning can be grasped only if we view it in terms of the Church.

Just as a family truly grows together and shares its vital experiences, learns the give-and-take of sacrifice and generosity, and builds up a sense of solidarity, in truth grows and matures in bodily health and psychological unity most especially by sharing a common food; so also Christ, ever adapting himself to man's ways, has guaranteed the growth, unity, and solidarity of his Church-family by providing as a kind of magnetic center the eucharistic meal of his own flesh and blood.

In its *Constitution on the Church* (November 21, 1964), the Second Vatican Council in more than one place explains how the Eucharist shapes the Church. In speaking of the bishop as high priest of the local Church, the council notes that

> The Eucharist, which he [the Bishop] offers or causes to be offered, and *by which the Church continually lives and grows* . . . the mystery of the Lord's Supper is celebrated, that by the food and blood of the Lord's Body the whole brotherhood may be joined together. In any community of the altar, under the sacred ministry of the Bishop, there is exhibited a symbol of that charity and "unity of the Mystical Body without which there can be no salvation" (S.T. III, 73, 3).[26]

That the Eucharist promotes the unity of the Church is clear also from other passages of the same document:

> Really partaking of the Body of the Lord in the breaking of the Eucharistic bread, we are taken up into communion with Him and with one another. "Because the bread is one, we though many, are one body, all of us who partake of the one bread." In this way all of us are made members of His Body, "but severally members one of another."[27]

The Eucharist is *sign* and *cause* of the Church's unity:

> Strengthened in Holy Communion by the Body of Christ, they [the faithful] then manifest in a concrete way that unity of the people of

---

[26] AAS, 57, 1, January 30, 1965, par. 26, p. 31; N.C.W.C. tr. Emphasis added.
[27] *Ibid.*, par. 7, pp. 9, 10.

God which is suitably signified and wondrously brought about by this most august sacrament.[28]

From the above conciliar statements, certain conclusions emerge concerning the ecclesial effects of Holy Communion. We may try to summarize these as follows.

1. **The eucharistic meal builds up the Church.** Viewed with the eyes of Christ at the Last Supper, the Eucharist emerges as the dynamic design for the ongoing creation of the Church. Christ's intention in providing the Eucharist was certainly much more than giving each one of us the personal gift of his presence. For the God-Man's expansive outlook concerns the whole people of God, indeed the whole of humanity. At the moment of the Last Supper, when Christ stands on the threshold of his redemptive exodus to the Father, his saving love reaches out to gather in the children of his Father who have been scattered abroad (cf. Jn 11:52). It is for this reason that he enters upon his salvific pilgrimage back to the Father. Through this passage from death to glory, Jesus opens up a New Covenant to bind together the peoples of the earth in a new humanity, a life of incomparable unity, freedom, and growth.

Great leader that he was, Christ would insure the inner dynamism of this new community of man through his Spirit; he would provide for his Church a sacramental power-nucleus, generating a mighty thrust outward to reintegrate torn and splintered humanity. But paradoxically, Christ chose for this purpose seemingly weak and inconsequential signs, the signs of food and drink.

Addressing himself to the all-important goal of the unity of mankind in the Church, Jesus spoke first to his own milieu. The religious history of his people knew the symbolism of bread and wine. Bread was often weighted with the significance of God's own unifying word; for "Not by bread alone does man live, but by every word that comes forth from the mouth of the Lord" (Dt 8:3). The yearly feast of unleavened bread and the Paschal lamb recalled Israel's exodus beginnings and mobilized her national identity in a renewal of religious and political unity. Nor did Israel forget the desert manna, which nourished and unified her sojourning forebears.

The bread symbolism for Israel's unity is transposed at times into the related image of wine or the vine (cf. Is 5:1 f.; Hos 10:1; Ps 79:9 f.). It is of the vine of Israel that Christ is thinking when he chooses to call himself the "true vine" (Jn 15:1), and thereby identifies himself with the true or new Israel. It is a term of unity; Christ is saying, "I am the

---

[28] *Ibid.*, par. 11, p. 15.

Church." In the same passage (cf. Jn 15), which John includes in his Last Supper narrative, Jesus makes a plea for union with himself. "I am the vine, you are the branches. He who abides in me, and I in him, he bears much fruit; for without me you can do nothing" (Jn 15:5). A double meaning seems intended here; the vine stands for Christ as the Church, and it also stands for Christ in the Eucharist.

Thus Christ chose profoundly weighted symbols for the unifying meal of his Church. Bread and wine, already carrying a rich symbolism of unity, become the outward sign that will embody the full power of unity in his Church. The community that feeds on this sacred banquet must necessarily become one with each other in Christ.

2. **Union with Christ's risen flesh and blood.**   In consecrating bread and wine into his flesh and blood, Christ centers the unity of the new people of God in the eucharistic meal. His sacramental body and blood in fact constitute and establish the new community in Christ: the new people of the Church are formed by bodily contact with his risen flesh in the sacrament. Linked to the risen Christ and his Spirit under the signs of food, we are one body with him and with one another.

When our bodies are nourished by ordinary food, we assimilate this food into our organism; it becomes a part of us. But feeding upon Christ, we are rather assimilated or absorbed into him. In very truth, we become what we eat; we become more and more Christian or Christlike. In this way all Christians are merged more and more into the total Christ, growing up to that fullness or maturity of Christ in his body on earth (cf. Eph 4:12, 13). The polarity of ecclesial unity is centered in none other than Christ himself, personally present to his Church in the Eucharistic meal.

3. **Sign and cause of fraternal charity.**   A meal is a sign of friendship, brotherhood, unity, and love. To give another person something to eat means to give him life; eating common food means sharing a common life. Now the unity that Christ wills for his Church is a unity of brotherly love. According to John, Christ spoke of nothing else at the first Eucharist than fraternal love, unity, and peace (cf. Jn 14-17). It was in this sacramental context that Christ gave us his new commandment of loving each other as he loves us (cf. Jn 13:34). It was here that Christ promised peace to his followers (cf. Jn 14:27). It was here that Christ prayed that his followers might be one in the redeemed family of man, for which he was about to consecrate himself a living sacrifice (cf. Jn 17, passim).

But Christ was not given to mere words. If God's Word in the Old Testament was efficacious, and Christ is the very personal Word of the

Father, then his eucharistic word must truly cause what he wills it to do. In that meal of brotherly love and peace, the risen Christ will be the personal unifying bond drawing men to the Father in the family meal of festive joy. No wonder Augustine could exclaim about the Eucharist: "O sacrament of love, O sign of unity, O bond of charity."[29] No wonder St. Thomas Aquinas could specify the special sacramental grace of the Eucharist as the unity of the Church-body of Christ in charity.[30]

Ultimately it is the force of divine love that drives us together in Christ. Contact with Christ in the Eucharist is an encounter of friendship and love. He gave himself for the redemption of man totally out of love (cf. Jn 13:1), and continues to give himself in love to us in that great love-sacrament, the Eucharist. If we all receive the same Christ in Communion, our friendship with him must not be restricted to a kind of private interior union. We must meet him also in our fellow Christians. Like radial lines drawing closer to each other as they proceed from the circumference of the circle to its center, so we Christians converging upon the Christ of the Eucharist must necessarily be drawn to one another. Eucharistic charity holds the secret for the vital unity of the people of God.

From this great reserve of power must flow all the vigor of the apostolate. At the eucharistic table, we are energized in that love and zeal necessary to implement our confirmation witness to Christ in the modern world. Christian penetration in today's milieu must be essentially a penetration of charity, the ultimate unifying force of society. Nowhere else but in the Eucharist will we come to know the love of Christ in his Spirit to such a degree and with such intensity that it must necessarily be amplified in love for the community.

4. **The Eucharist and unity of all Christians.** One of the world's great symbols of ecumenical love, the esteemed Augustine Cardinal Bea, has insisted on the unifying power of the eucharistic Christ. Tracing much of the current renewal of the Church to fervent eucharistic piety, the Cardinal looks to the same source for the inner renewal of all Christians that must precede a return to a structured, institutional unity.[31]

Pointing out that our separated brethren share with us many of Christ's gifts, such as God's written word, the life of grace, faith, hope, and charity, and the gifts of the Holy Spirit, he goes on to cite Vatican II's Decree on Ecumenism to the effect that

---

[29] *Treatise on John,* 26, 13; *R.J.,* 1824.

[30] *S.T.,* 73, 3 and 4.

[31] Augustine Cardinal Bea, "Eucharistie und die Einheit der Christen," *Stimmen der Zeit,* Vol. 176, No. 12, September, 1965, pp. 406 ff.

Brethren divided from us also carry out many liturgical actions of the Christian religion. In ways that vary according to the condition of each Church or Community, these without doubt can truly engender a life of grace, and, one must say, can aptly give access to the community of salvation.[32]

The conciliar decree in another section looks hopefully to Protestant celebrations of the Lord's Supper for the furtherance of Christian unity.

Although the ecclesial Communities separated from us lack the fullness of unity with us which flows from baptism, and although we believe they have not preserved the proper reality of the Eucharistic mystery in its fullness, especially because of the absence of the sacrament of orders, nevertheless when they commemorate the Lord's death and resurrection in the Holy Supper, they profess that it signifies life in communion with Christ and await His coming in glory. For these reasons, the doctrine about the Lord's Supper, about the other sacraments, worship, and ministry in the Church, should form subjects of dialogue.[33]

Cardinal Bea concludes that from such liturgical celebrations in good faith among our reformed brethren, there will certainly flow eucharistic unifying grace. The measure and exact manner is left to God alone.[34]

Can the exact religious value of the Lord's Supper as it is celebrated in Protestant congregations be more explicitly defined? To this question the eminent Dutch theologian Father Schillebeeckx addresses himself and seeks a solution along Thomistic lines.[35] First it is necessary to consider the general Protestant understanding of the sacraments. Certain basic doctrines underlie Protestant sacramental theology: (1) the gratuity of God's gift of grace which takes the form of a call to faith. God's word promising salvation is powerful to stir up faith in the promise of the Gospel that by grace God grants forgiveness of sin and life eternal because of Christ's sacrifice finished on the cross. This well-known doctrine of justification by faith constitutes the cornerstone of Protestant thinking on the sacraments. (2) The concept of the Church not as a saving institution, but rather as a community of believers who keep Christ's body in being and constantly reform it. True sacraments, they maintain, can be celebrated only within this context of believers.

Now God's revealing and saving word comes to man in two ways — through preaching and through the sacraments of the Church. Through both of these and through the act of faith aroused in man, man receives

---

[32] Decree on Ecumenism, November 21, 1964; AAS, Vol. 57, No. 1, January 30, 1965, par 3, p. 93.

[33] Decree on Ecumenism, AAS, loc. cit., p. 106; tr. America Press edition, par. 22, p. 32.

[34] Bea, op. cit., p. 410.

[35] Edward Schillebeeckx, Christ, the Sacrament of the Encounter with God (New York: Sheed and Ward, 1963), pp. 184–195.

a share in God's salvation. Preaching is primary; the sacraments re-emphasize the spoken word, give it a personal orientation to the individual recipient, and thereby effect and strengthen the individual's act of faith in God's grace-giving word. The sacraments confirm or strengthen our faith in God's word. Therefore it would not be correct to say that they are mere signs in the Protestant view; in Calvin's view they are "full of power, full of faith."[36] Besides pledging the divine mercy and generosity, the sacrament also seals our own sincere submission to God's action. The whole process of faith then is essentially a divine act in me, an act which has no reference whatever to my merit or good disposition.

Of the Lutheran view of the sacraments, Father Schillebeeckx has this to say:

> The Lutheran view is closer to the Catholic. Luther held determinedly to the objective power of the sacraments to save. . . . Writing on infant baptism, he says: "By the prayer of the Church which believes and offers [sacrifice], and for which all is possible, even a little child is changed, purified and renewed by the faith infused into it."[37] Faith which alone can save performs its miracle of grace in the very act of baptism itself. Luther affirms the objective realism of the sacraments much more strongly than Calvin. This is very clear in the Lutheran doctrine of the Eucharist, which comes close to the realism of the Catholic doctrine.[38] It would probably be correct to say that Luther believed quite simply in earthly signs which signify and bestow super-natural realities, but that this Catholic notion becomes distorted in his thinking because of his denial of the Church as a saving institute and of the office of the priesthood.[39]

In the light of these premises, we may now turn to the discussion of the Protestant Lord's Supper more directly. First of all, as Father Schillebeeckx points out, "The Catholic faith does not allow us to consider this a valid sacrament."[40] This is so of course because of the lack of validly ordained clergy in the Catholic sense, a requirement for valid consecration, and also because of the loss of the traditional concept of sacrifice as effected by the consecration. Nevertheless we would do well to examine the religious significance of such worship beyond its unquestionable value as the prayer of a company of believers confessing its faith in Christ.

St. Thomas maintained that even the pagan "sacraments of nature"

---

[36] *Ibid.*, p. 187.

[37] Martin Luther, *Opera Omnia*, Frankfurt ed., Vol. 3, p. 87; cited in Schillebeeckx, *op. cit.*, p. 189.

[38] As will be seen in the next chapter, Luther maintained a doctrine of the real presence of Christ in the Eucharist, while many of the other Reformers reduced this concept to a mere symbolic presence of Christ.

[39] Schillebeeckx, *op. cit.*, p. 189.

[40] *Ibid.*, p. 189; cf. *Decree on Ecumenism*, par. 22; *AAS*, *loc. cit.*, p. 106.

possess a religious value and contain a kind of implicit reference to Christ.[41] Moreover the "sacraments" of the Old Testament (like circumcision, ritual sacrifice, Passover, and other festal celebrations), which anticipated and pointed to the coming of Christ and his sacraments, were authentic expressions of a religious attitude before God and certainly must have occasioned God's dispensation of merciful grace. May we not expect a parallel religious value in the worship of sincere Christians of the Reformed Churches?

Since most of them have a valid baptism, according to St. Thomas they are inwardly oriented or directed toward the Catholic sacrament of the Eucharist. For valid baptism may be called an implicit "Eucharist of desire."[42] This is so because through valid baptism they have come to belong to the Church of Christ in some way. Therefore celebrating the Lord's Supper with a sincere intention of returning to Christ's true Eucharist and acting in good faith with the sincere conviction of doing Christ's will, our separated Christian brethren have a real "Eucharist of desire" and therefore in the celebration of their worship really participate in the essential grace-effect of the Eucharist, the unity of the body of Christ. Father Schillebeeckx would call this a spiritual reception of the sacrament itself. Acting in good faith, these Christians make vital contact with Christ even though they do not receive the fullness of eucharistic grace, which can be given only with the true reception of the real sacrament; nevertheless Protestant worship may be viewed as "a quasi-sacramental manifestation of an explicit Eucharistic desire which, moreover, implicitly looks forward to the true fruits of the Catholic Eucharist."[43] Subject to any further Catholic teaching to the contrary, Father Schillebeeckx concludes that the Protestant communion service has more than merely a subjective religious value.[44] "Through their celebration of the Lord's Supper they really grow in unity with Christ and with men."[45]

It should be noted that Schillebeeckx' above observations preceded the Ecumenism Decree, which says nothing about a "Eucharist of desire." Does the Conciliar decree go further than this in establishing the religious value of the Protestant Lord's Supper? Upon reflection, it seems that it does. Speaking of the liturgical celebrations of these ecclesial communities separated from the Catholic Church, the Council notes that "these without doubt can truly engender a life of grace, and, one must

---

[41] "Sacraments of Nature" refer to the religious acts of man apart from revealed religion, those ritual acts by which man sought to contact the Supreme Being to which nature around him bore witness. Ritual washings, sacrifice, tithes, penitential acts, and the like had the effect of disposing man for contact with God, however inadequately he thought of him. Cf. S.T., III, 61, 3.

[42] Schillebeeckx, op. cit., p. 192, quoting S.T., III, 80, 9, ad 3.

[43] Ibid., p. 194.   [44] Ibid.   [45] Ibid.

say, can aptly give access to the community of salvation."[46] Furthermore, the decree goes on to assert:

> It follows that the separated Churches and Communities as such, though we believe they suffer from defects already mentioned [lack of full communion with the Catholic Church in doctrine, discipline, and concept of ecclesial structure . . . (par. 3)], have been by no means deprived of significance and importance in the mystery of salvation. For the Spirit of Christ has not refrained from using them as means of salvation which derive their efficacy from the very fullness of grace and truth entrusted to the Catholic Church.[47]

Thus the Protestant bodies are acknowledged as true ecclesial communities acting as means of grace for their people. It is not simply, then, a case of eucharistic desire on the part of one or another individual Protestant. The whole Church community, professing the Christian faith and worshiping God in Jesus Christ, becomes a medium of God's saving action among his people. For them too, God's gifts of faith and grace are available in their celebration of the Lord's Supper, even though we cannot acknowledge the sacramentality of that act in the strict sense. Its basic value, then, seems to derive from the true ecclesial reality which these Churches represent, even though they fall short of the full *institutional* form of *ecclesia* embodied in the doctrine, worship, and authority of the Catholic Church. God's Spirit is at work in these communions also, "engendering a life of grace" and "giving access to the communion of salvation."[48]

D. The Eucharistic Meal and Eschatology

Primary to an understanding of Christianity is that it is historically conditioned. In common with the Old Testament, the Christian looks upon temporal history as a happening in the dimension of time created by God. All history moves toward a divinely conceived goal or end (eschaton; hence the name "eschatology"). The ancient Jews already looked forward to a day of fulfillment ("Day of the Lord"), which in time they came to link with the person of the Messiah. This time of future fulfillment was to bring the definitive rule or kingship of God among men.

Now it is clear that the New Testament authors were convinced that the end-time had already arrived in the person of Christ. Jesus the God-Man, had come decisively to establish the rule of God among men in the form of the Church. Joined to Christ in his Church then, the

---

[46] *Decree on Ecumenism, AAS,* Vol. 57, No. 1, January 30, 1965, par. 3, p. 93; tr. America Press.

[47] *Ibid.*

[48] *Ibid.*; cf. Gregory Baum, *The Ecumenist,* Vol. 3, No. 3, March-April, 1965, p. 43.

Christian, though he still remains in time, in a sense begins to live beyond time. He has been transferred "in Christ" into that kingdom where Christ entered at his ascension. This is the meaning of Paul's assertion that through baptism, God "brought us to life together in heaven in Christ Jesus" (Eph 2:5–6).

But how exactly are we to bridge the gap between this world and the kingdom of God in eternity, into which somehow we are already inserted? The answer is found in the presence of Christ's Spirit. His coming is connected with the last days, as Peter explained at Pentecost, "This is what was spoken through the prophet Joel: 'And it shall come to pass in the last days, says the Lord, that I will pour forth of my spirit upon all flesh . . .'" (Acts 2:16, 17). The risen and ascended Lord has poured forth his Spirit, who becomes in us the pledge or guarantee of the eternal possession of God's kingdom in eternity (cf. 2 Cor 1:21 f.). The Spirit becomes a great personal link between the risen, glorified body of Christ in heaven and his Church-body on earth. Now Christ, present to us through his Spirit in the Church, is leading us gradually through time back to the Father. This is the end and meaning of all human history.[49]

Already in the New Testament, this "coming" of Christ is associated with the Eucharist, which commemorates it and makes it present. Thus Paul associates the Lord's Supper not only with the Lord's death but also with his "coming": "For as often as you shall eat this bread and drink the cup, you proclaim the death of the Lord, until he comes" (1 Cor 11:26).[50] Moreover the language of the early liturgy, especially in the anaphoras or eucharistic prayers of consecration, like that of Hippolytus (A.D. 215), is filled with eschatological references. Through the Eucharist, then, we are already put in touch with the last days, inaugurated by Christ's Paschal sacrifice through which he acquired in his humanity complete sovereignty over man. In himself he already embodies that rule or kingship of God among us. Since we meet the risen Christ in the Eucharist, then the ultimate and final fulfillment of the rule of Christ as Lord of history is already realized. "Realized eschatology" refers to this paradoxical situation: we live in the present, and yet the future is already here; to put it another way, we are already redeemed through

---

[49] See the very interesting interpretation of the "Coming of the Son of Man" or Parousia, usually associated with Daniel 7:13, as referring not to a descent as at the time of the Last Judgment, but rather to an ascent to the Father. This interpretation by Dr. Lowther Clarke is noted in Gregory Dix, *The Shape of the Liturgy* (London: Dacre Press, 1945), p. 262, footnote 1.

[50] According to F. X. Durrwell, in his masterful biblical study of *The Resurrection* (New York: Sheed and Ward, 1960), p. 329, fn. 51, the Greek sentence here expresses finality. He concludes from this that the proclamation of Christ's death necessarily also proclaims his resurrection and therefore his final coming.

Christ's death and resurrection, and yet the ultimate fulfillment of this redemption will be realized perfectly only in heaven.

Thus it may be said that the Eucharist anticipates heaven. Even in the Old Testament, the prophets, groping for concepts or images of the future golden age, often described it in terms of a festive banquet. Christ built upon this concept and often spoke of the rule or kingship of his Father as being like that of a wedding feast (e.g., Mt 22:2–14; cf. Mt 25:1–13). Thus he prepared the way for the climactic banquet of the Eucharist, the meal that announces that the age of fulfillment has already arrived. Truly the Mass is the beginning of heaven; it is union with the risen Christ who with each Mass transforms us step by step that he may one day present us in the kingdom of his Father when his Church-body will have become most fully like his own risen body.

The Eucharist opens out a magnificent prospect of the future. It is truly the sacrament of Christian hope, the sacrament that borders on heaven, the joyous possession of our Father and of one another in an eternal reunion of perfect love. In a world fragmented by anxiety, tragedy, war, hatred, and injustice, the meal of the Eucharist remains the unshakable promise of eternal peace and order, in which alone there can be true joy. Fittingly we make our own the eucharistic prayer of St. Thomas, which synthesizes so well the whole doctrine of the Eucharist:

O sacred banquet in which Christ is received, the memory of His passion is renewed, the soul is filled with grace, and a pledge of future glory is given us.[51]

[51] Roman Breviary, Feast of Corpus Christi, Magnificat Antiphon for Second Vespers.

CHAPTER XI

The Eucharistic Presence

I. GOD'S PRESENCE IN SALVATION-HISTORY

True friendship thrives on togetherness. Two people in love long to be physically present to each other; enforced separation only intensifies the desire for presence.

Now the God of revelation is not only the most high God, the totally other, completely transcending his creature; but he is also the immanent God, who has willed to be very near to man (cf. Ps 138:7 ff.) and to show himself a Friend to man. As creator God, he is present to his works (cf. Wis 11:25; Rom 1:20), sustaining and conserving their existence. He reveals himself to the fathers — Abraham, Isaac, and Jacob — and enters into covenant with them. To Moses he reveals his name Yahweh, which some scholars have interpreted to mean "I am he who is always with you," that is, as a covenant-partner who is always at hand to keep his word.

God is present to his people as a savior God, particularly in the exodus-liberation. The supreme benefit of the covenant is precisely the promise of God's continued presence with his people. He who had led them from Egypt under the sign of the cloud would now continue to be present, leading his people across the desert to the land of Canaan (cf. Ex 33:14, 17; 34:9).

It was especially in the tent of meeting or testimony that God gave a sign of his presence. Here where the ark of the covenant was housed, Yahweh gave witness of his continual presence as a fellow camper, a tent dweller among them; and the visible sign of his presence over the ark was the cloud of glory. Much later, when Solomon's temple was dedicated, the cloud of glory reappeared as Yahweh "took up residence" at the center of Israel's liturgical life (cf. 1 Kgs 8:10–12).

With the destruction of the temple and the ensuing exile in Babylon, the cloud disappeared; yet the prophets Ezekiel and "third Isaiah" proclaimed the presence of Yahweh creating a living temple, a new people, embracing all nations (cf. Ezek 43:1–6; Is 66:18–23).

All these provisional and limited forms of Yahweh's presence in the old covenant would one day yield to an incomparable presence in a new kind of "tent," a more wonderful temple — the flesh of Jesus of Nazareth (cf. Jn 1:14, 2:21). The Incarnation made God present in the flesh; no closer identification of the Divine Person with humanity is conceivable; there can be no greater gesture of friendship than that "God so loved the world that he gave his only begotten Son" (Jn 3:16). He is truly Emmanuel, "God with us (Is 7:14; Mt 1:23; 28:20).

Even if Jesus would one day be taken up from visible sight, he would yet remain "wherever two or three are gathered together [in prayer] in [his] name" (Mt 18:20). He identified himself with the poor, the sick, the outcast, so that whatever charity was directed to them in his name would be done to him (cf. Mt 25:40) He would be present in the persecuted (cf. Acts 9:5). Finally he would be present in his Spirit, not only in individuals (cf. Rom 8:9, 14), but also in the multitude of believers being formed into God's temple (cf. 1 Cor 3:16 f.; 6:19; Eph 2:21 f.) and into the members of his Church-body (cf. 1 Cor 12:12, 13, 27).

Through the same Spirit, Jesus will live in those who eat his flesh and drink his blood (cf. Jn 6:56 f., 64); he will live in them as his Father dwells in him (cf. Jn 14:19 f.). Such a living union presupposes that Jesus has gone back to the Father and has imparted his Spirit (cf. Jn 16:28; 14:16 ff.); thanks to the gift of this Spirit, Christ's followers have in them the same love that unites the Father and the Son (cf. Jn 17:26); this is why God himself dwells among them (cf. 1 Jn 4:12). In fact all three Persons come to live in the just man: Father, Son, and Holy Spirit become present to the man who loves Christ and keeps his word (cf. Jn 14:23).

This presence of the Savior that Paul wishes for us (cf. 2 Thes 3:16; 2 Cor 13:11) will not be perfect before the deliverance of our mortal flesh (2 Cor 5:8). Then raised up by the Spirit who is in us (cf. Rom 8:11), we shall see God who will be all in all (cf. 1 Cor 13:12; 15:28). In the place which Jesus has prepared for us, we shall see his glory (cf. Jn 14:2 f.; 17:24), the light of the new Jerusalem, the dwelling of God with men (cf. Ap 21:2 f., 22 f.), the perfect presence of the Father, the Son, and the Holy Spirit in us (cf. 1 Jn 1:3; 3:24).

Such is the presence that Christ offers to all who believe. "Behold I stand at the door and knock" (Ap 3:20). It is not a presence accessible to the flesh (cf. Mt 16:17), that is, to mere natural man without grace; it is a presence not reserved for one people only (cf. Col 3:11), nor confined to one place (Jn 4:21); it is the gift of the Spirit (cf. Rom 5:5; Jn 6:63), offered to all who are "in Christ," who form his body wherein he is present in his fullness (cf. Col 2:9), and interiorly present to the believer who enters into that fullness (cf. Eph 3:17 ff.). In the fullness of the Spirit's power, the believer will hear Christ's final invitation, "Come" (Ap 22:17).

II. THE REAL PRESENCE OF CHRIST
IN THE EUCHARIST

All the various forms of Christ's continuing presence in his Church are brought into focus by the Eucharist. Here God's people enjoy the presence of their covenant-Friend in the New Covenant-ark, the eucharistic bread and wine.

This truth is really presumed by the other two great realities of the Eucharist discussed in earlier chapters, namely, the sacrifice of Christ and the sacred meal of his body and blood. For how could Christ really be offered in eucharistic sacrifice or consumed as eucharistic food unless he is truly there? Indeed Christ's real presence in the Eucharist is a fundamental eucharistic reality, without which the sacrifice-meal would be meaningless. Nevertheless, it is quite sterile to consider the sacramental presence of Christ as a mere static reality. The truth of the matter is that the Christ of the Eucharist is most actively, dynamically present, offering himself at the moment of the eucharistic sacrifice and solidifying his Church in charity through Communion and in His enduring presence. The eucharistic presence of Christ must never be divorced from the sacrifice-meal.

A. *Early Belief in the Real Presence*

The Pauline and Johannine teaching on the real presence of Christ in the Eucharist has been treated amply enough above.[1] Early in the post-Apostolic period, Ignatius of Antioch, on his way to martyrdom in Rome (about A.D. 107), denounced the Docetist heretics of the East for their denial of the real eucharistic presence. Basing their ideas on a dualistic philosophy which considered matter to be evil and only the spirit good, they failed to comprehend how the Son of God could unite a true body to himself at the incarnation; hence they asserted His body was only make-believe, merely an *apparent* human nature. Against them Ignatius writes:

> From Eucharist and prayer they hold aloof, because they do not confess that the Eucharist is the Flesh of our Savior, Jesus Christ, which suffered for our sins, and which the Father, in his loving-kindness, raised from the dead.[2]

Insisting on the real presence of Christ's flesh in the Eucharist once more, the martyr-bishop addressed the people of Philadelphia in the East saying, "Take care, then, to partake of one Eucharist; for, one is the Flesh of our Lord Jesus Christ, and one the cup to unite us with His Blood. . . ."[3]

This emphasis on the reality of Christ's flesh in the Eucharist recurs in a succession of patristic writings. In his *First Apology*, Justin Martyr (writing c. A.D. 158) describes the primitive Christian Eucharist (Chap. 65) and then asserts concerning the eucharistic banquet:

> We call this food the Eucharist . . . not as ordinary bread or ordinary drink do we partake of them, but just as through the word of God, our Savior Jesus Christ became incarnate and took upon himself flesh and blood for our salvation, so we have been taught, the food which has been made the Eucharist by the prayer of his word and which nourishes our flesh and blood by assimilation, is both the flesh and blood of that Jesus who was made flesh.[4]

A half century later, the great champion of orthodoxy, Irenaeus of Lyons, (writing about A.D. 177) maintains that "The bread over which thanksgiving is pronounced is the body of the Lord and the chalice of His blood."[5] This great polemicist and defender of true doctrine combatted the Gnostics, who like the Docetists denied the reality of the

---

[1] Cf. pp. 165–167.

[2] *Letter to the Smyrnaeans*, Chap. 7, par. 1; tr. J. Kleist, ACW, Vol. 1 (Westminster, Md.: Newman Press, 1949), p. 92.

[3] *Letter to the Philadelphians*, Chap. 4; tr. Kleist, ibid., p. 86.

[4] Justin Martyr, *The First Apology*, Chap. 66; cf. J. Quasten, *Florilegium patristicum* (Bonn: Hanstein, 1935), Fascicle 7, Part I, pp. 17–18.

[5] *Against the Heresies*, IV:18, 4; R.J., No. 234; P.G., 7, 1027.

incarnation and the resurrection of man's body. For Irenaeus, it is clear
that the resurrection of our own body is guaranteed by eating the very
real flesh and blood of Christ in the sacrament (cf. Jn 6:55).

Taking for granted the reality of the Lord's presence in the Eucharist,
the early Fathers and theologians began to reflect on two further points:
at what moment does Christ become present in the sacrament and in
what way is he present? To explain the former, the Fathers generally
appealed to the words of institution and/or the epiclesis (invocation
of the Holy Trinity or of the Holy Spirit); the exact relation of the institution words to the epiclesis remained unclear for some time, and the
exact opinion of some Fathers is often difficult to determine.[6]

In answer to the second question, i.e., how Christ becomes present, a
certain refinement of language is noted in the explicit reference to a
change from bread and wine to the body and blood of Christ. For
example, Cyril of Jerusalem notes:

> Of old in Cana of Galilee he changed water into wine of his own will.
> Is he less worthy of belief when he changes wine into blood . . . ?
> Therefore, do not look upon the bread and wine as bare elements; for
> according to the Lord's assurance, they are the body and blood of Christ;
> for even though the senses suggest this to You, let faith make you
> certain and steadfast. Do not judge this matter by taste, but by faith
> be certain beyond any doubt that you have been deemed worthy of
> the gift of Christ's body and blood.[7]

The same emphasis on change through the words of institution appears
in the writing of the Eastern theologian Gregory of Nyssa (c. A.D. 385):

> Rightly then we believe that the bread also which is consecrated by the
> word of God is made over (metapoieisthai) into the body of God's
> Word. . . . Here similarly the bread, as the Apostle says, is sanctified
> by the word of God and prayer, not that it becomes the body of the
> Word by the process of eating but that immediately it is transformed
> into the body by the word, as was spoken by the [divine] Word: "This
> is my Body."[8]

Moving once more to the Western Church, we encounter in the fourth
and early fifth centuries the towering figures of St. Ambrose of Milan and
his most noteworthy protégé, the great St. Augustine. It has been suggested that, in regard to the Eucharist, these two men are twin sources of
two theological traditions; one (that of Ambrose), the so-called "metabolist" tradition, which emphasizes the thoroughgoing change from bread
and wine into Christ's body and blood; the other, the "symbolist"

---

[6] Cf. Paul Palmer, *Sacraments and Worship* (Westminster, Md.: The Newman
Press, 1957), p. 207 f.

[7] Cyril of Jerusalem, *On the Mysteries*, IV, 6; *R.J.*, No. 846; *P.G.*, 33, 1101.

[8] Gregory of Nyssa, *Catechetical Oration*, 37; *R.J.*, No. 1035; *P.G.*, 45, 93.

tradition (Augustine's position), emphasizing the distinction between the outward sign and the reality of faith associated with the sign after Consecration, namely Christ's body and blood spiritually present.[9]

Ambrose takes the more practical and less patently theological approach, in terms of the liturgy. Time and again he emphasizes, in his great catechetical lectures *On the Mysteries* and *On the Sacraments*, that the sacramental words effect the real presence of Christ's flesh and blood. Writing about 390, Ambrose teaches:

> Surely it is the true flesh of Christ, which was crucified, which was buried; therefore it is truly the sacrament of that flesh.

> The Lord Jesus Himself declares: "This is My Body." Before the benediction of the heavenly words another species is mentioned; after the consecration the Body is signified. He Himself speaks of His blood. Before the consecration it is mentioned as something else; after the consecration it is called blood. And you say "Amen," that is, "It is true." What the mouth speaks, let the mind within confess; what words utter, let the heart feel.[10]

The same emphasis on the change that occurs through the consecration words appears in another text: "Christ is in that sacrament, because the body is Christ's. So the food is not corporeal but spiritual."[11] In his other work *On the Sacraments*, the Bishop of Milan insists that the author of the sacraments is the Lord Jesus himself and he alone. The sacraments have come from heaven. He goes on to say:

> You perhaps say: "My bread is usual." But that bread is bread before the words of the sacraments; when consecration has been added, from bread it becomes the flesh of Christ. So let us confirm this, how is it possible that what is bread is the body of Christ.

> By what words, then, is the consecration and by whose expressions? By those of the Lord Jesus. . . . Thus the expression of Christ performs this sacrament. . . .

> But perhaps you say: "I do not see the appearance of blood." But it has the likeness. For just as you took on the likeness of death [that is, in baptism], so, too, you drink the likeness of precious blood, that there may be no horror of blood and yet the price of redemption may be

[9] Cf. C. W. Dugmore, *The Mass and The English Reformers* (London: Macmillan, 1958), whose position is summarized in an article by the Rev. H. Benedict Green, "The Eucharistic Presence: Change and/or Signification," *The Downside Review*, Vol. 83, No. 270, January, 1965, p. 32 ff.

[10] St. Ambrose, *On the Mysteries*, Chap. 9, par. 53, 54; cf. Quasten, *Florilegium Patristicum*, Fascicle 7, Part III (Bonn: Hanstein, 1936), p. 135; tr. Roy J. Deferrari, *The Fathers of the Church*, Vol. 44 (Washington, D. C.: The Catholic University of America Press, 1963), p. 26.

[11] *Ibid.* Chapter 9, par. 58; Quasten, *op. cit.*, p. 136; Deferrari, *op. cit.*, p. 27.

effected. You have learned then that what you receive is the body of Christ.[12]

It may be noted then that in his first work, On the Mysteries, Ambrose paid scant attention to the form of bread continuing after the consecration; in the latter work, On the Sacraments, he took pains to mention that the consecrated reality (blood) remained under a "likeness." Beyond this he does not seem to specify any further the nature of this "likeness." In his concept of the composition of material being, bread would simply be given a new form of existence through the Real Presence of Christ.

Augustine introduces a more subtle distinction between the visible aspect of the sacrament and its inner spiritual reality. Cautioning against a crass, cannibalistic understanding of the presence of Christ's flesh in the Eucharist, Augustine paraphrases Christ's "bread of life" sermon (cf. Jn 6):

> Understand what I have said in a spiritual manner: not this body which you see, will you eat, and not this blood which they will shed who crucify me, will you drink. What I commended was a kind of sacrament: understood spiritually it will give you life. Although that sacrament must be celebrated in a manner that is visible, it must be understood in a manner that is invisible.[13]

Augustine's distinction between sign and content appears clearly in another place where he says, "The Lord did not hesitate to say 'This my body,' although he was giving a sign of his body."[14] The association of sign with content is particularly clear in one of Augustine's letters; after explaining that the sacraments have a certain similarity to those things which they signify, he applies this to the Eucharist:

> Just as in a certain way the sacrament of the body of Christ is the body of Christ, the sacrament of Christ's blood is Christ's blood, so the sacrament of faith is faith.[15]

From this last statement, as well as from several other selections of his thought that could be made, it is clear that Augustine is not contradicting the teaching of Ambrose. He believes just as surely as his mentor in the reality of Christ's presence in the Eucharist; but unlike Ambrose, he puts greater stress upon the sacramental sign in which and through which that presence occurs. Thus the so-called symbolist and metabolist, or

---

[12] St. Ambrose, On the Sacraments, IV, Chapter 4, par. 14, 20; cf. Quasten, op. cit., pp. 158–159; Deferrari, ibid., pp. 302, 304.

[13] Augustine, Commentary on Psalm 98, P.L., 37, 1265; R.J., No. 1480; tr. Palmer, op. cit., pp. 210–211.

[14] Against Adimantus, R.J., No. 1566; P.L., 42, 144. Cf. also On the Trinity, R.J., 1652, P.L., 42, 873.

[15] Epistle 98, 9; R.J., No. 1424; P.L., 33, 363.

idealist and realist schools of thought on the Eucharist are not far apart, at least in these two men. Later writers, however, will carry the divergence much further. The two approaches reappear down through the Middle Ages to the time of the Reformation — e.g., between Paschasius and Ratram, Lanfranc and Berengar, scholastic orthodoxy and Wyclif, even in a sense between Luther and Zwingli. Certain Reformers, claiming to follow Augustine's thought, overemphasize the spiritual nature of Christ's presence to the point of denying his real presence altogether.

As the theological understanding of the Eucharist develops in the Middle Ages, we find a certain oscillation between what Irenaeus called the earthly and the heavenly elements in the Eucharist, that is, between the visible and the invisible realities.[16] The early Fathers had often spoken of the outward elements of bread and wine in terms of "likeness," "representation," "sacrament," or "figure" of Christ's body. But such terminology must be interpreted in the light of the then-current notion of symbol as "that which manifests the underlying reality." It was unthinkable that the Fathers regarded these sacred symbols as empty or void of the divine reality. Nevertheless, later writers took exception to what they considered dangerous ambiguities. John Damascene of the eighth century (died 749) explicitly rejects the notion that bread and wine are a figure of Christ's body and blood and maintains that the bread and wine are the very body of the Lord and His very blood.[17]

B. Eucharistic Controversies in the Middle Ages

A forthright challenge to the doctrine that bread and wine are changed into the substance of Christ's body and blood was formulated by a priest of Tours named Berengar. Whether or not he denied the Real Presence altogether is still controverted by historians; nevertheless, most people of his time looked upon him as a heretic. Twice, in 1059 and again in 1079, he was ordered to retract his teachings and affirm belief in the Real Presence. The second formula, drawn up under Pope Gregory VII (1073–1085), and imposed upon him in 1079, affirms:

> The bread and wine, which are placed on the altar, through the mystery of the sacred prayer and the words of our Redeemer, are substantially changed into the true, proper, and lifegiving flesh and blood of our Lord Jesus Christ. After the consecration it is the true body of Christ, which hung on the cross as an offering for the salvation of the world, and which sits at the right hand of the Father. And it is the true blood of Christ which was poured forth from his side. And Christ is present

---

[16] For Irenaeus' statement, cf. *Against the Heresies*, P.G., 7, 1029.
[17] *On Orthodox Faith*, 4, 13; P.G., 94, 1144.

not merely by virtue of the sign and the power of the sacrament, but in his proper nature and true substance. . . .[18]

The next year (1080) the archbishop of Canterbury, Lanfranc, at one time abbot of a monastery in Normandy, France, wrote militantly against Berengar, and in so doing contributed much to the clarification of the relation between Christ's historical body and his eucharistic body. He distinguishes clearly between the appearances or species of bread and wine remaining after the consecration and the reality of the Lord's presence:

> . . . Therefore do we believe that the earthly substances which, through the priestly ministry are divinely consecrated on the table of the Lord, are, in a way that defies all telling and understanding, wondrously transformed by a power that operates from above into the essence of the Lord's body, the appearances (species) of these same remaining along with certain other qualities, lest the faithful draw back in horror at the sight of bits of raw flesh, and that they may receive a richer reward for their faith. And yet the Lord's body itself, which exists in heaven at the right hand of the Father, remains immortal, inviolate, whole, untouched, unharmed. To tell the truth, the same body that was taken from the Virgin we receive, and yet, not the same. The same, surely, as regards the essence and properties of true nature and its powers, and yet, not the same if we regard the species of bread and wine and those other qualities included above. This faith the Church has held from the earliest times and holds even now. . . .[19]

Someone has wisely observed that today's error stands in the service of tomorrow's truth. Out of the Berengar controversy there developed a new effort to clarify the doctrine of conversion in the Eucharist. While the term "substantial change" had been used on occasion to describe the effect of the consecration, the term "transubstantiation" had not yet appeared. From the twelfth century on, the application of metaphysical terms like "substance" and "accidents" became dominant in Western eucharistic theology.

Hugh of St. Victor and Peter Lombard approach the problem about how Christ becomes present in the Eucharist by first eliminating certain projected theories. The body and blood of Christ are not simply created at the time of the consecration (creation theory) nor are the bread and wine annihilated (annihilation theory), but there is a real transition from the material elements into the body and blood. While neither of these men used the term "transubstantiation," yet they clearly held the teaching expressed by it, that as a result of consecration the substances of the bread and wine are changed into the substances of the body and blood

---

[18] Denzinger, 325; TCT, No. 712.

[19] Lanfranc, On the Body and Blood of the Lord, No. 19; P.L., 430; translation in Palmer, op. cit., pp. 230–231.

of Christ with only the external forms of bread and wine remaining. The term "transubstantiation" is used by Hildebert of Tours early in the twelfth century, while the verb "transubstantiate" is found in Stephen of Autun in the first half of the same century.

In the twelfth and thirteenth centuries certain puritanical sects revived the basic tenets of the earlier Gnostic and Manichaean heresies. In their aversion for all things material, they included concepts like the visible Church, priesthood, and sacraments. They denied the incarnation of Christ and therefore the reality of his flesh in the Eucharist. It was in condemning one of these groups, the Albigensians of southern France, that the Fourth Lateran Council (1215) first officially used the term "transubstantiation" in regard to the Eucharist.

> Indeed, there is but one universal Church of the faithful outside which no one at all is saved and in which the priest himself, Jesus Christ, is the victim; his body and blood are truly contained in the Sacrament of the Altar under the species of bread and wine, transubstantiated by the divine power — the bread into his body, and the wine into his blood.[20]

In its choice of these terms "species" and "transubstantiated," what did the Council intend? Did the Council fathers intend to impose upon the Church the early Scholastic definition of transubstantiation or was it using these terms in a more general sense? First, it may be noted that the decree does not use the word "accidents" at all and there is no explicit statement that the substances of the elements cease to exist and that the accidents alone remain. Hence it has been maintained that the Lateran usage of transubstantiation has a more general sense simply denoting a mysterious change.[21]

In determining the meaning which the Council wished to give to the terms "substance" and "transubstantiation," it is pointed out that the Aristotelian definition of these terms was probably not intended by the Council. Up to the middle of the twelfth century, western Europe knew only Aristotle's logical works, preserved and handed down especially through Boethius. Prethirteenth-century logic contained certain metaphysical implications, but it was not until the thirteenth century that a metaphysical system as such came to the fore as a vehicle for propounding the theology of the Eucharist, notably in the work of Albert the Great and Thomas Aquinas. Therefore to read an Aristotelian interpretation into the technical vocabulary of the twelfth century may misrepresent the intentions of that era's theologians.

[20] Denz., 430; tr, TCT, No. 659, p. 259.
[21] Cf. J. H. Srawley, "The Eucharist (To the end of the Middle Ages)," Encyclopedia of Religion and Ethics, ed. by James Hastings, Vol. 5 (New York: Scribner's, 1912), p. 559.

It is difficult, moreover, to know the precise value of the metaphysical terms used in that period of development [that is, the twelfth century]. One would commit an egregious error if he read into the twelfth century expressions "accident," "substantial form," "first matter," etc., the doctrine of the late thirteenth century. With others, M. de Wulf thinks that "Many deficient and erroneous interpretations arise from having carried a logical theory into the metaphysical realm."[22]

In the light of such reservations, it would not seem justifiable to assume without further proof that the Lateran Council (or for that matter the later Council of Trent, 1545–1563) intended to canonize a particular philosophical system in expressing the revealed truth of Christ's presence in the Eucharist.

The thirteenth century witnessed a certain reform in the Church which gave rise to new religious communities like the Franciscans (established by Francis of Assisi, 1209) and the Dominicans (founded by St. Dominic, 1216). At this same time a new emphasis in eucharistic devotion developed as a natural consequence of the theological interest in the question of the Real Presence. Adoration of Christ present under the species inspired the erection of tabernacles attached to the high altar rather than to the side wall apart from the place of sacrifice. The elevation of the Host immediately after its consecration so that all the worshipers could adore Christ present there, the introduction of the feast of *Corpus Christi*, eucharistic processions, Forty Hours' devotion, benediction of the Blessed Sacrament — all of these liturgical developments centered upon the Real Presence aspect of the Eucharist and reflected the theological milieu in which they arose. Praiseworthy and firmly endorsed by successive ages of faith, these accessory rites must never be separated from the eucharistic celebration of sacrifice and meal, the native setting of the Real Presence.

C. The Scholastic Synthesis of St. Thomas

It is scarcely possible in our limited space to do justice to the genius of Thomas Aquinas' eucharistic theology. We propose to treat only the highlights of his doctrine and refer the reader to Thomas' own writings and the commentaries thereon.[23]

St. Thomas treats the question of the Real Presence in questions 75 to 77 of the Third Part of the *Summa*. Basic to Thomas' theology is the metaphysical structure that he borrows from Aristotle. His problem, of

---

[22] Raymond G. Fontaine, S.S.S., *Subsistent Accident in the Philosophy of St. Thomas and in His Predecessors* (Washington, D. C.: The Catholic University of America Press, 1950), Ph.D. dissertation, p. 45.

[23] *Summa Theologiae*, III; Questions 75 to 77; English translation, *The Eucharistic Presence*, introduction, notes, and appendices by William Barden, O.P. (New York: McGraw-Hill, 1965), Vol. 58 of New Dominican translation.

course, is to show the reasonableness of believing that a real change has occurred in the bread and wine through the Consecration, and that Christ is really present there, even though externally the bread and wine still look the same. To do this Thomas employs the notions of *substance* and *accident*. A substance, in the thought of St. Thomas, has existence without inhering in a subject.[24] We might call the substance the inner reality of something. It exists in itself, not in another. In itself substance as such is not visible to the eye, nor is it sensibly perceptible at all, but becomes so only through its *accidents*. An accident, on the other hand, exists *in* a subject.[25] In the ordinary course of nature, the accidental qualities (sight, color, quantity, size, shape, weight) will actually need a substantial subject in which to inhere and upon which they depend in order to be. We cannot think of whiteness, roundness, taste, aroma, without ordinarily thinking of something like bread which is white, round, tastes and smells like bread, etc. Ordinarily we are able to identify the substance of something by its outward appearances, its species, or its accidents. On the basis of this distinction, then, Thomas proceeds to outline a theology of transubstantiation.

First he insists that the body of Christ is really and truly in the sacrament, not just figuratively or as in a sign or symbol.[26] We know this, he says, only by faith, not through our senses. Christ is there, not extended in space but sacramentally, in the way of a spirit and by the power of God's Holy Spirit.[27] For Thomas, the Consecration of the Mass effects a profound change; the entire substance of bread and the entire substance of wine are changed respectively into the entire substance of Christ's body and the substance which is his blood. The substances of bread and wine do not remain after the Consecration, but rather as the words of Consecration indicate they are changed into the body and blood of Christ.[28] The body of Christ, he points out, is not brought in locally, that is, by movement from one place to another. Christ does not leave heaven and pass through space in order to get to the altar; nor in such a conception of local presence could it be understood how Christ would exist in different places simultaneously. Therefore Thomas affirms, Christ must become present in the sacrament by a real change of substance in the bread and wine. One substance (bread) is entirely changed into a new substance (body of Christ). In support of this truth, Thomas points to Christ's words "This is my body," in contrast with "Here is my body." The latter expression would allow for a coexistence of two substances simultaneously, namely bread and body of Christ (cf. Luther's

---

[24] *S.T.*, III, 77, 1, ad 2.
[25] *Ibid.*
[26] *Ibid.*, 75, 1.

[27] *S.T.*, III, 75, 1, ad 4.
[28] *Ibid.*, 75, 2.

teaching that Christ becomes present *in* the bread). Furthermore such a situation would have us worshiping both a created object (bread) and the adorable body of Christ.

The change, as Thomas explains it, does not involve an annihilation of the bread and wine, but a real passing from bread to Christ's body and from wine to Christ's blood. After the Consecration, nothing of the former substances of bread and wine remains; under the species or appearances of bread and wine is the new substance, the body and blood of Christ. All that remains of the bread and wine after the Consecration is their species or outer forms. After all, Thomas argues, God's power is not limited to changing outward forms; he can also change the being or the substance of a thing. It is obvious to our senses that something of the bread and wine still remains; Thomas explains this in terms of the bread's accidental qualities. Under these forms we are able to eat Christ in a noble way, commensurate with the supreme spiritual value of this experience. Thomas thus avoids any crass cannibalism in his explanation of the Eucharist. Finally he notes that the presence of the accidents of bread and wine without their true subject underneath makes our faith all the more meritorious.[29]

In the next question (Q. 76), Thomas takes up the manner in which Christ is present in the Eucharist. He first asks if the whole of Christ is there. This leads him to distinguish very carefully between two causes operating to make Christ present: the one, the sacramental sign itself; the other, the principle called "natural concomitance." In virtue of the sacramental words "This is my body," only the body of Christ is present. Likewise through the words "This is my blood," only the blood of Christ is present. But as soon as the first consecration ("This is my body") is pronounced, another principle or cause operates to make the whole of Christ immediately present in the species of bread. Natural concomitance means that whatever is in fact joined to the body or blood of Christ at that moment when the sacrament is celebrated becomes present along with that element to which the Consecration words are primarily directed. Christ is now in his risen glorified state; he can no longer be broken up into parts. Wherever a part of Christ is, there the whole of him must also be. Therefore as soon as the body of Christ becomes present through the words of the first Consecration, immediately all of Christ that is united to his body (blood, soul, divinity) in his glorified heavenly existence also becomes present in the sacrament. It is this theological principle that justifies the practice of giving Communion under only one species; for, as Thomas points out,[30] through the mutual operation of the two causes (the sacramental words and concomitance),

[29] *Ibid.*, 75, 5.   [30] *Ibid.*, 76, 2.

the whole of Christ is rendered present under each species. Not only this, but the whole Christ is present also under each and every part of the species; just as the whole nature of bread is contained under any part of the loaf, so the whole Christ is contained under any recognizable part of the form of bread.

Thomas next inquires whether the body of Christ is in the Eucharist in such a way as to take up a certain amount of space, is it there locally? He answers that the body of Christ with its natural dimensions is present but not extended in space. The whole manner of Christ's sacramental presence is conditioned by the sacramental sphere in which he exists; he is there after the manner of a pure and simple substance. That is, Christ's body and blood are present to the species, are related to the outward forms in such a way that when the species disappear, the relationship breaks off and Christ's body is no longer there.

Logically this leads Thomas in his last question on the Real Presence (Q. 77) to come to the very heart of the eucharistic mystery. We noted that ordinarily we are able to discover the nature of the substance of a thing by its external or outward forms or qualities. When a thing looks and tastes like bread, ordinarily we can affirm that the substance of bread is truly there under these qualities. Now in the case of the Eucharist, through the change called transubstantiation, the accidental qualities of bread are maintained in existence even though their proper substance (bread) is no longer "underneath" to support them. How then are they kept in existence? The qualities of bread certainly cannot exist naturally in a substance which is entirely foreign to them (body of Christ). For whoever saw a body which is white, round, tastes like bread, is fragile like bread, etc.? Therefore precisely here we touch upon the profound mystery of the eucharistic presence; here we must resort, says Thomas, to God's power to keep the accidents of bread in existence as the sign under which a totally foreign substance, Christ's body, is now present.

As though to minimize God's intervention to some degree, Thomas suggests that perhaps God keeps in existence by His special power only the dimensive quantity of the bread and wine, which takes over a kind of substantial function so that the other accidents inhere naturally in the quantity of the bread. The accidents are real; they remain in a natural state, so that whatever was done externally to the bread before Consecration may still be done afterward. This is why there will be no difference in the chemical analysis of the species of bread after the Consecration from what was true of the bread before the change.

Finally the clear thinking of Thomas sees the eucharistic presence of Christ as entirely unique; everything about the mode of Christ's presence there is sacramental. Hence Christ's body in the sacrament is beyond all change. Whatever is done to the species is done only to them; so that if the species are broken, Christ's body is unaffected by this action. Christ's body does not suffer; Christ is not a prisoner of the tabernacle; he is not locked up within the confines of a tiny space in the Church; he is not in the Eucharist locally (occupying a certain amount of space as we do) nor subject to suffering or change of any kind. Thus the clear teaching of St. Thomas eliminates pietistic aberrations, which have not been altogether absent from our devotional literature. We must not try to imagine how Christ can be present on several altars at the same time or in several particles, because his presence is thoroughly conditioned by the characteristics of sacrament. He is there after the manner of a substance as such, not physically extended in space.

The duration of Christ's eucharistic presence is therefore determined by the species, to the extent that when the species disappear, Christ's unique sacramental presence terminates. An astute refinement of this point is suggested by Father Karl Rahner, who identifies the dissolution of the species with the very moment in which they are no longer recognizable as bread. In other words, we must not think that Christ remains eucharistically present in our bodies for ten or fifteen minutes after Communion on the pretext that it takes this long for the species to be dissolved; for surely as soon as we have consumed the particle, the species are no longer there as *constituting bread*. Other reasons may be adduced for making an after-Mass thanksgiving; but this prayer should not be made dependent on a specious explanation like the above.[31] When Christ's human nature "leaves," he still remains present to the communicant through his Spirit and the power of sanctifying grace.

D. *Pre-Reformation and Reformation Controversies*

In the fourteenth and early fifteenth centuries we meet two men who in England and on the continent respectively were forerunners of the Reformation of the sixteenth century, namely, John Wyclif (1324–1384) and John Hus (1369–1415). John Wyclif, a priest and scholar of Oxford, England, initiated a movement based upon an exaggerated notion of Christian poverty. This led him to oppose Church property in government and ultimately to deny the divine origin of ecclesiastical authority. The Bible became the sole rule of faith (a cardinal principle of the Reformation).

Regarding the Eucharist, Wyclif opposed the doctrine of transubstantiation, repudiating the idea of accidents existing without a subject, and condemning the popular devotion as idolatry. Opposing the popular

---

[31] Karl Rahner, *The Christian Commitment* (New York: Sheed and Ward, 1963), translated by Cecily Hastings, pp. 179–185.

notion of a visible presence of Christ, he uses somewhat ambiguous language to assert his beliefs. For him the body of Christ is "virtually in the host as in a sign"; the host is not itself the body of Christ, but his body is sacramentally concealed in it. The bread is an "effectual figure" of the body of Christ; the sacrament is the *form* of bread and wine and not Christ or part of him — language directed against the materialistic ideas of his time.[32]

A great admirer of Wyclif, Hus translated his works into Bohemian and upheld Wyclif's doctrines with a new insistence. In eucharistic teaching, John Hus made a special plea for communion of the faithful under both kinds, presumably casting doubt on the fullness of Christ's presence under either species. Both men were condemned at the Council of Constance (1414-1418), the sixteenth ecumenical council of the Church.

About a century after the Council of Constance, Luther inaugurated his reform of the Church.[33] In the matter of the Real Presence, Luther tried to make the doctrine more reasonable by denying any real change in the substance of bread and wine; the Swiss Reformers went to the extreme and denied the Real Presence altogether as we understand it.

Adhering to the literal sense of Scripture, Luther maintained that Christ's words, "This is my body. This is my blood," must be taken at face value:

> What is the Sacrament of the Altar? Answer: Instituted by Christ himself, it is the true body and blood of our Lord Jesus Christ, under the bread and wine, given to us Christians to eat and to drink.[34]

In the *Large Catechism*, the statement referring to the bread and wine reads "in and under the bread and wine."[35] While Luther therefore continued to hold the doctrine of the Real Presence, he rejected transubstantiation as a statement of how Christ becomes present there. In his view, the elements remain true bread and wine even after Christ becomes present; there is a coexistence of the two realities. To his mind, transubstantiation was merely a Thomistic explanation, a purely theological opinion. As early as 1520 he was able to write:

> . . . it is real bread and real wine, in which Christ's real flesh and real blood are present in no other way and to no less a degree than the

[32] J. H. Srawley, *op. cit.*, p. 560.

[33] For a succinct summary of principal Reform attitudes toward transubstantiation and the doctrine of the Real Presence, cf. Cyril C. Richardson, "Word and Sacrament in Protestant Worship," *Ecumenical Dialogue at Harvard* (Cambridge, Mass.: Belknap Press of Harvard, 1964), pp. 162–166.

[34] Luther, *The Small Catechism*, VI, tr. in *The Book of Concord* (Philadelphia: Muhlenberg Press, 1959), p. 351.

[35] Cf. *The Book of Concord*, p. 447.

others assert them to be under their accidents. . . . the opinions of the Thomists, whether approved by pope or by council, remain only opinions, and would not become articles of faith even if an angel from heaven were to decree otherwise. For what is asserted without the Scriptures or proven revelation may be held as an opinion, but need not be believed.[36]

In 1529, Luther met the Swiss Reformers Zwingli and Oecolampadius in a meeting that was arranged for the purpose of bringing about unity in doctrine between the Lutheran and Swiss camps. In the course of the discussion, Luther remarked regarding the Real Presence:

I'm not sticking to my opinion without reason, enough for me the following, "This is My Body." I confess that the body is in heaven. I confess as well that it is in the Sacrament. I don't care whether this be against nature so long as it not against faith.[37]

In the Smalcald Articles of 1537, Luther wrote as follows:

As for transubstantiation, we have no regard for the subtle sophistry of those who teach that bread and wine surrender or lose their natural substance and retain only the appearance and shape of bread without any longer being real bread, for that bread is and remains there agrees better with the Scriptures, as St. Paul himself states, "The bread which we break" (1 Cor 10:16), and again, "Let a man so eat of the bread" (1 Cor 11:28).[38]

What causes the Real Presence to be accomplished in the celebration of the Lord's Supper? When the words of institution are recited by the minister, they are not words of consecration so much as God's direct address to the recipients of the sacrament.

No man's word or work, be it the merit or the speaking of the minister, be it the eating and drinking or the faith of the communicants, can effect the true presence of the body and blood of Christ in the Supper. This is to be ascribed only to the almighty power of God and the Word, institution, and ordinance of our Lord Jesus Christ. For the truthful and almighty words of Jesus Christ which he spoke in the first institution were not only efficacious in the first Supper but they still retain their validity and efficacious power in all places where the Supper is observed according to Christ's institution and where his words are used, and the body and blood of Christ are truly present, distributed, and received by the virtue and potency of the same words which Christ spoke in the first Supper.[39]

---

[36] M. Luther, *The Babylonian Captivity of the Church,* in *Luther's Works,* Vol. 36 (Philadelphia: Muhlenberg Press, 1959), p. 29.

[37] *Account of the Colloquy at Marburg,* quoted in Palmer, *Sacraments and Worship,* p. 244.

[38] M. Luther, *Smalcald Articles,* Part 3, Art. 6, in *The Book of Concord* (Philadelphia: Muhlenberg Press, 1959), tr. and ed. by Theodore G. Tappert, p. 311.

[39] *Formula of Concord, Solid Declaration,* Art. VII, 74, 75, in *The Book of Concord* (Philadelphia: Muhlenberg Press, 1959), p. 583.

The presence and activity of Christ in the Lord's Supper are connected with the entire external and visible action of the Supper as ordained by Christ: the consecration or words of institution, the distribution and reception, or the oral eating of the blessed bread and wine, the body and blood of Christ. Apart from this use it is not to be deemed a sacrament. . . .[40]

For Luther the eating of the Lord's Supper is a comfort to the Christian conscience and the assurance of the forgiveness of sin if it is received in faith. Once the Christian has faith that he has been redeemed by Christ, he shares in Christ's body and blood in order to increase this sense of confident faith.[41] An Anglican theologian comments on the continued influence of Luther's idea of the Real Presence as follows:

It is perhaps not surprising that Luther's doctrine of the objective reality of our reception of our Lord's body and blood in the Eucharist slowly declined in precision within the Lutheran churches. It is based simply on the literal understanding of the words of institution, and is logically unrelated and unnecessary to the Lutheran doctrine as a whole. It kept its place in the Lutheran doctrinal confessions, but it received and could receive no adequate expression in the Lutheran liturgies. When the bulk of the German Lutherans were united with the German Calvinists in the Prussians State Church in the early nineteenth century, it was in the result the Calvinistic Eucharistic doctrine which prevailed, though the question was formally left open for every communicant to decide for himself.[42]

As the Reformation developed in Switzerland, two points of view were expressed there on the Real Presence, namely the extreme view of Ulrich Zwingli and the more moderate doctrine of John Calvin. Zwingli, who as a monsignor had once been a chaplain to Pope Leo X, held a strictly spiritualistic concept of religion as a basic principle. Therefore logically we find him denying any vestige of the Real Presence in the Eucharist. In his *Account of Faith*, Zwingli wrote:

I believe that in the holy Eucharist, to wit the Supper of Thanksgiving, the true body of Christ is present to the contemplation of faith; by this I mean that those who give thanks to the Lord for the benefits bestowed upon us in His Son acknowledge that He truly assumed flesh, in that flesh truly suffered, truly washed away our sins by His blood, and thus everything wrought by Christ for them becomes present, as it were, by the contemplation of faith. But that the body of Christ is either really present in the Supper by way of essence — I mean the natural body itself — or that it is orally taken and eaten by the teeth, as the Papists and certain ones [Lutherans] who are nostalgic for the fleshpots

[40] *Ibid.*, pp. 584, 585.
[41] Gregory Dix, *The Shape of the Liturgy* (London: Dacre Press, 1945), p. 635.
[42] *Ibid.*, pp. 635–636.

of Egypt hold, we not only strenuously deny, but steadfastly assert to be an error contrary to God's word.[43]

Thus for Zwingli, Communion means a vivid recollection of the Passion of Christ as the source of our past redemption. The bread and wine are plain ordinary elements; and the sharing in this meal is a mere reminder, an expression of our faith in Christ's work of salvation. In keeping with his general sacramental theory, the Eucharist too is a mere sign or ceremony demonstrating to others one's saving faith in Christ. This notion comes out clearly in an after-Communion prayer which he composed for his revised ritual of 1525:

> Now remembering, dear brothers and sisters, what we have just done according to our Lord's command, namely that with thankful remembrance we have borne witness to our belief that we are all miserable sinners, but by His body given and His blood poured forth [that is on Calvary] we have been cleansed from sin and redeemed from everlasting death. . . .[44]

Further explanations that he gave of the words of institution by Christ exemplify his notion of a kind of figurative or purely symbolic presence, as when we point to a picture of someone and say, "That is so and so" — obviously far different from the physical presence of that person in our midst.

Between the conservative realism of Luther and the extreme symbolism of Zwingli, John Calvin, leader of the Reform movement in Geneva steered a middle course, a kind of ecumenical position between Zwingli and Luther. Calvin's doctrine is somewhat ambiguous: on the one hand he asserts most positively what he calls the Real Presence and yet on the other hand explains his thesis in somewhat obscure and seemingly contradictory terms. In his short *Treatise on the Lord's Supper*, he states:

> We have then to confess that if the representation which God grants in the Supper is veracious, the internal substance of the sacrament is joined with the visible signs; and as the bread is distributed by hand, so the body of Christ is communicated to us, so that we are made partakers of it.[45]

The sign of the Eucharist is not an empty sign nor a mere reminder of the past deeds of Christ as Zwingli thought; but rather it actually in some way puts us in touch with the body of Christ:

> . . . the communion which we have with the body and blood of our

---

[43] Zwingli, *An Account of Faith*, VIII, quoted in Kidd, *Documents of the Continental Reformation* (Oxford, 1911), No. 225, p. 474.

[44] Translation and quote in Dix, *op. cit.*, p. 632.

[45] Quoted from J. K. S. Reid, *Calvin: Theological Treatises* (Philadelphia: Westminster, 1954), p. 148.

Lord . . . is a spiritual mystery, which cannot be seen by the eye, nor comprehended by the human understanding. It is therefore symbolized by visible signs as our infirmity requires, but in such a way that it is not a bare figure, but joined to its reality and substance. It is therefore with good reason that the bread is called body, since not only does it represent it to us, but also presents it to us.[46]

The way in which Calvin conceived the union between the sign and its inner reality or substance may be deduced from the example with which he introduced the above passage. He drew the analogy between the baptism of Jesus and the Eucharist; just as the dove was the visible sign of the presence of the Spirit in Christ, so the bread and wine are visible signs of the presence of Christ in the Eucharist. This vision that was granted to John the Baptist was not an empty figure, but a certain sign of the Spirit's presence; therefore he could say in the Gospel that he saw the Holy Spirit because it was represented to him according to his capacity.

In other passages we find Calvin using what sounds like traditional language, such as the word "substance"; but for him this does not mean a kind of invisible core, nor, when applied to Christ's body, His natural physical body, but rather simply the basic reality of a thing. Hence he says, in language that sounds very realistic:

The matter and substance of the sacrament is the Lord Jesus Christ, and the efficacy of them is the gifts and blessings which we have by means of Him.[47]

Or again:

Christ with all His riches is presented in it [the Eucharist] no less than if He were set before our eyes and were touched by our hands.[48]

In summary, he could say:

We all confess, then, with one mouth that, in receiving the sacrament in faith, according to the ordinance of the Lord, we are truly made partakers of the real substance of the body and blood of Jesus Christ.[49]

Calvin was deeply concerned to disprove the local presence of Christ's body in the Eucharist. Calvin's uncertainty about the condition of the risen Christ's body appears in a further statement in his *Treatise on the Lord's Supper* as follows:

Now to maintain this [the localized presence of Christ], it is necessary to confess either that the body of Christ is without limit, or that it can

---

[46] *Ibid.*, p. 147.
[47] Reid, *op. cit.*, p. 146.
[48] *Instruction*, 1537, art. "Of the Lord's Supper."
[49] *Short Treatise on the Lord's Supper*, Reid, *op. cit.*, p. 166.

be in different places. In saying so, we come at last to the point where it appears nothing but a phantom. Hence to wish to establish such a presence that the body of Christ is enclosed within the signs, or is joined locally to it, is not only a dream but a damnable error, contradicting the glory of Christ, and destructive of what we ought to hold concerning His human nature. For Scripture teaches us everywhere, that as our Lord Jesus Christ on earth took our humanity, so He has exalted it into heaven, withdrawing it from its mortal condition, but *not changing its nature.* So we have two things to consider when we speak of our Lord's humanity. We may not destroy the reality of His nature, nor derogate at all from its glorious estate. . . . For if we wish to abase Him under the corruptible elements of this world . . . we annihilate the glory of His ascension.[50]

Opposing any enclosure of Christ in a local sense under the "corruptible elements" of bread and wine, Calvin maintains, in order

not to diminish the efficacy of this sacred mystery, we must hold that it is accomplished by the secret and miraculous virtue of God, and that the Spirit of God is the bond of participation, for which reason it is called spiritual.[51]

Christ's body remains in heaven, and his body and blood are associated with the sacramental signs through the Holy Spirit who serves as a "a kind of channel by which everything that Christ has and is, is derived to us."[52] Trying to explain this further, Calvin compares Christ to the sun and the Holy Spirit to the rays that carry the sun's warmth to the earth.

Calvin's conception of what has been called a dynamic presence or a presence of power in the Eucharist comes out clearly in a passage from his *Institutes:*

For though he withdrew his flesh from us, and with his body ascended to heaven, he, however, sits at the right hand of the Father; that is, he reigns in power and majesty, and the glory of the Father. This kingdom is not limited by any intervals of space, nor circumscribed by any dimensions. Christ can exert his energy wherever he pleases, in earth and heaven, can manifest his presence *by the exercise of his power,* can always be present with his people . . . just as if he were with them in the body; in fine, can feed them with his own body, communion with which he transfuses into them. After this manner, the body and blood of Christ are exhibited to us in the sacrament.[53]

The opinion expressed in the *Institutes,* composed in 1536, reappears over twenty years later in a letter to Bullinger, dated December 27, 1562:

---

[50] *Short Treatise on the Lord's Supper,* in Reid, *op. cit.,* p. 158 f.

[51] *Ibid.,* p. 166.

[52] Calvin, *Institutes of the Christian Religion* (London: Clarke, 1957 ed.), tr. Henry Beveridge, Vol. II, Bk. IV, Ch. 17, #12, p. 565.

[53] *Institutes of the Christian Religion,* Vol. II, Bk. IV, Ch. 17, #18, p. 570 f. Emphasis added.

Although the flesh of Christ is in heaven, we nevertheless feed truly upon it on earth, because Christ by the unfathomable and omnipresent power of His Spirit makes Himself so much ours that He dwells in us without change of place. . . . I see no absurdity in saying that we really receive the flesh and blood of Christ and that He is thus substantially our food, provided that it be agreed that Christ descends to us not merely by the exterior symbols but also by the secret operation of His Spirit, that we may ascend to Him by faith.[54]

The same emphasis on the power of Christ being in the Eucharist appears in one last text we shall quote from Calvin's *Commentary on 1 Corinthians*:

My conclusion is that the body of Christ is really, to use the usual word, i.e., truly given to us in the supper, so that it may be health-giving food for our souls. I am adopting the usual terms, but I mean that our souls are fed by the substance of His body, so that we are truly made one with Him; or, what amounts to the same thing, that a life-giving power from the flesh of Christ is poured into us through the medium of the Spirit, even although it is at a great distance from us, and is not mixed with us.[55]

Twentieth-century Calvinism seems to have adhered pretty much to its founder's original teaching in this matter. In 1931, the Synod of the Reformed Churches of France asserted:

As concerning the mode of the Lord's presence in the sacrament, believers can have different views, but they cannot differ on the fact of the presence itself; it is a real presence according to the Spirit and is inseparable from the elements of the Eucharist in the very act of celebration.[56]

The net result of such explanations seems to dilute the fullness of the Real Presence doctrine as taught by the Catholic Church. A presence in power is not the same thing as a physical presence under sacramental signs. Authority or power may be exerted at a distance, as Calvin himself intimates; this falls far short of the actual presence of the person exercising the authority. Furthermore Calvin's view seems to give undue prominence to the work of the Holy Spirit in the Lord's Supper and to minimize the presence of the body of Christ. It seems, in short, to confuse the Last Supper with Pentecost.

In England, Archbishop Thomas Cranmer, who governed the diocese of Canterbury from 1533 to 1555, was the first to put the Reform move-

---

[54] Quoted in Thurian, *op. cit.*, p. 118.

[55] Calvin, *The First Epistle of Paul the Apostle to the Corinthians*, tr. J. W. Fraser, 1960, p. 246; quoted in Thurian, *op. cit.*, p. 118.

[56] Thurian, *op. cit.*, 119; cf. Donald M. Baillie, *The Theology of the Sacraments* (New York: Scribner's, 1957), p. 101.

ment there on a theological basis. Historians continue to debate the exact nature of his theological inclinations, as to whether they were Lutheran, Calvinist, or Zwinglian. While many Anglicans and Episcopalians today are not inclined to take Cranmer as their source of authentic teaching, nevertheless we summarize his views here as a Reformation leader in England. Regardless of the opinions of some historians, it seems fair to say that his opinions were more definitely Zwinglian than Calvinistic or Lutheran.[57] Dom Gregory Dix, the Anglican monk, concludes that after a detailed study he is unable to distinguish the substance of Cranmer's teaching from that of Zwingli.[58] We may cite one passage dating from 1550 as an example of Cranmer's views:

> The eating of Christ's Flesh and drinking of His Blood is not to be understand(ed) simply and plainly as the words do properly signify, that we do eat and drink Him with our mouths; but it is a figurative speech spiritually to be understand(ed), that we must deeply imprint and fruitfully believe in our hearts, that His Flesh was crucified and His Blood shed for our redemption. This our belief in Him is to eat His Flesh and drink His Blood, although they be not here present with us, but be ascended into heaven. As our forefathers before Christ's time did likewise eat His Flesh and drink His Blood, which was so far from them that it was not yet born.[59]

E. Doctrine of the Council of Trent

The post-Reformation council, the Council of Trent, meeting in its thirteenth session on October 11, 1551, under Pope Julius III, published its decree on the Holy Eucharist. Concerning the Real Presence, the Council affirmed:

> To begin with, the holy council teaches and openly and straightforwardly professes that in the blessed sacrament of the Holy Eucharist, after the consecration of the bread and wine, our Lord Jesus Christ, true God and man, is truly, really, and substantially contained under the perceptible species of bread and wine. It is not contradictory to say that our Savior always sits at the right hand of the Father in heaven according to His natural way of existing and that, nevertheless, in His substance He is sacramentally present in many other places with us.[60]

Clearly opposing the mere figurative or dynamic (virtual) presence of Christ in the Eucharist according to the teachings of Zwingli and Calvin, the Council summarized its teaching in Canon No. 1 as follows:

---

[57] Cf. Palmer, *Sacraments and Worship*, pp. 248–250; Francis Clark, S.J., *The Eucharistic Sacrifice and the Reformation* (Westminster, Md.: Newman Press, 1960), pp. 159–164.

[58] Dix, op. cit., p. 656.

[59] *Defense of the True and Catholic Doctrine of the Sacrament*, III, 10, (1550), quoted in Dix, op. cit., p. 648.

[60] *Decree on the Most Holy Eucharist*, Chap. I, quoted in TCT, No. 719, p. 281.

If anyone denies that the body and blood, together with the soul and divinity of our Lord Jesus Christ, therefore the whole Christ is truly, really, and substantially contained in the Sacrament of the most holy Eucharist, but says that Christ is present in the Sacrament only as in a sign or figure, or by His power: let him be anathema.[61]

The Council summarizes its teaching on the mode of Christ's presence in the Eucharist as follows:

If anyone says that the substance of bread and wine remains in the holy sacrament of the Eucharist together with the body and blood of our Lord Jesus Christ, and denies that wonderful and extraordinary change (conversio) of the whole substance of the bread into Christ's body and the whole substance of the wine into His blood while only the species of bread and wine remain, a change which the Catholic Church has most fittingly called transubstantiation; let him be anathema.[62]

Defending Communion under only one species, the Council declared:

If anyone denies that in the venerable sacrament of the Eucharist the whole Christ is contained under each species and under each and every portion of either species when it is divided up, let him be anathema.[63]

Upholding the continued presence of Christ in the consecrated Hosts, including those which remain after Communion, the Council declared:

If anyone says that after the consecration, the body and blood of our Lord Jesus Christ are not present in the marvelous sacrament of the Eucharist, but are present only in the use of the sacrament while it is being received, and not before or after, and that the true body of the Lord does not remain in the consecrated hosts or particles that are kept or are left over after Communion: let him be anathema.[64]

Eucharistic Communion brings us the true flesh and blood of Christ; it is not a mere spiritual or figurative eating of Christ. The latter view is condemned by the Council in Canon 8.[65] In Canon 9, the Council reiterates the mandate of the Lateran Council (1215) concerning the Paschal Communion once a year.[66]

Finally in Canon 11, the Council summarizes the requirements for a worthy reception of the sacrament. Maintaining that faith alone is not enough for receiving this sacrament, the Council insists:

. . . lest this great sacrament be received unworthily and thus be received unto death and condemnation, this holy council has determined and decreed that those who have mortal sin on their conscience, no matter

---

[61] TCT, No. 728, p. 286.
[62] Canon 2, TCT, No. 729, p. 286.
[63] Canon 3, TCT, No. 730, pp. 286–287.
[64] Canon 4, TCT, No. 731, p. 287.
[65] TCT, No. 735, ibid.
[66] TCT, No. 736, ibid.

how contrite they may think they are, must necessarily make a sacramental confession before receiving, provided that they have access to a confessor.[67]

In the light of current discussion about transubstantiation, it is important to understand the meaning which the fathers of the Council of Trent intended to convey by their choice of the words "substance," "species," and "change (conversio)" in Canon 2 above. Historians of dogma point out that in the twelfth century, before the introduction of Aristotelian metaphysics into the West, theologians were already speaking of a substantial change in the matter of the eucharist. Alger of Liège (d. 1131) stated, "Only the sacrament of bread and wine is so changed that substantially it is not what it was; for the substance of it becomes the body of Christ, the form which remains signifies and contains that body."[68] One authority maintains that Alger's observation was repeated by the Council of Trent in its decree on the most holy Eucharist, Chap. 3.[69] That the Council of Trent did not wish to canonize the Thomistic and Aristotelian usage in explaining the dogma of transubstantiation would seem to follow also from the fact that the Council did not use the Aristotelian term "accidents" but rather chose the more indefinite term "species" or appearances. Furthermore the turn of the fifteenth century witnessed the rise of a positive theology based on the study of Scripture, the Fathers, and the Councils in the original text, a theology very often in conflict with scholasticism. Theology was in a state of transformation.[70] "The Council . . . was also hampered by the doctrinal divergences, precisely in this sphere [that is, sacramental teaching] between the great schools of theology. If anywhere, it was in connection with the sacraments that the problem of the relation of the Council to scholastic theology presented itself with particular acuteness."[71] Against such a background of controversy, it would not seem likely that the Council fathers would favor one school above another.

In any case it should be understood that the explanation of a dogma according to a certain theological school must be distinguished from the revealed truth as proposed dogmatically by the Church. It is the revealed truth which is a matter of faith and which is therefore the dogma, not

---

[67] TCT, No. 738, p. 288.

[68] De Sacramentis Corporis et Sanguinis Dominici, 1, c. 4, P.L., 180, 751; quoted in Leeming, Principles of Sacramental Theology (Westminster, Md.: The Newman Press, 1956), p. 565.

[69] Denz., No. 876; TCT, No. 721, pp. 282–283; cf. Leeming, ibid., p. 565, footnote 34.

[70] Hubert Jedin, A History of the Council of Trent, tr. by E. Graf (St. Louis: B. Herder Book Co., 1957), Vol. 1, pp. 392–393.

[71] Ibid., Vol. 2, 1961, p. 373.

any particular theological explanation of it. Therefore it would seem that we may understand Canon 2 above in the following way; *transubstantiation* means simply an "essential change"; at the Consecration in the Mass, the substance of bread and wine are changed by God's power into the substance of Christ's body and blood which thereby become present while the outward forms ("empirical realities or phenomena") of the bread and wine remain.[72] "Substance" means "that which, taken in its ultimate being and significance, makes the offering bread (and nothing more) or the Body of Christ; 'species' means that which in the world of ordinary human experience is accessible to us. By declaring that the species of bread and wine remain after the consecration, the doctrine of transubstantiation also expressly (and rightly) teaches us that empirical procedures cannot detect any physical change in the offering."[73] What we seek is the irreducible minimum of the revealed truth.

> The defined doctrine of transubstantiation (Denz. 884) does not attempt to give an explanation of just how Christ becomes present but simply to state in alternative terms that cannot be watered down that on the one hand what Christ gives us is, as He says, His Body and nothing else, and that on the other hand the empirical reality available to our sense may and must be recognized as that of bread. The sense of "substance" and "species" in the context of the definition as such must therefore ultimately be sought in this theological datum and not in the maxims of philosophy.[74]

On the basis of such a distinction between the revealed truth of the Real Presence and its formulation in human language, we have the justification for contemporary theologians to test new ways of expressing the dogma of the eucharistic presence in currently meaningful language.[75]

III. THE EUCHARISTIC PRESENCE IN CONTEMPORARY FOCUS

The perspective of Vatican II in which we must view current thinking on the eucharistic presence of Christ is that of a dialogue with the modern world. A twofold dialogue is in progress, first between theology and contemporary philosophy, and second between the Catholic Church and other Christians. One of the most exciting developments in Catholic theology derives from a forthright encounter with such philosophies as existentialism, phenomenology, and logical analysis. Theologians are

---

[72] Karl Rahner-Herbert Vorgrimler, *Theological Dictionary*, tr. by Richard Strachan (New York: Herder and Herder, 1965), p. 466.

[73] *Ibid.*

[74] *Ibid.*

[75] Cf. below under Section III-B.

driven to reexamine the traditional truths in the light of these new philosophic ideas; while God's truth is immutable, man constantly struggles to understand, to clarify, and to communicate the ageless truths of revelation in language and thought patterns meaningful to his contemporaries. The application of existential and phenomenological idiom to biblical truth affords rich new insight into God's ways with men and builds a firm bridgehead of communication with contemporary thinking man. Interdisciplinary dialogue of this kind further enhances the great conversation which the Church has initiated with her fellow Christians. As dialogue moves forward, discussion must eventually turn to the major concern of eucharistic worship.

A. Liturgical Reform and the Real Presence

The Constitution on the Sacred Liturgy (December 4, 1963) speaks of a manifold presence of Christ in liturgical celebrations:

> He [Christ] is present in the sacrifice of the Mass, not only in the person of His minister, "the same now offering, through the ministry of priests, who formerly offered Himself on the cross," but especially under the Eucharistic species. By His power He is present in the sacraments, so that when a man baptizes it is really Christ Himself who baptizes. He is present in His word, since it is He Himself who speaks when the holy scriptures are read in the Church. He is present, lastly, when the Church prays and sings, for He promised: "Where two or three are gathered together in my Name, there am I in the midst of them."[76]

Far from underestimating the traditional doctrine of the Real Presence, the Council rather places this truth in a new context. The believing Christian encounters Christ at Mass in a fivefold way. These several modes of Christ's presence are not explained by the Council but remain open to theological reflection.

That Christ is present at the eucharistic celebration in the person of His minister is clear from the words and actions of the priest. In Christ's name, the priest utters the Consecration "This is my body," allowing Christ to speak and act through him to make present his enduring sacrifice. Christ is the principal offerer at every Eucharist. At Communion, the priest acts in a dual capacity; as our brother, the priest receives the eucharistic food along with the Christian community; but as the agent of Christ, he is the medium through whom Christ himself feeds us.

As a gracious host, Christ speaks to us in words of friendship and brotherhood. Through Scripture, he calls us together in his redeeming love; he proclaims his saving deeds for us; he admonishes us to faith,

---

[76] A.A.S., Vol. 56, 2, February 15, 1964, par. 7, p. 100 f.; NCWC tr.

trust, and repentance. His word is life-giving to those who hear it in faith and commitment.

Drawing us to himself in faithful allegiance, he leads us in the action of sacrifice. Just as he is present as the principal priest of every sacrament, so in the Eucharist Christ is present to gather us into his own self-surrender to the Father. As the risen Christ, he enables us to pass over with him little by little at every Mass to the joyful freedom of his Father's house. In and through and with him, we renew our covenant-commitment, reaffirm our word of loyal obedience to the Father who gives us our daily life.

As our daily bread from the Father, Christ is present in the eucharistic meal to sustain his followers in the strength of mutual love. Feeding on his very substance, present under the species of bread and wine by transubstantiation, we mature in the new humanity which the risen Christ is fashioning on earth.

Christ as the source of a new risen humanity remains present in us in his human nature only as long as the eucharistic species endure; but he continues to be present among us in our fellow Christians. The risen Savior remains among us when we are at worship; he reveals his presence among us when we serve him in one another. As Christ is the sacrament of God, so the Church is the sacrament or sign of Christ. In this community he is present in a variety of functions: in the Church teaching, sanctifying, worshiping, gathering up all things in the love of his Father. The eucharistic presence then is a presence first to the community and then to each individual member. When we encounter him in eucharistic Communion, we meet him as head of the new humanity (cf. Col 1:22; Rom 5:12-19; I Cor 15:45-49; Eph 2:14-16; 4:22-24). No more radical encounter with our brother Christians is possible than meeting them through the eucharistic Christ.

B. Recent Theology of the Real Presence

Theology develops by dialogue. Current theology represents a twofold thrust: toward ecumenism and toward modern philosophy.

In the first instance, theologians of the reformed tradition like F. J. Leenhardt and Max Thurian have made significant contributions to Protestant eucharistic theology. Thurian's work The Eucharistic Memorial has given us much insight into ecumenical eucharistic theology. In a special chapter on the Real Presence, the monk of the ecumenical community at Taizé first sets out to explain Calvin's views on the Real Presence. He then summarizes his own views in a series of theses, where he unequivocally asserts his belief in the true, real, and substantial presence in the Eucharist of Christ's body and blood, humanity and divinity both.[77] Just what this means to him he attempts to explain in the following way:

This real presence of His body and blood is the presence of Christ crucified and glorified, here and now under concrete signs. The meaning of every corporal presence is to attest concretely the presence of that person that he may enter into a concrete communion. By the real presence of His body and blood, the Church knows that Christ is there concretely in the midst and it receives Him by means of a concrete sign. The substantial presence of Christ does not denote a material presence, in the natural sense, but the presence of the profound reality of the body and blood of Christ crucified and glorified.[78]

Like other modern writers, Thurian emphasizes the purpose of Christ's presence as a means of contacting him through signs. He is adamant in rejecting the localized presence of Christ's body in its natural sense, which can be understood in a perfectly orthodox way. The elements of bread and wine become a privileged place where Christ may be met and received. Christ accomplishes this through his Spirit and his word over the bread and wine.

As to the condition of the bread and wine, Thurian maintains that they are no longer ordinary bread and wine once Christ makes of them a sign of his presence. Their chemical nature remains the same but "behind this, faith must recognize the true and new substantial reality of the bread and wine: the body and blood of Christ."[79] The elements of bread and wine "are changed, not chemically, [but] in the sense that the glorified Christ takes possession of them to make them a concrete sign of His presence in our midst, to make them His body and blood, a place where He may be found locally, contemplated sensibly and communicated concretely."[80] The whole liturgical action, not merely the eucharistic narrative, accomplishes Christ's presence there. In accord with contemporary emphasis, Thurian notes that the Eucharist is not merely a sacred object but "an action in an act of communion. The signs of bread and wine are eucharistized for the sacrifice of thanksgiving and intercession, which are accomplished in the communion."[81] This is a true objective presence.

Advocating Communion even for the sick as an extension of the eucharistic celebration in church, he comes to touch upon the question as to whether Christ remains present after the celebration is over. Whereas Leenhardt maintains that the eucharistic Bread reverts to its natural status outside the context of the sacramental action, Thurian has this to say about the problem:

[77] Thurian, The Eucharistic Memorial, Part II, p. 120.
[78] Ibid., p. 121.   [79] Ibid.   [80] Ibid.   [81] Ibid., p. 122.

After the celebration has been completed by the communion of the faithful, including that of the sick in their homes, the real connection between Christ and the elements left over is a mystery that should be respected.

Since the conclusion of the Eucharist is the communion . . . we cannot define the nature of the relationship of Christ and the elements that remain after the completion of communion. There is no need to speculate about the continuance nor about its disappearance. The mystery is to be respected. Because of such an attitude of respect, it is fitting that the Eucharistic remains should be concealed after the celebration.[82]

Indecisively he leaves an open question the relationship of Christ to the elements remaining after Communion. He does not, of course, subscribe to transubstantiation in the sense of Trent; firmly upholding the real objective presence of Christ on the one hand, he seems to go not much further than Calvin in explaining just how that presence occurs. He concludes his treatment of the Real Presence with a moving paragraph on the Eucharist as sacrament of unity.

As indicated above, Thurian accepts the Real Presence in the objective sense but rejects transubstantiation to explain the mode of that presence. Indeed nearly twenty years ago he stated very forthrightly:

In the Catholic theology of the Eucharist, the dogma of transubstantiation is not an essential one. The central element of the Catholic belief in the Eucharist, as of ours, is certitude about the real presence. The dogma of transubstantiation has a protective and defensive purpose. It was explicitly formulated in the Middle Ages, and its sole purpose was to express the mystery of the real presence in an understandable way to the men of this period. . . .

It is surprising that for centuries Catholic theology has continued to explain the dogma of the real presence by transubstantiation, while human thought has moved forward so that this explanation has become quite out of date and unreal. . . . Indeed, it is an urgent matter that this dogma of the real presence be thought out again in modern concepts. Not only will this result in an increase of spirituality for Catholic faith and piety, but it will be one step more toward the unity of the Church.[83]

Addressing himself to this task of rethinking transubstantiation, Professor F. J. Leenhardt, a Reformed theologian, approaches the notion of substance in the light of modern philosophical analysis.[84] For him sub-

---

[82] *Ibid.*, p. 123.

[83] Thurian, "Toward a Renewal of the Doctrine of Transubstantiation," in *Christianity Divided*, ed. Callahan, Obermann, and O'Hanlon (New York: Sheed and Ward, 1961), pp. 197, 199. Translated from an article written by Thurian in 1946.

[84] His work *This is My Body* is the second part of O. Cullmann-F. J. Leenhardt, *Essays on the Lord's Supper* (Ecumenical Studies in Worship I), tr. by J. G. Davies (London: Lutterworth Press, 1958), pp. 24–85. Cf., also, Cyril Vollert, "The Eucha-

stance does not mean, as for Aristotle and St. Thomas, the substratum of accidents or the matter behind the form; but looked at existentially, substance is determined by the ultimate meaning that a thing comes to have in human relationships. In the matter of the Eucharist, the substance will depend upon the meaning that Christ gives. Thus when Christ says "This is my body" over the bread, he gives it a new meaning, a new finality; the bread no longer has reason to exist for nourishing the body, although it still continues to do this; the essential meaning of the bread will now be seen through faith as a sign through which we contact Christ. It is the will of God that gives the ultimate meaning or reality to things. Leenhardt professes to derive this premise from a study of the setting of the eucharistic words; he claims it represents the Hebrew attitude toward reality that God's word and will are the source of all meaning and reality. In this case the divine meaning that Christ gives to the eucharistic bread transcends its natural meaning as nourishment but does not completely cancel out its secondary purpose. Hence outside the Lord's Supper, the eucharistic bread reverts to its natural status.

But, as Catholic critics have noted, Leenhardt's position seems close to nominalism in that he has Christ imposing a "change" on the bread and yet no real objective change occurs there. "The author's lack of realism, his 'extrinsicist' teaching on 'transubstantiation,' seems to derive from pure nominalism."[85]

In the Catholic camp, such a philosophy of analysis has not been without influence. Two British authors, Herbert McCabe, O.P., and Charles Davis, have each made contributions that seek to restate the traditional doctrine of transubstantiation in modern terms.[86] For Father McCabe,[87] sacraments as encounter between Christ and his Church are a kind of sign language; they have a word function by which Christ and the faithful communicate with each other. In short, the sacraments are a dialogue; in the Eucharist we do not have a physical object statically before us, but Christ is there "as language in which we speak, the word in whom we pray and who speaks to us."[88] For McCabe, Christ's Eucharistic presence is a further specification of his presence to the whole Church-community as such. His presence, he maintains, is not a physical presence; to understand this in an orthodox fashion, one must take him

rist: Quests for Insights from Scripture," in *Theological Studies*, Vol. 21, 3, September, 1960, 427–434.

85 Vollert, *ibid.*, p. 433.

86 In the Netherlands, the discussion on the Real Presence has involved men like P. Schoonenberg, S.J., L. Smits, O.F.M.Cap., and E. Schillebeeckx, O.P. Cf. *Herder Correspondence* (New York), Vol. 2, No. 12, Dec., 1965, pp. 388–392.

87 Herbert McCabe, "The Real Presence," in *Clergy Review*, Vol. 49, No. 12, December, 1964, pp. 749–759.

88 *Ibid.*, p. 758.

to be opposing a "natural" presence, that is, one extended in space or occupying a certain part of space.[89]

Approaching the subject somewhat differently from Father McCabe, Father Charles Davis likewise ventures a new study of the manner in which the Real Presence comes about in the Eucharist.[90] He premises his study with the statement that the Council of Trent did not intend to canonize the Aristotelian theory of substance and accidents in expressing the dogma of the Real Presence. The Council Fathers did not use the word "accident" at all, he points out, but rather the word "species"; the word "substance," he asserts, is employed in a nontechnical, non-Aristotelian sense. Inheriting this term from long doctrinal usage, the Fathers of Trent used the term "substance" merely with the meaning of the reality of the bread or of the body of Christ. Applying this to transubstantiation, the Fathers of Trent meant that by a wonderful conversion the reality of bread is changed into the body of Christ; the outward manifestation, however, is not Christ's own but that of the previously present bread. What was bread is converted into the body of Christ without any perceptible change.

Father Davis finds a certain difficulty in the traditional Thomistic formulation. Taking substance as that which can exist by itself, he finds that in the bread and wine there is not a single substance but rather a conglomeration of substances accidentally united. But according to the Thomistic explanation, this would mean that a group of substances is converted into Christ's body; and therefore the Real Presence will cease even where no change has occurred such as to involve a substantial corruption. If we removed any of the components from the consecrated elements, such as water from the wine or starch from the bread, all this would amount to is a local separation involving no substantial change, that is, no change in the existing unities of activity. Yet the Real Presence would cease, because all agree that Christ is present only under the appearances of bread, not those of water or starch.

To obviate such a difficulty, Davis proposes a different approach to the notion of substance. What makes the reality of a thing and gives it its unity and intelligibility is the human purpose, the human meaning

---

[89] In the interests of ecumenical clarity, one might well observe two basic premises. First there is only one objective body of Christ; therefore one should not speak of the "sacramental body" as if it were different from the "natural body." Second, a distinction which is orthodox and admissible is to say that "the body is sacramentally present in the Eucharist, naturally present in heaven." Finally it might be best to omit the use of the term "physical" altogether and to speak instead of the "natural presence" as distinct from "sacramental presence." Cf. James Quinn, S.J., "Ecumenics and the Eucharist," in *The Month*, Vol. 33, No. 4, April, 1965, p. 216.

[90] Charles Davis, "The Theology of Transubstantiation," in *Sophia*, Vol. 3, No. 1, April, 1964, pp. 12–24.

which it comes to have. This is not to reduce reality to a purely subjective level. He cites as an example a painting which is a conglomeration of substances. On the level of physical reality there is no unity of being or activity here; the unity and intelligibility come from its relation to man.

Bread is this kind of man-made object which gets its unity and meaning not from its physical composition alone, but from its relation to man. Within limits, the physical composition of bread can vary considerably; but we give this matter a meaning and a purpose when we make it serve as human nourishment. This is not to discard altogether its objective makeup, that is, the physical substances of which it is composed. To know the reality of a thing is to know its purpose, its human significance; if this relation is unknown, the "substance" is itself unknowable.

Applying this to transubstantiation, we may say that the new reality which the bread has become through the consecration, namely the body of Christ, is unknowable except in the realm of faith. Therefore there is no measurable or perceptible change in the bread as such; such change will not be subject to scientific analysis. To know transubstantiation means to know it as a religious event, to know it in faith. What was bread now stands in a new relation to us as Christ himself; the material elements now convey to us the reality and action of Christ.[91]

But now it may be objected: isn't this saying that the bread remains bread, but it is merely used by Christ for a higher purpose and that there is really no change here at all? Is this not the Lutheran doctrine of a coexistence of the bread and the body of Christ? Father Davis answers that the Church has always admitted that on one level the material elements after the Consecration remain the same as the bread; they still look, taste, and act the same way as before the Consecration. Christ wished to preserve, not to destroy, this action of bodily nourishment, which is precisely what Christ made the sign and cause of sharing his own life with us.[92] Christ has altered the intrinsic meaning and purpose of the elements; in their relationship to man, these forms are now the body of Christ in the sacrament. Transubstantiation, then, is not a change of physical substance but a change of finality, a change in what this thing called bread means and does for man, therefore a change in what it is for man.[93] According to Father Davis, such an explanation restores the Real Presence to a truly sacramental status by which the externals, though not changed physically or naturally (as they are not in any other sacrament), nevertheless serve to signify a new reality through the consecration, namely, the reality of Christ's true presence.

It can be seen that in such an explanation or expression of the mystery

---

[91] *Ibid.*, p. 21.   [92] *Ibid.*, p. 22.   [93] *Ibid.*

of Christ's presence in the Eucharist, the notion of substance has moved from that of a metaphysical or ontological reality to the existential thing, described in terms of its characteristic function. While the chemical function of bread does not change in the Eucharist, the human or social function does change; a new sacramental function is assumed by the consecrated eucharistic bread in making Christ present. In so doing, the sacramental function must totally and objectively displace the mere human function of bread. There is therefore only one meaning and only one reality. The eucharistic bread which makes Christ present remains such for as long as the sacramental symbolism lasts. Therefore, in contrast with Leenhardt's view, there is no question of the Real Presence "abandoning" the eucharistic bread once it has been consecrated.

C. Paul VI, "Mysterium Fidei"

On September 3, 1965, Pope Paul VI issued an encyclical letter on the Eucharist, Mysterium Fidei (Mystery of Faith), purportedly to caution against certain recent errors among Catholic theologians writing on this subject. Among the proscribed opinions are those which

> discuss the mystery of transubstantiation without mentioning what the Council of Trent stated about the marvelous conversion of the whole substance of the bread into the Body and of the whole substance of the wine into the Blood of Christ, speaking rather only of what is called "transignification" and "transfinalization," or finally to propose and act upon the opinion according to which, in the consecrated hosts which remain after the celebration of the sacrifice of the Mass, Christ our Lord is no longer present.[94]

Insisting that the rule of language confirmed by the authority of previous ecumenical councils be preserved, the Holy Father continues:

> In the same way, it cannot be tolerated that any individual should on his own authority modify the formulas which were used by the Council of Trent to express belief in the Eucharistic mystery.[95]

Maintaining that such formulas are not tied to any specific form of human culture or a single theological school, but that they present reality in a way adapted to men of all times, the Pope suggests that it is the work of theologians to explain and defend such formulas. He does admit "that these formulas can sometimes be more clearly and accurately explained." In fact, the achievement of this goal is highly beneficial. But it would be wrong to give these expressions a meaning other than the original. Thus, the understanding of the faith should be advanced without threat to its unchangeable truth.[96] He insists that he does not wish

---

[94] Mysterium Fidei, AAS, Vol. 57, No. 11, October 30, 1965, p. 755.
[95] Ibid., p. 758.   [96] Ibid.

"to deny in those who are spreading these singular opinions the praise-worthy effort to investigate this lofty mystery and to set forth its inexhaustible riches, revealing its meaning to the men of today; rather we acknowledge and approve their effort."[97] However he finds it necessary to reprove the opinions which these theologians have expressed.

Later in the encyclical after reviewing the teaching of the Fathers on the presence of Christ in the Sacrament, the Pope repeats the phrasing of the Council of Trent in its decree on the Eucharist, Chapter 4 and Canon 2. He goes on to explain:

> As a result of transubstantiation, the species of bread and wine undoubtedly take on a new meaning and a new finality, for they no longer remain ordinary bread and ordinary wine, but become the sign of something sacred, the sign of a spiritual food. However, the reason they take on this new significance and this new finality is simply because they contain a new "reality" which we may justly term ontological. Not that there lies under those species what was already there before, but something quite different; and that not only because of the faith of the Church, but in objective reality, since after the change of the substance or nature of the bread and wine into the Body and Blood of Christ, nothing remains of the bread and wine but the appearances, under which Christ, whole and entire, in His physical "reality" is bodily present, although not in the same way that bodies are present in a given place.[98]

Thus it seems that at least some of the statements of Fathers McCabe and Davis noted above may well fall within the proscription of the encyclical; nevertheless neither theologian has professed to deny the revealed truth of the change or conversion of bread and wine into Christ's body and blood really present. They are merely seeking more viable language in which to express the revealed mystery, an effort which the Pope on his part has affirmed he does not wish to discourage.[99]

From such discussion, we can realize that theology is alive to the spirit of the times, striving to be in dialogue with the modern world, as both Council and Pope have urged. We can appreciate that theology is a human science, a groping science; the human mind is ever seeking greater clarity in the divine message. In all humility we must admit our own inadequacy; we don't know all the answers, not even to religious truth. God expects man to use his mind, always subject to the inspiration of the Holy Spirit and the guidance of the Church.

---

[97] *Ibid.*, p. 756.

[98] *Ibid.*, p. 766.

[99] For discussion of *Mysterium Fidei* and its implications for the above theories, cf. Joseph M. Powers, S.J., "*Mysterium Fidei* and the Theology of the Eucharist," *Worship*, Vol. 40, No. 1, Jan., 1966, pp. 17–35; Colman O'Neill, O.P., "What is 'Transignification' All About?" *The Catholic World*, Vol. 202, No. 1210, Jan., 1966, pp. 204–211.

D. Conclusion

Following the counsel of Pope Paul, the Catholic will acknowledge and cherish the great blessing of the New Covenant in having God among us in the sacramental species. But he will not conceive of this as a mere static presence; Christ reveals his presence by an *action*, renewing the great deed of his sacrifice and feeding us in the sacramental meal. Remaining in the sacramental species after Mass, Christ continues there to be present to us as the sacrificial victim risen and glorified indeed, the Paschal Victim leading us into that trinitarian unity which he requested for his Church the night of the first Eucharist: "That all may be one, even as you, Father, in me and I in you; that they also may be one in Us, that the world may believe that you have sent me" (Jn 17:21). The eucharistic presence should never be dissociated from the sacrifice-meal. Only within such a perspective can we preserve that integral view of the sacred eucharistic mystery reflected in the Benediction *Collect*:

> O God, Who in this wonderful Sacrament left us a memorial of Your passion, grant, we implore you, that we may so venerate the sacred mysteries of Your Body and Blood as always to be conscious of the fruit of Your redemption.[100]

[100] *Collectio Rituum* (Milwaukee: Bruce, 1964), p. 257.

CHAPTER XII

History of the Eucharistic Liturgy

INTRODUCTION

The theology of the Eucharist, surveyed in the past four chapters, reflects an ongoing process of creative understanding in the contemporary life of the Church. Concomitantly, by launching a reform of the eucharistic liturgy, the Second Vatican Council hopes to revitalize the Church's worship and to make it an authentic expression of eucharistic belief and ecclesial charity.

The quest for cultic authenticity, however, presumes a prudent regard for the historical evolution of the Mass liturgy. Only in this perspective does the current Mass reform become fully intelligible as tradition-based and yet pastorally oriented. Hence the concern of the present chapter with the centuries-long evolution of the Mass ritual.

I. THE LAST SUPPER

The first Eucharist was celebrated at the Last Supper, within the context of a solemn festive meal which had at least the atmosphere of a paschal feast. Adapting the supper ritual, Jesus transformed the bread and cup blessings, pronounced in the form of thanksgiving, into the twofold thanksgiving offering in which he consecrated himself to the Father for the world's redemption. Then sharing the sacrificial bread and cup with his followers, he invited them to join in his sacrifice even unto death.

It was Christ's intention to celebrate a covenant ritual at this meal. From this eucharistic covenant sacrifice, a new people of God emerged. As essentially a eucharistic community, they would give cultic witness to their identity as those who are incorporated into his body in the sacrament.

From the first Eucharist, the essentials of Christian worship appear as the thanksgiving offering (Consecration) and the complementary covenant meal of Communion. Developing a suitable matrix for the sacramental rite itself was left to the Church's own creativeness; in word and gesture, the local churches were to set forth for the faithful of their time and milieu the intrinsic meaning of eucharistic worship. From the very beginning, freedom of local adaptation prevailed.

II. THE EUCHARIST IN THE APOSTOLIC CHURCH

Since Christ had celebrated the first Eucharist within the framework of a meal, it was natural that the Apostles should do likewise. Fulfilling the Lord's mandate to do what he had done as a memorial to him, in Jerusalem and in the other early Christian centers, the Apostles and the presbyters assembled the local Christian communities for a weekly celebration of the "breaking of the bread." Since this meal celebrated the Lord's triumph over sin and death, accomplished on the first day of the week, the Palestinian Christians would have gathered either on a Saturday or Sunday evening (since the Jews calculated their day from sunset to sunset).[1] The type of meal with which they introduced the Eucharist would scarcely have been the Paschal meal with its complex and lengthy ritual; rather they may have chosen something like a *chaburah* (brotherhood) meal or at least the weekly Sabbath meal. From Acts 2:42, 46, we gather that these meals were taken in one another's home, since there

---

[1] Cf. The risen Christ's appearances at a meal on the first day of the week (cf. Lk 24:35, 43; Jn 20:19, 26); also Paul's celebration at Troas (cf. Acts 20:7); a collection for the poor at Jerusalem, taken up on the first day of the week, presumably at the weekly liturgy (cf. 1 Cor 16:2).

was at this early date no special house of Christian worship. In fact, the first Jewish Christians continued to frequent the synagogue and the temple until they were expelled; their uniquely Christian worship was celebrated at home.

Evidence for the Mass at this early date is piecemeal. The clearest New Testament evidence we possess for the Eucharist in the apostolic age is found in St. Paul's first letter to the Corinthian church (cf. 1 Cor 11:17–34). In Greek Christian communities like that at Corinth, the equivalent of the chaburah meal was called agapē (love), because they felt that fraternal charity, mandated so forthrightly at the first Eucharist, ought to be tangibly expressed in every eucharisic gathering of Christian table fellowship. Just as at the chaburah meal the members of the group each brought food for the meal, so at the agapē the participants contributed what food they could so as to share it with the poor.

In the Corinthian church, however, practice often fell short of the ideal. Small cliques of the well-to-do, arriving early for the meal, sat down and ate together without waiting for the working-class poor or slaves, who found nothing left to eat when they came to the feast. There was the added problem of excessive drinking. Such conduct, Paul insists, violates the key virtue of Christian love; it makes a caricature of the very meal designed to witness to Christian unity and solidarity in Christ.

The agapē meal was immediately followed by the Eucharist (cf. 1 Cor 11:23–29), with the whole service being called the Lord's Supper. From this description, as well as from other evidence, we can gather that the twofold consecration offering was expressed in the form of a thanksgiving blessing, placed at the end of the agapē.[2]

The agapē-Eucharist, finally, served as a communication medium between the churches. Paul's letters undoubtedly were read on occasions like this, so that all the faithful would hear the message of their spiritual father. In the next period of liturgical development, a full-blown liturgy of the Word, modeled after the synagogue service, would proclaim God's saving love for his people. With the eventual separation of agapē from Eucharist (certainly by the second century), the liturgy of God's Word came to serve as a fitting prelude, indeed an integral complement, to the Eucharist proper.

III. THE MASS AT ROME IN THE SECOND AND THIRD CENTURIES

Confining ourselves to the development of the Mass in the West, especially at Rome, we can discover the broad outlines of the Mass at

---

[2] For other evidence of this, cf. Kilmartin, *The Eucharist in the Primitive Church* (Englewood Cliffs, N. J.: Prentice-Hall, 1964), p. 147.

this period in an important document written by Justin the Martyr and entitled *The First Apology* (about A.D. 158), addressed to the Roman emperor as an explanation of the typical Sunday worship of the Christian community. Justin's description (par. 67) is as follows:

> . . . On the day which is called Sunday, we have a common assembly of all who live in the cities or outlying districts, and the memoirs of the Apostles or the writings of the Prophets are read, as long as there is time. Then when the reader has finished, the president of the assembly verbally admonishes and invites all to imitate such examples of virtue. Then we all stand up together and offer up prayers, and, as we said before, after we finish our prayers, bread and wine and water are presented. He who presides likewise offers up prayers and thanksgivings, to the best of his ability, and the people express their approval by saying "Amen." The Eucharistic elements are distributed and consumed by those present, and to those who are absent they are sent through the deacons. The wealthy, if they wish, contribute whatever they desire, and the collection is placed in the custody of the president. . . .[3]

From this account, it appears a well-established custom at Rome to begin the eucharistic celebration with a Scripture service modeled after the Jewish synagogue liturgy. Already at this early date, the basic twofold structure of today's Mass appears: the liturgy of the Word and the liturgy of the Eucharist.

To explain this form of worship to the emperor, Justin carefully employs the Roman idiom; the Christian day of assembly (the "Lord's Day") is called "Sunday" (*dies solis*). The Gospels are called simply the memoirs of the Apostles. Of considerable import is the parity accorded the apostolic writings with the older inspired works of the prophets. By implication, constant liturgical usage testified to the Church's acceptance of these writings as canonical or inspired.

At this early date, there were no selected pericopes or passages adapted to the different Sundays of the year; the reading was a *lectio continua* (continuous or serialized reading). At a given Mass, the celebrant signaled the reader when to stop; the next Sunday the reader would continue where the previous reader had concluded. Presumably the readers were minor clerics or laymen. The liturgical function was therefore structured according to the classical principle of the distribution of roles; the lesser offices, like that of lector, were performed by assistants, while the major role was performed by the celebrant.

The scripture readings are followed by the homily or instruction of

---

[3] J. Quasten, *Florilegium Patristicum* (Bonn: Hanstein, 1935), fascicle 7, part I, pp. 19, 20; tr. in Palmer, *Sacraments and Worship* (Westminster, Md.: The Newman Press, 1956), pp. 59–60.

the celebrant, which is considered an integral part of the liturgy. In answer to God's word spoken through Scripture and sermon, the faithful rise (in the traditional posture of prayer in the ancient Church) and offer up the litany of petitionary prayers for the needs of the Church and one's fellowmen, prayers which have once again been restored at least on Sundays and feast days — the so-called "prayers of the faithful."

Following these prayers, a simple offertory rite occurs, with the bread, wine, and water being brought to the altar. The celebrant then consecrates the offerings in a thanksgiving or blessing prayer of his own composition. Like the Jewish grace at meals in its grateful recollection of Yahweh's saving acts, this prayer would recall Christ's great salvation deeds for man, climaxing in the narrative of the Last Supper, Christ's death, resurrection, and sending of the Holy Spirit. The loud "Amen" of the faithful at the end of this eucharistic or thanksgiving prayer is the congregation's solemn assent to the offering, their way of saying that the sacrifice is not only the celebrant's own personal gift to God but their gift also. Congregational participation, dialogue fashion, is not a twentieth-century creation; it dates back at least to the mid-second century, and probably much earlier.

The Communion rite is briefly recounted as the distribution of the elements or the consecrated species of bread and wine to the faithful — presumably to all those present. Communion to the sick is noted as their way of participating or sharing in the blessings of the Mass. Finally, the loving solidarity of God's people is demonstrated by their contributions to the collection, which is given to the celebrant for the clergy and for the poor.

Such an account makes no mention of the common meal or agapē, although such a meal undoubtedly was retained in some parts of the Church (e.g., Egypt) until as late as the fifth century. From Justin's description it would seem that the common custom at Rome was to have the Eucharist celebrated at a single table, the table of the celebrant or the altar, with the worshipers gathered around it. As congregations increased in size and required a larger area for worship, the more spacious homes of the Christian aristocracy of Rome were opened to the faithful for the Sunday assembly.

Documentary evidence from the early half of the third century (about A.D. 215) yields important knowledge of the gradually evolving eucharistic prayer (Canon) of the Roman Mass. The Apostolic Tradition of St. Hippolytus[4] records and describes the rite for the consecration of a

---

[4] Hippolytus, a learned priest of Rome, born about 170, for a time antipope, was reconciled to the Church and died a martyr in exile, about A.D. 235. The Apostolic Tradition attributed to him was discovered in a library at Verona toward the end

bishop, followed by the bishop's Mass. For this special occasion, the scripture service is replaced by the ritual for the making of the new bishop — a sign of the flexibility of the liturgy prevailing at this time; the administration of another sacrament, like holy orders, could replace the liturgy of the Word.

The eucharistic prayer, developed after the manner of the Jewish grace after meals, has become the most prominent feature of the Mass. The following text probably does not record a fixed form of this prayer, but serves as a sample of a eucharistic or thanksgiving prayer which the bishop might use for his Mass.

In Chapter 4, the text begins with the salutation or kiss of peace rendered to the new bishop as a sign of welcome and allegiance.

1. And when he has been made bishop let everyone offer him the kiss of peace saluting him, for he has been made worthy.	Kiss of peace.
2. To him then let the deacons bring the oblation and he with all the presbyters laying his hand on the oblation shall say, giving thanks:	Offertory
3. The Lord be with you. And the people [*laos* — laity] shall say: And with thy spirit. Lift up your hearts. We have them with the Lord. Let us give thanks unto the Lord. It is meet and right. And forthwith he shall continue thus:	Preface dialogue
4. We render thanks unto thee, O God, through thy Beloved Servant Jesus Christ, Whom in the last times Thou didst send to be a Savior and Redeemer and the angel of Thy counsel;	Eucharistic prayer or Canon
5. Who is Thy Word inseparable; through whom thou madest all things and in whom Thou wast well pleased;	
6. Whom Thou didst send from heaven into the Virgin's womb, and Who conceived within her was made flesh, and demonstrated to be Thy Son, being born of the Holy Spirit and a Virgin;	
7. Who fulfilling thy will and procuring for Thee a holy people, stretched forth His hands for suffering that He might release from sufferings those who have believed in thee;	
8. Who when He was betrayed to voluntary suffer-	

of the past century. It was found in a Latin version as well as in other Eastern language versions as part of a so-called Egyptian *Church Order;* only in the present century, through important studies like those of R. H. Connolly and Gregory Dix, has the document been edited critically so as to yield a fairly accurate copy of what the original Greek manuscript must have looked like. Here is an example of how our present century has been able to open up new and vital insights into the ancient liturgy of the Mass. The Latin text may be found in Quasten, *op. cit.,* fascicle 7, part I, pp. 29–30.

ing in order that He might abolish death and
rend the bonds of the devil and tread down hell
and enlighten the righteous and establish the
ordinance and demonstrate the resurrection,

9. Taking bread and making Eucharist to Thee,   *Words of institution*
said: Take, eat; this is My Body, which is broken
for you. Likewise also the cup, saying: This is
My Blood which is shed for you.

10. When you do this, you do My *anamnesis*.

11. Doing therefore the *anamnesis* of His death and   *Anamnesis* or
resurrection, we offer to Thee the bread and   remembrance prayer
cup, making Eucharist to Thee because Thou
hast made us worthy to stand before Thee and
minister as priests to Thee.

12. And we pray thee that [Thou wouldst send Thy   *Epiclesis* or
Holy Spirit upon the oblation of Thy holy   invocation of the
Church] that Thou wouldst grant to all who   Holy Spirit
partake to be made one, that they may be
filled with the Holy Spirit for the confirmation
of their faith in truth;

13. That we may praise and glorify Thee through
Thy Servant Jesus Christ through Whom honor
and glory be to Thee with the Holy Spirit in
Thy holy church, now and forever and world
without end. R. Amen

There follows at this point the blessing of oil and other foods. Here
in the Mass of Holy Thursday, the bishop consecrates the oil for the
anointing of the sick. Then after the prayer and preparation for Holy
Communion, the people approach the altar in procession to receive the
sacrament while chanting the communion song. Holy Communion is
followed by a concluding prayer, an imposition of hands, and the dismissal by the deacon, "Go in peace."

Here then we have the oldest text of a Roman Canon dating from
about A.D. 215, but reflecting customs that were certainly established
well before this. The language of the Church at that time even in Rome
was Greek. This prayer clearly preserves the ancient character of the
Eucharist as an action imbedded in saving history. God's past actions
among men, from creation down through redemption and the creation
of the Church, are recalled here as the proper setting for that act in
which His redeeming work is made present and continued in the power
of the sacrament.

The whole prayer of Eucharist is a continuous and unbroken prayer;
there is no interruption, for example, in the institution narrative (par. 9)
nor is there an elevation of the sacred species. The elevations of bread
and cup were not introduced until the twelfth and fifteenth centuries

respectively. Directing the worship of the faithful to God through Christ as it does, this prayer clearly exemplifies the mediatorship or high priesthood of Christ; it is through Him that glory and honor is paid to God in the Holy Spirit. The Mass is Christ's whole priestly people engaged in worship; hence the preface dialogue between celebrant and people which has been retained almost word for word in the Roman Mass down to the present day. The return of the dialogue principle to the Mass of the twentieth century is certainly not innovation but restoration.

IV. THE GOLDEN AGE OF LITURGICAL DEVELOPMENT: FOURTH TO THE SIXTH CENTURIES

With the advent of the Emperor Constantine and the edict of toleration (313), the Church for the first time was granted legal status in the Roman Empire. Christianity became the state religion; the emperor himself encouraged the "new" religion by constructing magnificent edifices called basilicas over the tomb of Peter on Vatican Hill, and in honor of Paul outside the walls of ancient Rome, in honor of the most holy Savior or John on the property of the Lateran family (the pope's cathedral church and the original papal residence), and St. Mary Major, the great basilica in honor of the Blessed Mother.

Under such impetus it was natural for the Church, especially at Rome, to embellish and amplify the simple liturgy of the first centuries. Important developments therefore occurred during this period of liturgical growth.

Whereas the original language of the Mass in Rome was Greek, since the first converts were Greek-speaking people, by this time Latin had been introduced into the liturgy because this was the current language of the people. The earliest guideline determining the choice of a liturgical language for the Church was the vernacular principle. The Roman genius of language showed itself in the beauty of style and economy of expression, which became a hallmark of the Latin Mass prayers. Prayer and ceremony, too, came to reflect the noble restraint of the Roman spirit; emotion and sentimentality were kept to a minimum by the emphasis upon objective, dogmatic devotion.

A notable development of this period concerns the central eucharistic prayer. No longer was this left to the discretion of the celebrant; by the time of Gregory the Great (590–604), this great prayer of thanksgiving assumed a fixed form which has remained largely the same up to modern times. At some time between the fourth and sixth centuries, a series of petitionary prayers came to be inserted within the Canon (i.e., fixed formula or pattern) in a symmetrical fashion before and after the central consecration prayers. These prayers (for the Church and ecclesiastical authorities, in honor of the saints, for the living, for the faithful departed, a clerical petition for pardon and a prayer for all nature) very probably entered the Canon to replace the prayers of the faithful or litany of petitions which used to follow the liturgy of the Word (the scripture service). This prayer remained the great prerogative of the "president of the assembly" and was of course recited aloud in its entirety. At the end of this consecratory proclamation, the faithful, as they had done already in the days of Justin the Martyr, responded enthusiastically with their sign of approval and co-offering, the acclamation "Amen," their way of saying "Yes" to the sacrifice that had been offered in their name.

A new development occurred at the beginning of the ritual. If in Justin's time, the service began with the proclamation of Scripture, now especially when the Pope was presiding at the liturgy in one of the churches of Rome, a feeling for magnificence created a more formal entrance rite. The congregation was to be presented formally before almighty God. As this ritual unfolded, it included a solemn entrance procession of assisting clergy and the Pope, to the accompaniment of a processional hymn intoned by the schola or choir of chanters and repeated antiphonally or alternately by the congregation as a simple chorus or refrain. Generally this song was one of the psalms of the Hebrew psalter, adapted to the locale and circumstances of the liturgical celebration. This entrance or Introit song helped to create the atmosphere or mood of the day's liturgy. Similar processions accompanied by processional chants likewise developed at the Offertory (when the congregation brought gifts forward to be received by the celebrant) and at the Communion (when the congregation went forward once more to participate in the eucharistic meal). The songs accompanying the movement toward the altar helped to alert the faithful to the sacred meaning of their action of giving and receiving.

Besides the opening procession, the entrance rite also came to include a litany of petitions, of which the present "Lord have mercy" is the last vestige;[5] the "Glory to God in the highest," a series of acclamations to God originally introduced only on festive occasions; and a concluding prayer of petition, the Collect, by which the congregation was officially and formally presented to God. With the conclusion of the entrance rite, the scripture service was then held. Generally this included a reading from the Old Testament and from one of the letters of the New Testament, followed by an intervening psalm-chant (Gradual, Tract) which served as a meditation on the Epistle or first reading, and the Alleluia

---

[5] It was Gregory the Great who finally limited this litany to the ninefold petition to Christ that still remains in our Roman Mass.

psalm conceived as a joyful welcome to Christ about to address the assembly in the Gospel. After the Gospel, the Pope or bishop or celebrating priest preached a simple homily of an instructional and hortatory nature. This concluded the liturgy of the Word.

At the Offertory, the congregation came forward, bringing bread, wine, and other gifts for the support of the clergy and the poor; these gifts were received by the celebrant and his assisting clergy and placed alongside the altar for the rest of the Mass. Enough bread and wine from the offerings was placed on the altar itself for the Consecration. After receiving the gifts, the celebrant washed his hands without reciting any prayer; and then, returning to the altar, he proclaimed aloud a single prayer over the gifts, the only offertory prayer in those days.

Immediately after this he intoned the dialogue which marked the beginning of the solemn eucharistic prayer. After the thanksgiving offering was completed and the people's "Amen" had sounded, the Communion service began. As a kind of grace before the meal, the faithful together with the presiding priest or bishop recited the Lord's Prayer. This was followed by the *fractio* or breaking of the bread, necessitated by the use of small loaves of leavened bread which had to be broken with the help of the assisting clergy for distribution to the faithful. During this time the choir chanted a kind of litany, the "Lamb of God." When the *fractio* had been completed, the presiding priest received Communion first; then Communion was distributed to the clergy and the faithful under both forms. Following Communion the vessels were cleansed, a final after-Communion prayer was recited, and the notice of dismissal was given by the deacon. Such was the meaningful, active, and solemn liturgy in the golden age of worship, during the reign of Gregory the Great.

V. NORTHERN INFLUENCE ON THE ROMAN LITURGY: SEVENTH TO THE TWELFTH CENTURIES

If the Roman liturgy reached its peak development by the time of Gregory the Great, the next centuries were to witness a certain retrogression from the earlier communal and hierarchical pattern of worship. Medieval accretions tended to obscure the simple clarity of the earlier liturgy. A "sanctuary," pageantlike liturgy, "performed" by clerics and choir, reduced the congregation to silent spectators.

Many factors, of course, contributed to the rise of this situation. Despite the ninth-century growth of vernacular tongues like French and German, the Roman liturgy became frozen in Latin. The language barrier was to impede both understanding of the Mass and communication between altar and people. In its turn, architecture further hardened the status quo. The great Gothic cathedrals of the eleventh and twelfth centuries scarcely encouraged corporate prayer. Massive buildings, distance between congregation and altar, exaggerated embellishment of the altar screen and consequent deemphasis of the altar table — these factors helped to raise a wall of silence between sanctuary and nave, a barrier which is only now in the twentieth century being steadily dismantled.

How did such a decline in the communal spirit of the primitive Eucharist eventuate? Undoubtedly, one major factor was the influence of the imperial court. Charlemagne, who was crowned emperor by the Pope at St. Peter's on Christmas Day, 800, was so impressed with the splendor of the papal liturgy in Rome that he ordered his monks to take back with them to the Frankish court at Aachen manuscript copies of the liturgical manuals in use at Rome. At this early date there was not yet a fixed missal including under one cover all the prayers and rubrics of directions for the liturgy. Certain liturgical books, of course, had been compiled: *sacramentaries* (books containing the rubrics of Mass and especially prayers to be recited by the celebrant — Collect, Prayer over the Gifts, Preface, and After-Communion prayer);[6] *lectionaries* (books containing the scripture passages to be read on the different Sundays and feasts of the year); *Kyriale* and *Graduale* containing the major chants for the Mass.

Now the monks at Charlemagne's court not only set about copying the Roman liturgical manuscripts; but in the absence of centralized control, they felt free to make changes in the format of worship. Many features of Eastern provenance were introduced into the Roman liturgy which were in sharp contrast with the primitive format of worship — frequent use of incense; multiplication of bows and blessings; silent prayer to foster an aura of mystery before the great King; and, in general, the evolution of a ceremonial of pageantry akin to that of the imperial court.

Among the specific modifications of the Gallican monks was the reduction of the Canon or eucharistic prayer to silence. More silent prayer was added at the beginning of Mass (prayers at the foot of the altar, originally said privately by the celebrant either in the sacristy or on his way to the altar) and at the expanded Offertory ritual. In regard to the latter, the earlier simplicity of a gift procession, followed by a single prayer of offering, yielded to a ceremonial offering of host and chalice,

---

6 Principal sacramentaries of the early period are the *Gelasian*, attributed to Pope Gelasius, a fifth-century pontiff; the *Leonine* sacramentary, attributed to Pope Leo the Great, but probably of later compilation; and the *Gregorian* sacramentary, attributed to Pope Gregory I, but likewise probably of later authorship.

accompanied by explanatory prayers as though to make sure that God did not mistake the meaning of the gestures. In this rather infelicitous arrangement, one might say that bad liturgy is like a bad joke — it has to be explained to the listener after the telling.

Into these prayer forms, there crept a new note of individuality (cf. prayer for the offering of the host: "Accept, O holy Father, this spotless host which I, Your unworthy servant offer to You,"), a characteristic observable also in the breach between celebrant and assembly created by so much silent prayer at the altar. No longer did the whole congregation join in celebrating the Eucharist under the presidency of the bishop or priest; but rather the officiating priest alone came to be called the celebrant; for a good part of the Mass, he would attend to his own part, to the virtual exclusion of any community involvement. Fast disappearing was the original distribution of roles, where the celebrant truly presided and did not repeat the traditional assembly prayers like the Gloria and Creed, nor recite the scripture lessons proclaimed by the lectors.

Perhaps most disastrous of all was the fossilization of the Roman Mass in the Latin tongue. Up to this time, as we have seen, the vernacular principle guided the choice of liturgical language. But now, even though modern vernacular tongues began to develop,[7] the language of worship as well as of the academic world remained Latin. It has been suggested that the retention of Latin was inspired by the political desire to employ every possible expedient of unity; the widely diffused Latin worship would greatly aid in stabilizing the status quo of imperial unity. Be that as it may, Latin eventually made impossible the earlier dialogue format of the primitive liturgy. People no longer understood what was being said at the altar; with the altar moved back against the wall of the apse, the celebrant now turned his back to them; and finally the insertion of choir stalls between altar and nave moved the faithful farther and farther away from the focus of worship.

A further barrier of medieval provenance was the growing complexity of church music. As trained choirs and polyphonic composers combined efforts to produce a highly skilled music of worship, the congregation was effectively barred from its traditional role of community chant and song. Acclamations of joy, antiphonal songs, and even the simple responses to the priest's salutations fell away, as the lips of God's people grew silent.

Inactivity in song paralleled inactivity of movement. Early in this

---

[7] Cf. the Oath of Strasbourg (842), a move toward settling the division of Charlemagne's empire after his death, was taken in two languages, primitive French (Romanic) and early Germanic.

period, the Offertory procession was given up, at least in many places and gradually was abandoned altogether, except for very rare occasions like the offering of ceremonial gifts at a priestly ordination or the consecration of a bishop. In fine, the Western liturgy assumed the character of a stylized, formalized pageantry — to be watched and admired, but to be understood and participated in less and less.

The low ebb of liturgical understanding is reflected in the pious commentaries on the Mass produced at this time. Men like Amalar of Metz[8] began to interpret the ceremonies of the Mass in terms of the Lord's passion, so that the prayers at the foot of the altar were associated with Christ's prayer in Gethsemani, the washing of hands recalled Pilate's hand-washing at the condemnation of Christ, etc. Unfortunately, such exaggerated and unhistorical symbolism has prevailed in much literature on the Mass down to our own day.

VI. THE MASS FROM 1200–1600

During the previous centuries, Mass without chant (always to be regarded as a truncated form of worship) had come into vogue, in part at least due to the monastic situation where many ordanied priests lived in the same community. As each priest wished to offer "his own Mass," it was obviously unfeasible to carry out the full liturgy with chant in each instance. Hence an abbreviated form of the Mass came into use. In the absence of processions, precluding the need for lengthy processional chants, abbreviated versions of the entrance hymn, the Offertory hymn, and the Communion hymn appeared. When these processions were also abandoned at the solemn chant Mass (which was always regarded as normative for public worship) only one or two psalm verses were retained as a vestige of the longer hymn.

This period also witnessed the introduction of the two Elevations, that of the host in the twelfth century and that of the chalice by the fifteenth century. In keeping with the then-current emphasis on the static aspect of the Eucharist the faithful desired to look upon the sacred species to reaffirm their loyalty to Christ really present. But abuses were hard to contain; scholarly data record the custom of "elevation-hopping" — a custom which moved people to run from church to church to be there just to witness the Elevation and gain an indulgence. Inability to see the Host prompted some to exclaim in England: "Hold up, Sir John, hold up. Heave it a little higher."[9] The desire to see the Host

---

[8] Ninth-century churchmen and liturgical writer.

[9] Cf. Joseph Jungmann, *The Mass of the Roman Rite* (New York: Benziger, 1955), Vol. 1, p. 121, footnote 101.

afforded the opportunity for making a kind of spiritual communion at a time when the faithful scarcely dared to make a sacramental Communion.

On the occasion of greater feasts, there was added after the Epistle a prolonged commentary called the Sequence, composed in poetic form and set to simple music. Examples of this are the Sequence for the Easter Mass (constructed as a kind of dramatic dialogue between the faithful and Mary Magdalene on Easter morning) and the rather horrendous "Day of wrath, day of ire" of the Masses for the dead.

VII. THE EUCHARISTIC LITURGY FROM 1570 TO THE PRESENT

The variety of local customs and abuses, modifications, and exaggerations that had crept into the Mass liturgy during the Middle Ages led the Council of Trent (1545–1563) to consider a certain fixed and uniform liturgy for the Western Church. A postconciliar commission was appointed to look into the matter; seven years after the completion of the Council, Pope Pius V in 1570 imposed upon the Western Church the missal of the papal court. Only those liturgies which had existed two hundred years or more before this time were permitted to continue. In this way, the liturgies of some religious orders (Dominicans, Carmelites, and Carthusians) and the liturgy of some dioceses (Milan and some Spanish dioceses) still remain, even though they differ in certain respects from the Roman liturgy. With the publication of the *Missal of 1570*, the long period of liturgical expansion and local adaptation came to an end. From that time until the current liturgical renewal initiated by Vatican Council II, rigid uniformity has prevailed in the Latin rite of the Church. The reform of the Western liturgy currently in progress thus marks an historic milestone, for once again the principle of reasonable local adaptation will obtain.

A certain liturgical adaptation to changing cultural periods remained a phenomenon even after 1570. Developments of the Baroque period in ecclesiastical art and music can scarcely trace their inspiration to the authentic principles of earlier liturgical worship. It was the era of concertized Masses, external pomp and display, post-Renaissance neo-paganism, and sentimental love poetry fashionable in the drawing rooms and princely courts of the aristocracy. The liturgy was looked upon as a spectacle to be performed, much as the secular court was the scene of a grand and spectacular ceremonial. Much attention was lavished upon the externals of this grand spectacle, without much consideration for the true soul or inner meaning of worship. Opera, the great cultural creation of the Baroque era in the secular sphere, became a kind of model or paradigm for the "production" or "performance" of liturgical pageantry in the cathedrals.

Coupled with this overemphasis on formality was the fierce loyalty to the Church and a stubborn conservatism which refused to relinquish the legacy of the past in matters liturgical as in general religious ideas. It was a kind of post-Reformation siege mentality that sought to defend anything and everything associated with the Church that seemed to be under attack by its enemies. While this factor did serve to maintain the relics of the past, it did so in the case of the liturgy without transmitting the true soul of the worship of God's people. True spiritual life had to seek nourishment elsewhere (e.g., Stations of the Cross, Benediction, devotion to the saints), in ways perfectly good in themselves but certainly peripheral in comparison to the central mysteries of salvation celebrated in the Mass and the other sacraments. The neopagan emphasis of the Renaissance era affected intellectual Catholicism by supplanting the ancient biblical medium of the Fathers with the mythology of the Greco-Roman period. Artistically this massive mythological approach is already visible in the creative forms that Michelangelo employs to portray biblical concepts and figures. All of this redounded to a further divorce from the true liturgical mentality, steeped as it is in the imagery of Scripture.

A reaction was bound to set in. But the kind of reaction that developed in the nineteenth century cast aside superficialities and mythological tendencies of the Baroque period without solving its true mistakes. The countermovement, led by Dom Prosper Gueranger of Solesmes Abbey in France, turned out to be a romanticism that looked naïvely to the Middle Ages for an authentic liturgy, since the Medieval period was supposed to represent an era of solid Christian culture in Europe. But as we have seen above, this very period which they took as normative was already marked by a decline in true liturgical awareness and spirit.

Hampering the whole restoration effort of Gueranger was a lack of critical scholarship; the French Revolution and attendant political upheavals of the early nineteenth century had destroyed or at least impaired many of the university resources and research facilities, which could have yielded a more accurate picture of the earliest liturgy. Therefore, the romantic liturgical revival, oriented toward the Gothic period, unwittingly propagated two false emphases: the one, that the Roman liturgy of the Middle Ages was the true exemplar of authentic liturgy; the other, a disproportionate and sentimental attachment to the eucharistic presence, to the disparagement of the other eucharistic realities of sacrifice and meal. Gueranger's liturgical commentary centralized the eucharistic presence of Christ; in this view, the Mass exists solely to make the divine presence available for man's adoration.[10] The net effect of Gueranger's well-intentioned efforts was to create a kind of hothouse liturgy for an artificially created congregation (the monastery). Nevertheless he must be credited with making the first serious attempt in modern times at a liturgical renewal.

If liturgical development was to have a solid footing, it was necessary that scholarly research provide authentic principles for reconstructing a living liturgy adapted, not to a medieval congregation of long ago, but to contemporary Christians. It was the genius of another monk, Dom Lambert Beauduin, that he recognized the artificiality of Gueranger's reconstructions and that he turned rather to the task of preparing his contemporaries to participate in a rightly understood traditional liturgy. Other Benedictine abbeys like those of Maria-Laach and Beuron in Germany and Mont-Cesar, Maredsous, and Saint-André in Belgium continued the work of liturgical research and scholarship which was to pave the way for the liturgical reforms now being initiated.

At the beginning of our own century, Pope St. Pius X (1903–1914) signaled a new interest on the part of the papacy in the restoration of liturgical worship. His first *Motu Proprio* (executive decree) concerned the purification of church music. In the course of that document, Pius X enunciated a principle which was to become the watchword of the liturgical restoration:

> . . . the Christian spirit [must be acquired] from its first and indispensable source, namely, active participation in the most sacred mysteries and in the public and solemn prayer of the Church.[11]

This Pope made some efforts at simplifying the calendar of feasts and the divine office of the clergy; he fostered more frequent Communion on the part of the young by permitting first Communion at the earlier age of seven. But further serious liturgical restoration would have to await the results of critical scholarship.

In the meantime liturgical centers for research and pastoral experimentation were founded in Germany and France; annual conferences were established to publicize the fruits of liturgical scholarship and to enlist wider support for the growing liturgical movement. Bishops' committees were set up in Europe to guide and foster such developments; but in the United States such a move was long in coming. St. John's Abbey in Collegeville, Minnesota, spearheaded the liturgical movement in the United States through the leadership of Dom Virgil Michel, who

---

[10] Cf. Bouyer, *Liturgical Piety* (Notre Dame, Ind.: University of Notre Dame Press, 1955), pp. 12, 16.

[11] "Tra le sollecitudini," November 22, 1903; *Decreta authentica SRC*, No. 4121.

founded the journal *Orate Fratres* (now called *Worship*). Dom Virgil from the very beginning demonstrated a certain social concern, so that his liturgical interests were far from being a sterile academic exercise. Liturgical writing and annual conferences on the liturgy since 1940 identified the leadership of men like H. A. Reinhold, Martin Hellriegel, Godfrey Diekmann, O.S.B., Gerald Ellard, S.J., and Michael Mathis, C.S.C. Like the efforts of Dom Lambert Beauduin of Mont-Cesar Abbey, the American movement was aimed at the parishes, not merely the monasteries. In the long run this emphasis contributed to the social ferment ultimately responsible for the liturgical work of Vatican Council II.

Support was not lacking from the highest authorities. Pius XI complained of the condition where the faithful at Mass are so often mute spectators instead of active participants.[12] His successor Pius XII (1939–1958), contributed in a major way to the liturgical revival. On June 29, 1943, he published an encyclical letter on the social nature of the Church (*Mystici Corporis Christi*). In thus defining the Church as community, Pius XII prepared the way for understanding the sacred liturgy as the official public worship of the entire Church community, head and members together. On November 22, 1947, *Mediator Dei* appeared to give further direction to liturgical restoration by exposing carefully the true nature of liturgy and its centrality in the life of the Church. Liturgical scholars hailed this encyclical as a *Magna Charta* for their efforts to bring the faithful back to the chief sources of redemption in the Mass and the other sacraments.

The same Pope officially established commissions to revise the calendar of feasts, the breviary, and the missal; the work of these commissions certainly will accelerate the major revision of the liturgical books by Vatican II's postconciliar liturgical commission. The introduction of evening Mass, the restoration of the evening liturgy for Holy Thursday and Good Friday, and a special provision (mandated, 1955) for a restored Easter Vigil celebration on Holy Saturday night marked a major advance in liturgical renewal and indicated a genuine pastoral concern to give the faithful, especially the working classes, easier access to divine worship. The restored Holy Week focused attention once more upon the central mysteries of our salvation. The last decree that Pius XII signed was a decree on active participation (September, 1958) in which the Pontiff outlined and mandated at least dialogue participation at Mass. Pope John XXIII instituted further provisional reforms of the calendar and the breviary, but left more drastic decisions on liturgical revision to the entire episcopate of the world whom he summoned to Rome for the twenty-first ecumenical council (first announced in January, 1959).

---

[12] "Divini Cultus," December 20, 1928; *AAS* (1929), 21, 40.

Convening in the fall of 1962, the first session of Vatican Council II embarked upon the gigantic task of charting the renewal of the Church in the twentieth century. Basic to such a renewal, it was felt, is a total reform of the Church's worship with a view to making it more authentic and genuine for the people of our time. A truly pastoral liturgy was the first goal of the Council, as it began debate on a schema on the sacred liturgy. Challenging problems arose, like the use of more vernacular language in the Mass and the sacraments, adaptation to local cultures, intelligibility of the rite of the Mass, in short everything entailed in providing a living worship-form for God's people that might serve both for the authentic praise of God and the sanctification of the faithful. If the Church is to project the face of Christ to the world, it must first renew itself at the true sources of holiness, the Eucharist and the other sacraments.

The resultant discussions and revisions of the schema were time-consuming; it was not until December 4, 1963, at the end of the second session of the Council, that Pope Paul VI (who followed John as pope in June of that year) was able to promulgate in the name of all the bishops of the world a *Constitution on the Sacred Liturgy*, which would officially chart the path of liturgical renewal for decades to come.

After a brief introduction detailing the general purposes of the Council, this first conciliar document outlines in the first three chapters the norms for the general restoration and promotion of the sacred liturgy (Chap. 1), provision for the pastoral reform of the Mass (Chap. 2), and the other sacraments and sacramentals (Chap. 3). The Council reenforces the centrality of the liturgy in the life of the Church because it is the work of Christ and the faithful together (par. 7). Directives are issued for the liturgical instruction of the clergy, so that they in turn may instruct the faithful and lead them to an intelligent active participation, both interior and external, in the worship of the Church. That this worship might be as meaningful as possible to the people of our times and adapted to our understanding, the worship books of the Church are to be completely revised. The missal, the breviary, the pontifical, and the ritual are the four books involved in the revision. These books contain respectively the texts and ritual for the Mass, the divine office, the sacraments and blessings reserved for the bishop, and liturgical celebrations and blessings within the jurisdiction of the ordinary priest. The elements of worship deriving from Christ Himself are immutable; but the supplementary ritual that has grown up over the centuries (as we have seen in this chapter in the case of the Mass) is subject to adaptation and change with the passage of time and the demands of local culture.

In the implementation of this reform, the principle of decentralization of authority is an important one. Greater freedom has been accorded national bodies of bishops to supervise liturgical adaptations in their own countries. The use of the vernacular tongues and even incorporation of new cultural forms into local worship (e.g., in Africa and Asia) are endorsed in this epoch-making document. The *Constitution* accords a prominent place to Sacred Scripture in the liturgy of the Word; the communal and hierarchical nature of the liturgy is proclaimed so that, in its external appearances, the celebration of the Eucharist could emphasize the role of the community as well as the distinction of function on the part of the presiding priest, the attendant ministers (clergy, servers, lectors, commentators), and members of the choir. Active participation is to be encouraged so that the people take part "by means of acclamations, responses, psalmody, antiphons, and songs, as well as by actions, gestures, and bodily attitudes."[13] Difference in function is to be highlighted by eliminating overlapping and repetition (e.g., as when the celebrant would pray quietly what the choir is singing at such times as the Gloria, Creed, etc.).

To help with the understanding of the Mass, a clear distinction is to be observed between the liturgy of the Word (centered at a place other than the altar, e.g., at the celebrant's chair, or lectern, or the front part of the sanctuary facing the people) and the liturgy of the Eucharist (centered at the altar table, which if possible should face the congregation). In this way, the proclamation of God's Word is given a more authentic setting, while the sacrifice-meal aspect is thrown into bolder relief at the altar table. One effect of the Council's teaching is to discourage the disparagement of the first part of the Mass; to teach that there are three principal parts to the Mass from the Offertory through Consecration and Communion tends to downgrade the importance of the proclamation of God's Word in the first part of the Mass (cf. CSL, par. 56).

Finally two other provisions are made concerning the Mass. One concerns the reception of the Eucharist under both kinds, in cases to be determined by the Holy See, subject to permission of the local bishop. The unity of Christ's priesthood and a certain caution against a mere multiplication of Masses is expressed by the Council's restoration of more frequent concelebration of the Mass. This means that several priest-celebrants may join in offering Mass together, thus demonstrating that all human priesthood is a share in the priesthood of Christ; it also serves to make visible the sign of unity between priests and faithful.

---

[13] CSL, par. 30; AAS, Vol. 56, February 15, 1964, p. 108.

The ritual of the other sacraments is also to be revised with a view to making them more intelligible to the faithful. In this way, the liturgy of the Church in its sacramental life may become a powerful force for instructing the faithful and enabling them through worship to encounter Christ personally and more effectively. Here again as in the case of the Mass, the principle of adaptation in matters of language and culture is reiterated. Making provision for the celebration of these other sacraments, the Council urges once more the centrality of the Eucharist. It encourages a special Mass "for the conferring of Baptism" to be celebrated if possible after the baptism of adults (par. 66). Confirmation too, when convenient, may be given within the Mass (par. 71). The connection between matrimony and the Eucharist is stressed by the placing of the contractual exchange directly within the Mass, namely, after the Gospel and the homily. By worthy and meaningful community celebration of sacraments and sacramentals, the Church under the urging of the Council seeks to draw all men more effectively into union with Christ.

Upon the promulgation of the liturgy *Constitution*, a commission for the implementation of the liturgical reform was established, both to initiate the work of revising the liturgical books and to act as a clearinghouse of information for the various national hierarchies. The American bishops officially introduced the use of English at Mass on the first Sunday of Advent, November 29, 1964. Most dioceses also introduced a simple altar table facing the people.[14] On the first Sunday of Lent, March 7, 1965, further changes were introduced in the United States, most notable of which was the separation of the first part of the Mass from the altar itself. Changes made thus far are probably the most radical to be expected at least for our country; later changes (e.g., in the Canon of the Mass) will probably be less obvious than the dramatic modifications already effected.

---

[14] Facing the congregation, the celebrant is more readily seen to be presiding over a family meal; the host would scarcely turn his back upon the guests at his table.

CHAPTER XIII

The Eucharistic Celebration

I. THE LITURGY OF THE WORD

The Holy Eucharist is essentially the celebration of the family meal of God's people. A meal within the family or a circle of friends is normally a happy occasion when we do three things: we speak, we offer, and we communicate.

1. Conversation is in many ways the heart of table fellowship. Certainly it would be a dull meal if no one said a word. Ordinarily the evening meal is the time when the family exchange the news of the day, and talk over things of mutual concern. Friends renew their acquaintance, intellectuals discuss, statesmen confer and negotiate, businessmen close a transaction. Jesus himself spoke to the Apostles at the first Mass about what was closest to his heart, fraternal love.

2. A meal also entails an offering. Providing the family meal, both father and mother have given of their very selves to feed their children. The food on the table symbolizes the toil of the father earning the

family support and the skill of the mother preparing a palatable meal. Appreciative children contribute their gratitude and their willingness to help the parents as well as one another. A meal of friendship too involves a certain exchange; the host sets a good table, the friend often brings a gift. At Mass, our gift to God is Christ himself and ourselves united with him.[1]

3. A meal draws people together. If a meal is all it is supposed to be, it will involve a real sharing of life, symbolized by the eating of the same food. A meal is meant to bring families and friends together, as it does most notably on all the important occasions of our life, baptisms, anniversaries, birthdays, weddings, holidays of the year. No wonder the Jews thought of the coming golden age in terms of a great banquet, where they would all sit down with God's Messiah.

At Mass too we speak, we offer, and we communicate. In the first portion of the Mass we talk to God, he talks to us (beginning of the Mass to the Prayers of the Faithful); in the second or eucharistic portion of the Mass, we offer (Offertory and Consecration) and we communicate (Communion). We shall now discuss each of these in more detail.

A. *The Entrance Rite*

We saw in the previous chapter that in second-century Rome, the proclamation of God's Word from Scripture preceded the prayer of the congregation (cf. *The First Apology* of Justin Martyr). Between the fourth and sixth centuries, a more elaborate entrance rite developed at the beginning of the service. The present liturgy retains this entrance rite consisting of (1) the procession of clergy and servers to the altar, accompanied by an entrance song; (2) the confession of our sins in the *Confiteor* at the foot of the altar; (3) the *Lord have mercy*; (4) the *Glory to God in the highest* on festive occasions; (5) the *Collect* or prayer of the assembly, which sums up or collects the silent petitions of the faithful and concludes the solemn presentation of the congregation before God.

1. The entrance procession and song

As the procession makes its way to the sanctuary, we join in song to greet our risen Lord who has called us together as his people united in our passage toward heaven. The procession moving through the church reminds us that we are essentially travelers; for the trip through this world we need to stop at intervals to gain strength from assembly in Christ and participation in his Paschal mystery by sacrifice and meal.

---

[1] ". . . by offering the immaculate victim not only through the hands of the priest, but also with him, they [the faithful] should learn to offer themselves. . . ." CSL, par. 48; AAS, Vol. 56, No. 2, Feb. 15, 1964, p. 113.

We join in song because this is a happy occasion. Every Eucharist is a celebration, and singing is a natural expression of happiness and love. We are glad to be together as God's people; we greet Christ as the Father presiding over this family, this parish, this academic community, this gathering in the presence of our priest. The song we sing may be one of the psalms, those prayer songs inspired by the Holy Spirit himself. It is also to be hoped that in the coming revision of the Mass, allowance will be made for the use of religious songs native to the people, and truly expressive of their sentiments of brotherhood in Christ. For major feasts and seasons like Advent and Lent, Christmas and Easter, it is fitting that the entrance song carry the spirit of the season and reflect the community's religious mood — e.g., longing for Christ's coming (Advent), joy over the redemption (Easter). At a Mass where the entrance hymn is not sung, the commentator may read the entrance psalm that is printed in the missal; when there is no commentator present, the celebrant himself may read this passage after he has taken the place proper to him for the liturgy of the Word.

2. The confession of sins

The ancient *Didache* recommended: "First confess your sins, that your sacrifice may be pure" (Chap. 14). In the presence of the all-holy God, the "totally other," man, is moved to acknowledge his creatureliness, his sinfulness. The Confiteor, a kind of lengthy act of contrition, was added to the Mass in the later Middle Ages. Whether it will be retained in the revised Roman Mass remains to be seen; in any case it serves to dispose us to acknowledge our limitations, and to come with reverence and respect to the holy meal with God.

3. The kissing of the altar

After the prayers at the foot of the altar, the celebrant advances to the altar and kisses it in the middle before going to the chair or the lectern. The principal significance of this reverence paid to the altar is that of a greeting to Christ our High Priest and personal Altar of Sacrifice, who is present in our midst symbolically by the altar table. At a bishop's Mass, the bishop kisses the book of God's Word as well as the altar, a twofold symbol of the presence of Christ. To understand how Christ is represented by the altar, we may recall that John Chrysostom referred to him precisely in those words; sacrifice which we do at an altar is a return to God through the gift that is placed on the altar. Now since we cannot have Christ *visibly* present as our mediator with the Father, we return to the Father through the symbol of Christ: the altar table. Putting our gifts on the altar table is equivalent to placing them in Christ's own hands.

4. The "Lord have mercy"

Next the celebrant (or commentator) and assembly join in a ninefold petition to Christ for mercy. Part of an ancient Greek litany of petitions, limited to the number nine in the days of Gregory the Great, the titles addressed to Jesus recall Peter's Pentecostal sermon where he proclaimed "that God has made both Lord and Christ, this Jesus whom you crucify" (Acts 2:36).

5. The "Glory to God in the highest"

Taking its inspiration from the angelic praise at the annunciation of Christ's birth to the shepherds (cf. Lk 2:14), this song of joy came to the West from the Eastern liturgies where it was already in use as a morning hymn in the fourth century. It is actually a series of acclamations or shouts of praise in honor of the Holy Trinity. It was gradually introduced into the Mass on major festivals of the Church, and is still omitted on penitential days as during Lent and on Ember Days.

6. "The Lord be with you" and the Prayer of the Assembly

The presiding priest is now about to conclude the entrance rite. With hands extended he greets the congregation in a biblical salutation (cf. Ru 2:4; Lk 1:28), to which the congregation responds in an idiomatic Hebrew expression, "And with you also." The exchange signifies a union of celebrant and people in Christ. In effect it serves as an alert to the congregation for an action or prayer in which the priest will lead and represent them.

The celebrant calls the people to prayer with the exhortation "Let us pray." After a moment of silent prayer by the congregation, the celebrant "collects" the petitions of all into a united prayer of the assembly.

This prayer is always prayed in a standing posture and with hands extended according to the ancient orante figure, often seen on the walls of the Roman catacombs. Standing typifies the Christian risen with Christ; extending the arms with palms turned upward toward heaven imitates the gesture of Christ on the cross and suggests a solemn petition to heaven.

This is essentially communal prayer. The priest makes a speech (in Latin, oratio) on behalf of the faithful, addressing God usually in the ancient trinitarian manner of prayer to God the Father, through Christ, in the Holy Spirit. In a more or less classical and stylized pattern, the celebrant first praises God for a certain quality or attribute; or he may advert to the mystery being celebrated on a given Sunday or feast. In the latter half of the prayer, he petitions God for the special grace expected from this eucharistic celebration.

It may be useful to recall three or four of the ancient Roman Collect prayers notable for their economy of expression and lofty doctrinal content. As a first example, consider the Prayer of the Assembly from the classical Mass for the feast of Epiphany:

O God,	Invocation or formula of address
On this day you used a star to show your only begotten Son to the nations of the world.	Reference to the feast
Kindly grant that we who now know you by faith may one day behold your heavenly majesty:	Request for special grace of the feast
Through the same Jesus Christ, your Son our Lord, who lives and reigns with you as King in the unity of the Holy Spirit, God forever and ever.	Conclusion: a request directed to God through Christ our High Priest.
Amen.	The People's solemn assent: "This is our prayer too."

In Paschal time, Christians experience a new impulse from the risen Christ's Spirit of love; in this union of fraternal love, we look beyond the passing joys of this world to eternal security. All this is expressed in the prayer of the assembly for the fourth Sunday after Easter:

> O God, you made the minds of the faithful to be of one will. Grant to your people to love what you command and to desire what you promise, so that amid the changing things of this world, our hearts may be fixed where true joys are to be found.

A parallel prayer for the third Sunday after Pentecost is as follows:

> O God, Guardian of those who trust in you, without whom nothing is strong, nothing holy, increase your mercy toward us. With you as our Ruler and Guide, may we pass through the good things of this world so as not to lose those of the world to come.

To summarize the entrance rite and at the same time to point out its psychological unity, one might draw an analogy to a man asking his employer for a raise in salary. Before entering the office he cleans off his feet. This is the Confiteor or contrition prayer. He knocks on the door; this is the "Lord have mercy." Ushered into the employer's presence, the employee first elicits a spirit of good feeling by praising and thanking the employer for his past benevolence to his employees. This is the "Glory to God." Finally, he presents his request; this is the prayer of petition or prayer of the assembly.

B. *The Liturgy of God's Word*

Now that the community has been officially presented before God and received by him, we sit down and listen as he addresses us in his inspired words. The lay lector, if one is available, proclaims God's word from the lectern facing the community; the passage chosen is generally from the Old Testament or from one of the letters of the New Testament.

1. The First Reading

Sometimes the First Reading is a kind of prophecy, whose fulfillment is proclaimed in the Gospel of the same Mass. An example of this may be found in the Mass for January 6, where the Old Testament passage (cf. Is 60:1-6) announces the homage to be paid to God at Jerusalem by the peoples of the East while in the Gospel Matthew recounts the coming of the Magi to pay tribute to the Messiah (cf. Mt 2:1-12). When the first reading is from the writings of St. Paul, as on most of the Sundays of the year in the present cycle of readings, the Epistle generally has a moral tone exhorting the members of Christ to "walk worthy of the vocation" to which they have been called (cf. Eph 4:1).

It is quite probable that Paul's letters to the Christian community he had founded were first read to them at a eucharistic assembly (cf. 1 Thes 5:27; Col 4:15, 16). This would be a natural occasion for apprising the local churches of what Paul had written to them, in much the same way as today a bishop communicates with his diocese through a pastoral letter read at the Sunday Masses. The same kind of gathering would naturally lead the participants to recall the sayings and deeds of Jesus, a very important factor in preserving the traditions about the Savior for later inclusion in the written Gospel material. In helping to preserve the traditions about Jesus, liturgical celebration fostered biblical memory.

In Old Testament Scripture, the ancient Hebrew was very conscious of the power of God's Word.[2] To speak and to act were identical. In the New Testament, God's Word took flesh in the person of Jesus of Nazareth and later became "incarnated" in the preaching of his Church. *Kerygma* (public proclamation of the good news of salvation) and *catechesis* (instruction of baptized converts) not only propagated the knowl-

---

[2] Cf. above p. 19 ff.

edge of Christ, but in a sense continued to make him present. In the age of the catechumenate, candidates for Christianity learned the teachings of Christ from Scripture during the liturgical synaxis, which came to be called "the Mass of the Catechumens."[3]

From this we begin to see how closely allied is the Word of God with the sacramental celebration. The eucharistic celebration makes Christ present both in Word and sacrament. Unlike the private reading of God's Word, which of course is highly to be commended, the public proclamation of his Word at a sacramental celebration comes to have a special sacramental value. His Word not only instructs, not only proclaims his saving love for us, but it already prophesies, announces, and certifies what is to happen to us in this very eucharistic celebration. Just as in the celebration of any sacrament, the Word explains and effects Christ's action in his faithful, so here the proclamation of God's Word in the scripture service of the Mass announces to us and certifies the sacramental event about to take place. Later, at this very Mass, the Epistle and Gospel will leap into life. Speaking now through his apostles and evangelists, the divine Word will move in very substance among us to renew his Paschal mystery and cause us to rise again from willful selfishness and sin to the status of his own risen life.

Present by his Word in the sacred liturgy (CSL, par. 7, 33), Christ continues his saving deed among men at this very celebration. It is here by his Word that He constitutes us as His people, summoning us into sacred assembly even as he once constituted the Israelite refugees from Egypt into the sacred Qahal at the foot of Sinai. Here he forms a community of believers, constantly calling us to the summit of commitment by a whole life lived in and for him.

Here in the liturgy of the Word, there converge the creative Word, the saving Word, the sacramental Word. In his visible ministry among men, Christ announced the kingdom of his Father; he proclaimed and revealed his Father's love for man; he bore witness to the Father's redemptive love. After preaching and eliciting faith, Christ then healed. He still follows the same pattern in the Mass. In the scripture service, he continues to proclaim the kingdom of his Father among men. In the eucharistic sacrifice-meal, Christ brings us far more than a bodily cure; He brings us the sacramental healing of his risen life. In Scripture we hear the good news of our redemption; in the sacrament we celebrate with Christ his saving passage from death to life.

---

[3] This inexact term suggests a twofold faulty emphasis: (1) that the first part of the Mass is reserved for the nonbaptized, (2) that this part contains only instruction.

2. Meditation psalm

Following the scripture reading, a psalm is read or sung as a reflection or echo of God's Word. It is in the nature of a prayerful response and a meditative pondering on the rich treasure of God's Word. This is followed by a transitional chant introduced in seasons of joy by the *Alleluia*, conceived as a greeting to Christ about to address us in the Gospel.

While the chant is being sung or recited, the celebrant bows to the altar and privately recites a prayer of preparation, requesting purity and worthiness of heart for announcing the holy Word of salvation in the Gospel.

3. The Gospel

Although another priest or deacon may proclaim the Gospel, when no other priest or cleric is available the celebrant himself proclaims it. All rise in deference to Christ about to speak in the holy assembly — the same Christ who spoke in the thunder and fire of Sinai, who spoke in the gentle breeze to the prophets.

The word "Gospel" (from the Old English *god-spel*) means literally "good news." At every Mass, Christ proclaims the good news first brought to earth at the incarnation: "You have a Savior, the anointed one, the Lord" (Lk 2:11). With joyful enthusiasm and zealous attention, we open ourselves to His Word that it may renew, transform, and re-create us in the image of him whose body we are.

Thus the Gospel is a sign, an "audible sacrament" of what Christ intends to do to us in the "visible sacrament" of the Eucharist.[4] Both sacramental word and sacramental act make present to us the wonderful works of God. At every Gospel, Christ can say to us: "The words that I have spoken to you are spirit and life" (Jn 6:64).

4. The homily

In the ancient basilicas, the pope or bishop celebrating the Eucharist delivered the homily from the chair seated on the raised platform behind the altar. The chair is the symbol of teaching and ruling authority. It is the privilege of the presiding priest as the highest cleric present to deliver the homily, a simple instruction on the sacred Word of God proclaimed at this Eucharist.

In the *Constitution on the Sacred Liturgy*, the Second Vatican Council

---

[4] Cf. Linus Bopp, "Salvific Power of the Word According to the Church Fathers" in *The Word* (New York: Kenedy, 1964), p. 166. The entire volume contains provocative essays on the developing theology of God's Word.

insists that "the sermon is part of the liturgical service"; it "should draw its content mainly from Scriptural and liturgical sources, and its character should be that of a proclamation of God's wonderful works and the history of salvation, the mystery of Christ, ever made present and active within us, especially in the celebration of the liturgy" (CSL, par. 35, No. 2). The Council repeats in another place:

> By means of the homily the mysteries of the faith and the guiding principles of the Christian life are expounded from the sacred text, during the course of the liturgical year; the homily, therefore, is to be highly esteemed as part of the liturgy itself; in fact, at those Masses which are celebrated with the assistance of the people on Sundays and feasts of obligation, it should not be omitted except for a serious reason (CSL, par. 52).

As far as possible then, the homily or sermon should take its inspiration from the biblical texts of the Mass itself. From the days of the great Fathers of the Church, the homily appears as a pastoral explanation and application of the scriptural Word to the lives of the faithful. It is also the continuation of the great *kerygma* or proclamation with which the Apostles first announced Christ and his powerful deeds to all who would listen. Likewise it continues the primitive catechesis of which St. Luke speaks, that further indoctrination rendered to baptized converts that they might "understand the certainty of the words in which [they had] been instructed" (Lk 1:4).

5. The Creed

After a moving speech, the crowd cheers and applauds. The sacred assembly has listened to the moving and inspiring words of the heavenly Father; now it is our turn to show our appreciation. We "applaud," we thank him for his redemptive word by the public and communal recitation of the Creed. In effect we are telling God that we take his Word seriously, that we will base our whole life upon his Word in accordance with the scriptural saying: "Blessed are they who hear the Word of God and keep it" (Lk 11:28). For this is the way a son shows honest affection for his father; "If anyone love me, he will keep my word . . ." (Jn 14:23).

The Creed seems to have developed out of the triple interrogation associated with baptism. To the triple questioning of the priest, the catechumen answered each time, "I do believe," and then was immersed in the baptismal waters. By putting the questions together ("Do you believe in God the Father Almighty, Creator of heaven and earth, etc."), the pattern of a creed or summary of belief took shape. The early councils of the Church, like those of Nicaea and Constantinople, formulated creeds as a kind of digest or code of faith to be used as a test for orthodoxy. The Creed recited at a Sunday Mass first appeared in the acts of the Council of Chalcedon (A.D. 451), but ultimately reflects the beliefs proclaimed at two earlier councils, that of Nicaea (325) and Constantinople (381). Originally it seems to have been the ancient baptismal creed of Jerusalem.[5] The Creed was added to the Roman Mass at the suggestion of Emperor Henry II who expressed surprise on his visit to Rome in 1014 that the Creed, already a part of the Mass in northern Europe, was lacking in the Roman Mass.

For us today, the Creed may be said to have the following practical significance: (1) It is a renewal of our baptism. As a baptismal prayer, it is recited by the candidate for baptism or his sponsors on the way to the font. We renew our baptismal faith, our adherence to Christ and his teachings in the solemn public proclamation of the Creed at Mass. (2) The Creed renews our oath of loyalty to God. Every article of the Creed must not only be believed but also lived. (3) What the national anthem does to stir the feelings of patriotism for one's country, that equivalently the Creed does for citizens of the Church. (4) As the national anthem reflects the freedoms and privileges of citizenship, so our Catholic Creed reflects our Christian privileges of calling God our Father, his Son our brother and Savior, his Church our family of brothers and sisters, and claiming as our destiny the eternal inheritance of heaven. Therefore (5) the Creed is a jubilant recounting of the benefits of divine love, an admiring enumeration of the gifts of the loving God who gives himself. Every article of the faith, sealed with the blood of martyrs, is a new gift from God. It is one prolonged declaration of our faith in God's eternal love for us.

6. The Prayer of the Faithful

Just as in the time of Justin the Martyr (A.D. 150), so once more at the mandate of the Sacred Vatican Council (CSL, par. 53) the "Common Prayer" or "Prayer of the Faithful" is to be restored to the Roman Mass. It is a litany of petitions for the Church, for civil authorities, for the special needs of the parish or community or country, for all mankind, for the salvation of the world, for the sick, the poor, and the faithful departed. This prayer is purposely left flexible enough so that the special intentions of a given congregation may be included from Sunday to Sunday as occasion demands.

This prayer, recited by the faithful in a standing position, is the ancient response of the congregation to God's Word. It is essentially a response of fraternal love in which the congregation makes its own the desires

[5] Joseph Jungmann, S.J., *The Mass of the Roman Rite* (New York: Benziger, 1951), tr. Francis A. Brunner, Vol. 1, p. 462 f.

of the heart of Christ. Universal in scope, these petitions embrace the whole missionary vision of the Church as it calls down God's blessings upon the entire family of mankind.

II. THE SACRIFICE-MEAL

A. Preparation of the Gifts

1. The Offertory

The celebrant now leaves the chair or the lectern where he has presided over the liturgy of the Word and he goes now to the table of the Eucharist, the altar. It is now the moment to receive the offerings of the faithful. As was done in the ancient Church from about the third or fourth century to the eleventh, a symbolic Offertory procession may be held in which representatives of the faithful bring the bread and the water and wine to be consecrated at that Mass. In some places too the collection is taken up and brought to the altar as a tangible way of demonstrating the part of the faithful in offering this Mass. The gifts are received by the celebrant in the sanctuary while the congregation sings the Offertory hymn.

The same observations made above concerning the entrance hymn apply here; where the Offertory antiphon still printed in the missal seems beyond the ability of the people to sing, it seems justified to hope that it be permitted to substitute a hymn known to the congregation which adequately expresses the meaning of the offering. Under present circumstances, however, the printed Offertory antiphon must still be read by the lector or commentator. It is also to be hoped that a simplification of the Offertory rite will be provided in the future revision of the Roman Mass. The present pattern of silent prayer and gesture dates from the Carolingian or post-Carolingian period of Gallican influence. Far clearer and simpler was the earlier custom of having the celebrant simply wash his hands after receiving the gifts and then proceed to recite only one prayer, the Prayer over the Gifts, recited aloud and naturally in the people's own language. Furthermore, some of the other prayers now in use, like that recited at the offering of the host, strike a note of individualism out of character with the communal nature of the Mass.

After the bread offering, wine and a few drops of water are poured into the chalice; this also is held up as a gesture of offering, followed by a pointed prayer which concisely expresses the meaning of the offering: "May we be received by you, O Lord, and may the sacrifice we offer this day in your sight be pleasing to you." It is at this point that the celebrant comes to wash his hands, reciting Psalm 25, chosen simply because of one verse, "I will wash my hands among the innocent" (v. 6). Returning to the center of the altar, the celebrant recites a prayer to the Holy Trinity, then turns to the servers and asks their prayer along with his for the acceptance of the sacrifice. Then turning back to the missal once more, he prays aloud the prayer which the Gallican liturgy had reduced to silence, namely the ancient prayer over the gifts. Once again the faithful make their "Amen," their "Yes" to the offering.

2. Significance of the Offertory

The preparation of the gifts at the altar should remind us to give ourselves to God at this Eucharist. We are about to be taken up into Christ's great act of commitment to his Father, his Paschal mystery. Unlike parasites, our place and posture at the Eucharist must be that of co-offerers and co-victims. Christ wants to take us with him to the Father; he asks the gift of our minds and wills; he asks our willingness to submerge ourselves into the community, without of course losing our individual personality. He asks of us the attitude of fraternal concern, symbolized by the one altar bread originally made of many grains of wheat (cf. 1 Cor 10:17). Like the American coin with "In God we trust" inscribed on one side of it, so the Mass leads us first in the worship of God; but like the underside of the coin, E pluribus unum ("One federal republic comprising many states"), the Mass too engages the corporate dedication of the full membership of Christ to the glory of the Father.

The offering then reminds us to give ourselves unreservedly and unconditionally. It reminds us to give our toil, our sweat, our labor, and our tears; our joys, our sorrows, our anxieties, our fears, our hopes for the future, our prayers, our repentance — all of these we put on the paten and into the chalice to have them absorbed into Christ's offering. We give so little even in giving our total self; we are to receive so much back through Christ's sacrifice and meal. We may make our own the rapturous cry of the Christmas liturgy "O wonderful exchange"[6] — what a tremendous bargain!

B. The Thanksgiving Offering

All through Salvation-History, the fundamental quality that God demands of man is that of giving thanks. When the ancient Israelite brought his firstfruits to the sanctuary, he was to remember God's saving acts of the exodus with gratitude (cf. Dt 26:5–11). So intimately was his daily life bound up with God that the Israelite acknowledged

---

[6] Roman Breviary, Octave of the Nativity, First Antiphon, First Vespers.

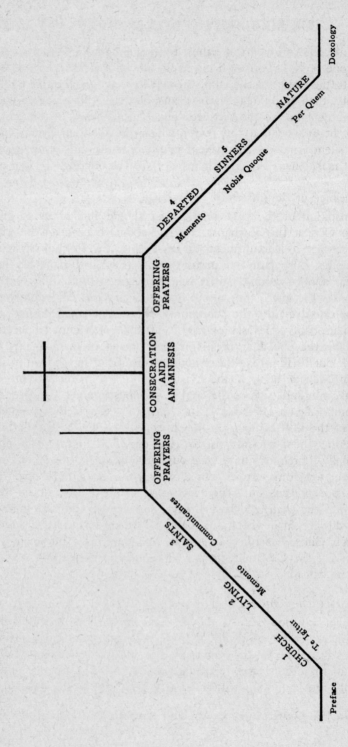

THE "EUCHARISTIC PRAYER" TODAY

[The numbered Mementos were inserted into the Eucharistic Prayer between the fourth and sixth centuries]

through the table blessing that all his food came from God; thanking God for it was itself a form of blessing.

Christ, the true firstfruits of his people and of all humanity, becomes a personal thanksgiving to his Father. Jesus of Nazareth is the human enfleshment, the very visibility of his eternal directedness toward the Father, whose perfect Image he is. This directedness might be termed "thanksgiving"; it is an eternal return to him from whom he eternally proceeds. Now this thanksgiving, as a relation in the Trinity, a relation of mutuality between Father and Son, must be all that the Father and Son are, that is, a subsistent Person, the very soul of this relationship of love and thanksgiving. Now it is this Spirit, the breath of life and love and personification of the returning thanksgiving of the Son to the Father that is present in us and to us as community in Christ. It is therefore through Christ united in the Spirit that we gather around our Father's table at Mass and celebrate our thanksgiving, our Eucharist to the Father. Christ, who gave thanks when he multiplied bread, when he offered himself at the Last Supper, when he consecrated himself as supreme "thank-you" gift for men (cf. Jn 17:19), now joins us in the sacrament of worshipful and grateful praise.

1. The Preface

Originally, the great prayer of thanksgiving, in which the sacrifice of Christ's Paschal mystery is renewed, was one unbroken prayer in which God was praised for all his salvation deeds of mercy from creation through the incarnation, redemption, and sending of the Holy Spirit.[7] But this prayer, as the effective Word of God in his members, not only thanks God for these past benefits but renews them sacramentally, so that redemption is a here-and-now event, in which we already encounter the Father in the redeeming, mediating presence of Christ.

The Preface we have today still maintains the ancient character of giving thanks. The word "Preface" may be interpreted spatially as meaning "to speak in front of," in the sense that the celebrant is now our spokesman to God gratefully recounting his salvation benefits. The priest is our toastmaster at the testimonial banquet of the Eucharist; after singing the praises of God, he will lead us in honoring the Father through our consecration gift.

One of the ancient liturgical books, the Leonine Sacramentary (attributed to Pope Leo the Great but actually of later provenance), included as many as 267 prefaces. The present missal has reduced them to fifteen; but certainly a greater diversity and enrichment is desirable,

---

[7] Cf. The Apostolic Tradition of St. Hippolytus, p. 268 above.

so that the Preface may truly express a broader spectrum of thanksgiving diffused through the feasts and seasons of the year. The Preface dissolves in the "Holy, Holy, Holy" (Is 6:3; Ap 4:8) as we merge our earthly worship with the homage of heaven.

2. The pre-Consecration Mementos

Between the fourth and sixth centuries, Memento prayers were inserted within the ancient thanksgiving prayer in a symmetrical and balanced way before and after the Consecration (cf. chart on p. 296). These prayers of remembrance and petition serve to gather up all three dimensions of the Church, in heaven, in purgatory, and on earth, and all of nature as well, that all may be restored to God through Christ in thanksgiving.

With Christ who prayed for the whole Church at the Last Supper (cf. Jn 17), we now with loyal devotion pray for our fathers in Christ, the pope and bishops of holy Church. Next we pray for our own family, relatives, and friends, and for all assembled around God's table. Our vision then rises to the fellowship of heaven, as we summon Mary, the Mother of the Church, and Christ's first disciples to our act of offering and praise.

3. The eucharistic summit: the Consecration

Immediately before the Consecration, the celebrant extends his hands over the symbolic gifts of bread and wine and thereby accepts them as the material of the sacrifice. After requesting that God take our humble gift and make it truly worthwhile by transforming it into the sacrifice of Christ, the priest proclaims the narrative of the Last Supper, a precious liturgical account already in use in the primitive Church before our Gospels were written.

We stand at the summit of sacrifice. It is the solemn covenant moment, when Christ in his own blood, sacramentally present under the signs of bread and wine, renews our kinship, our partnership, our friendship with the eternal Father. Once more, as at Sinai, at the Last Supper, on the cross, at our baptism, the Father takes us as his sons, treats us as though we were his own Son into whose very life we are at this moment incorporated. Our unprofitable lives, our tawdry possessions, our imperfect surrender are transmuted into something really worthwhile for God; as the bread and wine are changed into Christ's self-offering, so our gift is absorbed into Christ. Here is the supreme value of the Eucharist; our human sacrifice becomes the sign of divine sacrifice. Human gratitude becomes divine gratefulness. Finite appreciation becomes infinite consecration.

Here Christ is most at work reconciling the whole of humanity to his Father. Here his kingdom is most visible. It is the Church's most self-conscious moment; we are gathered together in the new Paschal life, the new victory life of the risen Christ. The Church is never more Church, community united with its Head, than when it celebrates the eucharistic mystery of Christ's Passover and ours.

4. Anamnesis: the post-Consecration Mementos

During the Eucharist as Christ's memorial (*anamnesis*), we enter into his triumphant return to the Father. One body with him through his Paschal mystery, we return with him in the covenant-sacrifice to the Father's presence. The thanksgiving of Abel, the obedience of Abraham, the priestliness of Melchizedek reappear in our own sacrifice.

We are offered by Christ, and we offer Christ to the Father. In this exalted moment, we do not forget our beloved dead who may be still on the way to heaven. We ask for their final victory with Christ in the life of total freedom in the company of the divine family. The clergy, cognizant of their own sinfulness, plead for pardon. And all these favors which the Church asks of an indulgent Father at the moment when the divine favor is most open to us, we gather up in the closing doxology or hymn of praise "Through Christ and with Christ and in Christ" — *through* Christ who introduces us to the Father, *with* Christ most truly one of us in our struggle for eternal freedom, *in* Christ as brothers facing our common Father.

As though to incarnate the doxology as a visible thanksgiving, the celebrant elevates Host and chalice in a magnificent gesture rendering "all honor and glory forever and ever."

The resounding "Amen" of the assembly, their enthusiastic and corporate "Yes" to the sacrifice, closes the solemn prayer-action of thanksgiving.

C. The Covenant-Meal of Eucharistic Fellowship

1. The family table prayer, the "Lord's Prayer"

The celebrant, our father in Christ, leads us now in the Communion prayer or the grace before the meal of the Eucharist. The Lord's Prayer is a baptismal prayer; we who became God's sons in the sacrament of initiation now lay claim to the sacred food of the family table. "Give us this day our daily bread."

But union with Christ presumes union with his body-members. "Forgive us our trespasses as we forgive those who trespass against us." Mutual forgiveness, reconciliation with our brothers (sometimes symbolized by a handshake, an attempt to update the ancient kiss of peace) will prevent us from acting out a lie. Fellowship in Christ's meal in fact as well as in sign is the only authentic Eucharist. Here the Church is truly "in communion," most visibly one body in Christ's Body.

2. The breaking of the Bread

At this point one of the New Testament names for the Eucharist is acted out as the consecrated Bread is broken. When leavened bread was used, this rite took some time, and a litany was sung ("Lamb of God") during the action. Now the celebrant breaks the large Host in half and then breaks off a third small Piece which he deposits in the cup. This latter ceremony recalls the ancient practice of the pope sending a consecrated Fragment (fermentum) to his neighboring bishops for insertion into their chalice as a sign of their common union in the one priesthood of Christ.

In silent prayer, the celebrant prepares to eat the sacred Food. And then he shares the covenant Food in this sacred meal of fellowship with the members of Christ. As the faithful come to Communion, the assembly sings of the fraternity it is renewing in Christ in the covenant meal. Mystery of unity, mystery of charity, the Eucharist is a dynamic catalyst of peace — peace in the family, peace in the community, religious peace, peace in the world.

3. Conclusion of the celebration

After the eucharistic meal has been celebrated, the priest cleanses the sacred vessels (chalice and ciborium). As leader of the community, he speaks a final prayer requesting that the eucharistic experience may be prolonged in the daily life of God's people, that their whole life may be eucharistic, giving thanks by restoring all things to the Father in Christ. As a final pledge of the Father's love, the priest sends God's children away with a parting blessing, that they may always remain sons of the Father, brothers of Christ, and one in the Spirit of love.

Selected Readings

I. THE FRAMEWORK OF WORSHIP

Baillie, Donald M., *The Theology of the Sacraments* (New York: Scribner's, 1957).

Baum, Gregory, "Word and Sacrament in the Church," *Thought*, Vol. 38, Summer 1963, pp. 190–200.

Bouyer, Louis, *The Paschal Mystery* (Chicago: Regnery, 1950).

——— *Rite and Man* (Notre Dame, Ind.: University of Notre Dame Press, 1963).

——— *The Word, Church, and Sacraments* (London: Geoffrey Chapman, 1961).

Brinktrine, J., *Die Lehre von den heiligen Sakramenten der Katholischen Kirche*, Vol. I. (Paderborn: Schöningh, 1961).

Butler, Basil Christopher, *The Idea of the Church* (Baltimore: Helicon, 1963).

Casel, Odo, *The Mystery of Christian Worship* (Westminster, Md.: Newman, 1962).

Cerfaux, L., *Christ in the Theology of St. Paul* (New York: Herder and Herder, 1959).

——— *The Church in the Theology of St. Paul* (New York: Herder and Herder, 1959).

Clark, Neville, *An Approach to the Theology of the Sacraments* (London: SCM Press, 1958).

Congar, Yves, *Mystery of the Temple* (Westminster, Md.: Newman, 1962).

Constitution on the Church, Second Vatican Council, November 21, 1964 (AAS, Vol. 57, No. 1, January 30, 1965, pp. 5–67).

Constitution on the Sacred Liturgy, Second Vatican Council, December 4, 1963 (AAS, Vol. 56, No. 2, February 15, 1964, pp. 97–134).

Cooke, Bernard J., *Christian Sacraments and Christian Personality* (New York: Holt, Rinehart, and Winston, Inc., 1965).

——— "The Sacraments as the Continuing Acts of Christ," *Catholic Theological Society of America Proceedings*, Vol. 16, 1961, pp. 43–68.

Davis, Charles, *Liturgy and Doctrine* (London: Sheed and Ward, 1960).

Durrwell, Francis X, *The Resurrection: A Biblical Study* (New York: Sheed and Ward, 1960).

Eliade, Mircea, *Patterns in Comparative Religion* (New York: Sheed and Ward, 1958).

Gaillard, J., "Faith and the Sacraments," *Theology Digest*, Vol. 9, Fall, 1961, pp. 161–167.

Haas, William P., "Phenomenology and the Sacraments," *Proceedings of North American Liturgical Week* (Washington, D. C.: The Liturgical Conference, 1960), Vol. 21, pp. 130–134.

Häring, Bernard, *A Sacramental Spirituality* (New York: Sheed and Ward, 1965).

Henry, A. M., ed., *Christ in His Sacraments*, in *Theology Library*, Vol. 6 (Chicago: Fides Publishers, 1958).

Journet, Charles, *The Church of the Word Incarnate* (New York: Sheed and Ward, 1955).

Leeming, Bernard, *Principles of Sacramental Theology* (Westminster, Md.: The Newman Press, 1960).

Lyonnet, Stanislaus, *De Peccato et Redemptione*, 2 vols., (Rome: Pontifical Biblical Institute, 1957).

Martimort, Aimé G., *The Signs of the New Covenant* (Collegeville, Minn.: The Liturgical Press, 1963).

McCabe, Herbert, *The People of God* (New York: Sheed and Ward, 1964).

McShane, P., "On the Causality of the Sacraments," *Theological Studies*, Vol. 24, September, 1963, pp. 523–536.

Mersch, Emile, *The Theology of the Mystical Body* (St. Louis: B. Herder, 1951).

––––––– *The Whole Christ* (Milwaukee: The Bruce Publishing Co., 1938).

Miller, John H., C.S.C., *Signs of Transformation in Christ* (Englewood Cliffs, N. J.: Prentice-Hall, Inc., 1963).

Norris, Frank, *God's Own People* (Baltimore: Helicon, 1963).

O'Callaghan, Denis, ed., *Sacraments: The Gestures of Christ* (New York: Sheed and Ward, 1964).

O'Connell, Matthew J., "New Perspectives in Sacramental Theology," *Worship*, Vol. 39, No. 4, April, 1965, pp. 195–206.

––––––– "The Sacraments in Theology Today," *Thought*, Vol. 36 (1961).

O'Neill, Colman, O.P., *Meeting Christ in the Sacraments* (New York: Alba House, 1964).

Philipon, M., *The Sacraments in the Christian Life* (Westminster, Md.: Newman, 1954).

Piault, Bernard, *What is a Sacrament?* (New York: Hawthorn Books, 1963).

Proceedings of the North American Liturgical Weeks (Washington, D. C.: The Liturgical Conference, 1940–1965).

Rahner, Karl, *The Church and the Sacraments* (New York: Herder and Herder, 1963).

––––––– "Personal and Sacramental Piety," *Theological Investigations* (Baltimore: Helicon, 1963), Vol. 2, pp. 109–133.

Richard, Lucien, "The Word and the Sacraments: An Ecumenical Approach to the Sacraments," *Journal of Ecumenical Studies* (Pittsburgh: Duquesne University Press, 1965), Vol. 2, pp. 234–250.

Robinson, J.A.T., *The Body: A Study in Pauline Theology* (London: SCM Press, 1955).

Roguet, A. M., *Christ Acts through Sacraments* (Collegeville, Minn.: The Liturgical Press, 1954).

Scheeben, M. J., *Mysteries of Christianity* (St. Louis: B. Herder, 1946).

Schillebeeckx, Edward H., *Christ, the Sacrament of the Encounter with God* (New York: Sheed and Ward, 1963).

––––––– "The Sacraments: An Encounter with God," in *Theology Today*, Vol. I, *Renewal in Dogma* (Milwaukee: Bruce, 1965), pp. 194–221.

Schmaus, Michael, *The Essence of Christianity* (Chicago: Scepter, 1961).

Semmelroth, Otto, *Die Kirche als Ursakrament* (Frankfurt-am-Main: J. Knecht, 1953).

––––––– *Vom Sinn der Sakramente* (Frankfurt-am-Main: J. Knecht, Carolusdruckerei, 1960).

Skydsgaard, Krister, et al., *The Church as the Body of Christ* (Notre Dame, Ind.: University of Notre Dame Press, 1963).

Stanley, David M., *Christ's Resurrection in Pauline Soteriology* (Rome: Pontifical Biblical Institute, 1961).

Stuhlmueller, Carroll, "The Sacraments in Scripture," *Studies in Salvation History* (Englewood Cliffs, N. J.: Prentice-Hall, 1964).

Sullivan, C. Stephen, *Readings in Sacramental Theology* (Englewood Cliffs, N. J.: Prentice-Hall, 1964).

Toland, Terrence, "Christian Sacraments: Sign and Experience," *Proceedings of the North American Liturgical Week*, Vol. 20, 1959, pp. 247–253.

Vagaggini, Cyprian, *Theological Dimensions of the Liturgy* (Collegeville, Minn.: The Liturgical Press, 1959).

Vollert, Cyril, "Church and Sacraments," *Society of Catholic College Teachers of Sacred Doctrine Proceedings*, Vol. 8, 1962, pp. 38–58.

Yearbook of Liturgical Studies (Notre Dame, Inc.: Fides, annually, 1960–1965).

II. BAPTISM

Casel, Odo, "Art und Sinn der ältesten christlichen Osterfeier," *Jahrbuch für Liturgiewissenschaft*, Vol. 14, 1938, pp. 1–78.

Crehan, J., *Early Christian Baptism and the Creed* (Westminster, Md.: Newman, 1950).

Cullman, Oscar, *Baptism in the New Testament* (London: SCM Press, 1950).

Davis, Charles, *Sacraments of Initiation* (New York: Sheed and Ward, 1964).

George, A., et al., *Baptism in the New Testament* (Baltimore: Helicon, 1964).

LeFort, Thomas, "The Waters of Death and Rebirth," *Worship*, Vol. 35, 1961, pp. 275–281.

Maertens, Thierry, "Historie et pastorale du rituel du catechumenat et du baptême (Bruges: Biblica, 1962).

Neunheuser, Burkhard, *Baptism and Confirmation* (New York: Herder & Herder, 1964).

O'Shea, Wm., *Sacraments of Initiation* (Englewood Cliffs, N. J.: Prentice-Hall, 1966).

Palmer, Paul, *Sacraments and Worship* (Westminster, Md.: Newman, 1957).

Ryan, W., "The Teaching of St. Thomas in the Summa Concerning the Baptismal Character," *American Ecclesiastical Review*, Vol. 149, December, 1963, pp. 361–385.

Schnackenburg, Rudolf, *Baptism in the Thought of St. Paul* (New York: Herder & Herder, 1964).

Stanley, David M., "The New Testament Doctrine of Baptism," *Theological Studies* (1957), pp. 169–215.

Stuhlmueller, Carroll, "Baptism: New Life Through the Blood of Jesus," *Worship*, Vol. 39, No. 4, April, 1965, pp. 207–217.

Verbillion, J., "Signs of Life: Baptism and Confirmation," *Cross and Crown*, Vol. 14, Summer, 1962, pp. 333–348.

Whitaker, E. C., *Documents of the Baptismal Liturgy* (Naperville, Ill.: Allenson, 1960).

III. CONFIRMATION

Beraudy, R., in *L'Eglise en priere: Introduction a la liturgie*, ed. A. G. Marti-mort (Paris and Tournai, 1961).

Bohen, Marian, *The Mystery of Confirmation* (New York: Herder & Herder, Herder, 1963).

Burns, Patrick J. (ed.), *Mission and Witness, The Life of the Church* (Westminster, Md.: The Newman Press, 1964).

Camelot, P., "Sur la théologie de la confirmation," in *Revue des sciences philosophiques et théologiques*, No. 38 (1954).

———— "Towards a Theology of Confirmation," *Theology Digest*, Vol. 7, No. 2, Spring, 1959, pp. 67–71.

Delcuve, Georges, "Confirmation: Sacrament of the Apostolate?" *Theology Digest*, Vol. 13, No. 3, Autumn, 1965, pp. 198–205.

———— "Is Confirmation the Sacrament of the Apostolate?" *Lumen Vitae*, Vol. 17, No. 3, September, 1962 (Brussels, Belgium), pp. 467–506.

Dix, Gregory, *The Theology of Confirmation in Relation to Baptism* (Westminster: Dacre Press, 1946).

Lampe, G. W. H., *The Seal of the Spirit* (London, 1951).

Luykx, Bonifaas, "Confirmation in Relation to the Eucharist," in *Readings in Sacramental Theology* (Englewood Cliffs, N. J.: Prentice-Hall, 1964), pp. 187–209.

———— *La Confirmation, Doctrine et Pastorale* (Bruges, 1958).

Marsh, Thomas, "Confirmation in Relation to Baptism," *Theology Digest*, Vol. 13, No. 3, Autumn, 1965, pp. 193–197.

Rahner, Karl, *The Christian Commitment* (New York: Sheed and Ward, 1963).

———— "The Sacramental Basis of the Layman's Position in the Church," in *Nature and Grace* (New York: Sheed and Ward, 1964).

Thornton, L. S., *Confirmation: Its Place in the Baptismal Mystery* (London: Dacre Press, 1954).

Thurian, Max, *Consecration of the Layman* (Baltimore: Helicon, 1957 and 1963).

IV. EUCHARIST

Amiot, François, *History of the Mass* (New York: Hawthorn Books, 1959).

Assisi Papers, The (Collegeville, Minn.: The Liturgical Press, 1957).

Aulén, Gustaf, *Eucharist and Sacrifice* (Philadelphia: Muhlenberg Press, 1958).

Baum, Gregory, *Progress and Perspectives: The Catholic Quest for Christian Unity* (New York: Sheed and Ward, 1962).

Bouyer, Louis, *Liturgical Piety* (Notre Dame, Ind.: University of Notre Dame Press, 1954).

Calvin, John, *Institutes of the Christian Religion*, tr. Henry Beveridge, 2 vols. (London: Clarke, reprint 1957).

Church and Ecumenism, The, Vol. 4 of *Concilium* (Glen Rock, N J: Paulist Press, 1965).

Clark, Francis, *Eucharistic Sacrifice and the Reformation* (Westminster, Md.: Newman, 1960).

Congar, Y., *Lay People in the Church* (Westminster, Md.: Newman, 1957).

Cooke, Bernard, "Synoptic Presentation of the Eucharist as a Covenant," *Theological Studies*, Vol. 21, 1960, pp. 1–44.

Cullmann, Oscar, *Christ and Time* (Philadelphia: Westminster, 1950).

Cullmann-Leenhardt, *Essays on the Lord's Supper* (London: Lutterworth Press, 1958).

Danielou, Jean, "Banquet of the Poor," *The Lord of History* (Chicago: Regnery, 1958), pp. 214–240.

——— *The Bible and the Liturgy* (Notre Dame, Ind.: The University of Notre Dame Press, 1956).

Davis, Charles, "The Theology of Transubstantiation," *Sophia*, Vol. 3, No. 1, April, 1964, pp. 12–24.

Decree on Ecumenism, Second Vatican Council, November 21, 1964 (AAS, Vol. 57, No. 1, January 30, 1965, pp. 90–107).

Delling, Gerhard, *Worship in the New Testament* (Philadelphia: The Westminster Press, 1962).

Delormé, et al., *The Eucharist in the New Testament* (Baltimore: Helicon, 1964).

Diekmann, Godfrey, *Come Let Us Worship* (Baltimore: Helicon, 1961).

Dix, Gregory, *The Shape of the Liturgy* (London: Dacre Press, 1945).

Higgins, A. J. B., *The Lord's Supper in the New Testament* (Chicago: Henry Regnery Co., 1952).

Holy Eucharist and Christian Unity, The, 43rd Annual Meeting of the Franciscan Educational Conference, August 6–8, 1962, Vol. 43 (Louisville: Bellarmine College, 1963).

Jeremias, Joachim, *The Eucharistic Words of Jesus* (Oxford: Blackwell, 1955).

Jungmann, Josef A., *The Early Liturgy* (Notre Dame, Ind.: University of Notre Dame Press, 1959).

——— "Eucharistic Piety," *Worship*, Vol. 35, July, 1961, pp. 410–420.

——— *The Mass of the Roman Rite* (New York: Benziger Bros.), Vol. 1, 1951; Vol. 2, 1955.

——— *Public Worship* (Collegville, Minn.: The Liturgical Press, 1957).

——— "The Over-All Historical Picture" [of eucharistic piety], *Pastoral Liturgy* (New York: Herder & Herder, 1962), pp. 1–101.

Kilmartin, Edward J., *The Eucharist in the Primitive Church* (Englewood Cliffs, N. J.: Prentice-Hall, 1965).

Lécuyer, Joseph, *Le Sacrifice de la Nouvelle Alliance* (Le Puy: Editions Xavier Mappus, 1962).

Lehmann, H. T., ed., *Meaning and Practice of the Lord's Supper* (Philadelphia: Muhlenberg Press, 1961).

Liturgy and the Word of God, The, the Strasbourg Papers (Collegeville, Minn.: The Liturgical Press, 1959).

Luther's Works (Philadelphia: Muhlenberg Press, 1959 ff.).

Marlé, René, "L'Eucharistie dans la division des chrétiens," in *Études*, April, 1963, No. 317, pp. 94–107.

Marshall, Romey, and Taylor, Michael, *Liturgy and Christian Unity* (Englewood Cliffs, N. J.: Prentice-Hall, 1965).

McCue, James F., "Luther and Roman Catholicism on the Mass as Sacrifice," *Journal of Ecumenical Studies* (Pittsburgh: Duquesne University Press, 1965), Vol. 2, No. 2, pp. 205–233.

Meyer, Boniface, "Sacramental Theology in the *Institutes* of John Calvin," in *The American Benedictine Review*, Vol. 15, No. 3, September, 1964, pp. 360–380.

Miller-Wright, ed., *Ecumenical Dialogue at Harvard* (Cambridge: Belknap Press, 1964).

Nicolas, Marie-Joseph, *What is the Eucharist?* (New York: Hawthorn Books, 1960).

Nocent, Adrien, *The Future of the Liturgy* (New York: Herder & Herder, 1963).

O'Shea, K., "Sacramental Realism: Some Thoughts on the Sacrifice of the Mass," *Irish Theological Record*, Vol. 30, April, 1963, pp. 99–145.

Paul VI, *Mysterium Fidei* (On the Holy Eucharist, September 3, 1965), AAS, Vol. 57, No. 11, pp. 753–774.

Piepkorn, A., "The Lutheran Doctrine on the Sacrament of the Altar, Ecumenically Considered," in *National Liturgical Week* (1964), Vol. 25, pp. 134–154.

Reid, J. K. S., *Calvin: Theological Treatises* (Philadelphia: Westminster, 1954).

Taylor, Michael, *The Protestant Liturgical Revival* (Westminster, Md.: Newman, 1963).

Thurian, Max, *The Eucharistic Memorial* (Richmond: John Knox Press, Vol. I, 1960; Vol. II, 1961).

——— "The Real Presence," in *Christianity Divided*, ed. D. J. Callahan *et al.* (New York: Sheed and Ward, 1961), pp. 203–222.

——— "Toward a Renewal of the Doctrine of Transubstantiation," in *Christianity Divided*, ed. D. J. Callahan *et al.* (New York: Sheed and Ward, 1961), pp. 197–201.

Vajta, Vilmos, *Luther on Worship* (Philadelphia: Muhlenberg Press, 1958).

Vollert, Cyril, "The Eucharist: Quests for Insights from Scripture," *Theological Studies*, Vol. 21, No. 3, September, 1960, pp. 404–443.

Vonier, Anscar, *A Key to the Doctrine of the Eucharist* (Westminster, Md.: Newman, 1946).

Wicker, Brian, *Culture and Liturgy* (New York: Sheed and Ward, 1963).

Subject Index

Altar table, 204 ff

Baptism, development of Christian, 94 ff; a dying and rising with Christ, 84 ff, 107 f; ecclesial effect of, 59; ecumenical perspectives, 110 ff; and Holy Spirit, 108; incorporation into the Church, 106; in New Testament, 20 f; prehistory of, 86 f; and priesthood, 109; rite of Christian, 97 ff; in salvation-history, 91 ff; sacramental character of, 61 f; theological synthesis, 105 ff; valid outside Catholic Church, 110 ff

Character, sacramental, of baptism, 59; of confirmation, 60; in Fathers, 58 ff; of orders, 62 ff; scriptural foundations for, 57; theology of, 59 ff
Christ, acts in sacraments, 41 ff; encounter with, theology of, xiii f; gives his life as covenant food, 162 f; messianic servant at Last Supper, 159 f; present in eucharistic food, 165 ff; sacraments as acts of, 35 ff; seals New Covenant in his own blood, 161
Church, sacrament of risen Christ, 12; sacraments as acts of, 35 ff; sign of Paschal Mystery, 60 f
Communion, builds up Church, 218 ff; and community, 218 ff; consummates sacrifice, 213 ff; frequency of, 210 ff; meal of freedom, 216 f; rite of, 207 f; sign and cause of fraternal charity, 220 ff
Confirmation, anointing for illumination, 138; anointing by the Spirit, 132 f; anointing for witness, 135 ff; and Christian militia?, 139; completes baptism, 129 f; ecclesial effect of, 60; ecumenical perspectives, 140 f; historical development of liturgy, 122 f; and Holy Spirit, 131 f; liturgy of, 122 ff; present rite of, 125 ff; a priestly anointing, 133 ff; theology of, 129 ff; witnessing with Christ in the Spirit, 116 ff
Covenant, eucharistic, institution of, 152 ff; meals, in Old Testament, 149 ff;

sacrifice, in Old Testament, 149 f

Easter Vigil, description and interpretation of, 78 ff
Eucharist, builds up Church, 219 ff; Christ's presence, 165 ff, see also Real Presence; climax of Christian initiation, 143; continues Christ's redemptive act, 163; fellowship in body of Christ, 143 ff; first, context of, 156 f; fulfills Old Testament Passover, 158; liturgy of, history, 264 ff, see also Mass; as meal, 199 ff; as meal, dogmatic synthesis, 213 ff; as meal, and eschatology, 225 ff; as meal, in Fathers, 202; as meal, liturgical traditions, 204 ff; as meal, of messianic servant of God, 158 f; in the New Testament, 22; Paschal context of, 156 ff; patristic testimony to, 145 ff; primacy among sacraments, 147; as sacrifice, dogmatic synthesis, 175 ff; as sacrifice, ecumenical perspectives, 196 ff; as sacrifice, in reformation theology, 181 ff; as sacrifice, theological speculations, 193 ff; as sacrifice, theology of, 170 ff; as sacrifice, at Trent, 189 f; as sacrifice, unity of, 191 f; a sacrifice meal, 143 ff; in salvation-history, 149 ff; texts of institution, deductions from, 159 ff; and unity of all Christians, 221 ff
Eucharistic liturgy, in Apostolic Church, 265 ff; see also Mass
Eucharistic meal, see Meal; Eucharist, as meal; Communion
Eucharistic presence, 228 ff, see also Real Presence
Eucharistic sacrifice, see Sacrifice; Eucharist, as sacrifice

Faith, of Church, 30; and fruitfulness, 34; and sacramental sign, 29 f
Finality of sacraments, 53 ff

Grace, characteristic of sacramentals, 66 ff; and ecclesial effect of sacraments, 64; sacramental, of each sacrament, 69 ff;

Index of Names

Ambrose, St., confirmation as illumination, 139; confirmation as priestly anointing, 134; confirmation as seal of spirit, 131; early eucharistic celebration, 146; eucharistic meal, 203; Eucharist as manna, 203; Real Presence, 232 f; significance of baptismal robes, 104

Albert the Great, St., on purpose of anointing the sick, 63

Augustine, St., confirmation and priesthood, 134; distinction between valid and fruitful reception of sacraments, 64; eucharistic doctrine, 179 f; Real Presence, 234; sacramental seal, 55 f

Aulen, Gustaf, Lutheran doctrine of eucharistic sacrifice, 184

Baum, Gregory, ecumenical perspectives of baptism, 113

Beauduin, Lambert, and liturgical movement, 279

Bellarmine, Robert, Mass-sacrifice, 193

Berengar of Tours, Real Presence, 235 f

Billot, L., Mass-sacrifice, 194

Bohen, Marian, confirmation as completion of baptism, 130; confirmation and witness, 135

Calvin, John, eucharistic presence, 246 ff; rejection of Mass-sacrifice, 186; views on confirmation, 140

Casel, Dom Odo, Mass-sacrifice, 194; mystery presence theory, 44 ff

Cranmer, Thomas, eucharistic presence, 249 ff; teaching on Eucharist, 187 f

Cyprian of Carthage, St., Eucharist as sacrifice, 177; rebaptism of heretics, 55

Cyril of Alexandria, St., eucharistic meal, 204

Cyril of Jerusalem, St., confirmation as priestly anointing, 133 ff; confirmation as seal of spirit, 131; eucharistic sacrifice, 177 ff; Real Presence, 232; rite of Communion, 207; sacramental seal, 59

Davis, Charles, confirmation and witness, 135; eucharistic presence, 259 ff; sacraments as presence of Paschal mystery, 48

De la Taille, Mass-sacrifice, 194

Delcuve, Georges, trinitarian concept of confirmation, 136

De Lugo, on Mass-sacrifice, 193

Dix, Gregory, Cranmer's eucharistic doctrine, 188

Eliade, Mircea, symbolism of water, 86

Franzelin, Mass-sacrifice, 193

Gregory VII, Pope, formula on Real Presence, 235

Gregory of Nyssa, St., Real Presence, 232

Gueranger, Proper, nineteenth-century liturgical movement, 278 f

Hildebert of Tours, transubstantiation, 237

Hippolytus, Apostolic Tradition of, baptism and confirmation, 123 f; celebration of Eucharist, 146; on Roman Mass, 269 ff

Hugh of St. Victor, Real Presence, 236

Hus, John, eucharistic teaching, 243 f

Ignatius of Antioch, St., eucharistic meal, 202; Real Presence, 231

Irenaeus of Lyons, St., effect of Eucharist, 202 f; Eucharist as sacrifice, 176 f; Real Presence, 231 f

John Chrysostom, St., Eucharist as sacrifice, 178

John Damascene, St., baptismal seal, 58 f

John XXIII, Pope, and liturgical renewal, 280

Justin the Martyr, St., description of early eucharistic celebration, 145; Eucharist as sacrifice, 176; Real Presence, 231; on Roman Mass in second century, 267 f

Jungmann, J., development of Mass liturgy, 276 ff

Lanfranc of Canterbury, Real Presence, 236